Hiroshima: Bridge to Forgiveness

"The Crane and The Butterfly"–
Takashi's Hiroshima Story

autobiographical memoirs by Takashi Thomas Tanemori,
with John Crump

2nd print edition

ii

© Takashi Thomas Tanemori & John Michael Crump, Spring 2007

TVP

657 SOUTH MONROE STREET, SAN JOSE, CA 95128
Tel: (408) 296-5935   E-Mail: jcrumptvp@earthlink.net

2st print edition—Summer 2008
ISBN 978-0-9817532-01

United States Copyright and U. S. Library of Congress

Tanemori, Takashi Thomas, 1937 –
Crump, John Michael, 1954 –

Hiroshima : Bridge to Forgiveness : The Crane and The Butterfly, Takashi's Hiroshima story : autobiographical memoirs / by Takashi Thomas Tanemori ; with John Crump – 2nd print ed.

ISBN 978-0-9817532-01

    1.   Tanemori, Takashi Thomas, 1937 -, Crump, John Michael, 1954 – . 2. Hiroshima-shi (Japan)—History—Bombardment, 1945—Personal narratives. 3. World War, 1939-1945—Children—Japan—Hiroshima-shi—Biography. 4. Atomic bomb victims—Japan—Hiroshima-shi—Biography. 5. Christian biography. I. Crump, John, 1954 - III. Title. IV. Title: Bridge to Forgiveness. V. Title: Crane and the Butterfly. VI. Takashi's Hiroshima Story. VII. Series.

Dedication

THIS BOOK is a gift I dedicate to my three children: Jonathan, my First Son, Nathan, my Second Son, and Roxanne, whom I call my "Princess." I give it with heartfelt gratitude to your Mother, who has sacrificially given her heart and soul, and helped to make my gift possible. In extension, I also give this gift to all the innocent children of the world, who are also my "spiritual" children, even though I will not have the privilege of meeting them all.

I hope that the spirit of my Hiroshima Story may become a part of the fabric of your lives, like embroidery with many different lengths of threads crisscrossing in many colors, adding to an iridescent tapestry of human dignity, someday to be showcased with all its splendors. This is my hope; this is my prayer.

We can create our lives by
Transforming our experience
Into something new,
Like a butterfly soaring freely
Into the splendor.

From your Daddy,
Spring 2007

Contents

Dedication iii
Foreword v
Acknowledgments vii

Hiroshima: Bridge to Forgiveness
"The Crane and the Butterfly" —
Takashi Tanemori's Hiroshima Story

Part One: "The Crane" — A Life in Japan **3**
  Chapter One: Curse of the Buddha 5
  Chapter Two: Takashi's Dream 21
  Chapter Three: Judgment Day 33
  Chapter Four: Black Engine to Kotachi 49
  Chapter Five: Blood Ties 61
  Chapter Six: Tales of a Hooligan 89
  Chapter Seven: Illicit Love in a Secret Garden 117
  Chapter Eight: Shakai-Jin 142
  Chapter Nine: Squeaky Shoes and the Black Cadillac 153

Part Two: "The Butterfly" — A Life in America **183**
  Chapter One: Sayonara, Mount Fuji 185
  Chapter Two: A Migrant Labor Camp 203
  Chapter Three: An American Snake Pit 223
  Chapter Four: College Life 259
  Chapter Five: Two Become One 296
  Chapter Six: Theological Seminary Training 314
  Chapter Seven: The Purple Robe 337
  Chapter Eight: California Ministries 370
  Chapter Nine: In Search of Salvation 387
  Chapter Ten:
      Reaching Americans Through Their Stomachs............ 396
  Chapter Eleven: The Return of the Butterfly 421
  Chapter Twelve: Saving Humpty 431
  Chapter Thirteen: From Ikebana to Bonsai 446
  Chapter Fourteen: The Epic Return to Hiroshima 464
  Chapter Fifteen: Crossing the Last Bridge 482
  AFTERWORD 503

Foreword

Words from the Author:
Yo`koso … **Welcome …**

MAY I invite you to journey with me to find ways to come home to the place called "Peace"?

This is "Takashi's Journey from Hiroshima … August 6, 1945 – August 6, 2005."

I was an accident, born in Hiroshima, Japan. I am a survivor of the Atomic Bomb which fell, devastating Hiroshima, on August 6, 1945. As a result I became *Hibakusha*, a street urchin, at the age of eight. I grew up with contempt, shame, and guilt in the rubble of postwar Japan—defeated.

My journey across the "Bridge to Forgiveness" has been long and difficult. It has engendered hatred and yet also love—human emotions in stark contrast to each other.

This is my personal story, beginning with the charred cradle of my childhood that propelled me forward on a harsh journey toward manhood.

In my youthful thinking, it was my teenage duty to seek revenge on Americans for the destruction of my family. I immigrated to America at age 18 on the eve of the 1960's, and struggled to survive in a nation swirling in social, moral, economic and political turmoil. America seemed to be at a spiritual ebb tide, struggling to make sense of the Vietnam War.

Paradoxically, my "life path" from Hiroshima demonstrates how a heart twisted by hatred and revenge can be transformed by forgiveness, and can evolve to a path of peaceful wisdom and the healing of human hearts. The gift from this process is the ultimate solution to human conflicts.

The path of my journey crosses many bridges. The Aioi Bridge in Hiroshima and the San Francisco Bay Bridge provide stern landmarks to the travels of my heart and the expression of my soul. I have been guided on this path by the radiant strength and dignity of the "Crane" and by the grace and gossamer beauty of the "Butterfly," a symbol of sacrifice and the transformation of its own life for the benefit of others—all humanity.

I hope *Hiroshima: Bridge to Forgiveness—Takashi's Hiroshima Story* will contribute threads of many colors to an iridescent tapestry of human dignity. This is my hope; this is my prayer.

May I meet you at the end of the journey, in my Japanese garden or at your place, celebrating together the tenacity of the human spirit while sipping hot *sake*?

May we learn to live for the benefit of others, for we are at our best in serving …

Takashi "Thomas" Tanemori
A Peacemaker

Acknowledgements

WE HAVE a saying in Japan: "Too many captains send a ship to the mountain top!" To guide a ship through raging stormy nights to its destination harbor requires an able captain with firm hands on the helm. His task, though, cannot be accomplished without the assistance of countless shipmates. *Hiroshima: Bridge to Forgiveness—Takashi's Hiroshima Story* is the past-to-present journey of my ship. Countless shipmates were needed for me to complete my odyssey through unknown water and unpredictable weather to the distant, then-unseen harbor.

I wish to gratefully acknowledge the help of many who invested precious time and energy over the last ten years, who have volunteered their hearts and souls as they have been able. My deepest apologies if I fail to name a contributor to these efforts.

I gratefully acknowledge Roger Nakayu, Ray Jager, Paul Schwartz and Robert McCullough, who have provided me with computer support and technical assistance. I express my utmost gratitude to Meg Jefferson, who helped me since the spring of 1994 to compare and contrast the many differing aspects of culture between my two countries: Japan and the United States.

I am most appreciative of Cynthia Long, whose capacity of heart allowed her to endure my oddity and hear me out, to be a sounding board for me. I also truly appreciate Lynn Thomas, who gave me special insight for weaving intricacy and complexity into my writings; Barbara Dinehart, who generously supported my efforts and the mission of Silkworm Peace Institute; and Norma Berger, who accompanied me and provided crucial support for my projects, including Showtime Entertainments.

In editing my story, many folks served as if they were stepping stones in the pond of a Japanese garden: they came, provided support, and then went. Some were like a half-moon wooden bridge, creating an enchanting environment; some were sounding boards and others gold-miners, sifting tons of gravel for "bright nuggets." My thanks to Don Kirchner of High Ground Productions;

Anthony M. Ruiz, owner of FASTFRAME in Lafayette, California; David Simpson, owner of the Lafayette Bookstore; and Ann Baker, proprietor of UPS of Lafayette.

Dr. Robert Hagler, the veterinarian for my two guide dogs, offered generous gifts of free services and financial support for my journey back to Japan; Mia Tagano, John Maroy, the newest "treasures," and Ann Albricht (known to me as Noble "Oxen" Woman, complementing my "oxen" spirit) have all been like an umbrella, shielding me from unexpected rain or blocking the scorching heat of summer. I thank you all.

Since November 1982, when I started retracing my journey from the ashes of Hiroshima, I have been like a baker creating a special cake. The help of each person to gather the cake's ingredients is immeasurable.

Glenn Newsum, a typical "Irishman" and former banker in Turlock, California, kept his sacred promise, and has faithfully been there for me for more than three decades since I met him. Glenn is a rare treasure.

Another man who has enriched my life is Toshi Nakamura, proprietor of Serika Japanese restaurant in Orinda, California. Toshi's "Japanese spirit" is nearly identical in many respects to that of my Daddy. I often see him as a *Henkutsu-man:* stubborn, but true to his integrity, even at his own expense. His virtue has sustained my own "Japanese spirit" for more than twenty years.

I am forever indebted to Mr. M. Iori, Chief Executive Chef of Hiroshima Kokusai Hotel. He has been the grain farmer in my cake metaphor, harvesting a quantity of key ingredients. Mr. Iori was the first man to receive me and embrace my heart on my original return to Japan. He has continued to be a bridge or link on subsequent trips as I reconnected the Hiroshima of my past with the adopted America of my present and future. Only with his generosity in providing accommodations and skilled guidance, did we accomplish our goals. With his giving spirit and love, I consider Mr. Iori a typical Japanese man deeply rooted in traditional culture, a rare treasure selflessly helping me time and again.

And my deepest gratitude is due to the Japanese Production Team of Perry Hallinan, Jeremy Biddle, Yukiko Judy Matsubara of Yokohama, and her daughter Kimina, whose hearts and spirits became special "gifts" for the last four years, helping me to complete my journey.

I am most thankful to John Crump, the chief editor of my book, who spent more than two years as a "special baker" on this project. I had gathered in one basket many grains, thinking all of them important to the batter. It is the task of the special baker to sift the flour exceedingly fine, to mix just the right amount of ingredients and ensure the oven's temperature is neither too warm nor too cool. John not only edited my raw writings, but has also become my spirit partner. I do acknowledge that behind the greatest man is a woman. John's wife, Barbara, has been very generous and gracious in allowing him to complete his work.

I hold a special place in my heart for Joy Jones, the poet, artist and "spokesperson for the homeless" I met at an event in San Francisco in July 2005. She connected me with Michael R. Burch, the producer/co-editor for the final preparation of my book for publication. He has taken this delicate cake into his own hands, icing it with masterful decorations of intricate pattern and design. I am grateful for his financing of this publication, but more than that, for his heartbeat and vision for global peace. Michael has energized me in finishing this book and I look forward to his energy in our common quests.

It is one thing to have a wonderful cake. It is another to "package" it beautifully for countless consumers. Joe M. Ruggier, the publisher of Multicultural Books, became the last "link" for our book to become a reality. I humbly realize that without the tripod legs of my editors and publisher, my Hiroshima Journey would not be a reality to share with readers. I am honored to make my "maiden voyage" with them, and with you.

I am also deeply appreciative to graphic artist Don Barnes, who translated the heart of my story into the cover which graces this book.

My special heartfelt gratitude is to Diane Carrera. She has been part of my heart for more than 16 years since I moved to Lafayette, California. She and her mother provided an enchanting cottage in her backyard, and allowed me to create my own Japanese garden there to escape the hustle-and-bustle lifestyle of San Francisco. Diane is the special person who nourished me for more than five years during my recovery from a total gastrectomy due to cancer. Her caring heart, compassion and love have been the source of my strength and encouragement. Whatever challenge I have been to her, she has overlooked and overcome, and I humbly acknowledge that I could not have written this book without her.

Finally, my thanks to my Father's spirit, guiding me like a ship captain's unseen hands firmly on the helm. Father's teaching of the *Seven Codes of the Samurai* held my heart and soul intact in turbulent seas, enabling me to bring my ship safely to harbor, and to fulfill my promises to myself and to him.

Takashi "Thomas" Tanemori
"Urban Samurai"
April, 2007

Hiroshima:
Bridge to Forgiveness
'The Crane and the Butterfly'

Takashi's Hiroshima Story

By Takashi "Thomas" Tanemori
with
John Crump

Part One:
"The Crane" – A Life in Japan

Chapter One: Curse of the Buddha

I AM Takashi, son of Tanemori. Long ago, I was lifted from the ashes of Hiroshima to find my way in the world. Before then, my Father patiently taught me to live by the ancient code, as his Father had taught him. The code was my guide during many years of searching. My Father rightfully thought me an impatient, unreceptive pupil, but to honor my parents and all those who came before them, I pass all I learned of the ancient code to my children, and wish that they shall do the same with their children.

To my children I leave this story of my life to help them prepare for whatever hand life deals them. The hand dealt to me was rife with trials of my soul's fortitude and beliefs. I wasn't ready, nor was I wise enough to face them. I learned how easy it is to wander and forget the path, and to pay the consequences of doing so. This is the message that needs telling.

Days flee from me now, like migrating birds. An anxious stirring prods me to tell the story of my family name, the lifting of the curse and the life-long search for a place of peace in my heart and on this planet. My children should know about Hiroshima, my Hiroshima, where the story begins.

August 5th, 1945

I searched for words that evening before splitting atoms swarmed and plumed into an umbrella of death. A slight breezy exhalation lifted off Hiroshima Bay and sifted through the city streets and windows, offering relief from the oven-baked afternoon. Cicadas chattered.

While they lived at home, my sisters Satsuko and Chisako aligned in a relentless barrage of teasing and scorning. They gloated over my failures in light of their perfect grades, demeanor, and behavior that pleased our parents. I was their little inept brother and whipping horse.

Then the Imperial Military Power of Hiroshima announced that all students above the third grade must be evacuated to preserve the seeds of future generations. So my parents sent Satsuko and Chisako to live with relatives in the village of Yoshida.

Time passed. Homesick and apologetic, they wrote a letter to me. I admit it; I did miss them even though their absence meant liberation from my tormentors. And under war rationing, I was grateful for having two fewer mouths at home. I searched for the right words to reply to them. Should I mock them or let them know that I felt the fierce tug of blood relationship? Or how much I wanted them with us again at our skimpy dinner table?

For several years, the city had lived in fear of invasion. The Second Headquarters of the Japanese Imperial Army swelled its ranks in Hiroshima. The rumble of trucks, tanks, cannons, and the regular thud of marching soldiers punctuated all our days. No longer did we ask if, but when, the war would visit our street.

I didn't understand the fear. I saw the uniforms and the weapons and the stern, confident faces of warriors. For me, the hubbub was thrilling. Going and coming from school my friends played war games, squealing with delight as we vanquished the evil American forces.

I struggled to find not just the right words, but any words, to reply to Satsuko and Chisako. I re-read my sisters' letter:

Dear Taka-chan,

Since we said good-bye, we have often wondered how you are doing. We are doing fine. Looking back, we realize that we teased you too much. But as the distance keeps us apart, we miss you so much. We will write to you again.

Until then, be strong and courageous and obey the teaching of our parents. Study hard and we will do everything we can to help you when we return.

The quiet night was disrupted. One, then hundreds of air raid sirens spiraled into a shrieking choir, silencing the cicadas mid-chirp. In a finger-snap, the city went pitch black. My pencil leaped from my hand. My heart pumped ashes through my veins. An unnatural chill dampened my neck.

Banks of searchlights sprung awake and drew large white circles randomly in the dark sky, sometimes crisscrossing. The hum of human frenzy filled the space left by the cicadas. Practice drills were forgotten. A teeming, desperate herd of unprepared souls, knees churning forward, arms clutching the youngest, stampeded to narrow entrances and funneled down steps to underground shelters.

Father led our family through the heavy darkness to our neighborhood bunker. We stepped into a hot, dark, airless container stuffed with shrugging bodies. No one breathed. No one spoke. Only the small voices of weeping children charged the silence. Somewhere in the hole, someone lit a candle. I saw eyes turning away and bodies trying to shrink as small as possible. My Mother, Father, and eldest sister sat in a row beside me. I smelled the sweetness of candle wax, wrapped my fingers in my father's hand, and thought of Aunt Takae.

From my visit in the spring, I could still see her tight smile, busy eyes, finely coiffed hair, and tiny hands. She lived on Miyajima, the Island of the Gods, in Hiroshima Bay. Only there would fat white clouds recline in the violet summer sky. Aunt Takae kept a cozy, spare home, with rice paper walls and serenely polished wood grain floors. She had a little meditation garden in the back.

She told me the island drifted, like an unmoored boat, over the bay's choppy waters where fish were said to shyly smile. She told me "family matters" that I should know about before I became a man.

My aunt rasped her throat clear, notched her brow. "Pay attention, Takashi, with the ears of a *Samurai*." She showed me a moldy-edged sepia photo of a military-erect, regal young man wrapped proudly in a *kimono*. His eyes pierced the brownish tint of the print, daring anyone to meet his gaze.

"That is your father." She pointed to the crest on the *kimono*. "That shows you the Tanemoris are related to *Maruni Tachi Aoi,* the ancient Tokugawa Shoguns. You are from nobility, Takashi. Be careful, because it does not free you from the curse."

Sunlight bent through the rice paper. Shoguns, nobility, a curse? I was confused, dizzy with fascination, fear. I couldn't tremble or sob. "Aunt Takae, what's going to happen to me?"

She shifted on the floor pillows. "First, we talk about the family name. It is like a jewel passed down through generations from son to son. It lives in you and beyond you, and gives you immortality. Your first obligation is to continue your bloodline. If it ends, then all of your living past dies. That is an unimaginable horror. Do not allow your forefathers and mothers to become extinct."

"Your mother was frantic about giving her husband a son. Her salvation depended on it." She leaned her head close to my ear. We were alone in the house, but she whispered anyway, "What I'm telling you about your mother is taboo, you understand. But you should know the truth."

"Yoshiko Nakamura, your mother, was the beautiful daughter of a very respectable Hiroshima family. Her parents owned a *ryotei*, a popular, high-class restaurant, steeped in tradition. But there was a problem. The good life was too much for your mother's father. He drank too much, gambled, and openly toyed with loose women. It was awful. Little by little, he plundered the family's fortune and the family's respectability. In town, your grandfather was known as a *nai sode o furuhito,* one who swings the sleeves of a shirt that he doesn't have. He died a young man in some desolate gutter."

"So your mother's mother, Setsu, fell to financial ruin, shame, humiliation, and disgrace. The comforts she was accustomed to were gone. She was destitute with a daughter and a son to raise. These were desperate times."

"Setsu, your grandmother, oh, she was resourceful. She sold the family restaurant to raise some immediate cash. And in the process, her coy charms won the heart of Mr. Rokuji Sakae, her major creditor. They soon married."

Takae wagged a warning finger. "An answer to one problem gives birth to another problem that demands an answer. The new marriage was a good arrangement, but two children, Setsu figured, were too stressful for this new union and would slow the return to the comfortable life. So she sold Yoshiko to a wealthy, childless couple in the village of Yoshida."

"Don't be startled Takashi. Japanese families often allowed their children to be 'adopted' to repay debts. Of course, sometimes, they were accepted into the new family, and sometimes, they were just used as indentured servants. But either way, for your mother, this sale shamed her forever. Yoshiko never, never spoke of it and trembled whenever the subject arose."

Takae paused and took a deep breath. She tapped the old photograph. "Every problem has an answer. And this one was your father. He came to the rescue. Sadao Tanemori, the handsome young man from a good *Samurai* family, was your mother's chance to escape her humiliation and gain a prestigious name."

Takae again wagged her finger. "Dreams don't come true so quickly. Sadao's parents were against the match. Yoshiko brought nothing to the marriage, they said. Her station, her value, her situation was out of balance with Sadao's social standing. They pleaded with their son, 'Please, please make a better choice.'"

I gripped the photograph of my Father, young, noble, powerful, and defiant.

"Sadao was a good and obedient son. But now he stood firm and took Yoshiko's hand."

"Sadao followed his heart instead of his parents' wishes. But he stayed true to the ancestral *Samurai* way: *Jidai-Yusen*, sacrifice one's own immediate needs for a higher moral purpose; *Mugai-Kyoeki*, revere all alike, respect each individual, and choose non-violence over violence whenever possible; *Jita-Kyoei*, live for the benefit of others; and *Seishin-Kyoiku*, nurture the spirit and soul with truth and ethical principles."

"He was a man of high principles and treated your mother with honor, with respect. And yet, although the marriage was good, it was incomplete. Without the blessing of Sadao's parents, the family name was in question. Only a male child could help Yoshiko win the Tanemori's acceptance and lift the black cloud."

"Expectations rose while Yoshiko carried her first child. She was excited and bubbly with hope. Buddha would surely honor her prayer for a son. She would prove to Sadao's parents this marriage was right and just. This first-born son would carry the bloodline and legally consecrate the marriage into the venerable family. Finally she would be the respectable Mrs. Yoshiko Tanemori, free of the name tainted by her father's sins. This birth would also cleanse your grandmother from the guilt of selling off her only daughter."

"Mrs. Hamachi, the midwife, ministered to your mother behind the *shoji* screen while your father paced like a caged animal on the other side. Then it happened. The first bellow issued from the newborn's lungs. The moment arrived; the veil was to be lifted."

"Your mother sobbed and choked quietly. The midwife begged your father, 'Forgive me, forgive me. *Zannen de gozai masho. Seiippai watashi wa tsukushi mashita. Nanto moshite yoi noka.* I have done my best, but I have caused you great disappointment and pain for not delivering a son.'"

"Serving the Tanemori family was an honor, especially mid-wiving for their firstborn, so Mrs. Hamachi wanted everything to be perfect, but it was not. She said, 'Tanemori-san, child and mother are well. And your daughter will grow into a beautiful girl, like her mother. And one day she will bear her husband many sons.'"

"Your father would not hear any of it. He retreated to his room, closing the *shoji* behind him. He paced again, holding his head in his hands. Hopes, expectations, all dashed. Yoshiko covered her head with sackcloth, spilling endless tears of shame. How could this happen to a proud Japanese family?"

Through her tears, my mother named her daughter Masuyo, which means "her seed will be perpetrated for a million years, endlessly, with prosperity."

"The news of the birth traveled quickly to Kotachi, my Grandmother Setsu's village. For years, your mother suffered the icy silence of her own mother and stepfather. And your father's parents, who lived only four blocks away from their son and his wife, never opened their arms to Masuyo. Your eldest sister was born an embarrassment and outcast."

"Each pregnancy after that brought new despair. Satsuko, 'the hastening of the castle to be honored,' was born, then Chisako, 'yearning the wisdom to know.' Both were beautiful, healthy babies. But both were girls. There were no celebrations, no patting of backs, no jubilant toasts to a bountiful future. Each female child was greeted by a stony, unspoken rejection."

"For a time, the reputation and respect afforded to your father's parents kept this story in check. But three girls in succession had to be more than a coincidence. It meant something. The town talked in hushed tones at street corners and over rice bowls about the grave misfortunes of the Tanemoris. The neighborhood *sen-gan,* the thousand-eyed Gossip Committee, fueled a more outspoken contempt. They feared the curse of Tanemori would contaminate them all. Misfortune was, after all, a punishment for past misdeeds. The three girls were proof something was amiss in the Tanemori family."

"Your grandparents commanded Sadao to abandon his worthless wife and restore honor to the family name. Now a tortuous dilemma faced the obedient son: to obey the wishes of his parents or to follow his heart. And once again your father defied his parents. The code to which he trusted his life was from a higher authority than even his parents' authority. He could not be a man and simply cast aside his wife and children. So he brought his torment to the Shinto Shrine of *Kokutai Jinja.* Every day, he prayed to *Amaterasu,* the Sun-Goddess, to view him favorably and grant his family a son. And then, for the fourth time, your mother was pregnant." Takae paused, letting her words hang in the air. "It was a time of great fear and worry."

"One day, your father was at work, when his parents, terrified the new birth would cause even further humiliation, secretly visited your mother. They planned on convincing her to leave that very day. If she really loved

Sadao, they argued, she should free him from any more misery. They offered her money, urging her to take her youngest daughter and disappear."

"Sadao returned from work and saw Yoshiko weeping from the depths of her womb. Sadao opened and clenched his fists. Weeks later, he opened a letter from Setsu, your grandmother. She too had learned of the secret visit to her daughter. Setsu feared this latest calamity had its seed planted years earlier when she sold Yoshiko. Panic, fury, I don't know what motivated her, but she wrote this letter:

> *Sadao, I am greatly disturbed that you have blamed our family bloodline as the root of shame and disgrace for your own inability to bring forth a male child.*
>
> *How long, Tanemori, will you make my daughter a public spectacle when it is your seed that is defective? Or perhaps your seed is like a dried seed, without the inherent power to bring forth a new life—a male child. It is you who failed to produce a male child!*
>
> *You are a spineless jellyfish. I can only laugh at your calamity. How could you paint yourself as blameless and innocent of guilt? Shoulder the responsibility of a Japanese man! Why don't you curse Buddha and die, for he has already cast you away like dung. His ears will not listen to you. His eyes will not see you. His hand will not touch you to restore your manhood. He will not bless you with a male child. You are a disgrace!*
>
> *As Yoshiko's mother, it is my heartfelt wish that you set my daughter free from further shame and disgrace. Disavow your marriage contract. Restore the purity of my daughter as if she were a budding, young shoot.*
>
> *Setsu*

"Your father read the insults, the 'weakness of his seed,' a manless man, one without *kintama*, testicles. A lesser man than the son of Tanemori, tossed about like a dead dog, would have been filled with rage and vengeance. He placed the vile page softly into the *hibachi*, letting it flare and turn to ash. But then he turned to the wall and asked if the curse would ever end."

I asked Aunt Takae, "*Oba-chan,* why wasn't father a soldier, fighting against the Americans, like Toshi's father?"

"*Taka-chan,*" as she liked to call me, "don't ever think evil of your father. He is a just and righteous man. Be proud of having him as your father."

"Never was there a lower time before. The Tanemori home was without spirit, without life, and without hope of seeing the bloodline continue and prosper like a forest. Sadao's honor and pride crumbled beneath his feet. His mouth tasted of sand."

"This war for your father's soul was fodder for the town gossips, especially since now the fourth pregnancy began to show. The *sen-gan* chided, 'Three girls, three worthless wooden nickels, you must have done a terrible wrong for Buddha to withhold his blessings. It is the curse of Buddha.' Neighbors went the extra mile to distance themselves from the unfortunate Tanemoris. The curse of Buddha turned the 'uncursed' into the righteously indignant, who often uttered their favorite mantra: 'The nail that sticks out gets hammered down.'"

"While she waited for the new baby, Yoshiko would sneak out, past the closed shutters of her neighbors, the *sen-gan,* to visit the statue of Buddha. She would prostrate herself before the benign presence, begging him to lift the curse. She had suffered so much shame in her life, could he not be merciful? If the baby she carried were another girl, her life would be over. She could no longer bear bringing any more pain to the man she loved and revered above all others. 'Please, Buddha, please give me a son.' The fate of her family was in the strength and purity of this prayer."

"Back in mid-December 1937, all Japan was busy preparing for *Oseibo,* the New Year. At this time of the year, everyone straightens up their houses, mends whatever is broken, discards what is no longer useful, and returns anything borrowed to its rightful owner. Of course cleansing the soul, atoning for sins, mending broken relationships, and forgiving transgressions are also important. That's why we give gifts."

"One cold, gray afternoon, Yoshiko's difficult labor began. Between contractions, she prayed for this baby to be the *Oseibo* gift that would reverse all the misfortunes she had brought upon her husband and her family."

"The familiar ritual was repeated. Sadao looked to heaven and sent Masuyo off to fetch Mrs. Hamachi, the same midwife who had attended all three previous Tanemori births. Poor Hamachi. She dreaded this day. She wanted to escape the cutting of the cord and the first look at the baby's genitalia. Hamachi moaned to the spirit of her dead husband, 'I still have time to say no. Another midwife could go. If he has another daughter, I will die.'"

"Hamachi's dead husband spoke to her, 'Naoko, remember, you delivered their three children. Don't betray their trust.'"

Aunt Takae pointed out how impressed Hamachi was with how her husband seemed to listen more intently now that he was gone.

" '*Oba-chan,*' Masuyo called out, '*Sah, hayaku ikimasho. Haha-ue ga matte oraremasu.* My mother is waiting for you.'"

"Hamachi reasoned that even if the Tanemoris were cursed by Buddha, it could not be her fault. And since she was the one the family had long depended upon, then she was obliged to go. She gathered her birthing bag and started down the street with Masuyo. Turning the corner of Kanyu Street, Hamachi slowed, as if feeling the eyes of the neighborhood upon her. At the last turn, Hamachi caught the furtive Mrs. Noguchi peeking around the corner at her from across the street. She was a well-known informer and messenger of the neighborhood *sen-gan.*"

"Yoshiko's moans and cries rang out into the street. Behind the *shoji,* the rolling pangs were strong and close together, but the baby was not coming. Hamachi fought to show a calm face. Something was wrong. It was taking too long. Maybe, Hamachi thought, so much is at stake here that Yoshiko is holding back. She clasped Yoshiko's fingers. 'Bear down, push, the Gods will surely smile upon you this time.' Your mother's face tightened into a warrior's *let's do it* look, and she yelled out, '*Otoko no ko ka shinuru. Boy or die.*' One last grunt and an infant emerged."

"In the next room, Sadao's pacing was frozen in place by the newborn's lusty wail. He held his breath. The midwife held the slippery blessing up for Yoshiko, who would not open her eyes. '*Yoshiko-san minasai. Otoko no ko desu. Omedeto Gozaimasu.* It's a boy. It's a boy. It's a boy.'"

"Crying, laughing, your father wildly charged the birthing room. He knelt by Yoshiko's bed. Your three sisters followed on his heels. '*Anata,* honorable husband,' Yoshiko whispered, 'Buddha smiles on us.'"

"With humble gratitude, Sadao raised his son to the altar of *Amaterasu*, the Sun-Goddess. She greeted the newborn, heir to the Tanemori line, and chased the scowling *sen-gan* off to their next victim. You were named Takashi, 'the Noble Man.'"

And now I was Takashi, seemingly far less than noble, crouched like a mouse in the shadowy dark of a bomb shelter, with my hand cradled in my Father's. Just beyond the weak candle, someone was crying. I was desperate to sleep, but the lonely crying persisted. Mother's head rested fitfully on Father's shoulder. I heard faceless voices mumbling names I had heard before on the radio: Correigedor, Iwo Jima, Guam, Tinian, Peleliu, Leyte, Luzon, Iwo Jima, Okinawa. The war roiled across the wide Pacific, hopping over tiny atolls and islands in the vast ocean space. Each leap moved the enemy nearer to Hiroshima.

The everyday chatter was only about the war. What happened today? What will happen tomorrow? How close are they? Everyone was affected. My friends, my city, my nation were blanketed with anguish as losses mounted. Invasion, the unspoken fear, skittered about like a bat flitting close to the ground.

I often heard the rallying cry, *yamato damashi,* die before surrendering, forced into conversation as the Imperial Military Government desperately demanded confidence on the home front, and greater personal sacrifice. I could almost palpably taste the fear of public opinion that might name *you* as the one who rejected the official attitude, resulting in ostracism, in your becoming a "walking ghost," a traitor.

Mother shivered and leaned closer to Father. She wore the Tanemori name proudly, and had given birth to my brother, Sadayoshi, in 1941 and my little sister, Sayoko, in 1943. She was fully dedicated, all four foot nine inches and 100 pounds of her, to her role of raising six children in a nation ravished by a faraway war that was inching closer every day, a plight that now had her huddled underground with her family.

In the house, she was an unending energetic dynamo. Born in the year of the Tiger, she scrubbed and polished and fussed over the cleanness and neatness of her children. Even in times like these, it was important to keep up appearances. We all put on the *Kabuki* mask for our neighbors. Unfortunately, her Number One Son did not cooperate.

The trouble started when Mother discovered that the long-awaited Takashi, the family's blessing, was, of all things, a left-handed boy with "nothing upstairs." Left-handedness was a deviant trait. It marked me as an "outsider" with the potential of being the laughing stock of the neighborhood.

In first grade, my teacher solemnly reported that I was jumpy and inattentive in class. And it was due to my being left-handed, the sign of a misfit. Mother wrung her hands, "Does Buddha have no mercy?"

She made it very clear. "Takashi, it is a disgrace for you to be left-handed. Your father will be ashamed. He will not be mocked by neighbors because you won't use your right hand." I was confused, shocked. How could this happen to *me*? I was the prized Number One Son, and now an embarrassment? Father never said anything or showed any disappointment about my favored hand. So how could it matter?

Mother's duty as a good wife was to mold me according to the dictates of our culture. No debate was possible. No effort was spared to make sure that I would measure up to community standards. Number One Son will be a right-handed boy. And so began the campaign to alter what nature had decreed.

Over my silent protests, she tied my left hand behind my back. I played, did homework, and ate with this clumsy disadvantage. My older sisters, Satsuko and Chisako, were delighted by my predicament.

They were both excellent students. They did everything right and resented my Number One Son status. They insulted me endlessly, even making up songs, "We search for a cure for our empty-headed brother; we even asked the *Suppon,* snapping turtle, for a reply. But he remained silent. The only way to fix such a foolish, dumb and stupid brother is for him to die young."

My oldest sister, Masuyo, was my only solace in this misery. But even Masuyo's comforting embrace didn't quiet my bitterness. With Mother's relentless badgering and hand tying and my sisters' barrage of taunting, I seethed with anger. I was steadfastly sullen and distant. Since I was prohibited from openly showing disfavor towards my Mother, I railed instead against my sisters, the "worthless wooden nickels."

The world made no sense to me. My right-handed friends, Toshi and Sumiko, were considered "normal," even though their schoolwork was just as bad as mine. I had nightmares about being the freak everyone said I was, one doomed to be scorned.

Mother lectured me every day and every night about doing things the accepted way. I felt my resistance yielding to her persistence. I was giving in, giving up, surrendering. My ears were swollen with shame and failure to conform, even though I believed in *yamato damashi,* dying before surrendering.

I endured the tying back of my evil hand, the lectures, the teasing, yet I never seemed to show any improvement. Mother became more testy, more frustrated with me. When she'd turn away, hand to her brow, I knew she feared she wouldn't win her battle to reshape me into a respectable form. I contained my anger, my hatred of her. I could not show disrespect, but I could let my rage blaze, deep in my hidden center.

I returned from school one day to a delicious aroma wafting from the kitchen. Peeking in, I saw the makings of a fabulous feast. Mother had mixed mounds of freshly steamed rice, stirred a frothy *miso* soup, chucked on succulent, broiling fish, and spooned steamed vegetables into a bowl. She had then garnished it with grated *daikon* radish and *nishime*. I knew of no reason to celebrate lavishly. In war-ravaged Hiroshima food was strictly rationed, yet here was a sumptuous meal Mother was preparing, on a school day no less.

The scent filled the entire house. The aroma of warm, savory food softened the edge of my anger. I waited for Mother to appear with the bonds to secure my left hand behind my back so that I could begin my homework until the serving. But she didn't leave the kitchen.

I tried to show some initiative and concentrate on my assignments. It should have been be easier since my left hand was now available. The aroma overwhelmed me. I couldn't make myself care about the lesson. My appetite was whetted.

Mother called us all to the table. Oddly, I didn't hear my name. My placemat was not to the right of my Father as it usually was. With a rope hanging from her fingers, Mother approached me.

"Takashi, your performance in school has brought shame to your father and to this family. This cannot continue," she said.

She tied both my hands to a nearby post. And bound I watched my family enjoy consuming this grand meal. Out of respect for Father, I remained silent. My sisters Chisako and Satsuko gloated. I wished my hands could wring their throats!

This great feast was not accompanied with the usual lively chatter. It was solemn. Father finished and looked me up and down. He exchanged a look with Mother, then rose, retreating into his room. I stood tethered like a dog for another hour in the empty room. I was imprisoned in my own house, before my own family. I didn't know if a human could sink any lower. I wanted to know whose villainous idea this was, my Mother's or my teacher's. I wanted someone to blame.

"Have you thought over your behavior? Do you understand why I tied your hands?" Mother untied my hands. I smirked and twisted away. She sent me to bed unfed. I lay there reasoning this through. Mother must be an *oni*, an ogre, a monster made to haunt and oppress me.

At that moment, I felt the cool knife-edge of hatred.

Mother never tied my hands again. It didn't matter. I harbored a festering hatred for her, even though I learned to use my right hand. I was still stubbornly left-handed, using it in secret, away from condemning eyes. But the right-handed indoctrination was so powerful that, to this day, I still feel twinges of guilt in my ambidextrous soul.

As the weeks passed under this uneasy family peace, I noticed Mother no longer ate meals with her family. She made up a litany of convenient excuses, "Go ahead, start without me," or "I've got things to do," or "I'm not that hungry tonight." I was certain she was hoarding all the good food for herself, eating it in private. This was my opportunity for revenge. I would spy on her, catch her in the act, and expose her duplicity to Father. I'd prove that I'd been wronged all along and that this *oni* was unworthy to raise Tanemori's Number One Son.

I sneaked out of bed and peeked into the kitchen where Mother was finishing cleaning up after dinner. Mother wasn't gorging on all sorts of rare and delicious treats. Instead, she scraped meager leftovers from her family's plates into her own rice bowl. From the caked bottom of the rice cooker, she salvaged a thin layer of rice. She crumbled it on top of the small clump of food leavings. Over this little pile, she poured green tea, garnished with a few slices of pickled radish.

I was ashamed. A place did exist for me, lower than the dining room punishment. I was stupid, selfish, the freak, unworthy of love. She was no *oni*. She was a wife, a Mother committed to loving her children, her husband, even me.

She went hungry so her family could eat. She hummed a lullaby and sipped her makeshift soup.

I regret never having the chance to tell her all this. If I sit quietly in the evening, sometimes I can faintly see tiny shoulders hunched over a bowl and hear a fading melody.

Chapter Two: Takashi's Dream

THE excitement of racing to the shelter was gone. Now the wait in the darkness, seemingly forever, would be uneventful. I was restless and stood up. Too many people were wedged into this small space for me to walk. I wanted to go home, to my house.

We lived within a mile of the heart of downtown Hiroshima on Tokaichi-Dori, a main road that stretched out to Ujina Harbor, the first naval base constructed during the Sino-Japanese War. This road was split in half. On one side, it bordered a sizeable residential district of modest homes like mine. On the other side of the road, as far as I could see, stood the walls of Tera-machi, Buddha Temple Town. Surrounding Temple Town, thousands of markers stood where dead spirits peacefully slept under Buddha's merciful protection.

In the summers, for fun and daring, my friends sometimes climbed these forbidden walls to steal hazelnuts and plums. Our bravado would sometimes take us across this silent landscape as a shortcut to the river. We splashed and jubilantly shrieked a hairsbreadth from the graves. It was exhilarating.

We would stomp out of the river onto the bank with laughter still dripping from our lips. But we felt *it*, the sobering, goose-bumpy chill of the place. Toweling dry couldn't wipe it off. We didn't understand what the Sino-Japanese conflict was; we didn't know what Pearl Harbor meant, nor that Hiroshima was the military capital of western Honshu, nor that its busy harbor was an invader's likely target. But the clouds of war and death were our constant companions.

I didn't know why my Father wasn't in the army. My friends' fathers were soldiers, away on maneuvers, battling on some Pacific atoll, or steering a warship into the wind. Why did he remain at home? Maybe his government job was too important for him to leave for military service. Such euphemisms helped fill the hollowness of my feeble answers. My friends' quizzical eyes, their sidelong glances, their suspicions flustered me. I, too, wondered if my Father was a coward.

My place was to defend my Father. No more shame would be placed on our shoulders. My Father, Sadao Tanemori, a man of few words, was an honorable man. He spoke in soft and measured tones, his language so simple and clear that no one could misunderstand his meaning. I wished his controlled monotone would occasionally sparkle with some excitement, emotion, or spontaneity.

I knew he worked for the government and that his integrity, honesty, selflessness, and work ethic elevated him to role model status. His word was a sacred bond. His conduct directly and clearly represented him as a person, Father, husband, and member of society. He reminded me often of the guiding principles to live by. He left a high standard to satisfy.

Only now do I understand my Father's view of the war and how it differed from our neighbors'. In his work, he was privy to information about how the war effort was really faring, not just the state propaganda. He saw reports about death counts on both sides of the battlefield.

He was a Japanese citizen, loyal and true, but his commitment to *Bushi-do*, the way of the *Samurai*, led him to honor all life as his own and to practice non-violence. His position as a high-level government employee and the wisdom of his beliefs contradicted each other.

Earlier in 1945, the demands of Japan's voracious war machine had drastically reduced the basic staples of life. Now, my Mother's self-sacrifice and inventive ways of stretching a meal could no longer stave off the loud complaints of our empty stomachs.

One day, I was surprised when she packed my lunch in a clumsy wooden lunch box instead of the aluminum one. *"Aah, Heitai san ga Taka-chan no Bento bako ga hoshii to itte torini korare ta noyo,"* she said. "Even your lunch box must be sacrificed for the war effort."

Military trucks soon roared in, collecting cast-iron rice cookers and all other scraps of metal. In the midst of this, I marched home bearing my second grade report card. I was now officially considered a proper right-handed boy and the report card was proof. My grades had dramatically improved. I basked in the pride of my parents and was eager to collect my reward. Father promised me a trip to the movies.

I skipped down Hacchobori-Dori, hand-in-hand with my Father. It didn't matter that the little theater had only newsreels of Japanese soldiers fighting bravely in the Pacific. I wanted to see our men combating evil for the Emperor.

In the flickering darkness, I saw enemy B-29 Superfortresses shot out of the sky. I saw large gray American warships sprouting plumes of black smoke and sliding to the ocean's bottom. Now that I was a good son, I couldn't temper my enthusiasm for parental praise. I shouted *"Banzai!"* and jumped up from the seat. It flipped back into its up position, a salute of sorts.

Just enough light emitted from the screen to show the strain on my Father's face.

"Baka mono, Takashi," he said, "No reason to rejoice. Many, many soldiers die on the battlefield on both sides. Think of how many children will never see their fathers, uncles, or brothers? War is not for cheering. It does nothing but bring sorrow to all."

I was stunned. Wasn't giving your life for the Emperor the highest glory? He gripped my hand and dragged me down the row of seats. Instead of going directly home, he took me to Kokutai Jinja, the Shinto shrine of the Sun Goddess *Amaterasu*. It was next to the Rijo Castle, where the Second Headquarters of the Japanese Imperial Government was situated. We'd go to the shrine to pay respects to those who sacrificed their lives for the greater cause. I vowed to become a brave soldier and give my life for the Emperor. Father had crazy ideas.

I squeezed my eyes and prayed to *Amaterasu*. "Please change my Father's heart so that we may share the joys of victory." I was brash and foolish. I shouted out, *"Tenno Heika, Banzai!* Emperor, Live Forever!"* I knew he couldn't object to that in public. Father turned his back in stoic silence.

We walked home without words. Everything, my report card, my left-handedness, my day of honor, fell away because of my dishonorable behavior. Despite all the instruction, punishment, and all my effort, I was still a misfit.

Father carried his worries like wounds. He sheltered me from the taut thinness of his lips, the crow's feet edging his eyes. He worried for Japan, for Hiroshima, for his street, for his family. He worried about Hiroshima becoming the final and decisive battlefield where he could lose his misfit Number One Son.

For me, Father was to be loved, perhaps worshipped. He was the sun around which I circled. I felt traitorous to our bond, dirty and stupid, whenever my thoughts disagreed with his. We could never debate openly.

We often crossed the Aioi-Bashi Bridge to downtown Hiroshima. This bridge was next to the Industrial Promotion Hall, later known as A-Bomb Dome. Nearby was the grand Fuku-ya Department Store. A small amusement park spread over its roof. I loved the little boats that moved in a continuous route around its small sea. I loved the bars to swing and hang from. In the summer months, the small ponds were filled with tiny *koi*. We could scoop up as many as our thin rice paper net could hold before it dissolved. Up there, on the roof, with my Father's benevolent eye upon me, beneath the gentle sun, amid the rides, and vendors' candies, and plentiful *koi*, I lived in a perfect world.

But those blissful times were interrupted by incidents that rained shame and worry on my parents. Mother usually doled out the punishment for my misdeeds, but I was only struck once, when I lied. I'm certain Mother saw the guilt in my face as soon as I transgressed. Lying, especially to your parents, is a serious breach of trust. I was mortified.

This was so bad, Father stepped in as judge and jury. "I taught you to honor and respect your Mother. The truth must be honored, regardless of consequences." He removed the wide paddle from the wall. "Ten strikes for not honoring Mother and for dishonoring your own heart by lying." He delivered each blow unsparingly, with exactly the same force, and within exactly the same interval.

Each whack rattled the *shoji*, but I took it with *mugon,* silence. At least I could salvage some honor by the manner in which I accepted the punishment. When he had finished, I could not sit. He then gathered my broken spirit into his embrace. My body stung, but it was nothing compared to the fear of losing the honor a Father could bestow upon his misfit son as he taught him how to live.

He reminded me that we were *Samurai* of *Maruni Tachi Aoi.* And as the Number One Son, I was expected to embody the stoic virtues of the *Samurai Way*: to exhibit courage, loyalty, and self-restraint, and to be prepared to sacrifice my own needs to serve a greater good. From then on, Father and I prayed together each morning, just before he left for work. In the evenings, we strolled through the main gate of Hirose Dai-Nippon Kokumin Sho-Gakko (my elementary school) to the shrine of Emperor Hirohito.

He drilled me in the ways of the *Samurai.* "The four key principles are what?" he'd ask. I'd stand and dutifully rattle off, "*Jidai-Yusen*, giving up your immediate needs for a higher moral purpose; *Mugai-Kyoei*, showing reverence for all life, respecting individuals, and practicing non-violence; *Jita-Kyoeki*, directing your life for the good of others; and *Seishin-Kyoiku*, nurturing your spirit and soul with truth and an ethical life."

That summer, on weekends, we walked down the shore of the Tenma River. Sand squeezed up through our bare toes. Father would pick up and study stones and shells while telling me a fable that exemplified a *Samurai* virtue. His narratives were timed to end just when we arrived back home. The stories were all about responsibility and accountability, honor and duty. I usually didn't understand them.

I wearied from the repetition of the stories. Over and over, "Remember who you are. Follow your heart, even if you must go against the norms of society. See your life only as a benefit to others. In return your life will benefit us all." I loved him for thinking I was worth the time he spent teaching me the lessons of life. He stepped through the lessons with urgency in his voice. It seemed strange. He had forever to train me. For some reason, he seemed to be on a tight schedule.

Once my knowledge of the four pillars of the *Samurai* was satisfactory, he introduced three more, to complete the Seven Codes: *Seiryoku-Zenyo*, giving your whole being up to goodness, righteousness and honor; *Tekii-Akugyaku*, learning to use misfortune to create good; and *Shinmi-Yuko*, letting your heart and soul govern all your actions.

These too he drummed into me and repeatedly tested me on. At times, I wondered if Father thought I was the Number One Son, the moron. But his urgency made each session important, of itself. This code of ethics either seeps into the molecules of your being, or not. There is no middle ground. I've spent the last fifty years of my life trying to probe and live by this code.

By the spring of 1945, the city simply accepted the inevitability of an invasion. In the parks, civilians rehearsed drills in defense techniques with bamboo spears. In the afternoons, Miss Tanaka *Sensei* took my second grade class into the courtyard to practice attacking rice and straw sacks. We pretended they were American soldiers. After we wrapped our heads with the *hachimaki*, the white bandana with the red circle on the forehead, we lunged again and again at the cooperative enemy, until he lay in shredded heaps on the cobblestones. The Land of the Rising Sun would not be caught unready to fend off the invader.

One day, after a defense drill, I returned home and found Mother weeping and shrugging. She held a thin letter in her hands. She thrust another envelope addressed to me in my face. "Here, Takashi," she said, "from your sisters."

This was the letter I was struggling to reply to when the air raid sirens sounded to scurry us all off to the shelter. As I read my sisters' lonely letter, I, their favorite scapegoat, understood why Father couldn't rejoice during the war newsreel.

I prayed for our family to be whole once more.

Now deep in the belly of the earth, in the small bunker, inside the suffocating airlessness and heat, I once again placed my hand in my Father's. I then fell away into the sleep of innocents, into a fast-moving dream.

Someone was gazing down at me. I tilted up on an elbow. My other hand rubbed at my eyes. I couldn't see anything in the foggy bleakness. A firm voice said, "Come, let me show you the way." I could now see a vaguely human form. "Let me show you the way. I will take you to see a friend." I was startled with fear and confusion.

"No, no. I want to stay here." I yanked my Father's arm and cried out. I was confused. I couldn't smell the stench of the shelter anymore. Father didn't respond to my tugging. He stared, glassy-eyed. No one else heard my pleas. The whole shelter was filled with zombies. Am I the only one awake? Am I alone with this thing? The world has tipped over, and I can't find the horizon.

"Leave me alone. I don't want to go. I don't know your friend."

"It is time to go," the voice insisted. I clamped my Father's arm in a death grip, but it was useless. I clutched only air. His arm was somewhere else. I glided away, abducted by strange hands. A strange force dragged me up, straight through the bomb shelter's ceiling, into an oddly quiet night. I could see nothing. My legs dangled foolishly.

"I can't see."

"Look inside yourself."

"What?" I looked downward, nothing. This can't be. How could I tell my friends? What would they think?

A shaft of light flashed from my chest out into the disinterested expanse. "Follow it, this light of your heart, to find your way."

I rose higher, gently higher, soaring on that beam. Below, my Hiroshima patiently waited. I saw my street, my house, my school, all seven of her delicate rivers, circulating life to the heart of the city. I saw her bridges arching, bowing over the quiet water, her seven surrounding hills, some sloped, some rugged, hugging the city like a mother's arms. Above, a canopy of stars blinked in the vaulted velvet night.

We swooped beyond the city into a dark green countryside. We sped past brooks and scrambling deer in the forest. The summery breeze smelled of autumn chill. Leaves changed into a fall mosaic and dropped to the forest floor.

Without warning, a bitter wind carried in a cold, gray winter. We flew over a frozen landscape, leaden and dead. In the distance, a desolate small cottage huddled low, its roof dripping with icicles. There were no giggling children on sleds, no barking dogs. An unholy wind howled and drained my body of warmth.

The long, arduous journey through this despair finally ended when the sun forced its rays through bleak skies. A huge, gnarled tree sprawled on the ground, dying. It looked as if it had fallen from one smooth death stroke through its trunk, just above the roots. A large bird, a kind I'd never seen before, with a huge wingspan, dove down and plucked a delicate seed from the scattered fruit of the tree. It ascended quickly to the clouds, flew out over a vast, dark ocean, and dropped the seed from its hooked beak onto some unknown, faraway soil.

Menacing black crows collected around the seed, pecking and clawing at it, trying to break it open. In turn, each bird claimed the seed and each claim was brutally disputed. While the crows cawed and scuffled, a small, light gray bird with friendly eyes rescued the seed. She gripped the seed awkwardly in her talons, but managed to carry it away and bury it safely in the ground.

We waited a good long while where the seed was planted before a young shoot raised its thin neck up from the soil. It grew to resemble the mother tree that had spawned it, maturing to bear fruit and becoming a safe haven for travelers needing food, rest and shelter from the blistering sun.

And from the original, toppled tree, a new shoot emerged. It sprouted slowly, enduring harsh winters, struggling beneath heavy snows. But in time it too blossomed and offered shelter and sustenance like its brother tree across the ocean.

The barren land filled with hamlets, towns, cities, and people, thousands of people everywhere. Then somehow, I was lugging a *hyotan*, a large earthenware pitcher, filled with water.

"What do you want me to do with this?"

"Give it to the people."

I hauled it up and down rugged trails, over mountain passes, and through deep valleys, giving quenching sips to all I met. The pitcher never drained. The *hyotan* grew heavier with every step. Exhausted, I stumbled and fell. The pitcher exploded into thousands of shards. Its infinite water supply gushed out, lost forever. Although this was tragic, I brightened, free of my burden. Thirsty hordes could find refreshment from someone else. With that thought, the pitcher seamlessly pieced itself together, filling once more with water.

"Why doesn't the water ever run out?"

"You will understand when you are older."

The day foundered a moment and switched to pitch dark. Again, buffeted by an unknown power, I rose like a feather and was deposited on a large, flat rock. A blinding burst of white-hot light fully consumed the darkness. My hands covered my eyes, but the light streamed through them. This odd light evaporated slowly, replaced by a merciless sun that withered the barren, empty field spread beneath it. One blade of defiant grass broke through the dust. From the hard-packed dirt, the solitary bright green sprig stood erect. Soon, other blades began piercing the dry earth. First two, then four, then hundreds, thousands, hundreds of thousands of blades carpeted the landscape.

The scent of lush garden flowers transported me. The yellow *Nano-Hana*, Rape Blossom, the emblem of Hiroshima, migrated quickly over the distant hills. This was an enchantment, a sweet seduction. I thought maybe I was in the garden Aunt Takae had told me about: the peaceful place where we all go when we cross to the other side.

A large, ancient tree, with twisted roots and branches, dominated the center of this great field of flowers. Its limbs stretched to the corners of the earth, each teeming with new life, buds unfurling and splashing into blossom.

All around it, new trees were taking root and there was a full forest.

I saw the irrepressible energy of fresh, dewy life pushing away the most hostile surroundings. I rode the wind. I became swift-moving, garden-scented air. My breaths were the life-spring force breathing me. I was the world of essential nature, the tendril showered by the soft spring sun.

"One day, you'll understand," the vague voice said, "I must leave. Wait here. A friend will meet you."

"Don't leave. Take me back home."

The form disappeared like steam. Again, I was lost, alone in a strange place; all bearings and reality anchors had fallen away.

An oboe cut the silence. "I have waited a long time for you." Could it be the voice of a boy my age? I scanned all around, searching.

"I'm here, Takashi."

A large white crane with a red topknot spoke to me. He cocked his head, as if wondering what was wrong with me. "I am *Senba-Zuru*, Mighty as a Thousand Cranes," he bowed low.

"You're a crane."

"Breathe deep from your belly, Takashi," *Senba-Zuru* said. He demonstrated. *Senba-Zuru* stretched his great white wings and inhaled. A long, continuous breath whistled through his beak. "Ahhh!" He exhaled up through his delicate neck and pounded his breast with his wings.

"Please, I need to find my Father."

He beat his wings. "Ahhh, the freshness of spring." A flock of cranes twirled and frolicked just beyond *Senba-Zuru*. One stood alone from the rest, isolated.

"Who is that?"

"It is me."

"How could …?"

Tears trailed down his downy cheeks. A great wing lifted to his eye. "I am from an ancient family of respected white cranes. I grew up in a happy family and then in an instant, it was all taken away. Once, my parents and I were gathering food in a field, when excited voices came at us from all directions. A host of hunters let fly a torrent of arrows. The sky was dark with arrows. My parents, pierced many times, wavered, and fell together on the summer grass. I escaped, though I wished that I hadn't. Living without them is empty and cold. Do you know why I survived, Takashi? Because I was taught to remember who I am, no matter what else may happen."

"How do you do that?"

"If I follow the way of my heart, then I know who I am."

A group of children played in the distance, in a schoolyard. A small boy wandered apart from the group. The pushing, squealing children wore freshly-pressed school uniforms. The outcast had only rags.

"The children don't let him play?"

Senba-Zuru looked straight at me. "That boy is like me. I don't know his story, but he too will survive." Abruptly, *Senba-Zuru* cocked his head and froze. A vacuum of silence consumed the air. The sky spawned a rushing, white unforgiving flash. A searing wind swirled. My scorched lungs coughed, feebly begging for air where there was none. I was drowning in a firestorm.

An earth-shaking growl penetrated the blasting wind and the white blindness. It came from everywhere at once and then blew apart, erupting like a nova, spewing a raging, hungry, massive demon. I faintly heard the crane say, "I will see you again when I return. Live your life, Takashi." The seething air sucked *Senba-Zuru* into the inferno's maw.

I was a stone. I couldn't call out. I couldn't move. I couldn't cry until the licking tongues of fire settled into ash and a galaxy of swirling embers. Then the blinking swell of red and orange sparks became thousands and thousands of butterflies. They swarmed around me and covered the sky above, the horizon. The jittery flight of this multitude, the wings that fanned my face, somehow all this came from the hellfire. A brief space cleared in the crowd of countless beating wings. A single white butterfly appeared and approached.

"Takashi, it's me." I heard *Senba-Zuru*'s oboe voice. I wept. The white crane had become a white butterfly. He lit softly on my palm. His wings slowly opened and closed.

"You too will learn to come back." I bowed. "Remember who you are. Follow where your true heart leads." With that *Senba-Zuru*, my white butterfly, was gone. My palm was empty.

I called after him. The rasp of my own voice woke me. My head was on my Father's leg in the stifling bomb-shelter. My family dozed. The all clear sounded.

"Let's go home," Father said.

I lay awake for the rest of the night, savoring my dream of the crane and the butterfly. It was a dream soon to be blotted from my memory for the next forty years.

Chapter Three: Judgment Day

A NEW morning, August 6, 1945, broke through bright and clear, ending the long night of air raid sirens and fear. A brilliant sun climbed the Hijiyama Mountains above Hiroshima with its 420,000 permanent citizens and 40,000 military personnel. The city awoke from its fitful sleep, thankful that no bombs had fallen during the night. Once again, Hiroshima had been spared the ruinous carpet-bombing of Tokyo, Yokohama, Kobe, Nagoya, and Osaka. Once again, Hiroshima was *testu no nabe*, an invincible cast iron cauldron.

This morning the city returned to normal wartime activities. A volunteer Army Corps had been organizing and mobilizing students of middle schools and girls' schools in the work of defending the city. The rumbling from the demolition of buildings and the widening of streets for "fire-breaks" was shaking the *shoji* screens in my home. The activity was one of many Army Corps Evacuation projects that had become a daily experience for quite some time, a final full-scale preparation for an inevitable invasion of the land by the enemy. Hiroshima would become the decisive battlefield. Buses and military trucks were already evacuating school children to prescribed destinations in villages outside the city.

As soldiers marched past my window, while people on the street cheered them, I lolled in bed, searching the corners of the ceiling for a sign of the great white crane or its soul mate, the white butterfly. The vivid dream pulsed through my mind.

My Mother, as usual, had been up since 5:00 a.m., preparing our breakfast. I wondered if she had slept at all the previous night. My Father religiously rose at 6:00 a.m.. He and I usually spent a few minutes just being together in the morning, before he went to work.

In recent days my Father had repeated the lessons of the *Samurai Code* with increasing intensity. It was now becoming obvious that his reason for this special time with me was to instill the ethics of the Code deep within me.

He had taught me the greatest victory is victory not over others, but over your own weakness. Giving out of abundance is not really true giving. True giving is when you freely give what you really need for yourself. Always make sure you give with your heart. Just because no one is around to witness your decision doesn't mean you are free to make wrong or selfish decisions. Always be true to yourself and honor yourself. Don't judge others. Always tell the truth regardless of the consequences. Don't idle your hands. Don't waste the time of others. Once time is spent it is forever gone. The greatest quality you possess is dependability, so people can always count on you. Once you make a promise, keep it regardless of the cost.

On this morning my door slid open and Father came in. He leaned over me, gently cupping my shoulder. Something was afoot. In the morning's bright light I noticed worry lines on my Father's dark brown forehead. His voice was composed but his hand shook as he closed the *shoji* screen.

"Oto-chan. Father." I was worried about him. I wanted to ask what was going on, but the words stuck in my throat. Neither did he have any words for me.

We shared a moment of powerful unspoken communication. He gently and firmly grasped my shoulders in a gesture of reassurance. I felt his strength flow into me, becoming one with me. I had rarely felt such intense intimacy with him, although we were very close. I understood just then, more than ever before, what it meant to my Father that I was his Number One Son.

Japanese people believe in a special insect called a *mushi* which reveals in secrecy a message of a catastrophe about to happen. I wondered whether my Father had been talking to a *mushi.* He asked me to sit with him and look into his eyes. I sensed a great urgency. He spoke with the same great deliberation as when he had repeated teachings on our walks by the river. It was as if he thought this was his last opportunity to instill the *Samurai* principles to the honorable son of Tanemori.

He told me, "Takashi, always remember to sacrifice your own immediate needs for a higher moral purpose.

Always observe reverence for life. And never forget to live for the benefit of others. These are the pillars of the *Samurai Code*. Takashi, listen carefully. I will say once more …"

Suddenly our talk was cut short as the sky erupted with shrill sirens warning of enemy aircraft approaching. At 7:09 a.m., on August 6, 1945 the radio blared the frantic announcement: "Enemy planes, B-29's, are in the skies northwest of Hiroshima, approaching sharply to the heart of the City."

Above us in the blue sky, the wings of three B-29s glittered in the sunlight as they flew in formation over Hiroshima City. The enemy planes no longer were shrouded by the darkness of night, but boldly approached in the brightness of day while Hiroshima's citizens were still recovering from the air raid less than five hours before.

"Three large enemy planes are proceeding westward over Saijo area ..." frantically came the voice of Mr. Masanobu Furuta, the radio announcer on duty at Hiroshima Castle's headquarters.

The screams of the sirens brought the city to a screeching halt. Our clock ticked in the silence as time seemed to stretch. For me, this was the first ever daylight air raid. We heard our running neighbors' footsteps as they rushed from their houses toward nearby bomb shelters. My Father hesitated before making his decision to stay in the house with the family. He called everyone into his room. My Mother, unexpectedly, showed her strength by supporting my Father's decision. We sat, holding our breath by our tiny radio, waiting for the next official announcement.

At 7:31 a.m., the announcer confidently delivered good news from Military Headquarters, "No enemy plane is in sight!" He repeated with a strong voice, "No enemy plane is in sight. It is all clear."

The radio said the *B-sans,* B-29's, had gone away. The "All Clear" was announced to great sighs of relief, loud applause and shouts of *Banzai* from all quarters of the city, like the ringing-in of a New Year! The clock started ticking again. Activity resumed as on any other day.

On the street, I watched my Father calmly greet neighbors emerging from the bomb shelter. I heard the voices of my neighborhood buddies, Taro, Katsutoshi and Kazuko, who had all played war games together, chattering excitedly about the events of the previous night.

"Were you scared when *B-san* showed its face this morning?"

Kazu fearlessly replied to Taro, "No! Why should I be afraid? Weren't they chased away by Japanese soldiers last night?"

"Yeah! But, you are acting like a little borrowed kitten, afraid of the big, monster American soldiers!"

"See, what did I tell you, Kazu. I just knew that *B-sans* were scared of Japanese soldiers. And they may have seen my Father's face. Ha, ha, ha! I bet they were scared like a little kitten."

"I am ready to fight. See. I have a bamboo spear. I am going to charge all Americans. It will be just like spearing fish."

"*Futari to mo Eikagen ni shinasai yo,*" Taro's mother turned to Kazuo. "You two stop nonsense talk. Instead of babbling, you need to return home and get ready for school."

She turned to Kazu and Masumi. "There is nothing to take lightly about the war. Your soldiers are fighting and dying to protect us. Your war games on the streets are no comparison to the realities of war. Instead of silly babbling, get ready to go to school."

I reflected about my Father, caught on the horn of his personal dilemma. He had an allegiance to the Emperor and he also had an allegiance to follow his truth and his heart. There were men from my neighborhood who were fighting in the thickest battlefields on islands in the Pacific Ocean. Many of their ashes had already been returned home in pine boxes.

At that moment, I felt shame for my Father, who had chosen not to be a soldier like Taro's father. I had to reassure myself that my Father was an honorable Japanese man even though he was not a soldier. He was, nonetheless, working for the Japanese Imperial Government. What was wrong with that? I had never heard him blaming any government or military leaders for this bloody war and the fate of Japan, which was in the hands of the same Japanese leaders who had made the decision to enter the war four years earlier. I should feel proud of my Father!

Taro arrived at our back door so that we could go to school together. I grabbed my *randoseru,* my official Japanese school backpack, and prepared to leave for school. Suddenly, a soft whimpering drew my attention toward a dark corner of our front room.

"Mommy?" I asked. As I moved closer, the darkness lifted to reveal my Mother gently rocking my baby sister Sayoko and quietly sobbing to herself. I instinctively extended my hand to touch her shoulder gently.

She looked at me with urgency in her eyes and asked me to stay with her a little longer. I walked to the door and told Taro that I would see him later, then returned to my Mother.

Just as my Father had, my Mother approached me with an inexplicable urgency in her voice. Her eyes were so transparent, I saw myself mirrored in them. Her unease was so clear, I took her hands in mine.

"Why are you crying, Mother?"

She seemed distant and withdrawn, but was finally able to speak in a soft, quivering voice as she composed herself, "*Chichi oya no oshie o kesshite wasure naide kudasai. Soshite Anata wa Tanemori no Chonan de arukagiri Samurai no chi o tsuide imasu. Sono koto mo wasure naide isshokenmei ganbatte ikite itte kudasai ne.* Always remember what your Father has taught you and never forget that you are the Number One Son, heir to a *Samurai* family. You have a duty to live victoriously as a Son of Tanemori."

"What's going on?" I asked. "Why are you talking like this all of a sudden? It doesn't make sense to me! Was anything happening this morning before I woke up?"

Then I squeezed my Mother's shoulder reassuringly and said, "It's okay, Mother, the B-sans will not come today."

"You are the Number One Son of Tanemori!" exclaimed my Mother. "Do not forget, you have a duty to live victoriously as a son of Tanemori."

"I understand, Mother." I said in a quiet voice. *"Oka-a-san, Nani mo shinpai shinaide kudasai. Takashi wa chonan dakara ne. Sayoko wa boku ga chanto mamotte yarimasu."* There is no need to worry. I am the Number One Son and I will protect my baby sister, Sayoko."

I reassured her that I would uphold the teachings of my Father.

She quickly turned away from me, perhaps to hide her tears.

"So ne. Oka-a-san wa nanimo shinpai shinai demo yokkata no ne. Takashi wa chanto wakatte kurete imasu ne? I shouldn't worry about you. You understand, I know. I don't need to remind you again, do I?"

She motioned me to go as she tried unsuccessfully to hold back a river of tears. "How silly I am," she said, wiping her tear-drenched face.

That was the first time I ever saw my Mother cry. Seeing so many tears was very unsettling for me. I had never seen her acting so strangely.

Through the open *shoji* screen of my Father's room, I could see my younger brother, Sadayoshi, sitting on my Father's lap. My older sister, Masuyo, was in the kitchen, finishing up dirty dishes before getting ready for school. No one had noticed the exchange between Mother and me.

"Sah, hayaku, hayaku! Hurry, hurry!" She tried to shoo me out the door.

I gathered up my *randoseru* and shouted, "I am going now!" then, to reassure her, *"Oka-a-san, B-sans* will not come back any more."

I watched military trucks, tanks, and the march of soldiers on the main street, only fifty yards from our house. Filled with excitement, I waved vigorously to the soldiers, giving them a big smile. I smiled because the sounds of marching assured me that *B-sans* would not attack the invincible city of Hiroshima. *"Heitai-san, Arigato!* Thank you soldiers!"

By the time I reached the Tenma Gawa River I had turned to reflect sadly on my Mother's flood of tears. The Tenma Gawa was one of seven rivers snaking through the city, and it ran right behind the school. I contemplated the footprints of sparrows or seagulls that marked the smooth, sandy beach left by the outgoing tide. I took a deep breath of fresh morning air mingled with the sea breeze saltiness, savoring the sensation.

Outside the main gate of the school, Kazu, a rambunctious second grade classmate, asked me why I was so late to join them on the way to school. Sumiko inquired, "What's the matter with you anyway? Where is your good old spunkiness?" They were mad at me for taking so long to join them.

"Come on. Let's play quickly!" Taro shouted at me. "We don't have much time, hurry!"

Suddenly, I returned to my "old" self, the rambunctious boy. We always played *Kakurenbo*, hide and seek, in the morning, and my friends had all waited for me to play our favorite game. I was excited, for it was my turn to be *"it"* this morning!

We all bowed deeply before the shrine of the Emperor at the school entrance and then ran past several hundred soldiers who were marching in unison and drilling with bayonets inside the school grounds. I couldn't shake off the memory of my Mother's sadness, as I gazed out the classroom's front windows at the soldiers while my classmates hid from me.

Being *"it"* while my classmates hid granted me a few calm seconds to overlook the schoolyard. I started to count *ichi, nii, san ...* the school clock moved towards 8:15 a.m. ... on August 6, *shi, go, roku ...* 1945 ... in my home town of Hiroshima! Through my covered eyes I saw my Mother crying. I counted, *shichi, hachi, ku, juu.* The chase was on. *Nine. Ten. Ready or not, here I ...*

The schoolroom clocked snapped to 8:15 and time stopped.

"ON THIS MORNING, THIS JUDGMENT DAY" the belly of the *Enola Gay* opened 24,500 feet above

"ground zero," as though the mouth of a giant were yawning wide, and out came "Little Boy"—three meters long and weighing four tons. Though its uranium weighed only one kilogram, the bomb's destructive power was the equivalent of 20,000 tons of TNT.

Two minutes earlier, air raid sirens had again shrieked and a warning had been broadcast from military headquarters. Mr. Furuta had read a news flash at exactly 8:13 a.m. This second warning had caught the people of Hiroshima by surprise, and I had not even heard it.

"Forty-Three Seconds Over Hiroshima" an atomic bomb detonated several hundred feet above Fuku-ya's Department Store where I used to trawl for goldfish. "... Oh, My God ... Hiroshima Strike!"

Without warning! BLINDING, BURNING, SHOCKING, WHITE LIGHT! I covered my closed eyes. I saw pure white light through my covered eyes.

A gigantic super sun blinded all creation. Thousands of suns all at once burst through a hole in the universe, consuming all colors within its whiteness. Even the blackness of a blind man's world would have been eradicated by its power. It consumed all, fused heaven and earth, ate every color, every shadow, every breath.

The *Pika-don!*—the flash bomb! Heaven and Earth were fused, One. The moment was captured in an eerie, dead silence. The silence was deafening. I saw nothing. I felt nothing! The ether froze in dead stillness. God's heart stopped beating. That was my last memory for an unknown length of time …

In an instant my school and all Hiroshima had evaporated. When I regained consciousness, I awoke in Hell! The three-story wooden frame school had collapsed into a heap of matchsticks. My third floor classroom lay shattered and flattened on the ground. Beneath the heap, I lay buried on my back, unable to move. I couldn't see anything. An immense pressure shoved me down and choked me so hard I could only manage a weak, silent scream of sheer terror. I could smell intense heat, and I sensed a molten fire moving toward me like an unrelenting river of lava.

I gasped for air like a fish out of water, as a super-heated torch seared my lungs and all the scorched air was sucked from the atmosphere. I lay gasping in an oven, choking for the breath of life. The weight of the inflamed air forced me down, far away. I was disappearing. I gasped the merciless air for breath. Except for a red glow, all was pitch black.

Though I couldn't see anything, I heard the screaming of my closest friends, Taro and Sumiko and others in the darkness. They were desperately crying out for *mizu*—water, water!

"Shinuru hodo atsui, atsui. I am dying."

We called out to each other, *"Kazu, Sumiko, Taro, Masa ..."*

We cried, too, for our parents. We all were screaming at the top of our lungs, but had little power to reach through this devil's wall of fire coming to consume us like a voracious, rampaging lion. Twisted black and yellow tongues of fire flickered through the red, blinding darkness, leaping at us like thousands of heartless vipers. We were all trapped with no escape, helpless as the caterpillars we used to burn just for fun, watching them writhe and be consumed in the blink of an eye among flaming leaves. We were doomed. Toshi's plea for life was the last agonized cry I heard.

"Atsui! Atsui! Mizu o kudasai! Water! Water!" One by one, the flames engulfed my classmates. Their cries for help were unanswered!

"Toshi, Gomen ne!" Please forgive me, Toshi. I begged him to forgive me because I couldn't help him. He sounded so far away. My second grade classmates were crying out for their mommies and daddies as, one by one, flames engulfed their small bodies. Now all my classmates were silent.

Trapped by debris, I couldn't move. Something hot and dripping burned my face. It must have been my own boiling blood which I felt dripping down my face, left arm and back. The fire was about to consume me.

"Oto-sa—a—n; Oto-saaan!" I screamed for my Father in total panic and desperation. My tongue stuck to the roof of my mouth like a weathered leaf. The roaring fire leapt to consume me. I was frozen in this fire! I knew I was a goner.

Time elapsed ... I don't remember anything more until I heard the faint voices of men. Mustering all my strength I screamed *"Ta—suke-e-e-teeeeee!* Help! Save me!"* I was surprised to hear my own voice! I was still alive! I screamed again. Then, I saw something or somebody:

"I am here!" A voice responded. *"Ooi Kocchida! Hayaku. Kocchi dazo!* Come this way quickly, come! *Dareka go kokoni iruzo!* I think there is someone right here underneath the rubble!"

The soldier moved the burning debris and grabbed hold of me, pulling me into his arms.

And so began my long journey ...

Many other soldiers were looking for other children. I saw one soldier carrying a child who was charred, blackened beyond any recognition, lifeless arms and legs dangling. It could have been me. This was the first scene of continuous days of horror I would witness. These images, branded in my mind, would haunt me for the rest of my life. Later I discovered I was 1164 meters from the hypocenter of the blast—about 7/10ths of a mile.

The soldier carrying me weaved in and out of throngs of people who were screaming in agony, charred, dead or just barely alive. People were creeping, stumbling, dragging their feet, crawling on knees and elbows, looking for any escape from the blazing inferno closing in on all sides. Parents were searching for their children, their vain cries and the shrieking of children incessant over the raging roar of the fire.

Writhing like worms, shrieking humans mangled under flaming debris were consumed in seconds. Their extinction made strange puffing sounds, like that of exploding fuzzy caterpillars. All the while I was being carried in the arms of my soldier, as he stepped over the dead, disfigured bodies.

Practically everyone was scorched, their clothes burnt and shredded. Some were naked and blistered, their hair singed. Many were unrecognizable, charred so black it was impossible to know whether they were male or female. Many children and grownups were groping at my rescuer, begging him to put them out of their misery. Others were pleading, *"Mizu, Mizu!* Water, Water!"

Smoke blackened the entire heaven and the sun refused to show its face. The stench of burning human flesh continued to ascend. I still didn't know what had happened. The voracious, roaring sound of fire was only broken by the piercing cries of children in search of rescue by their parents. Unrecognizably disfigured and mangled bodies fused with charred debris everywhere. Everything I saw was a filthy pitch black.

Those who could still move were moving en masse to the banks of the Tenma Gawa River. The disabled became helpless fuel for the irate fire. I witnessed the unforgettable horror of a mother, a headless infant in a sling on her back, screaming out the names of her lost children—looking vainly everywhere. She was unaware that the force of the blast had blown her baby's head off. What horror must have consumed her when she finally discovered the headless beloved bundle! My imagined semblance of her experience has brought me a realm of unspeakable grief ever since.

At the Tenma Gawa, throngs of people ran and pushed each other to claim some space on the sandy banks of the once clean and tranquil river. Grotesque dead bodies were floating like blowfish in the blackened sewage-like water, yet people rushed into it, voraciously drinking all they could swallow. The poisoned river claimed their lives and they disappeared into the current. Finally, the soldier carrying me reached the sandy beach of the river. He managed to find a place for us between the raging inferno behind and the angry river in front, as a throng of people claimed their "territory."

Then a miracle happened. My Father spotted me and called out my name. How on earth my Father found me I will never know, but there he was, clamoring over bodies to claim his son! In the midst of all this horror I experienced a moment of joy and gratitude. I knew I would be safe. I'm in my Father's arms now! My Father bowed many times to the soldier, profusely thanking him. I never saw a happier face on my Father.

"I am glad that your son is rescued, sir," said the soldier. "I must return to my company. I have a duty to perform. *Ogenki de ganbatte Ikite itte kudasai!* I trust you will be strong to live a long life!"

"*Anata wa Onjin desu. Arigoto gozai mashita.* You are a savior. Thank you, thank you for saving my son."

The soldier saluted my Father and disappeared back into the inferno. Long after the soldier had vanished into the smoke and crowds, my Father bowed after him with ultimate gratitude.

Father brought me to where Grandfather and Grandmother Tanemori, Masuyo, and my little brother Sadayoshi were gathered by the river's edge. I was in shock and didn't realize that Mother and little Sayoko weren't standing with them. The only thing I knew at this point was that my Father was holding me in his strong arms.

The flow of thousands of survivors flooded the river's narrow shore. All the bridges had fallen. This thin line of sand was the only oasis. A sea of faces grew. Those nearest the river's edge were nudged into the murky currents and swept away.

Those who had survived the raging firestorm, who had suffered burns of the worst degree and horrific wounds, complained most of an unquenchable thirst, pleading to heaven "*Mizu, Mizu, Mizu o Kudasai!* Water, water, give me water!"

Oddly enough, inky clouds from the northwest blew towards us. Swollen, black clouds blotted out the last few shafts of daylight. As the swirling darkness descended, anxiety spread like a rumor throughout the bleeding, cowering mass. What new horror was coming?

Jagged lightning tore the sky apart and a black, sticky rain fell. It smelled like the city's smoke.

Raindrops the size of golf balls dropped, pounding our scarred and scorched flesh. Every drop that struck me felt like someone hitting me with a hammer on open blisters. Through our pain, we were hoping the rain would extinguish the inferno. Everyone became wrapped in a black, sticky film. The downpour lasted for three hours, yet the city kept right on burning.

The rain angered the river. It foamed and rose quickly, eating at the hem of our refuge. Many were sucked into the flume. The huddling mass squeezed painfully closer, shrinking to preserve precious space. Some people pushed others away in order to save themselves from being sucked into the angry, black, oily river. Parents followed their screaming loved ones as they were swept into the current.

Trapped between the fury of the fire and the black *tsunami*, tidal wave, the only place to go was up. Some climbed on top of others. Some were crushed. Father was vigilant about monitoring the movements of this unwieldy crowd. He anticipated the direction of the surge and kept us in rhythm with the arbitrary thrust and parry of the massive beast. He led us to a high point on the riverbank. We struggled to keep firm footing on this slanted earth, while the Tenma became a gruesome river of corpses, a tide of thousands of bloated bodies.

I was covered with burns. In my Father's arms, I passed in and out of consciousness. Somehow, the rest of my family here on the riverbank seemed to have escaped serious injury. We stood under the black sky, by the swollen black river, with ravenous flames at our backs.

Day came and I woke, marooned with thousands of others on the beach. Blood smeared Father's hands and shirt. It was my blood. I was seriously injured. I could feel the damp, gaping wound under my left shoulder blade. I could see the oozing hole on the outside of my left knee, which prevented me from walking. Jagged glass shards were embedded in my head above the left ear. Skin hung off my left forearm. The morning sun pierced the smoky skies. I felt fire all over me again. My wounds suppurated.

The surging black river quieted. Yokogawa Bridge was destroyed, but its pilings snared debris and hundreds of bloated bodies. Desperate survivors attempted to cross over, using the pilings and bodies as stepping stones. Most often, the current or the water-slick corpses stole their footing. The weak collapsed mid-stride, contributing themselves to this bridge of death.

Father continually scanned the crowd, looking for Mother and my baby sister. For a brief moment, he saw a familiar figure in the crowd. "Yoshiko! Yoshiko!" He rushed up. The startled, disfigured woman was a stranger.

Father returned. We saw him fold to the ground.

Each new body added to the fragile stability of the bridge of corpses. At ebb tide, Father decided it was time to cross. If Mother and little sister were still alive, we would have to leave them behind. Maybe we'd rejoin later. Although we were weakened, we couldn't stay any longer on the riverbank with the spreading pack of frantic refugees, and expect to survive. The gruesome bridge offered a slim hope, but it was our only one.

We held hands and stepped across wide-eyed bodies. Father carried me, leading the others in single file, across the low tide to the other side. Father set me down on the bank and then solemnly touched each one of us, as if in blessing.

Sadayoshi asked for Mother.

"She'll be with us again soon," said Masuyo. Her cheek touched his.

The inferno burned behind the milling throng on the other side. When the tide rose again, the river burst through the grisly bridge, breaking the only escape route. Father bowed to his parents and asked for forgiveness. He could do nothing to ease their suffering. Bowing low, he vowed to find a way to bring us all to safety.

Lush rice paddies had once stretched out from this bank. But here the blast had left only a stretch of barren, smoldering clods. In front of us, a ragged field of blackened, limping skeletons inched their way to the rutted wagon road. We joined them. The march was silent except for the deep sighs and clumsy footfalls of the exhausted, injured, and dying. Father was my transport. He'd trip on brittle, desiccated bodies that, only moments before, had walked in front of us. And then Grandfather would help

Father lift me up again, to get in step with the masses before being crushed.

A little girl squatted by her mother, trying to wake her from her last dream. The glassy-eyed parade marched around and over the girl, fixed on one goal only. Keep moving. One step closer to relief from throat squeezing, from pain, from the reality of history. Keep moving. Nothing but death interferes with the next step.

Black flies swarmed out of the sun-brightened air, feeding on our blood and pus. I swatted at them, but it was futile. We were overrun. They fed fearlessly.

When evening fell, the flies retreated to rest their sated bellies. A cluster of farmhouses crouched in the near distance. Excitement rippled through our sorry lot, as we approached a hive of harried people.

A community relief effort was in full swing. Ordinary citizens threw themselves into acts of mercy, distributing hot food, tea, and medical supplies. Hundreds of survivors sat on the ground, resting, sipping tea. Others stood in long lines for food and medical treatment.

The only doctor, his white jacket striped with blood, bent over one soul, then over another.

He treated those who were in the most danger and yet had a chance of surviving. Several nurses, identifiable by their hats, moved from person to person, assessing who should be treated first. The triage process was an endless run of spur-of-the-moment life and death decisions.

A relief worker, an elderly man with a kind, weathered face, said to a victim, "We are very, very sorry, we cannot do more. We are only simple farmers."

Father remained patient. He helped those ahead of us in line receive their treatment. When it was my turn, a nurse's soft, kind hands cleaned my wounds with warm water and plucked the larger pieces of glass from my scalp. She squeezed soothing cucumber juice over my burns. It was the only medicine available.

A food distributor handed me some warm tea, a small rice ball, and a slice of *daikon*, pickled radish. After what we'd experienced, the tastes were new and exquisite. We settled on rice straw strewn outside the barn.

Hiroshima burned so brightly in the distance that night never appeared. I closed my eyes and saw again maimed, disfigured forms pulling themselves forward by their elbows, their seared skin dripping from their bones. These were the *yurei*, living ghosts. I saw them, nightmare creatures plodding relentlessly after me. I burrowed into my Father's arms.

That night I slept lightly, often waking up to the hiss of pyres being lit. Relief workers, covered in protective suits, quietly searched out the dead. They stacked them neatly in small pyramids on top of rice straw, then touched the kindling with a torch. The familiar smell of burning flesh threatened our newly found comfort. The Death Angels came for many people that night.

I must have finally given myself over to exhaustion and to faith: I was protected in the loving arms of my Father, because I didn't recollect any more. I had become a zombie lost in a realm of horror. I had probably reached a saturation point, a limit of the amount of shock a child can withstand. My haven, my home, my classmates, everything I had ever known and cherished, had all been extinguished.

> *Blameless souls forever vanish*
> *on this morning, this Judgment Day.*
> *Our silent cries, to heaven we appeal,*
> *scattered like the ash of withered leaves.*
> *Our ebbing souls*
> *cling to that lonely sky;*
> *we try in vain to escape this sea of flame.*
> *Oh, Hiroshima, once my haven,*
> *why has your life been sacrificed?*

I was left with only the loving arms of my Father, my scorched painful body and, I suppose, a will to survive. I have often wondered why I was spared.

Chapter Four: Black Engine to Kotachi

THE next morning, I woke to unendurable pain. My burns seared with fierce heat. Dark yellow, foul-smelling pus seeped from my left forearm. I shivered with the heat of my infection.

Father said we would reach the Yaguchi train station by late afternoon. The train was our salvation. It would take us to Kotachi Village, and the house of our maternal grandmother, Setsu, Grandmother Sakae. And so we stepped into the crowd, again beginning the *Mugon Shinigami Gyoretsu,* the silent death march. Black flies soon found us along the way.

At Yaguchi Station, three engines idled on separate tracks. The windows of their passenger cars were blown out. Shattered glass littered their aisles and seats.

The plodding, silent marchers broke into a ragged, frantic run, attacking the nearest door, scrambling for some small space on a train. They twisted and battled to place a foot on the step, and squeeze in. The weaker were pushed aside or trampled in the crush. Parents stranded on the platform passed small children through the open windows to strangers.

The situation inside the train did not improve. Wounded bodies contorted to fit in the crammed rail cars. Fights broke out as space diminished. Outside the cars, some who were able clung wildly to the roof or sides.

A man attempted to carry his dead son onto the train.

"Fool. Your child is dead," someone shouted, "leave it behind." Angry hands tore the body from the father.

"Make room for the living," another shouted.

A cheer rose when the *Ekicho-san*, the station manager, blew his whistle, and the trains pulled out, one after the other. Those left on the platform dispersed. On the platform and the tracks, several dead lay where they had fallen. This was their last race. Rescue workers cleared the bodies before the next train pulled in.

Father, ever alert and cautious, kept us at a safe distance from the mob. He wept and begged our forgiveness for allowing us to suffer.

Masuyo said, "We would not be living, if not for you."

"*Arigato*, Masuyo, *On ni Kiruzo,*" my Father bowed low, thanking her. She was sixteen then, his eldest, the first of his wooden nickels.

"*Sadao, suman sewa o yakasu no,*" Grandfather said, apologizing for being a burden. Father fought through tears and said that helping his parents was his greatest honor. Then he fell to the ground, covering his face. Grandfather touched his shoulders.

Two proud, disciplined *Samurai*, on the bare earth, inconsolable. I had never before seen men show such emotional vulnerability. I was awe-struck, beyond my pain and sickness.

A rescuer worker said a train from Kotachi Village would soon arrive. Father dusted himself off and began planning how to avoid the stampeding mob. Our lives depended upon him getting all of us onto the next train.

After a difficult wait, we heard a distant shrill whistle. We moved to the end platform. When the black engine groaned into the station, Father signaled us to rush for the boxcar, the very last in line. It was already crammed, but we barged in. Father found a spot under a blown-out window. With his back to the crowd, he held me in his lap with one arm, using his other arm to brace himself. He shielded me.

Masuyo and Sadayoshi found refuge in a nearby corner, their grandparents standing guard over them.

The late summer sun baked the train. Inside the car, the squeezed bodies broiled. The dank, hot air was laced with the smell of sweat and the odors of oozing wounds. The pained and disconsolate high-pitched wails of children were scattered throughout the silence of stone-faced adults. We waited. An eternity passed and another began, before the whistle blew and the train lurched forward.

As it gained rhythm and speed, the engine's smoke streamed backwards and seeped into our boxcar. We took shallow breaths. Through the smoke and shattered window, I saw lines of the torn and forlorn wandering beside the tracks, heading away from the horror.

Our destination was Kotachi Village, sixty-three miles by rail. There Setsu, our Grandmother Sakae, lived with her husband. I only vaguely knew her, but I imagined her waiting for us at the station.

The engine chugged us through a rolling countryside, far from the devastation. Serene landscapes of gentle hills, lush, green valleys and rice paddies. Bamboo groves lined the track, swaying in welcome as we sped by. The passing scenes lifted my spirits. We were going to be saved.

Then the engine noise and the rail clacking spiked. We held our ears while our little world on the floor of the train plunged into a deep, loud darkness. Hot, acrid smoke filled the car like never before. Fears of a fiery death returned. *"Astui. Atsui.* Hot. Hot." Father's arms tightened around me. Then, as quickly as it disappeared, sunlight returned and the noise quieted. Father said we had passed through a tunnel.

"Mizu. Mizu o kudasai. Water to cool my tongue."

"Takashi, gaman suru noda," Father said, "Be strong and say nothing."

I tried. But after the first, we went through tunnel after tunnel. The smoke and heat seared and choked my rasping lungs as we raced through the alternating light and darkness. I pleaded, *"Mizu. Mizu. Atsui. Atsui."*

At each station bodies, like cordwood, were stacked on the platform. Black flies thickened the putrid air. Rescue workers, white scarves over their noses, helped the living disembark from the train.

Villagers clustered on the platform, searching each face that emerged. Burned, disfigured, melted, many survivors were unrecognizable. An elderly farmer at one stop named his son as each person stepped down. "Are you my son? Are you?"

Once passengers exited the train, rescue workers with scarves and black armbands began the search for corpses. Their white gloves were soon painted red with bloody gore.

After a few stops, enough living and dead had departed to create room for us to stretch our legs. Sadayoshi, in Grandfather's arms, was thrilled by the ride on a train. He mimicked the sound of the black engine, "*Chu-chu. Chu-chu.*"

We neared Kotachi, and Father said, "Masuyo, we'll be there soon."

She never complained once during the ordeal. She held her head, sighing frequently. I wanted to be as brave as my big sister. My Father sat in a warrior's silence. He was strangely detached for the entire trip, a dark mask obscuring the face I knew.

At Kotachi station, he awakened from his trance. Cradling me in his arms, he stood to survey the car, memorizing every detail. He saw a man fall away just as we arrived at the station. The man lay curled near his wife. She begged him not to go.

"*Anata, naze. Anata wa naze.* Beloved husband, why have you left me? How can I care for our three children without you?" The wife and her children's keening sliced through Father like a sword. He may have thought of Mother and Sayoko.

I felt his chest tremble when he commanded our little family to prepare to disembark. The other passengers seemed relieved to have arrived, why wasn't Father? I thought we had escaped the Angel of Death, but something was still wrong.

The train hissed and heaved at Kotachi station. Villagers waved at us and cheered. With the train's arrival came the rippling excitement of families anticipating a post-apocalyptic reunion. The piles of unclaimed bodies dotting the platform didn't dampen the electric thrill. But I saw them, heaped like deformed manikins, and I understood that no one could escape the long reach of the bomb, even out here in the remote countryside of Kotachi.

We stepped down. The villagers massed, searching faces for kin. Father led us to the *hiroba*, the village square.

There we found temporary refuge from the crowd beneath an enormous black pine.

A woman, propped up by two young boys, staggered from the train toward her relatives. She was badly burned, but was coming here to bring her children home.

She bowed, "Thank you for waiting … so sorry to worry you. So sorry." She fell there.

"Miyoko?" her Father said. He carried her home.

What seemed to be a young man lay on the ground. Both legs were blackened stumps, his face a vague blur of features, both eyes soldered shut. In a surprisingly strong voice, he chanted his and his parents' names.

"I am Katsutoshi Yamato," he repeated like a mantra. "My parents live in Sudano Village. Please, help me find them." Katsutoshi means "year of victory."

His parents, an elegantly dressed elderly couple, stared at him. A few villagers urged the couple to acknowledge their son.

His Father bent over the young man and spoke something into his ear. His parents wouldn't step forward and claim their son. Loss of limbs, sight, or hearing were traditionally viewed as disabilities, karmic punishment for wrongdoing. Those less than whole were shameful to their kin and so must be hidden away in the shadows for their entire lives.

Mrs. Yamato delicately covered her mouth and tiptoed toward him. Her husband yanked her around sharply. He held her fused to his flank while splitting a path through the crowd, away from the nightmare.

"Yoshiko, Yoshiko wa kaette kita ka? Yoshiko, Yoshiko Tanemori, where are you?" Grandmother Setsu's voice sailed from the other side of the square. I heard her call my Mother's name. Why didn't she do the proper thing and call my Father? Father spoke up only when she walked right beside us.

"Sakae no Oka-a-san. Tanemori Sadao desu," he said, "Mrs. Sakae, Mother, I am Sadao Tanemori." He bowed to her and to her husband, Mr. Rokuji Sakae.

Grandmother Setsu looked at us and through us. She paled. Yoshiko wasn't there.

"We Tanemori have returned to you," Father continued, "I ask for your kindness and indulgence."

"Where is Yoshiko? You brought your children but not my daughter?"

Father bowed deeply, and in fear. He didn't raise his eyes, and awaited her response. I felt his heartbeats become louder and faster. He waited, unflinching. Neither did my Step-Grandfather, Mr. Rokuji Sakae, move.

"Why have you not brought my daughter home? What kind of a man are you? You save your own skin but leave your wife behind. Are you a coward?"

No one ever spoke to Father like that. In Hiroshima, people deferred to him. Now a woman was humiliating him in public. Grandmother was insane. Her husband didn't try to stop her.

My fists clenched. Father had saved our lives and now our own Grandmother shamed him. The outburst drew an audience.

"Where is my daughter? If you were a man, you would answer me. *Anta wa tsunbo ka no?* Why are you acting deaf and dumb? Don't you have any balls?"

Father did not protest.

What was unfolding before my eyes was contrary to all I had been taught by my parents. Seeing my own Father, respected as a proud Japanese man in the City of Hiroshima, being treated as a public spectacle was nothing but humiliating. My heart filled with anger and confusion.

Why should my Father be subjected to this breach of social code? Why were we not welcomed?

Japanese society was hierarchical, stressing the prerogatives of rank, sex, and age. My Father should be received with honor and dignity. The way of man was to observe the virtues of filial piety and obedience.

Model behavior for the woman was submissive obedience to the man. With all due respect to my Grandmother, she should have been aware of the consequences of defying the written and unwritten social codes and moral laws. She should have kept her proper place as a woman and honored my Father, or endured public punishment. What audacity she had! … to exercise her *will* in the public eye and humiliate my Father!

Further, I couldn't understand my Step-Grandfather standing afar, not only failing to intercede, but seemingly content to watch his wife ridicule my Father without pity. The distinguished Mr. Kamehachi Tominaga, a powerful village elder, stepped squarely in front of Grandmother. "*Se-chan.* Enough is enough. Your son-in-law has shown great courage by bringing your family to Kotachi Village. Be grateful. Open your heart, welcome them home."

Mr. Sakae took his wife's arm and motioned us to follow them.

As we walked in their wake, Grandfather Tanemori said, "Sadao, how painful it must have been to bear her attack. Thank you for your *mugon*, courageous silence. *"Yurushite kure.* We owe everything to you."

Under the arched eyebrow of Mr. Tominaga and the darting eyes of the small crowd, Grandmother Setsu yielded and took in our woe-begotten family. But we were not family to her. Yoshiko was not with us. Her daughter's blood no longer coursed through her grandchildren's veins.

A *naya*, a small storage shed for garden tools and supplies, crouched behind her house. Grandmother pointed to it. The *naya* boasted nothing but a roof and a floor, but it seemed a palace to us. We gratefully slept on the floor. Grandmother Setsu did knock once on our little door and delivered a bit of broth, rice, and tea. Masuyo used some of the tea to clean my wounds. Our life in Kotachi had begun.

The tranquility of this first night ended abruptly. Outside the shed's window, Grandmother shouted, "Coward. You left my daughter burning in hell. How can you live with yourself? Answer me."

I wished for Father to strike her quiet. But, as before, he withstood the verbal assault in *mugon*. She never understood his silence as strength and forbearance. It could only be sniveling cowardice. She slammed the door of her house. Her hysteria, unsatisfied, vanished with her.

The tainted scent of cremation fires crept into the shed from Kotachi Station. The *shini-gami,* Death Angels, were busy. I drifted into sleep until the sun was high enough to sneak through the slits and unsealed seams of the shed.

I woke to find Masuyo, wide eyes set in a strangely gaunt face, gazing into oblivion. Her dirty hair was matted in patches. She stared like the dead. "Masuyo *Ne-e-chan?* Are you all right?" I asked.

She stirred. *"Taka-chan.* Forgive me. Your sister is so worn out, so tired. Every bone aches."

"Oto-saaan, Oto-saaan. Masuyo, where is Father?"

"Don't worry, Takashi," she said, "Father went to Hiroshima to search for Mother and baby sister."

He was gone. He had left to revisit hell's inner circle. He wouldn't survive the return trip. And even if he did, how could he ever hope to find Mother and Sayoko alive? The risks for him, and for us without him, were numbing. But, I thought, Father knows how to survive and protect his family. He makes the right decisions. Maybe, if he finds Mother and she comes to us here in Kotachi, Grandmother might be more welcoming.

Masuyo also told me that Grandmother and Grandfather Tanemori had set out for Kametsuka, their old village. They knew they would never be welcome here, and that their presence in Kotachi would endanger their grandchildren. To save the children, they sacrificed themselves. They left early in the morning. I never saw them again. No one knows if they ever arrived at the village of their youth. No one mentioned them again. It was forbidden.

The daughters of Grandmother's husband, Mr. Sakae, wandered into Kotachi during the next few days. *"O-oi, Ba-a-san,"* he shouted to Grandmother, "they all have come home safe and sound. *Medetai! Medetai no.* What happiness."

Open arms greeted them. They were offered bedrooms in the main house and could eat anything they wished. Not one of them had any injuries.

Grandmother fussed over them, apologizing for the humble condition of the house, begging them to make themselves comfortable. These scenes were played out blatantly before me, as if my family was of so little consequence it made no difference whether I witnessed the favoritism or not.

When Uncle Tetsu Nakamura showed up, Grandmother Sakae threw a party to celebrate. In our dark *naya,* Masuyo, Sadayoshi, and I huddled and listened to the peals of merriment coming from the house. We dreamt about the feast they must be eating.

I despised Grandmother. My blood had boiled in the burning, collapsed schoolroom. Now here in the cool of the evening, in the dark shed, I felt it boil again with hate and outrage. I wished for the magic power to drain every drop of my Grandmother's blood from my body and replenish it with pure Tanemori blood.

The next day we had our own party. It wasn't a phantom dream! I heard familiar voices.

"Tadaima kaette kimashita. We're home now," was the greeting of my sisters, Satsuko and Chisako, when they came to the door of the *naya* the following noon. They had been evacuated from Yoshida Village and were carrying duffel bags containing all their possessions.

I had no idea whether they had already paid their respects to Grandmother and Mr. Rokuji Sakae. Neither could I speculate what Grandmother's reaction would be to my sisters' arrival. I had a feeling the *mushi* had told them where we were.

Satsuko and Chisako were jubilant in their reunion with Masuyo. Through tears and hugs they greeted her.

"No need to say anything," Masuyo comforted them. "We understand you had to undergo heavy burdens since we were separated. How we wished we were stronger for you. How we wish we could have done something to relieve your burdens. We are so sorry you had to bear such burdens alone."

They cried until there were no more tears. Sadayoshi was surprised to see his sisters.

"Ne-chan, Ne-chan! My sisters, my sisters!" he shouted, launching into their arms, broadcasting his first smile since the sky fell. He snuggled on their knees. Both sisters' tears blessed him, as they hugged him tightly.

By the time Satsuko and Chisako, my two former tormentors, came around to greet me and gently attend to my wounds, I had forgotten they were the mean sisters. Their teasing seemed so long ago and so trite now, after all the carnage we had seen.

My, they had really grown up since we said good-bye a little more than a year before! Satsuko, now 14 years old, reminded me of Mother both physically and emotionally. She had, as I remembered, the spirit of a tiger, strong and stubborn, with a big, pure heart.

"We are going to stay with you," Satsuko said. "Let's *yubikiri,* hook our little fingers together, and promise to each other that everyone will get well and will always stay together."

My two sisters stayed outside that night, waiting for Father to return from Hiroshima. The crescent moon illuminated the acrid smoke from the cremation fires.

I was overjoyed that my sisters had found us. I decided not to share what had happened between Father and Grandmother when we arrived in the *Hiroba,* the public square at the Kotachi Train Station.

"Taka-chan," Masuyo's weak voice implored of me, "I feel very tired and weak. I need to ask you to let me go lie down for awhile. And I want you to promise me you won't give any trouble to Satsuko and Chisako. Sadayoshi is now well cared for by Satsuko. I don't have to worry anymore. I need so badly to rest."

I called my other two sisters in. It hurt me to see how weak Masuyo was. As Satsuko placed a tiny pillow under her head, I noticed that Masuyo's innocent beauty was gone.

Satsuko wiped Masuyo's forehead with her bare hand. "No need to worry," she said, "it's important for you to get your rest. Chisako and I will take care of everything."

Now that Masuyo knew her little brother was in good hands, had she lost her will to live? I prayed the plumes of smoke would stay far away from our *naya.* We waited overnight, in vain, for the return of our Father.

In the morning, Masuyo sat up in a delirium, "I think our Father is coming home with good news. How I wish I could be at the train station to welcome them."

Satsuko promised Masuyo she would meet him. "I'm sure he'll be happy to have someone waiting for him," she said, and quickly disappeared.

The sun had risen over Seto-yama, a nearby famous mountain of the *Hachiman-san*, the Shinto-Gods who brought many good tidings to the locals. While the villagers returned to their normal summer season tasks in the rice fields, the mood of the village remained somber, over-shadowed by the gray cremation smoke continuously rising from the Seto-yama. The villagers were under the spell of the *Shini-gami,* the Death Angels.

Suddenly, the door of our shed slammed open. Grandmother Setsu marched in, planting herself directly in front of Satsuko and Chisako, like an *oni*—an ogre, a monster from hell.

"What in the world were you two thinking when you decided to come here?" she snarled. "First, your Father brought these three from Hiroshima and now you, two more! What are you two doing here? I have other family here. How insensitive! Have you no common sense? Why would you two come here to compound our difficulties?"

She wagged her finger. "No one knows when the War will be over."

Glaring at Satsuko and Chisako, she said, "The best thing is for you to go back to Yoshida, and take the others with you. This will help all around. We don't have room or food for so many extra mouths. I am surprised at your stupidity."

Satsuko tried to do her best to show proper respect. She cast her eyes toward Masuyo, who was barely able to raise her head, much less respond to Grandmother. Chisako, next to Masuyo, nervously rubbed her hands, looking to Satsuko for salvation.

Satsuko reassured her sister with a hug, then looked Grandmother straight in the eye, calmly saying, "Yes, Grandmother. After searching our souls, Chisako and I made our decision to join the rest of the Tanemori. We consulted with Mr. and Mrs. Izumi. They gave their blessings and told us we were correct to pursue our rightful place by joining our family. We are prepared for any consequences of our decision."

Grandmother tried to avoid Satsuko's clear, piercing eyes. "Satsuko," she chided, "why are you babbling? You aren't listening to anything I am saying at all! I will write a letter to the Izumis explaining my predicament. They will understand and have compassion for me. I know the Izumi family will be glad to take you back, as they have a great tolerance for you."

She repeated to Satsuko that she would write the letter right way.

Grandmother Setsu ignored the pleading of my sisters. "I will write to the Izumis explaining my situation. They will understand and take you back."

"Grandmother," Satsuko said, "the five Tanemori children will wait here, together, until Father returns. Perhaps, he will come tonight with Mother and Sayoko. Please be patient with us."

Grandmother Setsu turned away and slammed the door behind her. The shed's flimsy walls seemed to shake for hours afterwards.

Chapter Five: Blood Ties

I WAS not fully conscious of all that was happening around me. I saw things happen and acted or reacted accordingly, perhaps subconsciously. I sensed I was in a realm of the unknown, orbiting without coherence, and there were times when I felt I like a dead fish, drifting with the current.

There were other times when I felt that all my actions since the "Judgment Morning" of August 6 had been recorded upon my soul, like motion pictures with sound or silent snapshots, and all without my physical awareness. Perhaps they were being recorded for future reference, my soul serving as a camera, automatically capturing images and sensations. Whether these images were focused, overexposed or underexposed, I did not know, but they were burned into my deepest soul for decades to come.

Some of the pictures were in color and others were black-and-white. Only with the passage of time would I understand the purposes these pictures would be useful for, and see them in the proper light.

Would seeing them require my eyes or my soul?

During the next few days, the Sakae family was caught by surprise. In my Father's absence, I was forced to witness the entire Komatsubara family—the husband, wife and five children—appear in the *gen-kan,* the front entry room, at high noon. This was the family of the daughter of Rokuji Sakae, Grandmother's second husband, one of the two families that Mr. Sakae had been waiting for at the train station.

My leg injuries had healed enough to allow me to hobble and hop around to the front door of the main house when I heard a commotion. I witnessed the warm welcome Grandmother gave her husband's family. It infuriated me to see her bowing to the floor, begging them to feel at home. So this is what she looked like when she opened her heart!

I looked at them. They didn't have the slightest scratch on their bodies, and their clothes were all intact. And yet they were met with open arms and enthusiasm for their safely arriving home.

"O-oi, Ba-a-san," Grandfather Sakae shouted to his wife. "The Komatsubara family has returned! Everyone is fine! Oh what happiness!"

Grandmother Sakae put on her welcoming beautiful mask, but in her heart I felt she must have been holding out on true happiness for the sight of her own two children. Humbly she wiped her hands on her apron, like a servant. "Please accept my humble apology for my unpresentable appearance. This is your home. Welcome to your rightful place."

Mr. Rokuji Sakae saw to it that the Komatsubara family had comfortable accommodations in the main part of the house. Not only could they sleep on the *tatami-mat* floor, but they also had unrestricted access to the entire house without even *shoji* screen barriers to limit their activities.

The Tanemori family had to sleep on hay, in the n*aya.* Calling on the wrath of the Gods to fall upon Grandmother Sakae would not have troubled my soul. I was burned on the outside and seething on the inside.

The next day the entire Norikawa family—Mr. Sakae's second daughter, along with her husband and two boys, age five and three years old—returned to safety to Kotachi. Preparation had already been made to receive them comfortably upstairs.

At the same time Tetsuo Nakamura, my Mother's only brother and Grandmother Sakae's son, came home uninjured. There was a wonderful homecoming party that night for this 30-year-old bachelor, while the Tanemori children sat in the dark in the *naya*.

Only a few days before my Grandmother Sakae had insulted my Father, and now she was openly welcoming her son. Did we not have the same blood running through our veins?

My siblings and I bit our tongues! I wanted to deny having even a drop of Grandmother Sakae's blood. She disgusted me. I wanted to drain my blood and replace it with only the pure blood of Tanemori. I hoped and prayed Father would return home soon and we would have a family again.

On August 15, 1945, the day of *Obon*, when all dead spirits returned to their respected homes, I heard the voice of the Emperor Hirohito crackle over the single radio in the community, "… We suffered the insufferable; we endured the unendurable … We will endure the unendurable …"

Japan surrendered to America and the Allied forces. I wondered if the *"seed"* of Tanemori would endure.

Father came home from Hiroshima empty-handed. He had found no trace of my Mother or baby sister.

He made several more trips to Hiroshima over the next two weeks, these times to sift through rubble looking for their bodies. These were day trips, now that the trains were running almost regularly and most of the refugees had been evacuated from Hiroshima. While sifting through the ruins, my Father had no idea he was being exposed to radiation, and the constant exposure began to destroy him. Each time he returned he was more broken and despondent.

One night Father dragged himself back to us at eleven o'clock. Beyond exhaustion, he crumpled onto the floor trembling, in anguish, defeated—surrounded by his loving children. I could only imagine how horrific the experience must have been for him. Where could he have slept? Did any one give him food? The echo of his voice calling "Yoshiko!" over and over that fateful day was the reality of true suffering and pain that my Father had to endure. The eerie, echoing howling of dogs in the distance sent chills down my spine.

But tonight he had brought home a little chest cavity bone. His voice quivered as he handed it to me. He told me through his tears that he believed this came from our baby sister, and he that had brought it to us for burial.

"NO! NO! NO! Daddy, this is not Sayoko. Noooooo!" I beat his chest. "Daddy, tell me this is not true."

My sister Masuyo, now so ill she was in constant, violent pain, bore my Father's agony in silence.

He apologized over and over for not being able to find Mother. He had finally given up all hope of finding her, becoming a shell of a man, a ghostly shadow. Having reached the limit of suffering and grief, and being unable to communicate, he detached himself from life.

Under the flickering candlelight Father was almost unrecognizable, his sunken, weary eyes covered in filth. He was delirious, and I couldn't understand his words.

Awaking with the first light the following morning, I saw Father deep in slumber, like a dead man, in the corner of the *naya*. He wore the same filthy, stinking clothes he had been wearing for ten days or more.

I felt powerless to help, not even knowing to whom I could turn for assistance.

The last straw had come when Grandmother *Oni*—the ogre—burst into our *naya* while Father was in Hiroshima searching for our Mother and baby sister, vehemently insisting that because of Mother's death the direct link to her had been cut off. She accused us of taking up space, saying that we no longer had the "right" to occupy the *naya* for even one more day, and that the Tanemori were no longer part of her family circle.

Satsuko had decided not to inform Father about Grandmother's visit until the following morning. How much more hardship could Father withstand?

Ironically, our Step-Grandfather Sakae kept clear of any verbal dispute between our family and his wife. He always put on a cordial face for us, not out of any affection, but to avoid the ever-watchful incrimination of his powerful neighbor, Kamehachi Tominaga.

Tominaga, the elder who had come to our defense the day of our arrival, lived directly across the narrow street from our grandparents. In such close quarters it was easy for neighbors to know too much of each other's activities.

There was a power rivalry between these two men. Tominaga was wealthy. He owned a lot of land and a lumberyard. He had a political and social following, not only because of his wealth but also because he had a big heart.

Sakae, as his much less popular rival, was also a wealthy landowner of some of the surrounding mountains as well as rice fields which he rented out to farmers. They lived so closely under the watchful eyes of each other that they could hear each other sneeze when the windows were opened, and they would both be listening! Other villagers also watched the interaction between these two men. Sakae feared his rival in every aspect of his life in the village. And no one dared to stand opposed to Tominaga.

The morning after he learned of *Oni's* eviction notice, Father, with great trepidation, paid a visit to Tominaga. Concerned that he was in breech of social codes by calling so early, Father approached at the servant's entrance.

Tominaga apparently rejoiced in his visit, as afterwards Father told us in great detail how Tominaga received him. My tiny heart couldn't control the excitement and immense joy to the Tanemoris.

"Yokatta! Yokatta! Good! Good!"

Father said Tominaga had beckoned him to sit with him at the breakfast table and had called for his wife to come quickly with food and tea. Father had refused, pretending he wasn't hungry. But his stomach had made loud growling sounds, betraying the *Samurai* code of politeness in always refusing food the first time it is offered. This code is known as *bushi wa kuwanedo taka yoji*—no matter how hungry you are, never display hunger publicly. Although it was considered gauche for others, a *Samurai* could be expected to walk down the street cleaning his teeth with a toothpick, as if he had just finished eating.

"Oh, Tanemori-san? My heart goes out to you," Tominaga told Father. "I'm so glad you came back here safely with your children. I'm sure you're worn out. I want you to know I am rejoicing with you, and for your two daughters who returned and joined the rest of the Tanemori family."

When his wife brought the *miso*-soup Tominaga jokingly told Father that his wife was the worst cook anyone could find. "Mr. Tanemori, help me. I don't have any idea what to do with my wife. Look at me, how skinny I am. I really want to know what to do with her and, of course, I don't know what to do without her either."

He laughed loudly. "But one thing she can do well is make *miso*-soup." Tominaga, a man who loved to indulge in humor and life, patted his stomach, embarrassing his wife. It was a great relief for Father to, at long last, have cause for a good laugh.

Father's resistance to betraying his feelings was broken down by this warm reception. And the meal of *miso,* soup, *tsukemono*, radish pickles, and white fluffy, steaming *gohan,* cooked rice, created a most joyous and memorable occasion. Together, they had a good long cry.

Mr. Kamehachi Tominaga offered my Father his 14-by-20 tin-roofed garage, which was occupied only by field mice and spiders. It was four houses down from the Kotachi Train Station. At the time, this leaky, dingy, windowless, vermin-infested shed became a castle to us. My Father humbly accepted the offer.

Tominaga was very apologetic to my Father that he couldn't offer nicer accommodations. "There is no problem for us. I will talk to that Rokuji Sakae myself. Don't worry, it's going to be all right." Tominaga provided all the materials and his own employees to put in a raised wood floor, a door, and an out-house.

There is a Japanese proverb: *Suteru kami ga ire ba hirou kami mo ari.* There is a God who is merciless to those who cast down people like dung. There is also a God who is merciful enough to raise them up from falling.

A single 15-watt bulb illuminated our new bigger room, casting eerie shadows. It was, however, like a "beacon" of light on a dark stormy night that would guide a lost ship to safe haven.

Masuyo's condition had worsened terribly. We carried her very carefully when moving into our new place. Each day she seemed to be losing her battle for life. We had no idea what was afflicting her. She lay in pain, moaning on a paper-thin *futon*. My younger brother lay innocently next to her.

As the days progressed, she would occasionally beg only for water. We had no medicine to administer to her. She became a gaunt ghost, looking so *kawaiso!* I pitied her, wondering where the innocent, tender beauty of a 16-year-old had gone. I begged the Death Angels to go away!

One morning, while Satsuko and Chisako were out looking for food, Father handed me a pair of scissors and asked me to give him a haircut. He said he wanted to look handsome to see Mother.

With my heart in my throat I remembered my Father's words after he returned from his last trip to Hiroshima, "The only way to find your Mother is to go where she is!" I didn't understand what he meant. Did he mean that he would be going there to bring her back? Or did he mean ... NO! NO! Make this not be! "He cannot die and leave us behind!"

"Daddy, I'm afraid. I might accidentally cut off your ears," I said, trying to joke while holding back my tears. "Then, how could you hear me? Right, daddy?"

The scissors were so dull they couldn't cut *tofu*. I combed his hair with my fingers, preparing to cut it, holding the scissors in my left hand. To my shock, clumps of hair, roots and all, came out in my fingers, without the slightest resistance.

"No!" My tiny hands were shaking as I showed him the hair I held. I thought I had done something terribly wrong. "I'm sorry, I'm sorry!" I tried unsuccessfully to stick the hairs back on his head. I really didn't need a pair of scissors to give him a haircut; all I needed was to run my fingers through it.

He sank deeply into silence. Then, sometime later, he spoke to me very softly, saying, "Son, it's alright. Your Father is tired. I need to rest for a few minutes." I helped him lie down and put a little pillow under his head. I felt he wanted to tell me something more.

I stayed very close to him, listening to his labored breathing with long pauses in between breaths. He was so thin, pale and lifeless, like an *obake,* a ghost. Finally he slipped into a deep sleep. My world was caving in. The light of my life was slipping away.

My sisters returned with forage from the field when the afternoon sun peeked in though the door, casting its light into the dark room. The light must have awakened Father. He sat up, muttering something unintelligible to some unseen being. Then he shook his head vigorously, as if trying to shake something off or wake himself up.

"Takashi. I want you to sit right in front of me, squarely," he spoke softly, yet fervently, piercing my heart.

Perhaps some *mushi* had arrived with its secret only for him. I sat quietly, looking into his eyes. The fire had been rekindled in his eyes. He took my hands in his, with a great power of intention. I could feel his intensity, pulsing warmly and powerfully into my body. What had caused this newfound energy? It took him a moment to find the words he spoke to me from his soul. When the words came they were strong, clear and deliberate.

"I want you to understand with your heart. There is only one way to find your Mother. I must go to her where she is. And I intend to go there in just a little while."

My Father began to reiterate many things he had taught me while I was growing under his tutoring before the bombing of Hiroshima. Although his voice was soft, each utterance was very powerful, like thunder, and had the sharpest edge, like a two-edged *Samurai* sword tempered with *Kamikaze* spirit. Then, I knew his heart.

Here I was facing my Father, who was standing at the crossroads, instructing me once more. His message came in loud and unmistakable. I knew then that I must accept what he was telling me and allow him to go in dignity. I knew this was probably our last talk as Father and son, and I fell into a trance of absolute attention to his words.

"Never forget who you are. You are the firstborn son of Tanemori's family. You must always remember the virtue of being Tanemori. Do you understand?"

"You must always remember and follow the teaching and upbringing of your parents. No matter what comes your way! Do not soil or dishonor the Tanemori's name! Furthermore, hold to the truth and moral principles. They shall be your best friends on your life's journey!"

"And one last thing! Be strong and be sure never to be defeated by your own weakness. Be true to yourself. Do not be satisfied with yesterday's accomplishments. Rise to a new height each day. Conquering your own weaknesses with your will is the greatest victory in this world."

"I have lived my life by the principle of *Jidai-Yusen,* sacrificing an immediate need or goal for the sake of the greater good. I hope you have learned the principle of *Jita-Kyoei,* to always to be mindful of others, and to live for the benefit of others, and the third principle, *Mugai-Kyoei,* nonviolence and respect for all humanity ... Takashi, always remember who you are and follow your heart no matter what ... even if at times you might go against the norms of society ... and ... that's enough now!"

Pearls of tears welled up in his eyes, as if from his very soul.

"This is my last teaching. I believe you do understand! You are heir to the Tanemori name. I am counting on you to carry the responsibility with honor. And you must pass on to your children what I am passing on to you. Promise me, son!"

These were the teachings and instructions I remembered from my earliest days.

"Father! Father! I understand! I will guard and live by your teaching, no matter what. I promise you with all my heart. I shall fulfill your heartfelt wishes. Rest now, Father."

He never spoke another word to any living being. I stayed close to him all night, looking at him under the 15-watt bulb.

Death was common now in this tiny village of Kotachi, far from Hiroshima. The Death Angels were busy visiting many families. Our sky was being cursed by the dark, thick cremation smoke that hovered over the village, filling many villagers' hearts with terror. We have a saying in Japan that when smoke hovers over one's house that is the visitation of a Death Angel, beckoning a family member as a trophy.

It was 5:00 a.m. when he underwent muscle spasms and sat bolt upright, then collapsed to the floor, groaning and crying out incoherently. He gave one last convulsive movement, then his soul departed abruptly! I watched my Father succumb to the Death Angel.

"Oto-saaan" I shook him. "Father! Don't go and leave us behind!" I was screaming and crying hysterically. Satsuko and Chisako tried to pull me away from his body. Three neighbors came, and finally they were able to pry me loose. By then his body was cold and clammy, like a cold wax candle. His open eyes pierced to heaven, looking for Mother. His words echoed in my mind, "The only way to find your Mother is to go to where she is ..." I hoped he found her.

My Father died the morning of September 3rd. He was only 37 years old. His death came as a big surprise to everyone. He didn't have one scratch.

"Oto-san, Sayonara." We all said farewell to our Father and carried him to the cremation site the following day. A small fire was still smoldering when we picked up his remains. The remains in the ash of his bones, I was told later, were highly unusual, because they wouldn't burn. The cremators even lit another hot fire on top of them to turn them into the customary white crumbling ash, but his bones fused all the more, hardening into a gray-bluish color. Because they would not fit into the pine box for burial, his buriers had to leave the majority behind, only taking a few smaller ones.

In fulfilling their social obligation, Grandmother Sakae and one family member each from the Komatsubara and Norikawa families joined some neighbors at the cremation site. Tetsuo Nakamura, my Mother's brother joined them. When this group followed us to the final resting spot in the cemetery and stood over his final remains as if they cared, I was shaking in anger! This rite is reserved for the immediate family, and these people did not, in my mind, qualify either in body or spirit. It made my stomach turn. I despised them! Before my Father's spirit had completed its journey to paradise, the seed of rebellion against shallow, accepted social standards had been planted in my heart.

Perhaps my most beloved sister, Masuyo, was rushing to join him on his journey. She died during his burial rites. When we returned from his burial, we had to immediately prepare for her cremation. We were told she had passed away at 10:00 a.m.

When I fully realized we were now totally *oyanashigo,* orphaned, I was terrified. In less than one month, we had lost six members of our immediate family. My most beloved and cherished lights in the world had expired in smoke, leaving four of us to fend for ourselves. Sadayoshi was 3 years old, I was 8, Chisako, 12, and Satsuko, 14 years old. We four siblings of Tanemori were the only family in the community who lost both parents to the atomic bomb. And in Japan, orphans were worthy of only social contempt and disgrace.

What was it like to be fatherless in the postwar Japanese community of Kotachi Village? It was like the vast inky darkness of a bottomless ocean. We became a ship without captain, compass, or even any sails. Satsuko, by default, took the helm. I was a kite without a tail in a whirlwind—twisting and turning and tumbling in a raging storm. The last words of Father were my only anchor. I was unbearably lonely. I gritted my teeth. I became mute. My tongue felt as though it cleaved to the roof of my mouth. I was determined never to be defeated or bow to this unfortunate destiny. I was the Number One Son of Tanemori. I was given self-respect as the heir to the honorable family name, and with that name to establish my life, I would have to be like a lion, fulfilling my responsibility to restore the Tanemoris to their former honor and dignity. The task seemed insurmountable and terrifying!

I sometimes awakened in a cold clammy sweat. It reminded me of my Father's dead body. It was misery to be fatherless in Kotachi Village. Hope was confiscated, and I spiraled into a black hole, falling, falling and falling, groping blindly in the darkness, seeking any tiny bit of light in an endless, empty, hollow, heartless universe.

Oh! How I desired to see my future as if it were the August moon, the symbol of peace and prosperity. I heard a melody, *"Ju-u go ya Ottsuki sama hitori bochi ...* A lonely moon, casting its shadow darkly ..."

Abounding sadness within my heart . . .
drowning my loneliness in tears of self-pity.
Four abandoned children, once belonged in the fold.
To live until Tomorrow, our prayers we do raise.
Wishing to have a glimpse of my Father even once in
my dreams
The heat of yet another long night lingers.
Oh, Hiroshima, once my home.
My tears run dry waiting for the breaking dawn.

Instead, the only tangible shred of my Father I retained was a photo of him standing in his *kimono* emblazoned with the family crest—*Maruni Tachi Aoi.*

I went from being the treasured Number One Son, heir to an honorable family name, into being an *oyanashigo,* an orphan. I was terrified. I had been left to find my own way, left with three siblings to fend for ourselves.

I became a street urchin, trying to defend my personal dignity while scrounging for survival like a rat, searching waste sites and garbage cans for food, just to stay alive.

As an orphan cut off from the dignity inherent with maintaining my ancestral roots, my task of upholding the family honor would prove insurmountable. All that was holding me together was the knowledge of who I was, and the teachings and upbringing of my Father. He had instructed me and given me knowledge, making me aware of the distinct virtues, obligations, and rewards attendant upon my position as the family's Number One Son.

My Father had been third in line of four brothers and six sisters. Of his siblings, I had met only my favorite Aunt Takae of Miyajima.

Two days after Father's burial, a strange woman came to our door, claiming she was our Aunt Sumiko. How she had learned that Father had passed away was a mystery. She came to claim clothing and other items Father had brought to Kotachi for the Tanemori family, in the event that Hiroshima was bombed.

We were shocked. Satsuko, knowing these items and articles were a lifeline for us, begged her to let us keep them and clung to her like a *suppone*, a snapping turtle.

"*Sore dakewa yurshite kudasai. Korera wa watashi tachi kyodai no ikite yuku mono desu. Onegai, Oba-chan!*" She begged her to let the Tanemori siblings keep them. "Please, in the name of our Father, don't do that to us!"

Grandmother Sakae had cut us off already, and now Aunt Sumiko was icily claiming ownership by virtue of her closer blood ties with our Father, telling us to shut our eyes and mouths and never to speak of this to anyone.

She pushed my sister to the floor, shouting at her, "Satsuko, get away from me. You don't know what you're doing."

I tried to keep my aunt away from my sister. But my aunt knocked me down, and like a rabid hyena, carried away as much as she could while my sister crumpled to the floor in tears.

I chased my aunt to the train station in vain, yelling and gnashing my teeth, while a station agent held me back at the gate. Father would have turned over in his grave had he witnessed his sister's actions.

Grandmother Sakae distanced herself. I imagined she took great pleasure in the suffering of the Tanemori children. I watched my sister, Satsuko, cover her face in fear, crying out to our Father.

Though I was the Number One Son, I was still too young to undertake responsibility for the family. Even before I could assume authority as the head of the family, I had been deposed.

The weight of responsibility on the shoulders of Satsuko was too much for her to bear alone. She tried to hold us together with dignity and pride befitting the Tanemori clan. Many winter nights we all fell asleep, huddled together to keep warm, our stomachs empty. Sadayoshi and I would constantly plead for food, and this greatly frustrated Satsuko.

One day, Kamehachi Tominaga offered Satsuko a job at the lumber mill. She had taken the role of both father and mother, trying to guide us through these harsh times. At the mill, Satsuko was expected to work like a man, carrying heavy lumber. This heavy work on her young, frail bone structure forced a curvature of her spine and created other complications, which led to great suffering in her later years.

My brother and I looked forward to the days my sister was paid. With her meager earnings, she would stop by a store to bring home day-old loaves of bread. This was the only night of any week we had something to eat without fighting. But soon this changed. We demanded more loaves of bread, which drove Satsuko insane.

Shaking her head and pulling at her hair, she would furiously shout, "Could you two stop giving me hell all the time? You are acting like the *gaki,* imps from hell. You are always hungry. I wish you would just go back to the hell you came from. See if I care! I can't take it any more. Why do I have to bear this burden? I am not your mother or father! Why didn't you two die instead of Father!"

She looked like a witch! Chisako watched these outbursts from the sideline with a cool detachment, further fueling Satsuko's fury.

"*Omaeno bakamono ni Ne-e-san wa nanno tamini kuro o shinaito ikenai noyo.* You fool! I am not going to throw my life away for you and for anyone else, and for you Chisako ... *Sonna kao o shite*, what an ugly face you have."

Chisako screamed back at her, "I don't want to see your face either!"

They both exploded into tears. Dishes flew across the tiny room, shattering. I remember them both in tears, picking up broken dishes from the floor.

Chisako then walked out, not returning home until the next day. How often I wished for fewer nights of fighting among ourselves, and for more nights of sleeping with a full stomach.

Out of destitution, Chisako became a kind of outlaw, a *Yami gome Ne-e-san,* a black market rice sister. Postwar, rice was rationed. Chisako would take some of the villagers' rice crop in a specially designed pouch belt under her clothes to a black market in Hiroshima. She was well known there and honored by middlemen and consumers, as a "savior."

She was also well known by police, who would catch her in raids on a train or in the station. She told me that she had been photographed several times; her picture was plastered on every bulletin board in police stations.

Chisako told me this was the only way she knew how to help my sister Satsuko. "Did you know Takashi? I made a 'face' for the lineup for the 'wanted' bulletin."

She was a "marked" woman! Yet, while her "crime" was smuggling rice, and policemen confiscated the rice in the name of "Justice," for us this was a matter of survival. I deplored the authorities, "I bet those Police have taken rice to their own homes, filling their stomachs at my sister's expense while we are starving, penniless."

The spring following Father's death, feeling the village was closing in on me, I decided to go look at my old hometown, Hiroshima. Perhaps there was the possibility of finding refuge from the miserable realities of Kotachi Village.

Since I didn't have any money, I decided to take my chances by sneaking onto the train to Hiroshima. It was accepted knowledge among the villagers, and we were told in school, that Hiroshima's devastation was so extensive that nothing would grow there for the next 75 years. It piqued my curiosity to see how life was there, how people were surviving. I also needed adventure, a break from my small, miserable world.

It turned out to be easy to sneak onto the train and to avoid the conductors collecting tickets. The train took me to the central Hiroshima Station. There I saw many little cardboard shacks of vendors selling the basics of life, from food to clothes. Many more people were on the streets than I expected to see, bringing grim hopes and fears about whether they could continue to live there. I stood in the smoke of a stand whose owner was grilling little sparrows. I inhaled the fatty smoke of the grilling meat, pretending I was really eating the tender morsels. It made my stomach groan and ache.

For some reason, I didn't want to venture to the street where I had lived. Instead, I walked by the river near the station, reflecting on the days when Father and I had walked by the river. I could almost feel his presence next to me.

I sat down and watched the water flow by, deep in profound sadness. To my surprise, I noticed a single blade of grass right next to me. A defiant little green blade of grass emerging from the ruin—"*a blade of grass ... in a dreamless field.*"

I scooped it up, cradling it in my hands like a precious friend. I felt as if I were one with that blade of grass. I was no longer alone. If that blade of grass could live on, so could I! There was a powerful energy within me, screaming "life!" and bringing me great hope and joy.

In my heart I knew I must have perseverance. Returning to Kotachi, I knew I could not escape the reality of life there, and so I must make a go of it.

The role of the *sen-gan,* the Gossip Committee of Kotachi, a self-appointed group of civic leaders, was to monitor and regulate social behavior in the village. They took great pity on Satsuko for the misbehavior and moronic behavior of her younger brother. No one came forth to offer me advice, nor any compassion for what may have been motivating my apparent misbehavior.

The suffering of my struggling heart was met only with disparaging words and criticism. I was a reject, a misfit, in constant need of being watched.

I sometimes did stupid things out of anger. For instance, I took the opportunity to step on a pair of glasses that had fallen to the ground from one of the *sen-gan*. Infuriated, the man chased me, and stumbled. I cynically laughed and thumbed my nose at him as he ran in circles trying to catch me. I felt so good!

The path I carved to my Father's gravesite was well worn. There were indentations where I would fall to my knees on the ground next to my Father's dilapidated wooden grave marker. This was my shrine, my haven. It cleansed me and protected me. Each season there held a special magic for me. During my conversations with Father, the iridescent green of the forest of tall black pines and maples protected me from all outside evil energies. I wrote a *haiku, "Para para to—ochiru iroha no—Akino fukasa.* Dancing of—colorful leaves to the earth—reveals deep autumn."

Deep-seated in my soul, the image of *"a single blade of grass in a dreamless field"* became the inspiration which helped hold me together through the following decades.

While Grandmother Sakae and her husband's relatives were filling their bellies with rice, we foraged weeds. Neighbors and Grandmother Sakae gave us oats, which were animal feed.

I often pleaded, "Grandmother, are we not your grandchildren like Komatsubara and Norikawa?" I begged to be treated as an equal in her family, but nothing really penetrated her.

I would find solace visiting my Father's grave, knowing that he was watching over me. "Daddy, it seems impossible to follow your teaching," I would pray to my Father. "I don't have a kind heart toward my Grandmother Sakae. She is snubbing you, daddy. Please help me!" But I always reassured him that I had not forgotten who I was.

I have seen the hands of merciful "Gods" during the summer and the harvest seasons, when we would eat well on wild berries and nuts. One particular farmer, whom I called *Oba-a-chan,* Grandma, would let us forage for vegetables in her field. She often stood up to defend me against other villagers' complaints.

In the winter it was quite a different story. Sometimes when snow blanketed the fields, I would forage for weeds with my *akagire,* chopped, bleeding bare hands. To help ease the sharp, piercing pain, I would stick a whole hand, one at a time, into my mouth to keep it warm. The pain was often beyond what I could bear, and I would often come home with a basket empty of edible weeds. Many times I told my sister that I couldn't find anything under the snow, when the truth was I couldn't bring myself to look hard and long enough for forage.

She accused me of not carrying out my responsibilities and told me I would have to sleep on an empty stomach. Bearing my shame, I searched trashcans and garbage piles for food at the dumping place by Seto River. Villagers, and not just children, teased me by eating food in front of me and throwing the bones in my path.

The moral teachings of my Father could not fill the hunger in my stomach. One day, when I knew step-Grandfather and Grandmother Sakae were out of town and no one was in their house, I crept like an alley cat to their back door.

"How come? How unusual it is to see the back door locked from the inside," I murmured to myself. Without a second thought, after making sure no one was watching, I broke the glass window next to the door with my left hand. I stood on a wooden box and stretched my arm through the broken window to unlock the door.

Sneaking into the *daidokoro*, dining area, I felt like a professional thief, stealthily moving to the hutch where cooked white rice was kept in the *ohitsu,* rice tub. I spat on the track door to obscure any squeaking sound, then silently slid open the screen. My stomach growled loudly when I beheld beautiful cooked rice filling the tub to the brim. With a small rice paddle I tried to artfully shave the top of the rice mound so no one could tell it had been touched. I stuffed it gleefully into my hungry mouth.

"*Shimatta!*" No. It was too late. I noticed I had a cut on my finger from breaking the glass and a drop of blood had landed right in the center of the white mound. It looked like a Japanese flag! I was amazed.

I thought about making a design with the drops of blood, but a stern vision of the face of my Father appeared in my mind's eye. I realized I couldn't leave the rice stained with blood. With the paddle in my right hand I took a big hunk of it and stuffed it in my mouth, destroying all my careful sculpting. I felt so stupid for using my left hand to break the glass. Why didn't I use a brick or stone to break the window? It was surely *"atono omatsuri!"* It was too late to cry over spilled milk.

Now there was clear evidence of my thievery. This would be the perfect opportunity for Grandmother Sakae to put me away for good!

The next day, carrying a bamboo stick about 70 inches long and two inches in diameter, Grandmother Sakae caught up with me. The cloth tied around my left pinky revealed my secret.

"I am going to beat the tar out of you. I'll see to it that you won't be able to use your left hand ever again. I wish your Father had taken you with him instead of leaving you here. I want your broken hand to be a sign so that people will know what you did!"

Grandmother Sakae struck me with all her anger and frustration. Through gritted teeth I received my punishment. I took her beating like the son of a *Samurai*. I could hear Father's teaching echoing in my consciousness, "With every action there is always a consequence." I stoically took the beating without crying or flinching. My left hand and arm were swollen when she had finished venting her rage.

That night I visited Father's grave with *kuyashi namida*, tears of remorse, dripping on the ground. I had allowed my selfish will to dictate my actions, without considering consequences and without accountability. I had shamed him! I had been defeated by my own weakness! I knew I had failed in the eyes of my Father! I begged his forgiveness.

News of my transgression traveled fast. When I returned to school on Monday, everyone knew. The scars from the beating on my left arm and hand were still painfully obvious. The bullies were having a heyday, cynically mocking me for the punishment of my own Grandmother. "Let me 'nurse' you, oh, poor, poor little *oyanashigo*, orphan. Poor you—nobody to take care of you?" They mocked me with cynical laughter!

"Chikusho!" They spat upon me. My determined heart would not let them trample my dignity. I started a fistfight.

Then our sympathetic fourth grade teacher, Takahashi *Sensei*, teacher, came to my rescue and stopped the fight. My homeroom teacher was the picture of beauty. She was like a *Hakata*-doll, with peach-colored cheeks; her smile was like beautiful flowers; her sparkling eyes showed the beauty of her soul. She always stood up for me and showed her compassion for me in many different ways.

She would often give me her lunch, pretending she wasn't feeling well.

"Takashi-kun, I snacked too much and I don't think I am able to finish my *bento,* lunch. I wish you could help me. My mother doesn't like for me to bring any leftovers home."

I often heard her say to the entire class. "Now, look! He has lost both parents. His life is very difficult. He has no comforts, no food to satisfy his hunger. Instead of bullying him, why can't each of us show him some kindness and extend a helping hand?"

One Saturday afternoon after school, she invited me to her home. Her parents were well-to-do, respected landowners in the community.

"Sensei, doshite Takashi ni sonnani yasashiku shite kudasaru no desu ka?" I couldn't understand why she was so kind to me and why she would risk her own social standing and her family's respectability. It was a cold day. I was shivering, but my heart was filled with the warmth of my teacher. Her parents and brother joined us and heartily extended their welcome.

Takahashi *Sensei* offered me a hot bath. I was filthy. Like any street boy, I must have smelled pretty awful. I happily followed her into bathroom. Oh the scents and beautiful hot bath water!

Grandmother Sakae let us bathe in her house in the same tub of water her whole family had used before us. It was always lukewarm and kind of skuzzy by the time we could use it. This was different, and wonderful.

I tried to hide my embarrassment. I felt so fantastic. She washed my head and scrubbed my back like my Mother, without hesitation or awkwardness.

"Takashi-kun, how did you manage to get so dirty?" She scrubbed and scrubbed, washing my smelly hair. She gave a hug to this wet boy. I couldn't tell whether she was crying or laughing due to the sound of rinsing water. I hadn't felt such tenderness since the day of the bombing. I cried for the first time since my Father died because someone was really caring for me.

"You don't need to cry," said Takahashi *Sensei*, "I am with you."

Then, I cried more and louder. As she embraced me again to her bosom, I could recall the warmth of my Mother, faintly in my memories. Oh, how I wished she was my Mother!

"Sah. Yahaku oyu ni tsukari nasai." She urged me to get in the hot tub.

"Sensei, will it be all right for me to stay a little longer in the *ofuro*? It feels so good."

"Of course, Takashi-kun. Stay in the *ofuro* until you melt." She left me alone.

As I stuffed myself at dinner with *gohan*, white rice, broiled fish and *daikon* pickles until my seams nearly burst, she was crying. I had a fourth serving of *gohan*. Then *Sensei* and I sat dangling our feet from the *roka*, porch, looking at the sparkling stars. It seemed they were having a sparkling conversation.

"Sensei, look—a *nagare-boshi*, shooting star!"

"I think that bright star over there is your Father talking to you. He is watching over you. And all the other stars are cheering you on."

I promised her then that I would live strong and would not take second place to anyone. I told her I would be stronger, live a straight line, and make her proud.

"Takashi-kun, nanimo wasurete yukkuri to yasumu no yo." I want you to forget everything and don't worry. *Sensei* is here. I want you to have a deep sleep tonight."

It had been more than two long years since a *futon* had been prepared for me. Clasping me to her bosom and telling me not to lose heart, she then tucked me under a thick and fluffy futon as soft as a cloud, as my Mother had in the past. I loved being pampered by the tender being of

Takahashi *Sensei*, as I crawled into bed for the first time in ages with my stomach full.

By the time my teacher came to wake me, the sun was peeking through dark clouds. She pampered me again as the sun cast its huge smile on me. After breakfast, she handed me a five-pound bag of rice and sent me home. My heart was so light, I felt like a fluffy piece of cotton. I skipped and hopped like a *rabbit* ... until I turned the second bend over the hill. Suddenly, I met the same bullies who had challenged me in school. I clutched the bag of rice tightly under my arm.

"So, you are the teacher's pet. You are like a little puppy. What did she do? Smother you like a mother? Ha, ha, ha, ha! You make us laugh!"

"Let me see what you got from your teacher? *Yurusa naizo!* We will not let you go, shouted the leader of bullies."

I tried to protect the rice; it was for my sisters and younger brother. "No!" I shouted defiantly, "Get away from me. You're not going to take the rice from me."

One of the bullies punched my stomach, while the other tried to grab the bag. I knew I had no chance against them. I tried everything to prevent them from taking the bag, but I would not give them the satisfaction of having it. I ripped the bag, and the grains of rice scattered onto the ground. I stamped on it, grinding it into the dirt.

"Stop him! *Omae wa kichigai da!* You are mad!"

"He's a stupid, crazy imp from the Hell of starvation. Let him be. Let's go."

They all spat on me as they left. A cow witnessed the humiliating scene through the fence. I screamed furiously and swore after them. When they were out of sight, my tears changed to a kind of insane laughter.

"What happened to you," Satsuko asked, when she saw my swollen face. "Oh, I fell down the stairway at Korimbo Buddha Temple," I responded.

"What? You were at Buddha Temple? You mean to tell me that you stopped by the Temple for no reason at all? You never go to the Buddha Temple."

I couldn't tell her about my humiliation, about not being able to protect the beautiful gift of rice. It would have infuriated her. And if my teacher ever heard about it, I would have to contend with the bullies again. The rice was gone. I grimly swallowed my anger and said nothing to anyone.

By the time of the third autumn I knew well the trials of the long winter ahead. These would be days of shivering in the late afternoon sun against the west-facing wall next to our house, and falling asleep with no food in my stomach. These would be days of freezing hands as I dug in the snow for weeds to eat. I had no gloves or winter clothes to protect me from the penetrating north winds.

There was one goodhearted woman, Mitsukawa *Oba-chan,* who allowed me into her barbershop, a place where I was always welcome. I would crouch in the warm, dark corner behind her potbelly stove and fall asleep with my empty stomach.

The sound of my stomach growling would awaken me to the scent of sweet potatoes being baked on the top of the stove. Mitsukawa *Oba-chan* was known as *Oba-chan,* sweet potato, because she baked the potatoes on her potbelly stove for customers. They received royal treatment from her.

When giving them haircuts, she also washed their hair, shaved them, trimmed their eyebrows, cleaned their ears, and massaged their shoulders—all for one price. The process usually took one hour per customer. Customers waiting their turn enjoyed sweet potatoes around the potbelly stove.

From my dark corner I watched them shuffle the hot baked sweet potatoes from hand to hand, blowing to cool them off before popping them into their mouths. Pretending to be asleep, I kept one eye open for a chance of snatching a bit of potato skin someone might toss into the trash.

It was there that I dreamed several times and saw my Mother's tender face. In my daydreams I visualized my Mother, sometimes confusing her image with the face of Mitsukawa *Oba-chan.* Especially when she smiled at me, a potato in her hand.

"I think this is a little bit too burnt for the customers. If you don't mind ..." Sometimes she said, "I think I roasted one too many. I hate to waste it. You may have it."

She made these excuses because at first I would decline. I was the son of Tanemori. My Father had taught me to be reserved and modest, that I must behave with restraint. But she probably heard the growling of my stomach and witnessed me swallowing potatoes in two gulps. Sometimes I ate slowly and then regurgitated, like a cow, savoring each morsel. But later I grew to expect that she would give me a potato.

How I wished that Grandmother Sakae would act kindly like Mitsukawa *Oba-chan*. Even a little bit of tenderness would have made a difference in my behavior.

Her barber shop was a place where people would gather to talk about the goings-on in the community. Around her potbelly stove, folks shared their feelings. For me, it was the place where I found warmth, comfort and support.

Kotachi Village had many landlords, including my Step-Grandfather, who owned rice-fields and rented them to local farmers. This way the landlord could grow fat on the toil of poor farmers.

Not one landlord allowed the Tanemori children to use even the corner of a rice field to grow vegetables. One day, we found an unclaimed 8-by-14 foot patch alongside the railroad tracks, full of rocks and overgrown with Johnson weeds. We nicknamed it *Haisen-Batake,* the defeated patch, and worked diligently for one week pulling weeds and removing rocks to prepare the ground for vegetable seeds.

The first few days were fun. We counted one-hundred then two-hundred-fifty rocks! The more we cleared, the more rocks we found. I closed my eyes and wished the ugly rocks away. I pitied myself as I looked "broken"—hands scratched, skin torn and bleeding. My raw hands looked up at me with anger.

Finally, when the rocks and weeds were gone, we rejoiced. I stretched out on the soft ground in the sun, inhaling the fragrance of the coming spring. I could almost see my Father's approving face as I gazed up at the clouds. I wrote a *w a k a* : "*Fumaretemo—Mata fumaretemo—Taeshinobu—Mugon de matsu mo—Toko Haru ya.* Having been trampled like a horsetail—over and over again—endures suffering— endures in total silence—awaiting heart of spring."

Suddenly, a cold chill awoke me from my reverie to see the sun setting over the Goryu-zan, Five Dragon Mountain. Crows called to their children in their nests. It reminded me of a folk song my Mother sang about a crow and her seven children.

Karasu Naze naku no,
karasu wa yama ni,
kawaii Nanatsu no ko go iru karayo.
Kawaii, kawaii to Karasu wa naku you,
kawaii, kawaii to nakun dayo.

I didn't know that I could carry a tune. I was proud of our first claimed land, and I walked around it, marking every inch for the Tanemori family.

"Yes! We did it! This land is ours; it belongs to the Tanemori!" I shouted.

"Oh, boy! *Ne-e-chan,* sister, we will be planting seeds tomorrow. Let's start early in the morning." This was perhaps the first time Satsuko showed me any approval. I was proud, very proud.

I had a hard time sleeping that night. I heard the wall clock bong at two o'clock. I was ready with my vegetable seeds when the sun peeked up over Seto Yama (Seto Mountain). I happily carried our waste along the path in buckets to fertilize our new land claim. I felt as crisp and energized as the fresh air of the spring morning. I heard the whistling of a train as it came around the hill just before the Kotachi station, with a jubilant whistle this morning. My entire body felt as if it was riding on a pillow of joy.

"NO!" I screamed as we arrived at the field. The rocks we had so diligently cleared had been thrown back onto our patch by some villagers overnight. Who could have done this? I flew into a rage. "Whoever you are; wherever you are hiding, no matter how long it takes we will find you." I wept bitterly.

We again cleared the rocks and planted sweet potatoes. At first I was proud to be carrying our dung in buckets to the sweetest sweet potatoes in our patch. I could taste them. But as time went on, I had to put up with recurrent taunts from children whose parents would be the ones to carry those heavy buckets. I grew to hate carrying the dung to the "Field of the Defeated." I often labored under the moonlight just to avoid the *sen-gan* and the taunts and insults of other children. I felt so ashamed that I shunned almost everyone.

One muggy summer afternoon, when all the village kids were splashing and cooling off in the *Eno*-River, I was resentfully obeying Satsuko's demand to carry our dung to the patch. I was thinking more about my self-pity than watching my footsteps, when I lost my footing on the slippery gravel between the rice fields. The next thing I knew I was soaked in excrement.

I swore at whoever had put the stupid gravel there. "Who is in charge of taking care of this path? This loose gravel should be packed down."

The entire world, it was clear, was against me. At least I didn't have to carry the heavy buckets all the way to the patch. I left the buckets where they lay and went to jump in a nearby creek. My favorite surrogate, Honda *Oba-achan,* discovered me covered in dung and humiliation.

"Taka-chan, Omae doshita noja? What happened to you? You look like a stinking rat," she said, with a smile in her voice. She called me over and I was able to tell her the whole story, and how I felt so bad about the whole world and myself.

"Oh, kawai sonino. Maa, kega ga nakatte yokatta, yokatta" She was glad that I wasn't hurt. She told me how proud she was of our family, growing up so quickly without any parents.

"Come with me, we'll get you a change of clothes. You smell awful. You have your wish now, Taka-chan. Don't you want to go jump in the river?"

Every day we went to our patch to give our wonderful sweet potatoes tender care. I talked to them and carried them the human dung they deserved for becoming our food to sustain us through the winter.

I discovered another bonus of having a *haisen-batake* right by the train tracks. Food thrown from train windows frequently littered the tracks. Even as a proud son of Tanemori, I lowered myself to look for food. I felt ashamed in the eyes of my Father, as he judged my groveling behavior from heaven.

Still I was always drawn into searching, just in case I got lucky. When I arrived at the field, before doing anything else, I would quickly rush to the railroad tracks. Many times I ended up in tears, kicking myself for not finding anything edible. At those times I berated myself for forgetting I was a proud son of Tanemori.

But one day I got lucky. I saw a box of *Morinaga Kyarameru,* a caramel candy made by Morinaga Confectionery Company. I tripped over my own feet and scraped my knee scrambling for the tiny box. When I opened the box I discovered a million tiny ants busily devouring my treasure.

"You dirty old buggers! Get away from this. It's mine!" I shouted. At first, I tried to politely remove the ants so as not to waste any caramel candy. But I became too impatient. My mouth watering, I popped whole candies into my mouth, ants and all! After I swallowed the ants, I happily savored the sweetness of the candy, my first taste of caramel in many years.

When the harvest season came, we waited for the optimal time to pick our crop, which would become a vital part of the Tanemori's survival.

My sisters and I carried several large gunnysacks and a basket to gather our harvest. It was an agonizing moment for all of us when we discovered our whole harvest had been stolen in the night. Not one potato to show for all our care and labor and love. It ripped me apart.

Unanswered questions wracked my soul. Was this the same hateful person who had thrown the stones back into our field? Was there any way I could get even with the horrible villagers? Would springtime ever come to the Tanemori family? Was there any way I could avenge the wrongs continually being perpetrated upon us?

Seeds of vengeance against the *sen-gan* and villagers became deeply implanted in my heart.

Chapter Six: Tales of a Hooligan

THE first post-war years had been devoid of merriment in the hearts of the villagers. There was no *taiko,* drumming; no bells or flutes; no *shamisen,* singing; no vendors with glittering trinkets and crafts; no amusement rides or *tejina,* magic shows; neither were there *yatai,* food booths, to tease the nostrils; nor any gala of any kind. Kotachi Village was no different than any other village in those dark days of Japan.

Finally, though, the villagers prepared to welcome the god *Fuku no Kami,* who brought good fortune and good harvests to Kotachi. The leaders organized the first *Omatsuri,* a harvest festival at the Shinto shrine of *Hachiman-san,* a local *Ujigami,* sun goddess. As the festival approached, laughter returned to the village. Even the birds sang brighter, as if reflecting the sunlight. The colors of the changing maple leaves were more intense.

Vendors came to set up their *yatai* booths. Aromas of hot *sake* and grilled *yakitori,* chicken on bamboo skewers, and *tako-yaki*, pastry, filled our nostrils. Crowds from Kotachi and surrounding communities came to celebrate the harvest.

The incident of our winter potato theft had driven me into isolation. Ready at last to emerge, I decided to check out the festivities in the early evening. The scents of the *yakitori* made my stomach ache with hunger. Without one *yen* in my pocket, I simply mingled with the throng.

I saw a little boy and girl, about my age, holding their parents' hands. The sight stirred up an ugly larva that had lain dormant in the pit of my stomach since my Father's death. The children were clean and dressed neatly in nice clothes for the occasion.

In contrast, I was shabby, torn and dirty. They were happily strolling from vendor to vendor, munching away on *yakitori,* smiling and laughing. I hated them. I wanted to beat them up. They were looking sideways at me, as if I were the scum of the earth.

"Baka mono. Nani o jiro, jiro mite iru noda? Kisama tachi wa nanimono ka? Oyaga inai kara to itte

bakani suruna!" I screamed profanities at them and finally I burst into *kuyashi namida*, tears of self-pity. Feeling as though my insides were bound with barbed wire, I wiped my tears with the back of my dirty hand. They disappeared into the crowd.

It was then that I fully understood for the first time what it meant to be an *oyanashigo,* orphan. It became perfectly clear.

It was the Americans I had to blame. They had killed my parents and destroyed my childhood. I ran down the winding path to my Father's gravesite—which was only about five hundred yards from the shrine—and fell to my knees.

"*Oto-chan,* why, why, why? Why did you go and leave me behind? Living without you is far worse than my death could ever have been. Why didn't you come back for me after you found Mother?"

I made the vow then and there that I would avenge his death. I raged against Americans. I vowed with my heart and soul, whatever it would take, however long it might take, revenge would be my friend, my constant companion! This feeling of revenge fed me an unlimited surge of energy from the depths of my soul!

When Step-Grandfather Sakae decided to enlarge his house to accommodate his houseguests more conformably, he built large and comfortable houses for the Komatsubara and Norikawa families. To avoid the pressures of the *sengan,* he was forced to build a small, single room house with a kitchen for the Tanemori children, annexing a tiny room for my Uncle Nakamura, my Mother's brother. Although we did not share a common entrance, we did share a common wall and toilet.

One day Uncle Nakamura bored a hole in the wall in order to peek into the bathroom at my two sisters. On another occasion he made inappropriate advances to both Satsuko and Chisako. I felt I must rise to the defense of my sisters, even though I was like a field mouse going against my uncle. How sick my heart was. I knew this would create waves in the village.

Relations with Grandmother Sakae took a turn for the worse when I confronted her with my complaints about him.

"Oba-a-chan, I am telling you the truth about him. We cannot have him live next door to us. I want him to move and stay away from my sisters."

She vehemently denied that her son was capable of such actions. "You are mad!" Grandmother Sakae shouted. "You have your Father's blood running in your veins."

The next day, I happened to run into my Uncle and Grandmother, together in the public square. It was an opportune moment to confront them together.

"You are *kichigai,* a mad dog. Why do you have to make up such lies? What are you trying to do? Are you trying to destroy his character? You will be sorry!" Grandmother scolded as she shook her finger at me.

My Uncle stood sheepishly by, squirming like a worm being cut in half.

I continued, "Grandmother! What are you afraid of—the truth?"

"One day policeman will come and drag you away. Your Grandmother will see to it," said my Uncle.

No matter what I said, or what evidence I provided, Grandmother refused to listen. I knew the Gossip Committee was aware of my Uncle's misbehavior, but they were like three little monkeys: *Mi-zaru, Kika-zaru* and *Iwa-zaru,* with sealed eyes, ears and mouths! I threatened to call the police to bring a formal charge against him. But even if I had, no one would have believed me. I had to accept reality. Satsuko sternly forbade me to mention it to anyone. I only hoped my Uncle did not cross the line and soil the honor of my sisters.

The village leaders, the *sen-gan,* complained often to Satsuko about my clearly defiant attitude towards the moral standards of the village. Maybe they didn't like to see me rummaging for food in garbage heaps.

The leaders of Kotachi Village were no different than leaders in any other village or hamlet nearby. Their task was to make sure every villager conformed to the social standards and judgments they set forth, and they tried to enforce standards upon common villagers that applied only to people who were subordinate in rights and duties.

I understood the community ethic and I opposed it. The entire community was motivated by a collective ethic. Group goals were more important than any individual goal. Individualism was considered selfish. For the community to survive the villagers had to seek a collective goal. Rights and authority were defined by birthright, and villagers could only prove their individual worth by subjugating their individual wills to the will of the whole. The sacrifice for the whole extended to physical well-being, principles, families, and perhaps even to life itself.

To maintain societal unity, submissive behavior showing deference to social superiors was demanded. Individual villagers needed to constantly find approval with their peers and superiors. Psychological security required constant reassurance. Villagers would behave in such a way as to win approbation at any cost. Worth was measured by the acceptance of others. But in my estimation, if someone denied the mandates of his own spirit merely to be accepted, he would ultimately sell his own soul.

The *sen-gan* insisted upon a hierarchical pyramidal social structure, stressing the prerogatives of rank, sex, and age, simply to control those born to lesser classes. Of course under this system orphans, the disabled, the disadvantaged, women and children suffered the most. Kotachi Village was steeped in a deep tradition of "collective" ethics—the goal of the group was far more important than the goal of any individual. Pressures toward community solidarity and personal conformity to the consensus of the entire village were very powerful.

The *sen-gan* made no attempt to help me survive, let alone live an easier life. When a decision was made, it was to be obeyed by all, or else. Any defiance or breach of the village codes or the general consensus were most often met with harsh *mura-hachibu*, the cutting off of violators from all normal human contact, even if they chose to remain in the village.

Consequently, common villagers were but a "society of be-ers" and not a "society of do-ers." They were expected to maintain community and social "harmony" by blindly obeying the leader. Such a rigid social structure was aptly described by the Japanese adage: "the nail that sticks out gets hammered down."

There seemed to be a great community delight that the Tanemoris were being driven to the edge of a cliff. As I grew into adolescence, I was not only filled with disdain for the authority of the village leaders, I was openly defiant and contemptuous of them. Unfortunately, there was as much freedom in Kotachi as in a prison. Making waves in Kotachi was like dropping a pebble in a transparent glass goldfish bowl: it was as though a tidal wave had been set in motion. Any hermit could live in the middle of any big city and do whatever he wished, and nobody would be bothered. But if you sneezed in the Kotachi, you'd better worry about what the villagers would say. And Kotachi was a microcosm of Japan at the time.

Satsuko, now 18 years old, earned great empathy and respect from the *sen-gan* for her deportment and sacrifices on behalf of her siblings. Her survival mechanism was to pander to their expectations. I was in no way like her. My *ego* ruled my better judgment. I held on to the knowledge that I was the Number One Son of Tanemori!

After one rainstorm that lasted nearly a full week, the mood of the villagers was ugly. They had a feeling of having nearly been drowned. On the first day the sun peeked from the dark clouds, many villagers were out and about.

As I returned from school, a couple of *sen-gan* invited themselves over to talk with my sister Satsuko about my behavior. Sitting on the edge of our one-room house they sipped tea from the sides of their mouths. I held their presence there in utmost disdain.

My sister began her nonsensical jabber to the *sen-gan.* Her motions were those of a drinking-bird toy, bowing and bowing like an automaton, thanking the s*en-gan* for their seeming kindness.

"It is because of you and your goodwill that we four siblings are able to live a healthy life. I am deeply indebted to your kind hearts and consideration of our well being."

I tried to slip unnoticed out the door.

"Takashi, will you show your respect by greeting our guests?" Satsuko insisted that I sit down like a good boy to pay my respects to the men.

They chided me for my disapproved behaviors and tried to make small talk.

"*Oh, Takashi-kun. Kimi wa okiku sodatte iruno!* Oh my goodness! You have grown so strong and big. How happy I am for you," said one of the *sen-gan*.

I internalized my rage, thinking, "You liar! What is that to you? You are all hypocrites!"

But then my sister zeroed in.

"Brother I have wished you were dead like a dog. Then I would have no part of your shame and disgrace. Do you know what the villagers say about you behind my back?"

Unrelenting, she charged at me like a bull at a matador, "If you show respect, honor these leaders, and follow the required social codes, you will be accepted as they have accepted me."

I kept my mouth tightly shut, lest insults should pour out uncontrollably. What audacity, I thought, as one of the *sen-gan* spluttered, "Why can't you be like your sister, *Satsuko-san*, who willingly submits to our leadership. She is a noble young lady."

I simultaneously laid into them and my sister. "What leadership have I rejected? What authority have I disdained? You have had nothing to do with the Tanemori family since the day my Father passed away. When we were hungry did you offer us any food? In the winter, did any one of you come to give us warm clothes?"

I treated them with the same disdain and disrespect that I felt they had shown me. Whenever I had the opportunity to show them my contempt, I did so. Their complaints were more about my attitude than my actions.

"I have been the target of your insults and assaults, and the object of constant suspicion. All you have done is treat me like a rubber ball, bouncing me here and there at your will. You have all underestimated me, for I am not like my sister, who—like a sheep on the way to the slaughterhouse—meekly subjects herself to your authority. You have forced me to defend my shredded dignity and to protect the honorable Tanemori name. You have tried unsuccessfully, day-in and day-out, to exert your self-appointed power to bring me to your feet, just as you have exerted your dominance over others in the community. How I pity you! You're all such small people!"

"That's right! If your father could see your behavior, he would turn over in his grave," said another *sen-gan.*

"Hold it right there!" Satsuko challenged. "Don't you ever, ever bring my Father into this, or even utter his name!"

She was beside herself with frustration and anger as she turned back to me. "I will never forgive your misconduct. Quickly, without any reservation, bow your head so deep that you cannot see the sun and then beg their merciful hearts to forgive you. I will, for the sake of our Father, seek their forgiveness on your behalf. Do so quickly before their patience runs out!"

"That's enough, my sister. Can't you see they are having great fun at your expense?" I retorted. "They see you as a puppet of their will. Why should I ever consider seeking their mercy! I have no desire to feed their pleasure!"

"Takashi," my sister bowed before them, "I demand that you apologize and seek their mercy, right now!" She was afraid to raise her face, hoping to invoke forgiveness on my behalf.

"Ne-e-chan. Iikagenni shinsaiyo. See! That's what I mean. I bet Father is choking, as he watches from heaven. You are a spineless jellyfish! Get your own act together before you condemn my actions. Oh, heavens no! Give me a break! How dare you bring Father into this."

Defiant spirits, disdaining authority, we were labeled *Furyo-shonen,* hoodlums. My sister sternly warned me to make a 180-degree turn, or there would no hope for the Tanemoris to survive in the community.

"If there is a remote chance to redeem the name of Tanemori by removing you, I will not hesitate to do so," she admonished me. "What a relief it would be if I could do just that. Your brother and sister and I will not bear the brunt of your shame. Don't you feel ashamed? These men are here out of the kindness of their hearts, to help us."

"That's it!" I yelled back. "Satsuko, shut up, idiot! That's enough bullshit!" I couldn't believe I was saying all those words in *Japanese*! My Mother would have sternly punished me by washing my mouth with soap and salt!

The Tanemori blood in my veins had reached the boiling point! I couldn't hold my peace.

"You fools! Get out of here right now!"

They decided to leave quickly, without properly taking leave of Satsuko. I grabbed a bowl of salt and scattered it where they had sat, to show my contempt and to purify that space.

From then on, my relationship with Satsuko was extremely strained. The battle of our wills was constant. Ultimately, the Gossip Committee, the school officials, and the community leaders all subjected me to constant scrutiny. I became the victim of the most powerful social code, the principle of *mura-hachibu,* ostracism. But I had no choice but to stay in the village and submit to my fate.

In one fell swoop, I had lost what remained of my family and my village. It was too late to change what had happened. I had to take my anger and frustration into the shadows of the darkest recesses of night. I could not accuse or excuse myself. I had no energy even to cry. Externally I would not subject myself, nor show even a hint of vulnerability. Yet internally my soul was in a wringer. I had to remain intractable, by being absolutely right in my position against my sister's perceived groveling. If not for this, I would have lost all my power, identity and strength of spirit in my own self worth. I refused to admit any conflicting emotions over what I had lost. I felt like a bird without a branch, like a honeybee without a wildflower.

Satsuko believed she was fulfilling the instructions laid down by our Father to make every action be for the good of the whole of society. She was doing everything in her power to insure the survival of the Tanemori name with an honored position in the village.

On the other hand, I was following the instructions of our Father to be true to my heart, even if it went against the norms of society. This was the only way I could see to fill my obligation to my birthright. Maintaining my integrity was more important than blindly following social expectations.

In retrospect, I have come to understand Satsuko's approach to have been wiser and more appropriate under the circumstances. It would take most of my life for me to come to this humble acknowledgement. I honor her and give her thanks for her strength and wisdom. If not for her, the Tanemori name may not have survived.

By 1949, as a fifth grade student, I noticed that the gap between the rich and poor had widened. This bred even more fury in my heart. The entire community became intolerable to me. We were considered extra baggage for the community to bear, yet they took even less interest in our welfare. The teachings of Father about *Jidai-Yusen,* making one's life benefit the greater good, and *Jita-Kyoei,* living one's life for the benefit of others, were causing a huge conflict in my conscience. I could not find it within my capacity to live by these teachings. I lived with only a feeling of resentment for our treatment by the community as a whole.

I especially resented witnessing Buddhist priests gaining wealth for services which had become much in demand since the bombing. They were well paid for their duties of praying for the protection and guidance of departed souls who may not have reached "enlightened realms."

It was sickly amusing me to watch the mercenary lifestyles of these Buddhist priests, as their humble service to the community was superseded by clear desires for material gain. The priests used their spiritual position to breed fear in the hearts of many who had lost loved ones, and the Tanemoris were no exception. For over three years since we had buried our Father, my sister gave the priest an obligatory offering of money or food—our food—for praying over our parents' and sisters' souls. This charade made me wonder what had become of the humility, meekness and compassion that had been the guiding principles of the Buddhist priests I had known in Hiroshima.

Satsuko, now 18 years old, had labored long and hard, winter and summer for four years, at her backbreaking lumberyard job. Each and every day she sacrificed herself to feed our family.

She also sacrificed to feed the priest who showed up at our door, on the third day of each month, for his handout. At the end of the month, from her pitiful earnings, there wasn't a cent left over for a piece of bubblegum. Sadayoshi and I would beg her to bring home a freshly baked loaf of bread on her payday. If she did so, she had to forego some other essential item.

Satsuko made the monthly sacrifice to maintain her standing in the community. It was one of the hundreds of social demands that Satsuko was required to meet. Each time the Buddhist priest would show up at the door, clean, warm and well-dressed, with his big fat stomach and bulging gunnysack, I couldn't understand why she was giving this *tanuki*, this fat raccoon, an offering.

I had held my tongue for the last several years as I watched my sister dutifully dole out scarce money or food so that *O-bo-san*, the Buddha priest, would say a few phrases of gibberish in memory of our parents. He would stay about 30 or 40 minutes at most, chant what seemed to be gibberish, and make hocus pocus in front of the *Butsudan*, our altar. There were times he came when no one was at home: he would pick up his offering from the *Butsudan*, leaving a trail of incense behind him. Who knew how long he made his invocations on behalf of our loved ones?

There were times when Satsuko asked me to sit in for her while he did his service. In the beginning I did so, but I became so upset with what I deemed his insincerity, and the fact that he was taking my bare necessities of life with him, that I finally lost all patience to participate in his folly.

One stormy day, I angrily confronted Satsuko with my doubts about the sincerity of his ministrations. The priest showed up, huffing and puffing under the weight of his gunnysack, bulging with vegetables and fruits. When he set the sack at the door and exchanged social greetings, I could no longer contain my disdain. I blurted out, "Sister, why is it that you have to give money or food to him every month, damn it? We are hungry and in need. You know that many nights we have huddled together for warmth and have fallen asleep with empty stomachs." I was so upset I was shaking.

She erupted and slapped my face. "What I do and what I give to our priest is my business. You have nothing to say. I decide what is best for the Tanemoris."

"Don't tell me that what you are doing is what is good for the Tanemori family," I countered. "Aren't you ashamed? We don't even have enough money to buy bread. You don't have enough money to buy hand cream. Look at your chapped hands."

She glared at me with a raging fire. "Who is working so hard? I am! Your sister, and nobody else! I am giving my life for you. Don't you ever tell me what to do! When have you earned the right to speak so 'high and mighty' against what I choose to do? I have to suffer to survive. You haven't the slightest idea why I work so hard. How easy my life would be if you had died instead of Father. I deplore his death!"

She continued in her fury. "Takashi, you are vile and selfish! I will not permit you to dishonor the memory of our parents and bring such disgrace to the family name!"

The priest sat quietly before the *butsudan* listening to our raging. I took his silence to mean he was incapable of understanding our difficulties. I judged him to be incompetent as a priest.

"You are scum!" I told him, forgetting all propriety and manners. "How can you claim yourself to be an *Obo-san,* a priest, let alone a compassionate one? I have no idea what kind of priest you are. But I need an answer: how can you take money from my sister every month? Can't you see our situation with a kind heart and not demand offerings or gifts from her? I beg you to consider my sister's burdens. She is only 18 years old."

Satsuko threw herself before him. "I beg you to forgive us the folly of my young brother. I beseech the pity of *Amida* Buddha through your kind remembering, and I implore that you will place no blame on our parents' spirits."

She slapped my face again with her open hand. "I will never allow you to continue to bring shame and disgrace to the Tanemori family. You have no idea what you are doing. I am sacrificing so the priest will continue to remember our parents kindly and their spirits will not suffer." She implored him to begin his service. He knelt before the altar, lit the incense and candle, and began his incantations.

I watched for a moment, but I didn't feel in my heart that our parents' spirits were in a state of suffering. I had to speak! "Resting in peace? Where did you get that idea? How did our parents' spirit come to be at the mercy of prayers by this priest? I won't accept it. Do you have any guarantee that this priest has remembered our parents kindly for all these years, or has helped their spirits find solace?"

"How dare you talk to our priest this way! Your behavior towards him is all the more reason our parents are suffering."

"How could you ever believe such nonsense?" I argued scornfully.

By now she had prostrated before the priest, begging him to look upon me with mercy, so that our parents would receive the dispensation of his grace.

"They are not suffering. This is idiotic."

My anger became so vehement I began to shake. Satsuko changed her tone and addressed me with utmost seriousness, demanding a humble apology from me. She begged me, for the sake of our parents, never to repeat this behavior.

I knew in my heart that Father understood my pain. This alone gave me peace! My knuckles were turning white and my hands were shaking uncontrollably. "You get out of here! Right now!" I yelled at the priest.

He stopped chanting, but did not move at all, nor even blink his eyes. He reminded me of a statue of Buddha in the temple.

"Takashi. Tsutsushimi nasai!" She shouted at me for my interceding. *"Kokoni atamao sagete Hotoke-sama ni owabi o shinasai!"* She begged me to prostrate myself before the *Butsudan* altar and seek his mercy before my soul was eternally destroyed.

"Hayaku dete yuke, kono kuso Bozu. Get out of here con artist Priest!" I again raised my voice.

I felt pity for my sister, whose soul had been strangled by fear. As the priest stood to leave, my sister apologized and asked forgiveness while presenting him the envelope. He placed it in his purse, bulging with offerings, and gathered his gunnysack. I couldn't look at him. Mumbling and grumbling he left our house.

After that incident, my sister would send me off to do errands for her whenever the priest was expected to come and offer prayers. I thought my sister had changed her heart by trusting me with these new responsibilities.

How naïve I was! And yet I had become resigned to letting them "do their thing" in front of the altar in our house without disturbance or condemnation. Outwardly it appeared as if I had had a change of heart.

But from that moment on, I knew the breach between me and my sister was unbridgeable. I was tarnished with unpardonable social sin, and things were about to get worse. Many decades later, Satsuko admitted to me that the priest had been ousted from his Buddhist sect and had to leave his position in the village. But this does not alter my mature regret over my hooligan-like behavior toward my sister and her beliefs at the time.

As news about the incident with the priest traveled fast and far, the Gossip Committee was busy trying to figure out exactly what had happened. I could have enlightened them, but they didn't come to me. So the whispering continued.

When I was in the sixth grade, my old wonderful homeroom teacher, Takahashi *Sensei,* used her influence and trust to vouch for me to get a job as a paperboy. The newspaper, based on my bad reputation in the village, was hesitant to hire me, but did so under certain probationary conditions.

The first week of each month, I collected money from subscribers, and was humiliated to have the Gossip Committee follow and watch me as I did so. A mosquito-eyed man, Nishita, watched me like a hawk throughout the route, until I turned all the money over to the owner of the paper. The word was that the *sen-gan* wanted to make sure the owner got all his money.

This seemed idiotic to me. How could they think I would jeopardize my job by stealing money? The money and receipts were all at their disposal, and the figures had to match. It seemed they were purposely insulting me.

One morning, about 5:00 am, I bundled up in the worn, two-sizes-too-large overcoat that had been given to me by my surrogate *Oba-a-chan.* I made ready to meet a heavy, snowy paper route. Snow fell silently. Shivering against a north wind, I made my way down a street covered by snowdrifts. When I slipped and fell, I berated myself for my clumsiness, until I felt something under the snow where I had fallen. It was a neatly wrapped bundle of cloth.

"What in the world is this?" I asked, under the porch light of a business establishment. I looked around to make sure I was completely alone, and opened the bag.

"What?" My heart beat faster and louder, like a *taiko* drum. "Wow!" This was *"Tana kara Bota mochi!* A gift from heaven!" I had found manna, lots and lots of money, a bank account booklet and, above all, a *hanko,* seal, which served as an authorized signature giving the bearer rights to all legal transactions at the bank. I rubbed my eyes in disbelief, looking all around and up to heaven to make sure not even the Gods or Buddha could see my prize through the snowy clouds.

"No! It can't be!" I exclaimed to myself in silence. My heart increased its *taiko,* rhythm. I excused myself of any sense of wrongdoing because I hadn't stolen the package. It was there for the picking, a personal offering! It looked like the early bird just got his "worm," a whole bunch of worms!

When I picked up the papers, I counted them, as always. But this morning, trying to hide my treasure under my overcoat from the other paperboy, I was awkward. All I could think about was my boon and escaping the watchful *sen-gan*. I had to run to the bathroom, behind a locked door, pull the bills out and fondle them. It felt fantastic to hold all that green cash. It was a stack about five inches thick, in big denominations. I had never even seen that much money at once, and it was mine! I would be the richest boy in the village. This would go a long way towards food and clothing for my two sisters, brother and me. Oh, what a wonderful feeling it was!

I had yet to own a new school uniform, while other students, including my cousin, wore black spanking-new uniforms with shiny gold buttons and matching hats. Neither did I have any leather shoes. I didn't have rubber boots without holes, nor even good *geta*, wooden shoes, that were good enough to wear when I saw my friends.

I knew that with my newfound fortune I could buy lots of things and would be like a normal boy in the village. I wore a satisfied smile and tipped my head toward heaven.

As I started my paper route, I felt two dogs in my heart: one was white and the other black. They were arguing, then began to fight ferociously.

"Take it to the policeman. Remember what your Father taught you! Remember who you are. Who is crying out for truthfulness and justice?" asked the white dog.

"Why should you do that? Finders keepers! You didn't steal it. It was there for you. You're just a lucky guy. Somebody is looking after you!" said the black dog.

They argued back and forth

"NO! It doesn't matter whether anyone was watching or not. The money you found doesn't belong to you. It's not for you to keep."

"Yes. Look how much money you have! Just for you! Think how much food you could buy, you'll never be hungry again. Think what else you could buy with that money—a brand new school uniform, squeaky new shoes, boots, a bicycle—or anything you want. Just like the rest of the neighborhood kids. You have been deprived. Now it's your turn, you deserve it."

"No Takashi! Don't listen to that voice. Remember your Father taught you one of the most important moments in life is what to do when you are all alone. Didn't he tell you many times that your greatest victory is to overcome your temptation, to have victory over yourself. Don't defeat yourself by your own weakness!"

"Oh, come on! This is your chance to live a normal life like the rest of the people. Look at those Gossip Committee members: don't they live like they own heaven? Go ahead, do something big! This is your chance, don't miss it."

Continuing my paper route, I passed the police station and noticed the door was open and the light was on.

"That's strange. I don't remember seeing the light on at that time of morning ever before." My heart beat faster and louder when I approached to deliver their paper. I noticed two different sizes of footprints in the snow.

When I turned to continue my route, the dogs were fighting again. I hesitated momentarily, and then heard the weeping of a woman in the station. I did my best to ignore the dispute in my mind while I finished delivering papers. At the end of the route I discovered several extra papers still in my bag. I tried to rationalize why I had those extra papers.

My mind turned back to the bundle. This money would be mine to keep.

"Of course!" I shouted! "This is a way to get money back from that fat *Tanuki* who has stolen from my sister for years. That's settled!"

Somehow my footsteps led me back to the front door of the police station. The woman was still inside weeping and pleading. A policeman was trying to console heart.

The black dog spoke. "Your family has suffered, so let this woman suffer, too!"

"*Oka-a chan. Kore kara doshite tabete yukuno. Korekara Chieko wa onakaga suite yuku no ne.*" I heard the voice of a little girl asking her mother how would she be able to eat. Her tiny heart was bursting in tears.

I visualized her, clinging to her mother, burying her head in fear. I experienced her fear, which brought tears to my eyes.

The temptation was almost too much. I was being consumed in my own feeling of justification, torn between what was right and wrong. The more I tried to reason why I should keep it, the clearer it became that the question was not what is right or wrong. I knew the answer!

"Takashi, remember, who you are," the spirit of my Father spoke from the deepest chamber of my soul. "Be true to yourself! Be strong. To overcome oneself is the greatest victory."

I walked into the station and proudly presented the bundle.

How amazed they were to discover such an honest boy in their midst. They gave me a reward of 500 yen, about $5. Stepping out of the station, a hungry 12-year-old boy had suddenly become a tall, strong man. I could feel Father's approval. He was smiling so proudly. I knew I was the son of Tanemori! This was my first private money. I kept it secretly for a long time, spending it slowly on caramel candies without ants. I never told anyone about the incident.

As I grew, however, my reputation progressively worsened, especially during my junior high school years. I was known as the *chibi-chan,* the smallest or shortest shrimp of the entire Oda Junior High School. Although I did not seek to fight, I often managed to be caught in the midst of ruffians, until one day I banded with several other bad boys for "self protection." People would call us the "three bandits."

We spent our time committing minor acts of vandalism, drinking, and smoking cigarettes, which we rolled from dried weeds or even newspaper. We thought we were very cool and tough. My friends would find alcohol and we would bring ourselves further public shame by acting as though we had been drinking. We would chase trucks, trying to hit the drivers with slingshots. We stole eggs and fruit and food offerings to the Buddha statues. One day we moved the *Ojizo-san,* the Buddha statue at the crossroads, a route marker.

I became labeled a *furyo-shonen,* hoodlum, and was under constant suspicion by school officials and Gossip Committee members. Whenever something was missing, I was instantly called into the Principal's office for questioning.

My relationship with Satsuko had become one of stony silence, completely poisoned. Each time she heard of my antics from the Gossip Committee, it made our relationship icier and more distrustful. I had risked *mura-hachibu,* officially sanctioned ostracism. Grandmother Sakae joined with Satsuko in the chorus of voices crying for me to be sent to some kind of reform school.

One afternoon, two policemen researching a theft arrived at Grandmother Sakae's doorstep. When she saw me coming down the street from school, thinking this was the perfect opportunity to send me away, she rushed to grab me by the arm and gleefully tell me of my imminent banishment to a reform school.

"*Omawar-san* are here. I told you before that I was going to see you put away for good. You will not create any more embarrassment for me. Everybody knows you are my grandson, but remember, your mother is dead. Now I won't have to be seen as your Grandmother anymore. Your sister Satsuko has agreed and finally sees it my way."

My sister was raging, unable to withstand the public shame I had once again brought to our family name. She screamed at me and begged the policemen to take me to a Juvenile Retention Institution. Yet the police found no evidence, and I was not arrested. To my saving grace, one of the policemen had been in the station that cold snowy morning two years before, when I had proudly returned the bag of money. He recognized me and affirmed that I was indeed the same heroic boy.

"*Hai! Sodesu!*" I responded to him proudly, "That was me!"

What money bag? What woman? What little girl? When did it happen? The story was revealed to Grandmother and the rest of the *sen-gan*. They were in total disbelief that the *furyo-shone* who should be in reform school had displayed such moral integrity. Seeing their startled expressions, I couldn't help but smile. The added bonus was that the police never bothered me again.

Having failed to put me in reform school, the spirit of Satsuko became like that of a twisted, angry ox. She grew increasingly desperate. She wished I was guilty, as did Uncle "Peeping Tom," who supported my being put away.

Into these whirlwinds of conflict, my sister brought a young man, Kitsune Kuroki. From her first fumbling introduction, I realized this young man was her "knight in shining armor" who would save us from our desperate situation.

The moment I met him, I could see an absence of soul in his eyes. It would only be a matter of time before his true nature, the *oinari-san,* the fox of deceit, astuteness and cunning, would be revealed to her. Here was another person, egged on by Satsuko, to stand by her side to condemn my behavior. I fiercely challenged his manhood and made it clear to him that it was my responsibility to protect the Tanemori line from pollution. I took it upon myself to try to dictate to Satsuko what I felt was appropriate for her, and for us. I made it known to him I would not accept him marrying my sister.

Kuroki was undeniably handsome and superficially quite charming, but I found his shifty eyes ominous. One I perceived this shifty quality, I began to pile on other, perhaps imagined, negative attributes. He was too smooth-talking, especially in his overtures to my sister. I began building a huge case against him, absolutely sure he couldn't be trusted.

Kuroki's presence intensified the battles between Satsuko and me. These always dissolved into shouting matches, in which all my faults were enumerated for the whole village to hear.

"Can you show respect to Mr. Kuroki, who is willing to give his life for the Tanemoris? You have yet to welcome him with open arms, let alone an open heart."

The fury of her discontent lashed me like a serpent's fiery tongue. "Takashi. I have done what it took to keep the promise I made to our Father on his deathbed. He asked me to take care of you, but how often I have wished you dead! I wish you had died in Hiroshima like the rest of them."

Grandmother Sakae and Uncle Nakamura supported my sister totally; they would have liked nothing better than for my head to be roasted in the ashes like a sweet potato. They did their best to stack the deck against me, using Kuroki as a fulcrum. They also tried, with Satsuko, to turn Chisako against me, but she did her best to remain neutral.

One morning Satsuko was all over me to do the chores, pulling off my covers while letting Chisako and Sadayoshi sleep. "Stop pestering me," I grumbled, holding the covers tight. I wondered why she didn't go after Chisako and Sadayoshi.

"I deplore the death of our Father." She spat at me. "I wish he had taken you with him. Now, see what I have to go through."

Returning home from the chores, my back stiffened when I saw Kitsune Kuroki fondling my sister. I displayed my distaste to them.

Satsuko responded "I am only your sister. I have no moral or legal obligation to take care of you. Why should I suffer and give up my life on your account? You are good for nothing, nothing but a troublemaker. You will amount to nothing. Do you understand what I am saying? You will amount to nothing! Don't you have any shame?"

She went into her normal tirade against me, accusing me of rude and heartless behavior. She continued. "All he gets from you are snubs and contempt. You make him feel uncomfortable for even being here! You are a most ungrateful brat!"

Feigning surprise, I asked, "Oh, my dear sister, who are you talking about?" Have I not tried to show my grateful heart and my honor to you by giving you your proper place as my big sister? Do you mean you are asking me to conduct myself like a gentleman, toward this ... this ... man?" I was making it clear that I could never consider him a man, especially since I believed he was trying to move into our single room instead of inviting Satsuko to come live with him.

Kuroki stood up, cowardly, protecting himself behind my sister. "It is because of you that Satsuko has had to bear public humiliation, and unnecessary burdens. She cries day-in and day-out with shame caused by your hoodlum misbehavior. Even if you die young, it will not rectify what you have done to her."

I laughed so hard at his audacity that I almost choked. Who did he think he was talking to? He was not worthy to breathe the same air I breathed. "Don't make me laugh! You are disgrace. You call yourself a man. You have no dignity and no honor. You have no right even to use the name of Tanemori. You are subjecting the Tanemori family to public shame!"

When I vowed to both of them that this half-worm would never marry my sister, my sister burst into a rage. "Even if I could roast you or stew you in an iron pot, this would not satisfy my heart. I could kill you with my bare hands and feel no remorse over your carcass. I would be doing society a favor. The village elders would thank me. After what you have said, there is nothing I can do to make it right with Mr. Kuroki."

I felt betrayed. "If you want to sleep with this worm, born of a horse, then go ahead," I retorted to my sister. "But I will never allow you to even utter the name of Tanemori again. Neither will your children take the Tanemori name. You will be cut off from Tanemori."

My sister exploded. "I have kept the promise I made to Father on his deathbed. He asked me to take care of you, and I have, even though I have wished you dead!"

I lost my temper. I spat at him. "What right have you to appoint yourself to the *Samurai* class? Even the snake that crawls in the dust has sense to hide in the hole when shamed!"

He stood behind my sister while playing the role of her defender. I would never have believed my sister would reach so low for any man. NO! His presence blocked the way for a much more worthy suitor.

"That's it!" My rage overcame me. I yelled back at her. I ran to my sister's corner of our small house, where she kept her make-up case, and grabbed that precious symbol of her womanhood. While she begged me to put it down, I wanted so very much to break the mask with which she was forever ingratiating herself to the community. I threw the contents of the makeup case around the room and smeared her lipstick on the walls, breaking the window in the process.

Kuroki did nothing to stop me or to help my sister. I was secretly hoping he would act like a man and defend her, to prove he was a man of substance. But he failed the test, just standing passively as Satsuko crumpled to the floor with a broken heart. Before my final condemnation of his wimpiness, he quietly slipped out the door.

Many years later, after I had left Japan, Kuroki again pursued Satsuko and won her hand in marriage. She bore him two boys and one girl. When the children were still small, Satsuko divorced him, and raised another family as a single mother. She reassumed the name of Tanemori for herself and gave her children the "right" to bear the Tanemori name. This explosion was the last either of us could tolerate. We had tried our best to avoid each other.

I, the Number One Son, and Satsuko, the oldest child, both felt it our duty to guide and protect the family and its honorable name! Our ideas about how to do this were diametrically opposed, with no room for compromise.

Each saw the other as a threat to both our family honor and our own existence. The gulf between us was so great, the wounds so deep, that our relationship was beyond redemption. Satsuko saw my unwillingness to bend to social pressure as a direct threat to the survival of the family. In my mind she was actively destroying the essence of Tanemori each time she sold her soul for acceptance. She lived like a *jo-zu na yowatari,* a chameleon in the forest.

I wondered how she could live without her own spirit. The day would surely come when she would strangle to death for lack of her own breath. Dead silence had become our only communication. She was my enemy, a dragon helping others to destroy me. I detested everything she stood for.

My own isolation, terror and rage were overwhelming any other feelings I had. The Gossip Committee, in twos, and sometimes in threes, began showing up frequently at my home, as if they were afraid to confront me alone. I wanted to cut their tails, inch-by-inch, so they could see how they were stripping my sister of her identity. I kept my tail even more protected, baring my teeth and growling at them. With each visit I was driven deeper into my isolation and bitterness. The hole I dug for myself had no exit. I dug deeper and deeper into my miserable world of anger and hatred.

The typhoon season arrived like a lion with the month of September. The villagers were bracing themselves, preparing for the final stage of the rice harvest. The harvest would tell whether the Gods would reward the villagers' labors with bountiful crops. In our folklore, the Gods would smile if the village had cared for the needy and unfortunate ones, the fatherless children.

In contrast, brilliant mosaic colors stretched out through the hills, valleys and gorges. I could almost taste, feel and touch that my passing through this harvest season would be most painful. I believed only one of us could survive—either my sister or me. The breaking point had come, and following the harvest season the entire village would become a gray landscape. I shivered at a feeling of death.

No one knew that the path to my Father's gravesite was almost worn out by my pilgrimages there. There were two marks deeply imprinted in the ground by the dilapidated wooden marker where I often knelt. Today all the hills were covered with white snow, leaving no trace of my tears.

Into these swirling winds of my emotional conflict, the preparation of *Oshogatsu,* the New Year, came upon us. The essence of this season is *Oseibo,* the time to make amends and reconcile with those you may have offended or who may have affronted you. In *Oseibo,* houses are cleaned and shined from top to bottom to chase off evil spirits. Through the pounding of traditional rice cakes, the *omochi,* evil spirits, are driven away.

Everyone is responsible for cleansing their sins and transgressions through apology and forgiveness. Gifts are exchanged to demonstrate contrition. In the Temple at midnight, the gong is struck 108 times to appease the 108 Gods. Thus the New Year is welcomed with a clean slate.

One day during the heart of *Oseibo,* Satsuko broke the silence with an unusual request. Her voice was sticky-sweet and tender, *"Taka-chan,* will you take the gift of *Oseibo* to Tamura *Sensei?"* He was my homeroom teacher in junior high school, and he had also taught Satsuko. In fact, he had been her favorite teacher and he understood our family's plight, especially her problems with me.

"Why do you want me to take the gift?" I asked cynically.

"Aren't you the rightful representative of the Tanemori family?"

I quickly built walls against her. I was more than suspicious. I could see a very carefully wrapped gift, clearly representing her intention to honor him, a typical fulfillment of the social and cultural demands imposed upon her.

"No! Give me one good reason why I should do this errand for you? It's your thing. You go right ahead. I have nothing to do with you or your gift."

"He would like to see you," she timidly responded.

Suddenly a warm snuggly feeling snuck into my heart. Could it be she is trying to make amends? NO! Better to keep my heart frozen! Was I some kind of simpleton to imagine for even a split second any goodness in my sister?

But because it was the *Oseibo* season, I acquiesced and held out my hand for the pretty package and the round trip train tickets to Tamura *Sensei's* village, just one stop away. Oh, well, I hadn't ridden the train since my last secret trip to Hiroshima.

It was December 28, 1952. I was 15 years old. I rode the train with foreboding.

"What in the world have I gotten into? Perhaps I had made the wrong decision. Was I acting like a fool?"

Tamura *Sensei* lived in a magnificent traditional house, which revealed that he was a descendant of a *daimyo*, a powerful feudal warlord. The house sat on a hill, overlooking land holdings, the rice fields which he rented. The Tamura family was wealthy and well-respected in the community. He was also highly respected as a teacher.

When I arrived at the front door of Tamura's house, he was clearly expecting me. His effusive welcome was disingenuous. We exchanged formal greetings, and I extended my sister's best wishes to him and his family.

An unusual quiet and coldness in the house gave me a creepy sensation. Where were the others? Even an alley cat would have felt apprehensive.

Tamura *Sensei* directed me to his study. He invited me to sit in the *kotatsu,* the foot-warmer, and then appeared with a beautifully arranged tray of food. We regarded each other silently. I felt as if I had been captured. This was the first time Tamura *Sensei* had ever invited me to his house. He had singled me out for misbehavior in school, but it was highly unusual for a teacher to have any private relationship with a student.

He offered me the array of food, which I did not touch. He poured himself hot *sake*, drank it quickly, then poured another. He acted as if he had something to say, but didn't know how to begin. Each time he would start, he decided to have another *sake*. I had seen my Uncle Nakamura drunk on many occasions and I remembered how ugly and violent he would get.

"*Sensei*, are you all right?"

Finally, fortified with *sake*, he said, through bleary eyes, "Tanemori." I swallowed hard as the seriousness of the meeting became apparent. He downed another *sake* and with a deep breath looked straight into my eyes.

"Tanemori, it has been reported to me that your behavior has caused great concern to your sister. You have brought distress, shame and disgrace to your family. I am sure you are aware of your reputation, of your misconduct."

"*Konchikusho! Kono fatari wa oreo uragitta na!*" Now I knew my sister's madness within her method. I had fallen into Satsuko's trap! They had both betrayed me.

"Tanemori, are you listening to what I am saying? Do you have shame in your heart? You, the firstborn son, have brought reproach to your honorable family name."

He walked to the *shoji*-glass doors that looked out onto the Japanese garden. He motioned me to stand next to him.

"Do you see the black pine tree, its branches stretching over the pond in the center of the garden? It has taken more than thirty years of twisting, bending and adapting to the weather to shape it that way, reaching between heaven and earth. I am going to beat the spirit and the will of that *bonsai*, that proud and powerful tree, into your soul."

With all his strength, he slapped me across my face, back and forth over and over. As he laid into me, I stood my ground, gritted my teeth and accepted the punishment with *mugon*—silence. Fury at my sister's betrayal intensified my defiance and desire for retaliation. As long as he saw fire in my eyes, he continued, but he couldn't kill my fire.

After what seemed an eternity, *Sensei* walked out into the beautiful garden next to the powerful *Bonsai*-tree. He stood trembling, releasing his energy. He had not been able to draw one tear from my eyes, although I, too, was shaking with a vengeful energy against my sister, and now toward my teacher, who had blatantly planned this entrapment. My face was swollen and hot. I could have left at that point, but I did hold him in enough regard to wait for my dismissal.

By the late afternoon sun he beckoned me to come out to the garden. He gripped my shoulders and looked squarely into my eyes. I was stunned to see tears rolling down his cheeks. They reminded me of my Father's tears. This was the first time I saw my Father's tears coming from another person. His eyes bored into my frozen heart. Slowly and deliberately, he begged me to understand why he had beaten me. His lips were quivering. He asked me to consider again the black pine tree and how it grew to become the centerpiece of the garden.

"Tanemori, you must change your life. Anyone can choose to be a bully and live a life of a hooligan, wallowing in the river of selfishness. It takes a strong fish, a mighty *koi* to be able to swim upriver against the power of the waterfall. Put the teachings and admonitions of your parents to the test. See if they are right. If, after an earnest test, you find they don't work for you, you can come back and tell me. Only then will you will have no reason or obligation to follow them."

He looked into my eyes one last time—trying to reach down deep into my ice-covered soul. Then he turned around again, toward the black pine tree.

I saw him from behind, his shoulders shaking with sobs. I wondered whether he was crying from the guilt of having beaten me, or if he was crying for me.

I made several trips to my Father's gravesite, seeking consolation. I began to understand what it meant to uphold the honor and responsibility of the Tanemori name. I was willing to put the admonition of *Sensei* to the test.

If I nurtured my Father's teachings as he gave them to me, Tanemori, like the meaning of our name, would flourish. I reflected at his grave and shrine on the literal translation of the name Tanemori: *"The life within a seed will bring forth its fruit in due season. The life within the seed has its own volition, will bloom independently, and prosper like a forest."*

Nearly twenty-five years later, when I returned to Hiroshima for the first time since immigrating to America, I learned from Tamura *Sensei* the depth of my sister's agony over me.

She had begged Mr. Tamura *Sensei* to put me away that evening, to quietly snuff out my life, so that the Tanemori name would be dishonored no further. But even with all that *sake*, he couldn't bring himself to commit the act, and spared my life against her wish.

Satsuko must have been surprised and very disappointed to see me walk in the door that evening with my swollen face. Even though I spoke only in cold cordial tones to her, after that New Year observance she would frequently comment on the change in my overall demeanor.

Chapter Seven: Illicit Love in a Secret Garden

FROM the first day of Middle School, I was no stranger to any of the teachers at Oda Chugaku Junior High School. My wailing going into and out of the Principal's office remained almost a daily activity. What had changed, though, was the way I carried myself. Where in my early days I had lowered my head like a "marked" sheep in a slaughterhouse, for the last two years I had acted boldly, as though I owned the place.

My face was familiar to all the teachers and nobody paid much attention when I was subjected to disciplinary actions for my misbehavior. Sometimes the angry voice of the Principal raged throughout the office. At other times, the sound of the "board of education" being applied to my "seat of learning" rattled the windows. Yet not once did I shed tears, gritting my teeth instead with an inner fury.

I had definitely earned the brand of *furyo-shonen,* hooligan.

After having had the *tamashii,* the spirit, the tar, beaten out of me by Tamura *Sensei* a few days earlier, I found myself at my Father's gravesite, bathing in his spirit.

My mind returned to the image of the Japanese black pine. I was caught up with the explanation of how the *Bonsai* pine tree stretched over a pond in the garden. I could hear Tamura *Sensei's* voice again, coming from deep in my soul, "It has taken over thirty years of twisting, bending, and adapting to its circumstances to shape the way it stands, reaching between heaven and earth. The true grace of the *bonsai* is expressed in the space described by the tree's branches. It is called *yugen,* the grace of movement within eternal stillness—a truth that is beyond words."

These words were already burnt, or indelibly imprinted, on my heart. I didn't appreciate how difficult it was for Tamura *Sensei* to honor my sister's request until I reflected on his weeping that afternoon. He had counseled me to learn the virtues of a still mind, so that I would be able to walk the path of my life in the spirit of *yugen.* It was like hearing my Father's own words. I began to feel that at last there was someone who cared about me, someone willing to help me reshape my life.

On December 31, 1952, I made my first appearance at the local Shinto temple to make New Year's resolutions, promising to really turn over a new leaf.

Among the throngs of people coming to make resolutions were members of the Gossip Committee. They were incredulous to see me humbly bowing my head in reverence and admiration before the Shrine of the Sun Goddess. I could see them pointing, hear their whispering and scornful laughter.

One committee member put his dirty hand on my shoulder and asked me, "Are you real? How long will it last?"

On the morning we returned to school from winter break, Tamura *Sensei* asked me to stay after school. For the rest of the day my heart was in my throat, as I wondered what he would do to me. I sat in the outer office, rubbing my hands, my mind racing in every direction, trying to figure out exactly what he wanted from me. Waiting for him to finish his work seemed to take an eternity.

"Tanemori."

To my surprise, I sensed a smile in his voice. He was very welcoming and friendly, and asked me to do him a favor. I wondered what new trick he had up his sleeve.

He urged me to write down everything that was ripping apart my soul—all the anger and resentment—and to be truthful about my feelings. On one hand I was happy to have one person in my life show an interest in my feelings; on the other hand, I was not sure I wanted to bare the truth of my despicable internal world. Nonetheless, I agreed and poured my ugly guts onto paper for him.

Tamura *Sensei* edited my stream-of-consciousness expression of fury into an intelligible essay, accurately portraying feelings that had been locked in my heart. Then he asked me, "Would you be willing to read your life story in speech class?"

"Why, Sir? My life story is nobody else's business. Why should anyone care what happened to me, let alone about my feelings? No, Sir! Sorry, I refuse."

He smiled knowingly. He had tricked me. "Well, it's a class assignment."

The day came for me to give my presentation, and I stood in the front of a jeering classroom.

"Can he read?" asked one student.

"What does he have to say worth listening to?" sneered another.

"Does a rotten tree bear good fruit?" another shouted.

Tamura *Sensei* allowed the students to hiss at me, which surprised me. This made me even more determined to stand my ground and not be intimidated by punks.

Over their jeering, I began to read my story about how lonely and difficult it was to grow up as an orphan. I questioned why we had fought in the war.

As my story continued beyond my expressions of anger, I looked for solutions. I felt that if there was anything people could do in the aftermath of such a terrible event as a war, it would be to honor the dead. Instead of mourning for them, I felt we ought to rejoice for them.

Most importantly, though, society needed to make sure survivors were taken care of, because they were the ones who were really suffering. They had witnessed horror which they would never forget, and they had lost everything in their lives that had been precious.

I felt the raging storm of my experience passing over the class. The girls, especially Atsuko Tamura, Chiyoko Nishikiori and Sumiko Kawamoto, were immediately affected and yelled out at the hecklers, "Listen to what he has to say. Have you ever experienced such loneliness or suffered hunger, naked and ..."

Tamura *Sensei* had become teary-eyed along with many of the girls as they listened. The whole class became dead silent, as if in the eye of a storm, listening with their full attention and sympathy.

During the following weeks, it seemed everyone's mood toward me changed. I couldn't believe what was happening, as no one attacked or insulted me, not even the worst of the bullies. Tamura *Sensei* even gave my essay to the Principal and other teachers to read.

It was then that Tamura *Sensei* urged me to consider giving a public speech. Before I knew it, I was entered in the *Benron-Taikai,* the Public Speech Contest, a student competition sponsored by the Public Speech Club. I was standing before the entire student body and all the teachers, telling my story.

Shortly after the intramural tournament, Tamura *Sensei* called me into his office.

"What have I done now, that I'm being called in for?"

I had acquired a deeper respect for him, seeing him as a father figure. I often reflected on his image of the black pine tree in his garden.

Most of the teachers showed little or no reaction as I walked into the office. But Tamura *Sensei* saw me and waved for me to come quickly.

"Tanemori, I have good news for you. As a matter of fact, I think it is wonderful news for the school."

His approving smile seemed to approve the calmer and less aggressive way I had been behaving since my New Year resolutions. It seemed the promise of new budding was on the horizon.

"What's good news? There is no such thing," I said under my breath.

He told me I had been chosen by the Principal to represent the school at a regional tournament for public speaking. He detailed the event, to be held at Yoshida Junior High School, about 50 kilometers, 15 miles, away. There would be twelve participants from six different junior high schools contending in three levels of competition.

"Are you mad?"

I couldn't believe my ears. I was not a "joiner" of any kind, and couldn't envision myself in a Speech Club, much less representing the school in a regional tournament. I tried to shrink from the request, but *Sensei* wouldn't take no for an answer. And so I joined the *Benron-Kurabu,* the Public Speech Club.

I questioned Tamura *Sensei's* sanity again and again. The Club had yet to disprove its perceived image of lack of achievements. So far, no major awards were to be found in the display case. The student body thought of kids in the Club as *henkutsu,* social misfits, eccentric and weird nerds and intellectuals who sat around and talked *tetsugaku,* philosophy, beyond the realm of reality.

I couldn't embrace the idea of joining up with this group of defiant social rejects. They just weren't like the so-called normal kids in other clubs. But it wasn't long before I felt very welcome, joining in earnest conversations about deep and important philosophies. I had found my nest.

As the tournament date closed in, the Principal came to give us a pep talk. When he directed his talk at me, I realized my speech would be the cameo message for our club, and that he expected me to bag a trophy for the school. This was a totally new experience for me. I had never been the center of attention. I had always been looked upon as an example of what *not* to do!

I was being required to grow, to evolve, to shed my insecurities and change, dramatically. The students and the faculty, caught up in the excitement of a possible victory, made special efforts to wish me all the best, especially while I was practicing my speech.

The stakes were very high: a make it or break it situation for me. This was either a new beginning of acceptance, or an undertaking which could end in disgrace.

Instead of going directly home from school, I made a beeline to my Father's gravesite, my shrine of cleansing and purification, my only source of love and acceptance through these miserable years.

Now it could be my turn to shine. I felt like the delicate horsetail grass, trampled down, yet resurrected in the spring. I came away with confirmation that I was on the right track and that I should take courage to meet the new challenges presented to me. This could also be a new beginning for Oda Junior High School.

Tamura *Sensei* had always been known as the school's most disciplinary teacher, showing firm conviction and commitment to his teaching and to his students. I had certainly tasted his harshest form of discipline. He took it upon himself to mold me in a very different way when he worked on honing my speaking skills. He was warm and tender, except when he could see me slacking off and giving less than my best.

He required the best from all of us, and he could see through our pretences. When he felt we weren't giving a task the necessary commitment, we had to put in an additional hour of practice, or do extra garbage detail. On the other hand, he would give us honey and hot water for our throats.

I slowly improved my public speaking style and skills. Tamura *Sensei* and I had bonded, and I faithfully held to the promise I had made at my Father's grave to follow *Sensei's* advice. His prescription was working. Positive changes were taking place in my life; a new course was being charted.

One afternoon, I ran into Mimae *Sensei* in the hallway. Every student avoided this teacher at all costs. I detested his slight and minimal physical movements as much as his attitude, wishing he would act with the large, definitive movements and motions of a man.

"Oi. Omae wa byoki demo shite iru no de wa nainoka?" He wanted to know whether I had taken ill, since he hadn't seen me coming into the Principal's office for punishment lately.

"Did you get a new religion?" He poked fun at me for my constructive behavior of the last several months.

"Hey, Tanemori. I heard you're going to the tournament. It sounds to me like *kitsune*. Ha, ha, ha!"

He thought I was under the spell of a fox, an evil spirit. As his cynical laughter echoed through the hallway, I quickly excused myself without reacting to him.

The night before the speaking event, I bathed my soul with my Father's spirit at his gravesite. The full moon cast its smiling face, its approval. I had never seen before such white clouds floating like cotton candy against a dark canvas, an exquisitely beautiful night.

The tournament was to be held in Yoshida Village, a town of historical importance dating to the Asano Clan of the Tokugawa Shogunate, the center of political power for Western Japan.

For the Tanemori, the village held special significance. This was the village where my sisters Chisako and Satsuko had been sent to stay with Aunt Kakihara during the evacuation of Hiroshima.

That I was going to the same village reminded me of when we had all been one family. The last time we had all been together was the day my sisters departed in the rickety bus to Yoshida Village. As I now rode the same rickety bus, those precious memories flooded back.

I remembered Chisako fearfully and tearfully clutching Satsuko, who would become her surrogate parent. Masuyo had held baby Sayoko while Mother painstakingly attended to every detail of their departure, thinking perhaps she might never see them again. Her inner strength had been revealed as she wiped away her girls' tears.

Father had held my baby brother Sadayoshi in his arms, carefully guarding each word as he delivered his soul as though giving my sisters his last instruction. His brow had been furrowed to hide his deep sadness, as he realized this might be the last time he would be able to tell his children how much he loved them.

The remembrance of this final farewell of my parents, brothers, and sisters, and all the small details surrounding it, flashed vividly in my memory. It held a much deeper meaning for me now. It was so long ago and so far away, in another lifetime.

After we arrived at Yoshida Village, Tamura *Sensei* escorted us into the small school auditorium. As he did so, Aunt Kakihara approached, looking for my nametag. I had not invited any family, as I did not want to create the possibility of inviting more criticism. Besides, in my speech I named those who had mistreated me, and that could embarrass certain family members.

I wondered how Aunt Kakihara had found out about the speech tournament. I had to admit I was happy to finally meet her, and was pleased that she cared enough to come hear my story. We cordially exchanged our expected social greeting. Her figure reminded me of my Mother's.

Looking out at all the faces in an auditorium filled to standing room only was nerve-wracking. I took a seat and felt panic rising as I heard my heart beat louder and faster.

The first three speeches were flawlessly delivered by other contestants who clearly set the tone and overall standard. I sat motionless, focusing on my own message. During a short intermission, Tamura *Sensei* tried to bolster my self-confidence with encouraging glances. I would be the first speaker after the intermission. The wait was more than I could bear.

When I stood to deliver my message, I focused on remembering all I had learned in weeks of coaching. I just let my story play like a wound-up phonograph! About halfway through, I gained the courage to look into the audience. They were in tears. My agonized soul had for the first time found a soft pillow of acceptance and healing.

I described the scene of my Father's haircut, and opened up to the audience to passionately plead for them to understand the plight of the *oyanashigo,* orphans of the atomic blast. I spoke clearly and courageously.

"It has been customary, on the anniversary of the bombing of Hiroshima, to hold a public commemoration ceremony to pray for the souls of those who died. Yes, we must honor the souls of those who died, but perhaps we also should think of the future. The suffering of the departed souls is over, but what about those whose suffering continues? Perhaps we should also pray for the souls of those of us who survived the bombing and are left behind with all the suffering, memories and deprivation we must endure."

My message, however simple, came from my heart. It lasted but fifteen minutes, and as I finished, the auditorium filled with applause.

Yet, even in the midst of the applause, I heard loud cries of disapproval, angry voices making it clear that the emphasis of my message should have been only on those who had died, whose lives had been confiscated and denied a future. These voices questioned why we should pray for those saved from death.

At the end of the contest came the awards ceremony, and with it, an astonishing surprise. Clearly I had gained the empathy of the judges, teachers and most of the audience. Tamura *Sensei* was beaming proudly. When I was awarded the first-prize trophy, several people loudly declared their disapproval. I gratefully turned the trophy over to Tamura *Sensei.*

"*Yokatta! Yokatta!*" He grabbed my shoulders, unable to hide his emotion.

"*Sensei. Arigato gazaimashita. Subete wa Sensei no okagedesu.*"

I told him the victory and joy we shared were due to his compassionate heart, dedication, and sacrifices on my behalf. It was he, not I, who had created the delivery of my truth.

Feeling a need to escape the stifling auditorium, I excused myself to dash outside. I noticed my Aunt Kakihara out of the corner of my eye and wondered whether she approved of my message and the trophy.

Several adults were hot on my trail, following me out the door, reprimanding me for the selfishness of my message.

They angrily asked, "What made you the one deserving to have life?"

I was taken aback, my heart fluttering from this unexpected confrontation. I froze in silent response to demands to recant my position. My eyes begged for their understanding and then watched as teardrops hit the tops of my shoes.

A few steps away from these villagers stood a beautiful woman watching me as if she were my mother. Her beauty struck me as she approached, extending her warmth.

"*Totsuzen de taihen shitsurei towa omoi masu ga,*" she apologized as she came up to me, as if she wished my permission to receive her unexpected intrusion. Flushed with embarrassment, I bowed to her, wondering what she could possibly want from me.

"Is that you Tanemori-san?" she asked.

My words caught in my throat, "*Haaaaaai*! May I ask who you are?"

She invited me to stroll in the garden. In the height of cherry blossom season, the ambrosia in the air, so beautiful at this moment, made my head spin.

We stopped behind a black pine tree; its broad branches shielded us from the sun. She turned to me and took my hand in her soft hands. I could feel her heart beating with mine.

She told me she was a teacher at Yoshida Junior High School, and shyly confided how deeply she had been moved by my message. I watched the gentle breeze play in her silky hair as she told me of her compassion for my suffering and grief.

I was simply enchanted and mesmerized by the beauty of her simple "curves." My heart was captivated by the light in her coy eyes, her delicate gestures and her touching expression of empathy. I couldn't understand why she would risk being seen alone with a student, in the midst of total strangers who denounced me.

It took a buzzing bee to awaken me from the reverie of being in her presence. She spoke of how my message had entered her soul and asked if I would mind listening briefly to her wish.

I silently wondered, "What could she want from me?"

We sat on the roots of the pine tree. She told me my message and spirit would be helpful to her students. I had no idea in what way I could be helpful, but it really didn't matter.

When a member of our team came to tell me Tamura *Sensei* was looking for me, it was hard to tear myself away from her enchantment.

She again took my hands into her soft hands. Gazing into her dark, luminous eyes with hints of jade—a sea filled with sparkling jewels of understanding, sadness, and peace—a small bud in my heart had opened along with the cherry blossoms. It was a new experience for me.

I knew I had to see her again. We picked another time and place to meet. It wasn't soon enough for me. I took my leave from her with a longing in my heart. *"Sensei, arigato! Sayonara, Sensei. Sayonara."*

On the rickety bus back to school, I reflected on my discoveries of the past few hours. Meeting with Miss Nakamura *Sensei* had brought a bright light into my life, like a pin-hole shaft of light coming into a dark attic, penetrating the depths of my soul. My worth had been acknowledged. I couldn't believe she had chosen me as someone worthy to bring a gift to her students. The horizon was bright. The air was fresh. The ambrosia of cherry blossoms was delicious. *"Takashi. Imagoro doshita noyo. Kimochiga warui hodo kawatte kite irune."*

My sister couldn't believe the changes she saw taking place in me, exasperating her beyond words. I started looking everywhere for clean handkerchiefs. At night, I creased my pants between newspapers under the futon. I washed meticulously behind my ears, clipped my fingernails and combed my hair. I was no longer stealing eggs or committing vandalism.

No one believed my sincerity. Everyone thought I had been possessed by the *kitsune ni tsutsu mareta*, the spirit of the fox, a trickster who makes one do things one later regrets.

Even the *sen-gan* joined with my sister, ridiculing my sincerity. In actuality, Nakamura *Sensei's* beautiful goddess of kindness and compassion had touched me!

The result of the speech tournament brought me a new level of acceptance. Only two weeks after the event, as usual, I was called to the Principal's office in the early morning for some disciplinary reason. Often, I was used as a scapegoat for any mishap in the school. I had bent over so many times to receive the board of education that my backside had calluses. It hardly fazed me anymore. I was bored by the whole procedure.

Involved in mundane schoolwork in the afternoon, I was again called into the office. The Vice Principal's

Secretary walked into the class calling out my name, inciting my anger.

"*Tanemori, what did you do this time?*" Tamura *Sensei* moaned, as the smirking laughter of students filled the classroom. "*Shikata go nai yatsuda. Hayaku itte koi.*" He expressed his disapproval, but urged me to go quickly.

I followed the Secretary to the Vice Principal's office, steaming and ready to defend myself against some accusation. The Vice Principal surprised me with a proud smile. He handed me a telephone receiver, urging me to respond to a caller. I had only spoken on a telephone twice before in my life. I was afraid of speaking into the receiver. My voice was unusually soft.

"*Aaaaaah, Moshi, Moshi ... Ttttaanemori desu.*"

"*Ah, Tanemori-san?*" Responding to my mosquito voice was Nakamura *Sensei!*

I couldn't believe it. My heart leaped for joy. Our conversation lasted several minutes, while the delighted Vice Principal watched my bubbling enthusiasm. When I hung up the phone I was in heaven.

We had set a date and time for me to speak to her students. Whatever conversation the Vice Principal had shared with Nakamura *Sensei* before my arrival had put him in a great mood. When he escorted me to the door, he squeezed my shoulder gleefully, indicating his warm approval. All the quizzical eyes of the teachers in the office followed me to the door. I thanked him and returned to my class, beaming joy from ear to ear.

My feet hardly touched the ground on the four mile walk home. The teachers, students, villagers and my siblings all thought I was possessed by *kitsune*.

I didn't speak about the meeting to anyone. There was no question I was head-over-heels in love with this 25-year-old teacher who had shown me warmth and kindness. I began to consider all the reasons this arranged meeting was against social codes. If my fantasies had been realities, they would have violated every acceptable social norm. I enjoyed the clandestine nature of my fantasies and built a strong case in my mind as to why no one else should know of this meeting.

In the Japanese school system, we attended school for a half day on Saturday. All I told my sister was that I would not be back home right after school.

My secrecy annoyed Satsuko more than my seeming desire to avoid working in the rice fields. It was an important village code for everyone to work in everyone's fields. The *taue*, the preparing of rice paddies, was an overall community endeavor.

Harmony amongst the villagers in planting and harvesting a rice crop was important above all, because the activity honored the Gods of the harvest. They would, in turn, reciprocate by supplying a bumper crop to the village.

Satsuko most likely thought I was up to no good with my hooligan buddies, and this was another kick in her face for my avoiding an important community ritual.

How could I tell her the real reason? How could I reveal whom I would be meeting? That would definitely have been "suicide."

This Saturday morning, I was unusually spiffed up. My handed-down school uniform was as neatly pressed as I could make it, with a hand-washed white handkerchief in the breast pocket. My classmates commented on my dress and demeanor.

"Tanemori, what is the matter with you? Have you lost your mind?"

"You look so stupid. What in the world are you trying to do?"

I just smiled a secret smile and passed the morning, blushing in my daydreams about Nakamura *Sensei's* soft curves and tender touch. I didn't tell Tamura *Sensei* about the meeting, as I couldn't risk his disapproval. I couldn't risk anyone seeing through my ulterior motives. I needed to hold my love for her as privately away from judgment as possible.

When the bell rang, I ran to the bus stop at the bottom of the hill. It seemed such a long wait for the 12:30 bus. How many times I looked toward the top of hill to see if the bus had arrived!

Finally, seated in the old, rickety bus, I pondered what goodness Nakamura *Sensei* saw in me, and why my sister and others couldn't see the same goodness? Of course! Nakamura *Sensei* does not live with me day-in, day-out! Again her soft-curved lines and tender touch flashed through my mind, making me blush.

When I stepped joyfully off the bus, I imagined the unspoken truth of her love, truth revealed in her eyes, truth I was longing to hear. I imagined she understood the social danger of this meeting, danger she had chosen to overlook for the sake of her students and me. In reality, she was most likely innocent of my class worries.

"Tanemori-san," said Nakamura *Sensei,* welcoming me with a clear, crisp voice filled with tenderness. Three students, two boys and a girl, were timidly standing, dressed in clean, pressed uniforms. I saw the traces of hardship in their shoes. Why she had taken a personal interest in us, I never really understood.

The value of that day proved to be in the great fun we all had together. Nakamura *Sensei* took us on the bus to the *Goryu-Jo* site, the castle ruins of one of the most powerful Tokugawa Shogunate rulers. The ruins' high vantage point offered a magnificent vista. We saw in the near distance Kotachi Village, once considered as *Shita-machi,* subjects who lived under the powerful warlord. Looking over the cliff we saw two rivers merging, serving as a protective moat for the castle.

Nakamura *Sensei* left me and the other students alone for a while, disappearing into the woods. We didn't talk much in her absence, exhibiting shyness on this first meeting. But it seemed we all had some unspoken common understanding. Nakamura *Sensei* wanted to allow any discovery to come naturally.

When the visit ended, Nakamura *Sensei* joined us to descend to the village. I window-shopped for the first time, and with no Gossip Committee, no judges, and no paranoia, I felt absolutely free and happy. We all began to laugh and goof off, to forget everything about everything. We felt our wings.

We jumped in the merging rivers we had seen from above, splashing in the water and skipping stones. We giggled wildly and freely. This was the first moment unfettered by judgments, the first moment of joyous, belly-laughing fun I could remember since my days with my Hiroshima buddies. Nakamura *Sensei*, too, hiked up her skirts and played with us—we five happy children. Departing was such a contrast for me as I sadly said *sayonara* to everyone at the bus stop. When Nakamura *Sensei* asked me to promise to meet her again soon, I felt the electrifying warmth of her love energy travel through my hand and into my heart, the same feeling as at our first meeting. I wondered if she felt the same from me. We hooked our little fingers, making *yubi-kiri,* a pact, and promised we would be together again soon.

As the rickety-click bus climbed up toward the country road, I stood waving my arms until the bus disappeared. When I arrived home the crows were returning to their nests to care for their little ones.

In contrast to the beautiful afternoon, I was met at the door of my house by a scowling ogre—Satsuko.

"Takashi. What did you do? Were you with those hoodlums? How many times have I forbidden you?" Satsuko scolded, demanding to know where I had been.

I refused to divulge my joyful experience. I held the memory of that day locked in a treasure chest which would open for me in my darkest hours in the years to come.

The stark contrast between these new realities was difficult for me to reconcile in my understanding. I had seen a side of myself I hadn't even known existed. *Sensei's* compassion and love had shown me my higher self. I would not *buta ni shinju,* cast pearls before swine, and open up the purity of my experience to any ridicule. The only time I spoke of it was at the shrine of my Father.

Nearly two months later, Nakamura *Sensei* and I secretly met at the Yoshida Guchi train station to go to *Tanabata Matsuri,* a summer festival, in the midst of *Ochu-gen,* and just a few towns down the train line.

The *Ochu-gen* is the season for preparing and welcoming the *Obon* festivities, Buddha's ritual honoring all deceased spirits. Many people who had left hometown villages for cities to find work would return home to pay homage at family gravesites, setting out lanterns to light the way back for departed spirits.

Quietly I sat by the window, across from Nakamura *Sensei,* as the train rocked and clacked down the tracks. I could feel the electricity between our nearly-touching knees. My heart pounded with excitement. She smiled tenderly as if to affirm this meeting was good and right.

When our eyes met, she gently whispered, asking if she could call me by my first name, "Takashi," but only privately, of course. My head was spinning. I lost my sense of reality.

Then she took my hands into hers, looked into my eyes and softly uttered my name. I had never heard "Takashi" voiced so warmly and tenderly.

Would she ever share her intimacy with me? Would I ever hear her whisper "Takashi" so softly into my ear? Hearing my name coming from the lips of Nakamura *Sensei* caused something to be released from the very depths of my soul. Her heartbeat pulsing with mine swept me up in a tide of wild emotion. I was drowning. A sleeping leviathan had been awakened.

The town of Mukaibara was one of several major towns along the *Geibe-sen* line connecting Hiroshima and Miyoshi. Not a soul there knew either of us, so we were able to amble, hand-in-hand, free of judging eyes.

I felt like a young ram in a green pasture. We walked to the *Ujigami-san,* Shinto Shrine, amid high-spirited music of flutes, *taiko* drums and cymbals, all mingled with the chattering of town people.

Ahhh, the fresh air and the scent of roasting *yakitori,* skewers of chicken! She bought us both a skewer and we delectably shared the juicy meat with each other. I watched her with delight as she licked her lips.

We wandered into the woods and disappeared behind a big tree. As she leaned against the tree, I told her how I loved to be with her. Wanting to feel the closeness of her body, I pressed against her and put my arms around her waist. She received my warmth with hers. My head was against her bosom as it rose and fell with her deepening breath. We stood there in the bliss of each other's love. She whispered my name in my ear and I whispered *Sensei*. I could have stayed there forever, drinking in her being and love.

After a while, she suggested we go back home.

With one last sigh I held that final moment for an eternity in my heart. When we departed from each other at the train station, we hooked our little fingers and promised to meet again.

The summer was over, and the entire village was gearing up for the rice harvest. Practically every villager would be demanded to fulfill his or her own *shoku-bun,* a fulfillment of place, rank, responsibility and obligation to the community, by working in the field. This fulfillment would happen before the roosters awoke and would continue long after the crows had nested for the night. In this way, Kotachi Village maintained unity and harmony, and reinforced a sense of belonging, to all.

As she had so many times, Satsuko harshly reminded me of my duties and responsibilities as well as the consequences of defying the village consensus. For me, however, the harvesting season was an absolutely great time. Many of the *sen-gans* and Gossip Committees were too busy to keep their evil eyes on me. If I couldn't breathe freely, at least I could breathe a little more normally.

Yet there was deep pain inherent in the fall season. All the hills and gorges were painted like a mosaic prism, with colorful leaves dancing their brief shuffle to the ground. They left behind the "skeletons" of trees, delicate victims of the north wind as it penetrated the Village, turning it into a grave landscape.

I felt like a lonely traveler, moving from place to unknown place, or to a place from which there would be no return. Then the cold, white blanket would cover all.

I had gone through fall seasons alone many times in the past, for no one understood my heart. This year was no different, except that I had, beside my parents' gravesite, a special place to go—the riverside where Nakamura *Sensei* and I secretly met.

Again I felt melancholy. I felt pains in my heart for her.

One evening was unusually painful and lonely. I left the house carefully, to avoid being seen by my sister, and returned to the river bank. There I stood, where our "little fingers" had touched, avowing our mutual promises. Amidst the rustle of falling leaves, I saw clouds chased by the soft breeze glide across the dark velvet background, hidden by a *Mika-zuki-san,* three-quarter moon. It gave me an eerie feeling.

I longed for Nakamura *Sensei*'s tender touch, desiring to bury my head in her bosom. No! I just wanted to be with her, to be near her. I asked the *Mika-zuki-san* for the answer. It peeked out from the cloud; with silence, it touched my heart tenderly, causing me to cry.

"Aki kaze ni
Nagareru kumo mo
Sadame nara
Samishisa makuru
Waga kokoro."

[As the winds carried clouds like a predestined allotment, the loneliness filled my heart to bleed.]

With much anticipation, I began the second semester of my last year at Oda Chugaku Junior High School. The second semester was the crucial term for students bent on furthering their education. It was also the time to select a high school and set a course for the future.

Students whose parents were financially well off and who sought political gain could easily buy entrance to elite schools. Oh, the power of money! However, for me the second semester crossroads revealed a dark and unknown future.

If I hoped to regain social status and redeem the family honor, higher education must not be sacrificed. In Japan, education is equated with success and the "value" of an individual's life. I questioned what I, an *oyanashigo*, a war-torn young orphan boy, could do to achieve it. I painfully realized my vulnerability, standing against social tides and traditions. Perhaps my sister was right to subject herself to the social codes, even if merely to survive.

No one knew how often Nakamura *Sensei* and I had our secret meetings. And it would be more than six months after the Yoshida Junior High School speech tournament before our next public meeting took place.

Since the Yoshida Junior High School tournament, I had entered several speech contests, receiving recognition. Tanemori became a "household name," along with the name of Oda Chugaku, my junior high school. I had begun to enjoy the attention I was getting.

I was pleasantly surprised when Nakamura *Sensei* came to my school, mid-January, for a meeting with Tamura *Sensei* to discuss an upcoming Western Regional speech tournament in Hiroshima in March. Then she attended my speech club meeting, sharing her joy at my being chosen to represent the school.

I was absolutely elated to see Nakamura *Sensei*. She whispered into my ear, "Takashi-san." Suddenly, my heart started beating faster and louder than a bass *taiko* drum, almost bursting my chest.

As soon as the speech club had been dismissed, I implored her to come to see my "secret hiding place" on the hill behind the school. No one knew of my refuge! She allowed me to take her hand and lead her to a magical secluded hollow by a giant black pine. After school, I would come for protection and security beneath the peaceful boughs of this ancient tree, my new, trusted, and closest friend.

I told Nakamura *Sensei* of the many times I had conversed with the tree, asking it for advice, or just listening. The tree would moan and sway, applauding for me, or sometimes just listening to my lamentations in silent empathy. I felt the tree was always present for me. Nakamura *Sensei* was moved by my passion and deep connection to nature.

Many people were bewildered by my newfound recognition, especially Satsuko, who still couldn't accept the change everyone else seemed to notice. I was beginning to be treated with some celebrity and was acknowledged as the favorite student of Tamura *Sensei*. All this new attention was going to my head and creating turmoil in my stomach. Daily, I practiced with Tamura *Sensei*, working out every detail, punch line, and even the timing for pounding the podium to emphasize points. It was exhausting work.

As I progressed, Tamura *Sensei* expressed increasing concern, and requested that I change the thrust of my message. He wanted the entire speech rewritten. When I had initially given the speech, it had met with resistance from the audience. There was resistance to my belief that those who had died immediately were indeed the lucky ones, and that the survivors had lost everything except horrific memories and continual suffering. Our loss of loved ones and possessions had been compounded by a society which stripped us of our dignity and birthright.

It was my belief that our suffering should be honored by society and recognized by the religious community. Tamura *Sensei* felt this point of view, the substance of my message, should not be mentioned at all. Because my speech would be given in Hiroshima, he felt very strongly that I should speak only in honor of those who had died.

I had to look deep into my heart. This was a serious conflict with the one male figure I had finally come to respect and trust. It seemed the entire school was encouraging my message except Tamura *Sensei*. Everyone else had high hopes for me to bring back a trophy.

One week before the tournament, I was confronted with an agonizing choice: to follow the advice and demands of my teacher and mentor, or to follow my own heart.

He had taught me about the wisdom of the trees, and now the black pine in my secret place was my guide. I revered this ancient tree as the mother of all trees, whose branches reached the heavens and whose roots tapped the heart of the earth. She collected the wisdom of the entire world and lived only to give life. I felt as if she held the answer to my dilemma.

One day after school, I made my way to my "secret hiding place," as snow began falling. Torn and confused, I sobbed into her ancient embrace. Between sobs, I begged out loud for the tree to please understand that I only wanted peace. I knew the dead had found their peace: no pain, no more anguish. They had passed from darkness into the better place we all yearn for, a state of blessedness.

But for those of us left behind, there was no dignity in our struggle to survive. We simply existed, hanging by a thread, begging the Death Angels to relieve our suffering. I told the tree I believed from the bottom of my heart that we must honor the souls of those who died. But we must also think of the future and the suffering of the living. My final request of her was to know whether I was asking too much to pray for the souls of the survivors.

My plea ascended toward the sky, as soft *botan-yuki* blanketed the hills. Would my cry reach heaven?

As if in answer to my prayer, I felt a soft touch on my shoulder and the voice of my beloved teacher, Nakamura *Sensei*!

"I have heard everything, and I understand your anguish," she said. "Don't be afraid. I will be with you. You are no longer alone."

She wiped my tears softly with her hand. "How cold you are, Takashi-san. Let me warm you."

She hugged me warmly and tried to cover me with her overcoat. Huge snowflakes covered my head and shoulders. Then she took my hands, "Oh my, your hands are icy." She warmed them with her arms. I could feel her breasts, and a wonderful warmth there.

Nearly drowning in her warmth, I cried into her bosom like a little boy. She stroked me and hugged me tightly. I felt so at home with her touch, I became like a baby reconnecting with the long lost love of my Mother. I could no longer contain my emotions. Inside her *mayu,* cocoon, my heart was bursting.

"*Sensei* ..." I could no longer hold back my tears.

"*Nanimo iwanaide iino yo!* Takashi-san, you don't need to say anything." The language of "silence" created a world belonging only to us. Holding my face in her hands, she looked deep into my eyes, "Takashi-san, the most important matter in this life is your heart—the essence of who you are. I listened just now while you poured out your heart, considering what I would do if I were you."

Her eyes welled with tears, as she continued softly and clearly, with immeasurable love and firmness of conviction. "Most importantly you must deliver the message in accordance with your heart. All you can give is your soul. It is up to the judges and audience to receive your message. The ultimate outcome is not your responsibility. To compromise for the sake of appeasement is self-betrayal. I know what you will do, Takashi-san. I believe in you! Go for it! Don't worry."

She understood me. She confirmed my desire to follow my heartbeat without concern for consequences. She took her handkerchief, licked one corner, and wiped my tear-stained face.

As we returned to the school building, Nakamura *Sensei* told me to go directly to Tamura *Sensei* with my resolve. I wanted to put off the confrontation for as long as possible, and asked to escort her to the gate. She was so brave! She added strength to my resolve, confirming in me what it meant to live life according to the *kokoro,* the heart, the essence of who I am.

"Sensei, Wakari mashita!" As a Japanese proverb says, *"Koi no taki nobori.* It takes the will of *koi,* carp, to swim straight upward to the top of a waterfall." Knowing that Nakamura *Sensei* understood my heart and would be there for me gave me great inner strength.

She told me that she wished to accompany me to the tournament, but circumstances would not permit it. She would be praying for my success—not so much for a trophy, but for the victory of my heart. Looking around to see if anyone was watching, we hooked our little fingers, *yubi-kiri,* renewing our promise to each other.

Tamura *Sensei* and I had a showdown. He was sure I couldn't win the tournament with my message. I made it clear it was not my foremost objective to win, but to share my heart. At a certain point in our dispute he almost persuaded me to change my mind, when he mentioned my sister and the hardships she endured because of me. Yet I knew what I must do, and there was nothing he could say to deter me from pursuing my own heart!

My defeat at the Hiroshima Western Regional Speech Tournament came on the first trial. I was crushed. I had lingered too long enunciating words and ran out of time. The judges cut me off before I could deliver the heart of my message. I needed two more minutes.

I was bearing a great guilt. I felt I had let everyone down—the school, Tamura *Sensei*, Nakamura *Sensei*, my family, and myself.

The train ride home with Tamura *Sensei* was very uncomfortable. I thanked him for the opportunity to enter the coveted tournament, but also apologized for my failure. We exchanged few words as I sank deeply into my own cocoon.

He tried to encourage me. "There is nothing to be ashamed of. After all, you are the first and only student from Oda Chugaku to enter such a prestigious tournament. And no one enters except by invitation. You have honored Oda Chugaku, and as your teacher, I am elated by this honor. I should be thanking you."

Returning to my parents' graveside to report, I could stand proudly. I had honored the principles Father had taught me. I knew my parents smiled upon me. This was victory for me, engraved in my soul!

That weekend I met Nakamura *Sensei* again. I tried to tell her that I had failed to share the message.

"It was meant to be so," she said, quickly interrupting me. "While it's important that you strove for first place in the tournament, it's far more important to be the conqueror of your own soul."

She continued, "What would have happened had you presented your point of view, in accordance with your heart? Then the heart of your message would have challenged the judges and audience. Think of what this would have meant to Tamura *Sensei's* position. As your teacher and the Speech Club's director, and more importantly, as your special mentor, he would have been humiliated. The way it worked out, you saved his honor without compromising your heart."

There was a brief silence, as we looked at each other. I could accept that everything had worked out for the best. It warmed my heart. She hugged me and spoke again.

"As I said before, it is far more important to live according to our own hearts! I rejoice that you did as your heart dictated. In this defeat, you saved Tamura *Sensei's* honor, something far more important than bringing back a coveted trophy at the expense of his face."

After the tournament, we became very discrete. No one ever suspected that Nakamura *Sensei* and I were meeting where the eyes of *sen-gan* couldn't penetrate. But my sister constantly watched to see if I would reveal my true nature, *kitsune no shippo,* the nature of the fox, by returning to my former hooligan behavior.

My long-awaited graduation finally came. I had to abandon any thoughts of high school and college. Public education was compulsory only through the ninth grade, and anyone wishing to attend high school must pay tuition. Japan's educational system was for students of elite financial and social status.

Amid mixed emotions and tears, we students all began to sing the familiar song of every graduation from the halls of Oda Chugaku— *"Hotaru no hikari, mado no yu ki, fumi yomu Tsuki, hi kasane yuku ..."*

Some teachers were crying too—perhaps, for the joy of finally getting rid of us. I cried with relief, eager to open a chapter I hoped would bring a new self image and sense of dignity.

I would be entering *Shakai-jin*, becoming a member of society. To my astonishment, the Principal made a brief remark about me at commencement. He noted the way my life had turned around after I had joined the Public Speech Club, and he gave credit to Tamura *Sensei*.

There was an outburst of laughter by some students and teachers. I could almost feel a sigh of relief. Tanemori would be gone for good! The community leaders wished nothing less than my exile from Kotachi Village.

Meanwhile, Nakamura *Sensei* and I continued our secret rendezvous, soon developing a tender, profound, poetic love. We met in remote fields, at secluded riversides, and sometimes in other cities.

Our relationship—between student and teacher, not to mention younger boy and older woman—had become so precious. The relationship was textbook social "taboo." If we were ever caught, there would be no escaping judgment as harsh as in the story "The Scarlet Letter." We would be subjected to *mura-hachibu,* public ostracism, shame and disgrace. We would be "marked" for public spectacle.

Thrilled at the opportunity to leave the village to work in the city of Kobe with Maruhachi Company, a financial firm that owned pawnshops, I was nevertheless in torment over leaving Nakamura *Sensei.*

Chapter Eight: Shakai-jin

A FTER graduation, the Vice Principal found work for my classmate, Kenji Kayama, and me. We were to be errand boys at the Maruhachi Company in Kobe, one hundred miles up the coast from Hiroshima. I was sure he was a kindhearted man with a big heart.

At first I was elated, eager to get away from the prison that was Kotachi Village. This was my chance to burst free of the *jozu na yowatari,* the social code that was strangling me. I soon learned, though, that I was merely exchanging one jail cell for another.

I would be working ten hours a day, six days a week, for approximately $1.80 per week. More galling was the discovery that my employment was part of a complex social relationship between the Vice Principal and Mr. Ueda, the Vice President of Maruhachi. Apparently, Mr. Ueda had only accepted Kenji and me because of his duty to his former *senpai,* mentor, the Vice Principal.

I bristled at the thought that my life was still not my own. I would be closely watched, every action evaluated. If I performed well, the Vice Principal would be honored; if not, I would bring him disgrace and shame. Certainly, I planned to do my best, but this added obligation rankled me.

It was with great sadness that I said farewell to Nakamura *Sensei.* We spent our last day together in nearby Miyoshi, window-shopping and strolling hand-in-hand, freely, without being scrutinized by anyone. We paused at a shop window containing a pair of shiny black "squeaky" shoes. Constructed of exceptionally stiff leather, such shoes made a distinctive noise with each step. They were very expensive; only men with good jobs could afford them. Consequently, they had come to represent success and respectability.

Turning to Nakamura *Sensei,* I vowed, "The next time you see me, I will be wearing a pair of squeaky shoes just like those." Then, searching her face, I asked, "Will you miss me?"

She smiled gently, taking my hands in hers, "Yes, I'll miss you, but … it's time to open the window and let the bird fly free."

Then, seeing my face, she added, with a reassuring smile, "Never forget that my spirit will always be with you. You will never be alone."

How different was my parting from Satsuko. "Don't disgrace me," she said in an icy voice. "I will have to live with your mistakes. And don't come back until you are a *Shakai-jin,* a respectable member of society."

When Kenji and I arrived at Sannomiya Train Station in Kobe, Mr. Ueda and one of his subordinates met us on the platform. Mr. Ueda was a large man, about mid-fifty, with grayish hair. He greeted us with a gentle smile, which helped to ease my anxiety. "I am Ueda."

Tremblingly, we introduced ourselves with utmost care and respect. We bowed so low that our heads nearly grazed the walkway. I quickly extended greetings from our Vice Principal, saying that he was healthy and doing well.

I felt like a country mouse, without city etiquette or savvy, surrounded by wild alley cats supreme in their domain. Ueda snapped orders at his subordinate as though speaking to a slave. I was startled, wondering whether this was the treatment I would soon receive.

Mr. Ueda must have noticed my surprise. He sized me up, and then tried to cover up his embarrassment by laughing.

"Don't worry, Tanemori. Is that all you folks brought with you?"

I had all my worldly possessions in one duffel bag and my head was filled with dreams of possibilities.

While we were traveling to the Nada branch of the company, Mr. Ueda informed us he was *kohai,* junior to the Vice Principal Akiyama, to whom he owed several obligatory favors.

This was discomforting news. I wondered what kind of favors Mr. Ueda owed him? The relationship of s*enpai,* senior, to *kohai,* junior, in which the *senpai* often acts as a mentor, had been a deep tradition in Japanese society for more than a century. This relationship carries strong bonds of obligation, often lasting a lifetime and demonstrated in reciprocal obligatory deeds, a form of mutual favoritism.

Success or failure for my work at the Maruhachi Company would largely depend on how well I honored the obligatory relationship between these two men. My need to exercise utmost humility in this *shoku-bun,* workplace, in light of my greater personal obligations became painfully clear to me.

Arriving at the store, it was obvious that even at this early hour, employees were waiting to give us a proper social and ceremonial welcoming party.

I was introduced to the branch manager, Mr. Ise, a man so diminutive that, at first, I was not even sure he was an adult. Possibly to make up for his lack of stature, Mr. Ise had adopted an overbearing, belligerent attitude toward others. Already drunk, he seemed to go out of his way to belittle those around him. I disliked him immediately.

Turning away from Mr. Ise, my attention was drawn to a beautiful young woman who was serving food. Her air of innocence and graceful beauty made my heart beat faster. As I instinctively moved closer to her, Mr. Ise yelled at her from behind me, ordering her into the kitchen to fetch him more *sake*. Later that evening, I learned this gorgeous creature was his wife! Her name was Mrs. Mayumi Ise. *Mayumi* is translated "the cocoon of a silkworm."

All evening Mrs. Ise rushed in and out of the kitchen to do her husband's bidding. At one point, I excused myself and started to follow her to offer my assistance.

Sensing my intention, Mr. Ise yelled after me, "Tanemori, stay in your place!" Pretending not to hear, I continued on into the kitchen.

Mrs. Ise, although embarrassed, was clearly touched by my offer. When we brought out more food, Mr. Ise demanded to know if I had heard his command.

Mr. Ueda quickly intervened, "How nice to see a young man with such sensitivity to recognize your wife needed help." He then offered me some hot *sake*, a very honorable gesture. Mr. Ise fumed silently.

By eight o'clock Mr. Ueda, Mr. Ise, and Mr. Miyazaki, another boss, sought privacy behind a closed *shoji* screen to discuss what to do with Kenji and me. I waited anxiously, not knowing what to wish for. Although I already detested Mr. Ise, my attraction to his wife was undeniable.

While they were gone momentarily, I took the opportunity to be nearer to Mrs. Ise, offering to help her clean up the mess. Her embarrassed smile conveyed her approval of me.

After fifteen minutes, the bosses returned to announce their decision. Kenji was to go with Mr. Miyazaki and I was to be the *decchi-bozu,* errand boy, for Mr. Ise's pawnshop. I wondered about the motive behind this decision when Mr. Ise remarked that I was an *oyanashigo,* orphan. He seemed pleased and gloated about how hard he was going to make me work. I bowed deeply and held my tongue.

As Kenji prepared to leave with Mr. Miyazaki, we grabbed each other's shoulders, encouraging and reassuring one another that we would stay strong and meet the dismal challenges of our new life.

My objective was to work hard and save money so that I could one day afford a brand new pair of squeaky shoes, and then be honorably looked upon by society. Like a moth, my heart was pulled towards the flame.

After the party, Mrs. Ise led me down the narrow *roka* to my room at the front of the main building. The room was situated so that I could also serve as night-watchman—the first to awaken in the event of a break-in.

The corridor was so cramped that I accidentally brushed up against my boss's wife. I was instantly aware of her rounded curves, her soft femininity. Her eyes filled with warmth, dangerously. Would this mean big trouble for me?

It was immediately apparent that, under her housecoat, she was with child. Nonetheless, all my senses were aroused by her proximity. I felt a pang of longing for Nakamura *Sensei.*

Shyly, Mrs. Ise told me how pleased she was that I would be working for her husband.

"But," she cautioned, "Mr. Ise can be a difficult man. Learn to walk softly."

Then, taking a deep breath, she promised to stand by me until I turned 21 and became a *Shakai-jin,* a proud member of society. Deeply touched, I humbly asked if I could call her *Okusan*, a term meaning "honored lady of the house."

She gave me a blushing smile.

Okusan's warmth was the only thing that sustained me in the following months, months of long days filled with drudgery. Rising at five o'clock every morning, I would clean the store until seven o'clock, eat a small breakfast, and then work until ten o'clock at night.

Even this would have been bearable if not for Mr. Ise's continual harassment.

Having taken a dislike to me that first night, Mr. Ise went out of his way to torment me. He constantly criticized and belittled me, and even encouraged his five-year-old daughter to taunt me. So like him in body and spirit, Sazae spied on me, reporting every misstep to her father. My boss seemed to derive malicious glee from seeing me humiliated by a five-year-old.

Mr. Ise had a hot, erratic temper. Laughing hysterically one minute, he then would suddenly explode into rage. I never knew when a ruler, a pair of scissors, or a full cup of tea might come flying at me. But, despite his belligerent ways, I was not frightened of him.

I could not take him seriously as a full-grown man; rather I thought of him as some kind of evil imp. Whenever he became upset or lost control, he would jump into a cab and head for his mother's house … like a small child running for his mother's skirts.

Sadly, he worked his wife like a slave. As her belly grew full with child, it became more and more difficult for her to comply with his unreasonable demands. It hurt me to see her out of breath as she clumsily scrubbed the floor or grimaced under the strain of a heavy load.

Finally, I could stand it no longer. One morning I humbled myself and asked Mr. Ise if he would permit me to help his wife.

"If there is a fool in this world, it is you," he grinned, pointing a crooked finger in my face. "That woman belongs to me."

Then, becoming agitated, he shouted, "Have you been talking to my wife?"

Again, I bowed deeply. "No, Sir, this is my own idea. I have not spoken to your wife and am only asking because I can't bear to see her struggling. Will you allow me to ... "

He cut me off. "*Bakamono!* You fool! What have you two been up to behind my back?" he screamed.

Just at that moment, *Okusan* appeared with a beautifully prepared breakfast tray.

"What!" he yelled, "You expect me to eat this offal?"

He grabbed the tray and flung it at the *shoji* screen, splattering food everywhere and shattering the dishes. Then he lunged at her. I tried to step in between them, but was a split second too late. He slapped *Okusan's* face hard, and then grabbed her hair, bringing her to her knees.

"Ise-san," I pleaded. "What are you doing? Why are you hurting your wife? Are you a madman?"

He flung her away and stormed out into the street, hailing a cab.

I could sense *Okusan's* heart breaking into a thousand pieces. She doubled over, holding her belly. I had no words to comfort her. My attempt to help had only brought her greater suffering. Tears flowed down my cheeks as I began to clean up the mess on the *tatami*.

Hearing of the incident, my company *senpai*, superior, Gondo, warned against any further intervention on her behalf. "Tanemori," he said, "Don't be a fool. Leave her alone. She is not your business and you are jeopardizing your own chances for success."

Perhaps, he was right. Did I really want to remain an errand boy for the rest of my life?

That winter was one of the coldest I had ever experienced. A piercing wind rushed down Rokko-zan Mountain and blasted the inhabitants of Kobe, turning our blood to ice water. Try as I might, I couldn't stay warm in the drafty store. Although I still wanted to be a good worker, I could barely move my frozen arms and legs. My desire for squeaky shoes was the only thing that got me out of bed at five o'clock each morning.

Cruelly, I had been forbidden to use hot water to wash down the store each morning. Putting my hands into a pail of frigid water was agonizing. I repeatedly asked Mr. Ise for the still-warm bath water from the previous night's *ofuro*. The answer was always the same.

"Tanemori, there is no hot water for you."

On one particularly cold morning, it took all my courage to plunge my chapped and swollen hands into the icy bucket; I couldn't hold back my tears as I felt the skin on my hands crackling … I sobbed in self-pity … "Oh, let my tears warm this icy water!"

"Tanemori-san," Her soft voice startled me.

"*Oooooku-san,*" I whispered, "What are you dong up so early?"

"Shhh," she warned, putting a finger to her lips. "It's so cold that I couldn't sleep. Here, take this water to use."

She handed me the *ofura* water, insisting that it would be all right. And she asked me to forgive her husband.

"He becomes frightened when anyone questions his actions," she apologized.

Okusan urged me to get my work done quickly so that, afterwards, she could put medicine on my hands before her husband arose. The warm *ofuro* water felt so comforting and the ointment so soothing that my heart began to melt. I was startled to see that her hands were as chapped as mine.

For the next two weeks *Okusan* got up early to give me *ofura* water and put ointment on my hands. Shyly, she allowed me to massage the healing balm on her hands as well.

Silently, I vowed that no matter what happened, I would do everything in my power to protect her.

After several weeks of this tender treatment, my hands were almost completely healed. Then, one morning as *Okusan* was carefully drying my hands with the corner of her apron, I suddenly heard feet rushing down the hallway. I turned just in time to ward off a blow from Mr. Ise.

"*Kisama!* Bastard!" he screamed. "How dare you insult me like this?"

"It is not what you think!" I yelled. "Do not hurt your wife. She is innocent!"

I shielded *Okusan* with my body and defiantly faced Mr. Ise as he repeatedly slapped my face from side to side. The ultimate consequences of disobedience to his authority would be catastrophic for me. I did not hit back and did not back down. My only concern was for *Okusan's* safety. I could almost hear my Father's voice; this was a test to honor my heart—the inner essence of who I am—Tanemori.

As he pummeled me, my mind flashed back to Kotachi Village, to the blacksmith shop. There, many times, I had seen the blacksmith temper a *Samurai* sword with heat, water, and by pounding it with a heavy hammer. He would beat it over and over again until all the impurities were removed. When he finally felt the spirit enter the blade, he would hold it up for the Goddess *Amaterasu* to bless.

I was like that sword now—every blow made me feel stronger, truer. My soul seemed to swell with the blessings of *Amaterasu*.

Okusan, begging her husband to stop, pushed me aside and ran to her room. She didn't appear for the next two days. Whenever he saw me, Mr. Ise smiled smugly at my swollen, puffy face. Finally, Sunday arrived and Mr. Ise took his daughter to his mother's house. When I was sure the coast was clear, I went looking for *Okusan*, softly calling her name. She was not in her quarters.

"Tanemori-san." Her faint voice guided me to a small storage room. There I found her shivering on the cold bare floor, her face battered and bruised, her once innocent beauty now anguished and disfigured. I burst into angry tears. That bastard!

She leaned on me as I helped her slowly and painfully to her room. Barren and stark, it looked like a prison cell, except for a tiny dresser and *kyo-dai*, make-up mirror stand, her only possession, which had been given to her as special gift from her parents for her wedding. A few sparse clothes hung in the closet. Her little private surroundings looked so *kawai,* lonely and pitiful.

"Is your baby safe?" I asked. She nodded.

I ran to the kitchen to get a warm, wet towel. My hands shook as I bathed her swollen face. Then I fetched a cup of hot green tea and held her in my arms as I raised it to her lips. My heart swelled with love and tenderness for this wife of another man … her face so bruised, her soul so battered. Somehow, I felt the presence of Nakamura *Sensei* surrounding us and blessing us. There I was, holding her in my arms!

After she finished the tea, I gently laid her down on her futon, covering her softly with the quilt. Making sure that water and tissues were within her reach, I reassured her that I would stay within earshot and come immediately, if called.

"*Tanemori-san, ikanaide,*" she whispered. "Please don't go!" She pulled me against her, burying her head in my shoulder, and began to weep. I felt the warmth of her body. We were entering dangerous territory but … I couldn't resist her deep need of comfort.

"*Okusan, Okusan,*" I murmured, stroking her hair as she sobbed out her sad story.

She told me how her husband kept her a virtual prisoner, not even allowing her to visit her parents in far off Aomori Prefecture. She was deeply ashamed that she had not been able to pay proper homage to her parents after the birth of her first child. Now, five years later, she was expecting again.

Thin strands of black, silky hair fell across her bruised face as she sobbed out her unhappiness. Her sensuous breathing aroused an intense energy inside me which seemed to whirl out in all directions.

"*Daite, shikkarito daite.* Hold me tightly, please."

She buried her head in my shoulder and began weeping. It was a fearful moment, as I didn't know whether I was strong enough to receive her trust and desire to be held by me.

"*Tanemori-san, onegai … daite …* " she breathed.

I was free falling. There was nothing I would not do for her, no mountain I would not conquer.

When he returned, Mr. Ise, possibly out of some hidden reservoir of remorse, left both *Okusan* and me alone. Her bruises gradually faded, but her eyes were ringed with the dark shadows of fatigue. I worried about her tiny body, so swollen with child. When Mr. Ise was not looking, we would exchange secret looks of hope and encouragement.

Then, one day when the boss was out for the afternoon, *Okusan* suddenly let out a moan and clutched her belly. I rushed to her side.

"It's the baby!" she cried. She put my hand on her abdomen so that I could feel the intense contraction.

"*Okusan*, let me go next door and get Mrs. Ueda."

Something behind me suddenly caught her eye, and terror crossed her face. Turning around, I saw Mr. Ise entering the store, weaving back and forth from too much *sake*. His eyes exuded pure hatred. He started screaming obscenities at us.

"Please, Mr. Ise," I begged. "She's having her baby."

"*Anata ...*" *Okusan* began.

"Shut up you shameless whore!" He screamed back.

Not knowing what else to do, I threw myself at his feet, begging him not to hurt the baby. Luckily, this seemed to jolt him out his alcoholic rage. Coming to his senses, he yelled at me to go get Mrs. Okada, the midwife.

An hour later the lusty wail of a healthy newborn brought relief to my heart. There was, however, no rejoicing in the Ise household. The baby, two weeks premature, was a girl. Cursing *Okusan*, Mr. Ise left immediately, once again hailing a cab to his mother's house.

Adding insult to injury, everyone agreed the new child was *uri futatsu,* the spitting image, of *Okusan,* while her older sister looked like her father. It was painful to hear Sazae say, "My sister looks just like Mother. When we visit Grandmother we won't have to take that ugly baby with us, right, Daddy?"

In the months that followed, *Okusan* devoted herself to her new baby. I kept away, trying to remain emotionally distant from his abuse and her unhappiness. Mr. Ise continued to regard me with cold suspicion, treating his wife even more disrespectfully whenever I was around.

One morning as *Okusan* was hanging up diapers, I noticed her chapped hands were bleeding. Without thinking, I offered to help. She quickly brushed me away. I couldn't bear to see her suffering like this. Gathering courage, I went to Mr. Ise.

Bowing low, I asked humbly, "Ise-san, I beg of your kind heart that you allow me to help *Okusan* take care of the baby!"

He began to cackle hysterically, as if I had touched his funny bone.

My fellow employee, Gondo, quickly intervened. "Why not?" He asked. "See if Tanemori can help keep the situation under control and keep the baby from crying."

Gondo promised Mr. Ise that he would supervise me strictly. "If he even so much as winks at her," he vowed, "I will report him immediately." Then, conspiratorially, he added, "It is only a matter of time until he does something stupid. Then you can rip this thorn out of your side."

"So, I see!" Mr. Ise said smugly, diabolically satisfied by Gondo-san's plan, "I am not the only one who thinks Tanemori is stupid. But, Gondo, watch them like a hawk."

I loved being able to openly help *Okusan*. I held the baby, changed her diapers and washed her clothes. No task was too insignificant for me to show my love. I was very dutiful to her, and grew very attached to the baby. My attention was divided between working in the shop and helping *Okusan* with the baby. I kept the focus of my emotion completely on the baby.

Chapter Nine: Squeaky Shoes and the Black Cadillac

COLD winds ushered in *Oseibo,* the gift-giving season, a busy time for the pawnshop. Many people came to redeem their goods, in order to have money to buy gifts. The majority demonstrated gratitude and loyalty—except where I worked.

I had many sleepless nights, worrying about *Okusan,* who did not have money to buy gifts, let alone make a trip back to see her parents. Now with her second child, she was very anxious to make that homage to her parents. How could I help her? *Okusan* was deeply into her own world, wondering how she could possibly accomplish this.

Another Sunday arrived, with only the cry of a baby in the house. It looked like everyone had gone for the day.

"Okusan?" I called through the *shoji* screen.

She invited me into the room. Several times Kato had appointed himself as the eyes of our boss, to eavesdrop on us because our boss might unexpectedly sneak home from downtown.

Okusan looked totally run down, exhausted, and she was crying. It seemed as if she let the baby cry so that she could have company crying.

"My husband told me if I want to go home to my parents, to go right ahead!" she explained. "But he would not help me with any money to go to them."

I couldn't imagine what kind of deal had been made between her parents and the parents of Ise, for *Okusan* to have been forced to marry such a despicable human being. She was ashamed of sharing such an intimate family matter with me.

I was at a loss for words. Her tears dripped onto her baby's face. My heart felt her deep wound.

"Please, don't cry." I wiped her tears, my hands shaking like leaves, encouraging her to be strong and courageous, for her baby's sake.

She told me not to worry and to forgive her husband. I couldn't understand how I possibly could forgive such a detestable person, or why she would request me to do so, knowing what I knew about him. She could not speak through her tears.

The baby in her arms had no idea how desperately her mother searched for answers. I wanted to find some small way to help. My young heart reached for a source of strength. I promised I would do anything to help her.

Then it occurred to me! I had carefully put aside money for a brand new pair of squeaky shoes. I already had them picked out, along with a spiffy navy blue suit to match.

But could I touch that money, after having promised Nakamura *Sensei* I would save with singleness of purpose, for a pair of squeaky shoes which symbolized achievement in society?

Could I sacrifice my dream? I had already saved the price tag of the squeaky shoes and suit. I was in a huge quandary about what to do when the voice of my Father piped up unexpectedly: "*Jita-Kyoei*. Live for others. It benefits all." Suddenly, the decision became simple. I felt a sense of peace.

Muga muchu, singleness of heart, without concern for anything else, overtook me. I ran into my room and brought my bag of savings to her. She was shocked and immediately refused it. My tears flowed onto her hands.

She sternly rebuked me. "I did not share my troubles to get money from you. I just wanted you to know how important you are to me and to my baby."

I cut her off. "This is given in purity and without guile. This is for you to understand how much I care for you both."

She flatly refused, urging me to take good care of the money. Perhaps one day we could go to the store together to buy the shoes. My heart filled with her love and thoughts. We did *yubikiri*, crossing our little fingers, promising each other we would endure until the day we would shop together for the shoes.

Okusan accepted my heart. I saw for the first time a sparkle lighting her eyes, changing her tears into twinkling gems. This image of her was so precious. She burst for joy like a little child, her face lit against a dark canvas!

"Tanemori-san. I have an idea." Her smile grew and grew. "Let's go to the store and buy your shoes right now. If there is any money left, I will accept your gift toward my trip."

I had my cake and could eat it too! The Earth shook with my happiness. We all went out together and bought my brand spanking-new pair of shiny, squeaky, black shoes—which fit perfectly.

Wearing the shoes home from the store, I felt six feet tall and handsome beyond belief. I had accomplished my goal.

I slept with my shoes, keeping them warm in the futon. Even though I hardly slept that night, I met the morning chores, and the icy water on my hands, with a song on my lips.

It was Monday. My boss called me into the office, and asked me to close the door. I wondered if he might acknowledge me for a promotion for working hard and faithfully helping *Okusan* with the baby.

"Tanemori," he addressed me in his nauseating, high-pitched voice, a voice filled with hostility, "I heard you bought a brand new pair of shoes."

How quickly he had learned of my prized purchase. No matter how minute the incident, nothing went unnoticed by the boss. I thanked him for acknowledging the purchase of my shoes. "Would you like to see them, Ise-san?"

"Stupid," he responded, "where did you find enough money to buy brand new shoes?"

I was shocked. This was none of his business. "Oh, Ise-san." I responded innocently. "Thank you for asking me. I have been saving all my earnings from day one. Would you like to see where I kept the money?"

"What!"

His voice pierced my eardrums. I ran to my room and returned with an empty shoebox. "Here it is, Sir!" I grinned as I handed it to him. He thought I was poking fun at him, showing him a worn-out shoebox. He opened it and looked inside.

"I don't see anything that tells me that you've saved enough money for such expensive shoes!" he shouted. "Confess!"

He demanded that I confess to stealing the money from the cash register. "Don't you see yourself? Your guilt is clearly written all over your face!"

He must have known how absurd his accusation was, as I never even went near the cash register. I had been so closely scrutinized that, even if I had been a clever thief, I would have been caught in the act.

I adamantly denied the charge, but the boss persisted by citing my new shoes as evidence of misbegotten wealth. A sinister look betrayed his hidden motive to make sure there was due cause to fire me. I felt like a helpless mouse cornered by a ferocious alley cat.

"Just remember, nothing happens here which escapes me! You think my eyes are knot holes, you idiot? You think I am blind?"

Okusan was the only one who could help me declare my innocence. But if she were to testify and support me, the boss would crucify her mercilessly, which could only make the situation worse.

No matter what happened, I would not drag her into this dispute! I gritted my teeth as I made this difficult choice. It was agonizing to try to assume the role of hero. I chose instead to defile my honorable family name rather than jeopardize the lives of two people whom I deeply cared for—especially the innocent baby.

I begged my boss for the opportunity to speak with Mr. Ueda.

Mr. Ise just smiled his detestable smile. "You're a little bug caught in a spider's web. There is no way out." He called Kato.

I had told nobody about my new shoes, yet somehow Kato had told the boss about them. He walked in like a proud, victorious fighting cock.

My boss rendered his verdict and fired me. I was ordered to clean out my room by the end of the year and was forbidden to ever have another interaction with *Okusan*.

He called her in and told us there would be dire consequences if we were seen speaking to each other. Every move I made would be watched.

My soul was buried under a ton of bricks. What I feared most was news of my dishonorable discharge reaching Kotachi Village, giving my sister new fuel to feed her rage. I was doomed!

The report of my dishonesty would be registered on my official dossier and I would be crushed by the burden of disgrace. Unable to find other work, I begged Ise-san to please investigate the matter.

He would not let me speak with Mr. Ueda.

Was there no protocol to resolve the situation?

I prostrated myself before him. "I will do anything to clear my name. Please, please, allow me to defend my innocence. I beg of you to investigate the matter. It is only fair, Sir, to look carefully at who might be the thief. There may be errors in our cash records."

"Tanemori," he responded, "I told you I suspected for a long time that you would reveal your true colors. The only thing I did not do was catch you red-handed. What more proof do we need?"

Kato piped in, "We've got the evidence. You should be glad that we won't take the shoes away from you. We will just keep them for awhile. Won't we Mr. Ise? Hah! Hah! Hah!"

I gritted my teeth. "Who do you think I am, sir? I am a son of Tanemori! I would not do such a thing. I am not a thief!"

When I had said goodbye to Nakamura *Sensei* my heart was set on the day I would return with pride to Kotachi Village. I had told myself countless times I was ready to offer my body to reestablish the honorable family name.

Being accused of selling my soul was like being burned at the stake. My whole being was consumed with rage against Ise. I couldn't sleep at night for fear of nightmares.

I reflected on the bag of money I had found during my newspaper route. I had conquered that temptation! I remembered the policeman patting my head for returning the money. I was only 12 years old then, but I had felt like a man. I had kept my family name with honor and had maintained my self respect.

Oh, how I wished I was close to the temple of my Father to console my soul! Being far from him, I could only silently scream in my tormented despair *"Okusa-a-a-n!"* The cold wind penetrated my bones. Every employee was icy. They all treated me like I had the plague.

I was forced to eat all my meals alone. My tears mingled with the rice. I clung to warm thoughts of *Okusan* when she brought me food. I knew her love was cooked in the food for me. I forced myself to close my eyes when she came into the room because I could tell by her quivering lips that whenever she saw me she was holding back tears.

Late one night I found myself at the Buddhist temple. Protected by a blanket of darkness, I found my way to the main sanctuary where the Buddha sat immovable as a rock. The scent of candles brought back memories of the bomb shelter.

I was alone before the statue of Buddha, my tears dribbling to the floor. The Buddha received me with folded hands, as if he too refused to touch me. His eyes were stony, hard and cold; his lips were sealed.

The deadly silence informed me that his ears were deaf to my cry! I expected that at least the Buddha would acknowledge my hour of agony. But he did not move toward me, not even a millionth of a millimeter.

There was nothing in the world left to receive me. Hot lava exploded in my retching stomach. My heart burst into ten thousand pieces. I screamed in anguish. I could barely stand and grope my way through the temple out into the dark street. I was being sucked into a bottomless pit, where my soul mingled with sewage.

That night I resolved that the only way to salvage the honor of the Tanemori and clear my name was to take my own life. Would my Father call me a coward for choosing this way out?

For about a week I contemplated the method to use. I thought about hanging myself—gasping for air would be an excruciating way to die. I thought about throwing myself in front of a train—but the grossness of my body being scattered was sickening.

I thought about jumping into a lake—yet the fish would pick my flesh. The best way to die, without trauma, was in my sleep.

I went to every drugstore in Kobe to purchase enough sleeping pills. I figured 100 tablets would do it. I knew what I must do to salvage the honor of the family name.

In the stillness of the night I took a fountain pen and scrawled the last *Yui gon,* the expression of one's heart, to my Father, so that he would be prepared to receive me. This is the ceremonial practice before *seppuku,* suicide. I wrote:

My Honorable Father, I am at the crossroads, facing the great and momentous duty as your son to give honor to the family name. I have been accused of stealing money, but you know I am not guilty. I have no way to clear my innocence. Ise-san has denied my right to be heard.

I must maintain my integrity and respectable family name. I must be declared guiltless for the alleged crime and be restored to an honorable position before the public eye, before all employees.

My Father, what could I have done to avoid this? As long as I am in this body, I can think of no other way to prevent disgrace to the Tanemori name. I have tried my best to maintain my integrity and family honor since you left us four children. All the time growing up I upheld the moral teaching and principles you taught us. Yet I could not subject myself meekly to the social code of the Kotachi elders. I had to survive in my own way to maintain the integrity of Tanemori, for I am a scion of a *Samurai* family.

I found no answer in Buddha's heart or in the heart of my boss. It is very painful, but I have made an irrevocable decision. My utmost desire is for *Okusan* to live her life in fullness; and for her new baby to live with hope for the future. Thank you for teaching me precept upon precept, and by your example. I am a proud Number One Son of Tanemori.

Father, please honor and accept my heart's decision. I trust it will not cause trouble to your spirit or to Mother's, and that my sisters will not unduly suffer on account of my action. I pray that Buddha will extend his merciful hands to you. I find solace in my decision! I will be with you shortly. Please accept me with open arms when I arrive at the *Hatoba*, port.

Longing to see you, my Father. Your son, Takashi.

I wrote a second letter, maintaining my innocence, to my boss, and tucked both letters under my pillow. I bathed and put on my cleanest clothes as the symbol of my purity and innocence.

Peace came to my heart. In my pocket I put a hand-sized mirror to reflect the *Amaterasu* to guide me through my journey. A razor blade would protect me from evil spirits who might dissuade me from my chosen path; a coin would pay the ferryman to take me across the river to *Hatoba*, the port of the Pure Lands.

As I lay back to embark upon the journey, I heard howling dogs in the distance. They empathized with the pain in my heart. I then embraced the warmth of Nakamura *Sensei* and *Okusan* and bade them farewell. As I drifted away, the last sound I heard was the temple gongs ringing the midnight hour. When I awoke, I would be on another shore.

I awakened in a strange world, surrounded by strangers. Someone was leading me by the hand, as I walked between two separate, unrecognizable realities. I saw figures which might have been men or women, or perhaps *hotoke*, angelic beings. They looked as if they were formed of thick fog, and were motioning me to come toward them.

In a trance, I came upon a path which lead into a dark tunnel, seemingly without end. I descended, and was taken by surprise when my descent accelerated, down and around.

I screamed "No! No! No!" my voice echoing off the tunnel walls, my speed increasing. I was totally alone, descending into endless darkness, feeling the sensation of falling through a dark canal as if I were a baby being born into a new world.

Suddenly, it was as if I had reached the abrupt end of an elastic tether. I was suspended momentarily and then propelled upward. It seemed I spent an eternity traveling in that infinite, inky void.

Then I came through a gate which opened just long enough for me to pass through. After the gate shut behind me, I could see no vestige of an opening behind me.

I rubbed my eyes. I was stationary.

The darkness dissipated into foggy whiteness. It was so beautiful as the fogginess cleared. I was at the edge of a precipice, and curious to see the other side. I could begin to see the definition of the place before me. It felt comforting, as if ready to welcome me. I began to emerge into this new world, a wide open field, vast as the ocean and as expansive as heaven. Yet nothing made sense.

A thick fog rolled in, and I reentered a dark passage. The blissful silence was broken by the distant sound of clicking shoes on a hard floor. The sound grew louder and louder until it was deafening.

I couldn't bear it! I held my ears and my head rang as if I were inside a large *kane,* bell of Buddha's temple. The pain was excruciating, splitting my head, and there was no way to escape.

Faintly, I saw the outline of a human watching over me. Gradually I discerned a woman in a white dress.

I heard my own voice screaming "No! Who are you? Are you a *hotoke,* guardian spirit?"

Suddenly I saw a most beautiful flower garden, and I recalled Aunt Takae telling me years before on Miyajima about a garden in the Pure Realms where my parents were waiting for me.

I called out, *"Sensei!"*

The figure went away. Someone was banging my head with a sledgehammer. My stomach was now being consumed in a furnace; my throat felt as dry as fish scales! My swollen tongue stuck to the roof of my mouth. I was gasping for air. My body was pounding like someone had made *omochi,* pounded rice cake, out of me.

"Tanemori-san!" Someone shrieked at me.

Deafening voices reverberated painfully in my head. "I think he is regaining consciousness. The critical hour is past."

"Help me! Did someone stick a dagger in my stomach? Where am I? What am I doing here? Why are you here? Who are you?"

I opened my eyes. A man and woman in white uniforms were looking at me.

"Please, someone tell me where my Father is. Father! Father! Where are you, Father?"

"Tanemori-kun, we were able to save your life just in the nick of time." A man's gruff voice told me *kamisama*, god, helped him save my life.

"*Kami-sama?* What did *kami-sama*, have to do with saving my life? What happened to Buddha? What do you mean … you've saved my life? My Father was expecting me to meet him, I need to go there. Please let me go now. It looks as if I have gone the wrong way. Please, please let me go!"

Suddenly, I realized I had not crossed the river to the other shore.

"Tell me, what happened to me? Why am I wearing this white gown? What happened to my clothes and the razor blade, mirror and coin? Give them back to me. Please! Please!"

These women in white uniforms were not spirits. They were nurses, and the man in the long white coat was a doctor. The realization ripped me apart to the bottom of my soul. From deep in my *hara* spewed a wail of unspeakable grief!

"No! No! Why didn't you let me go to my Father?"

I buried my face in shame! Even in suicide I had proved a total failure. My Father had rejected me. The Number One Son of Tanemori was not even worthy of suicide!

There was no exit. I would have to live with this unbearable accusation from my own soul. I had replaced the depths of despair with an even deeper pit of abysmal dejection.

The doctor stopped at my hospital room later that evening, apparently to give me encouragement toward the next step in life, whatever it might be. He commented about my physical strength. He said my body was strong and healthy.

He added, "Son, you have an excellent set of *kintama,* balls. Make sure at least you use them before you die!"

I took his admonition with grace.

The next day, Mr. Ueda paid a visit, standing across the room as if he were sizing up the situation.

I was not quite ready to see anyone. I buried my head. I was furious. I detested him, wanted to spit in his face. It was too late for him to come to my rescue. He had been such a wimp, he couldn't even stand up to that worm of a man, Mr. Ise. I felt like asking him if he had lost his *kintama.*

I bit my tongue! I pitied him and didn't want to dignify him by looking at his face. He slunk to my side and reached out to touch me and told me I shouldn't be mad at him.

"Mr. Ueda, please. Don't even touch me!"

Eerie silence filled the room. I sat up and looked straight into his eyes. My head was throbbing, my hands shaking, my throat parched, and flaming anger leapt from my eyes. I waited for Mr. Ueda to speak before I would let him have it!

A nurse interrupted the charged silence. She greeted Mr. Ueda and echoed the joy of saving my life.

I could have strangled her with my bare hands. The doctor walked in and asked me how I was feeling. I growled under my breath.

The doctor looked at my chart, peered closely at my eyes and walked out without uttering a word. The nurse hurriedly checked my pulse and temperature, then excused herself, conveying her best wishes to Mr. Ueda, who acknowledged her with a slight bow.

Once again a negative charge filled the room. It was suffocating me and I grabbed my throat.

Ueda had not come to talk about the weather. He began by accusing me of disgracing him.

"You have dishonored the name of the company. I suggest you leave the Kobe area as quietly as you can. I want you to disappear without a trace. You will be discharged by tomorrow morning. We will have your duffel bag packed and brought here. I will personally see you step on the train. No one will ever know you have worked here. Do you understand?"

I took a deep breath and sat upright, my throat burning as I addressed him. "Are you finished Mr. Ueda? I would like the opportunity to defend my innocence. I have never stolen any money. According to your own words, you owe a favor to my Vice Principal, Akiyama, and to my Step-Grandfather. Why can't you investigate what actually happened?"

My heart was pounding. I hoped that Mr. Ueda would open his heart to my plea.

"Mr. Ueda. Why have you been so fearful of speaking to Mr. Ise? Isn't he a subordinate to you? You owe it to yourself to investigate this, so at least your conscience will be clear. Don't you think so?"

He tried to brush it off. There was nothing he could do to reverse the decision.

"What you have done is a social sin. We cannot afford to keep you for even one more day. No one must know what you have done or know anything about our decision."

"If you are not willing to listen to me," I countered, "Let me speak to *Shacho*, the President of company. I am certain he would listen. If you are talking about the integrity of the company, then why would you not want to find out the truth?"

Mr. Ueda dropped his head. "Sorry, there's nothing more I can do."

He handed me an envelope. I pushed it away.

"You understand, I must give this to you," he said as he opened the envelope. "See, here is your train ticket and, ahem, some money. Please, take it and just go!"

He insisted that I verify the money in the envelope—3,000 yen, about $50.00. This was comparable to seven months' wages.

"You know very well what society would say if we didn't extend this token to you! We are doing something extraordinary for you after the immeasurable disgrace you've brought to our company, which is impossible to rectify." He paused momentarily. "At least, no one else knows what you have done, except a doctor and two nurses. Kato and Gondo will not breathe a word for any reason. You know that, don't you! They are the kind of employees who know what is honorable."

I felt like gagging on the last supposition. "So, I see, Mr. Ueda, this is hush money." I looked squarely into his eyes. "You don't know who I am, do you? I am a son of Tanemori! Are you afraid of what I might do? Perhaps you are afraid of the truth! That's it, isn't it? Actually, I can see you are running scared of that madman Ise-san."

"Are you afraid of some kind of retaliation in the event he would find out you believed in me enough to investigate the matter?" My face was burning with rage. "How shameful you all are, including *Shacho*!" I burst into cynical laughter.

"Tanemori, even though this is a small token, it will come in handy one of these days. It will help you at least buy food for a few weeks. I want you to keep it. Ise-san does not know anything about this. It came from *Shacho*. He conveys his best wishes to you."

The next morning, Mr. Ueda and his slave met me at the hospital with my duffel bag. I implored him for an opportunity to say goodbye to *Okusan*.

"Tanemori, I am here to personally see you step on the train."

I was being led like a sheep to slaughter to the Shinkansen train station. When the train pulled in, Mr. Ueda bowed, asking me to understand and accept his decision. On the long train ride to Hiroshima, my thoughts were filled with regret for not being able to say goodbye to *Okusan* and her baby. My tears ran, and I let them come. It did not matter whether anyone saw me. There was no shame in my tears.

The face of Nakamura *Sensei* flickered like a candle in the wavering reflections in the window. I was a double failure, a failure in life and a failure in death! To the rhythm of the rocking clickity-clack of the train I repeated over and over the mantra, "My name is Takashi. I am the Son of Tanemori. My name is Takashi. I am a scion of a *Samurai!* My name is Takashi, Son of Tanemori ..."

They had stolen my squeaky shoes.

I lurked in the shadows of Kotachi Train Station until I was sure the night would blanket my presence. No one must see me coming back. No one must find out about the incident in Kobe, not the Gossip Committee, not Satsuko, and above all, not Nakamura *Sensei*.

When I remembered the enormous social risk she had taken by daring to offer me her love, it pained my heart. Although the truth might be found out sooner or later, I must guard it now. This village was the last place I would ever want to show my face again. The bridges I had burned were still smoldering, leaving only footbridges to the memory of Nakamura *Sensei's* sweet love, and to the temple of my Father, the only place in the world where I could seek and truly find solace.

I also had an important matter to settle with Buddha, whom I felt had betrayed me. Even though I had thought myself to be walking aimlessly in the wintry night, I found myself at the foot of the long stone steps to Korimbo Buddha Temple.

Directly behind me was my old school, Oda Higashi Elementary. The familiarity of the school was uncanny. It seemed an eternity since I'd been there.

As Buddha was inside the Temple and I needed answers, I climbed upwards, leaving footprints in the fluffy snow on the long steps. I tried several doors until I discovered an open sliding door into the main sanctuary.

The scent of burning wax in the Temples of Buddha always brought back memories of traumatic times. The Buddha in Korimbo Temple was renowned as the Buddha of infinite mercy and compassion. I stood before him, aggressively seeking my answer. My hands were balled into fists, and tears trailed down my cheeks onto the *tatami* mats. I expected Buddha to reach out his hands, to welcome and embrace me.

I could see my breath in the candlelight, while all around me everything felt cold and impersonal. Waiting, with no response from the Buddha, for what seemed like hours, I decided to change my approach. I humbly fell prostrate before him, not raising my face for fear of impropriety.

Out loud, I proclaimed my innocence and waited, drowning in my tears. I held my breath, listening to my heart skipping beats in great anticipation of feeling his touch. Soon, he would tenderly wipe away my tears.

I pleaded loudly, "If you see with your eyes, please tell me I am welcome here. I beg you, please touch me with your tender hand, for I need your comfort. Please fill my heart with your compassionate understanding. Declare me innocent. I have done nothing wrong. You knew why I couldn't ask *Okusan* to verify my innocence. Why didn't you intercede for me then?"

I waited for his response. Time waited with the silence. It was utterly still. My heart could no longer bear the weight of this punishment, waiting upon Buddha!

I screamed at him, "Look at me! Hear me! Touch me! Feel my heartbeat! What happened to your compassionate eyes? You won't see me! What happened to your comforting words? You refuse to speak to me with understanding! What happened to your merciful hands? You are afraid to wipe my tears! What happened to your tireless feet? You sit there, motionless! What happened to your forgiving heart? Why don't you show it to me by embracing me?"

How could I have slipped beneath the compassionate eyes of Buddha? No other Gods, and now not even Buddha, would come to my rescue. Didn't the artisan who created this effigy know Buddha's eyes could not see? His ears could not hear? His mouth could not comfort with words? His hands could not touch the needy?

He was simply a piece of matter unable to deliver me from my misery. My heart sank into a deep black hole.

Suddenly someone touched my shoulder. "What is the matter, my son?"

My heart froze. I had thought the temple was deserted.

"Is there anything I can do to help you?"

I held my breath! Blood drained from my head. Caught! I covered my face with trembling hands to keep myself from being identified. The solemn voice behind me sounded warm and confident, like my Father.

"My son?"

Had he been listening? No! He must never find out who I am! I dashed out into the darkness. He tried to pursue me.

"Son, wait for a moment!" His deep voice echoed through the sanctuary. I ran as fast as I could, slipping and tumbling down the long steps in a panic until I had no more energy.

The quarter moon clinging to a starless sky felt as lonely and desolate as my heart. A dog's howling confirmed it.

The Buddha had betrayed me. What a fool I had been to believe in the promises of Buddha!

I have no recollection of where I went that night. I remember only wandering in the cold, burning with rage. The image of the stone-cold Buddha tormented me. I covered my ears to block out the pleading voice of the priest calling after me. Finally, when I could hear the silence between my heartbeats, I realized I was kneeling at the gravesite of my Father.

I told him about the unjust world which had spit me out to be an outcast. I told him about death not even accepting me; about *Okusan* and our brutal treatment by my boss; about the squeaky shoes, and how the whole episode had led me to be condemned to an intolerable life. I told him about being shunned by the Buddha as if I were the useless shuck on an ear of corn.

I was at a total loss about what to do to salvage my family name from the gutter. My anger boiled and exploded like a volcanic mountain against Buddha's immovable statue.

I embraced my Father's grave marker. As cold and hard as the Buddha's statue, it gave me no assurance. I could not feel the spirit of my Father there.

"Daddy, I know now what I must do. The only way to restore honor to the Tanemori name is to take revenge on the American people who destroyed our family and robbed me of my birthright."

I vowed, "No matter what I must do, however long it might take, I will avenge your death. Americans must suffer as I have suffered!"

My alternatives were to remain in Japan in disgrace or to make a drastic step into the unknown. With my vow I decided to redeem my life by taking revenge on Americans!

By the time I felt the warmth of the morning sun on my back, I felt reassured that it was safe to return to face Satsuko. When stillness came into my heart, I knew Father had embraced me with his spirit and accepted my innocence

When I came upon Satsuko, ambling down Main Street, with my same duffel bag and in my same dirty clothes, she dropped her jaw as if the hinges of a trap door had fallen open.

"Is that you, Taka-chan? What in the world are you doing here?" She shoved me into the alley behind her, "Has any one seen you? Look at yourself!"

Without allowing me a breath to respond she hoarsely whispered, "Didn't I tell you never to come back here unless you returned to honor the leaders of community with proper gifts?" She was shaking in fury. "How do you expect me to explain this to everyone?"

She detested me because she was sure I couldn't take the pressures of living up to my worth in society. She couldn't even stand to look me in the face.

Relentlessly she laid into me, "You spineless wimp! When will you ever become a man? You're disgusting. I don't even want to think of you as my brother."

I couldn't get a word in edgewise.

She ordered me to leave the village immediately before anyone spotted me. When she saw a neighbor approaching, her plan was thwarted. Her harangue wound down like a used-up phonograph. The lilting high voice of my favorite community elder, Grandma Honda, was like the fragrance of spring: the voice of the Merciful God *Kami-sama.*

"*Oh, Sattsu-chan ka?* Oh, is that you, Takashi!"
I bowed deeply to my savior.
"How good it is to see you!" I thanked her for her opportune arrival. She smiled, showing her few blackened teeth, a symbol of wealth and social worth.

"Oh, by the way, *Sattsu-chan*, after I come home from the vegetable field, would you mind if *Taka-chan* came over to visit me? I have something I have wanted to show him for long time."
Without waiting for a response, she disappeared.
Satsuko fumed, spitting anger. Her angry, contorted face was too amusing. I burst out laughing. It was good medicine to have my funny bone tickled.

Now Satsuko had no option. She couldn't send me away before the holiday season was over without being frowned upon as a heartless sister. She dared not go against the powers that be. She gave me the grace to stay for the holidays but made me promise to leave no later than January 8th.

In some ways it was good to be back in Kotachi Village. It was much more fun hanging out with my old cronies than my miserable life in Kobe had been. But every day I lived in fear that the truth about the tragedy in Kobe would be found out.

I told everyone I had been laid off due to the business doing poorly. By all appearances I was doing fine, ready for life's next stepping stone.

I saw Nakamura *Sensei* on the evening of the class reunion. When I saw her, I didn't breathe a word about what had happened. Nor did I tell her of my resolve to avenge my Father's death.

While there were still a few days before the holidays, I made several trips to the city of Hiroshima to find out how I might be able to emigrate to Brazil or Argentina.

I was directed to a government official who asked me to fill out the papers necessary for emigration. I told him of my intention to avenge my Father's death. I had heard about Japanese colonies in those countries, and of people striking it rich.

If it was money I was after, he suggested I go to America.

I couldn't believe my ears, and I responded, "No! You are a mad man. Why in the world would you tell me to go to America? You are out of your mind! What do you know about America?"

He had to be deranged. I immediately headed for the door, shouting behind me, "Do you know that I lost my parents by *Pika-don*? If it wasn't for those barbarians ..."

I couldn't hold back my tears and ran into the hallway, and then out into the street, venting my anger and almost breaking my toe kicking a rock.

I heard his voice beckoning me, "*Kuso baka mono.*"

I cursed him under my breath. He was a fool of fools!

A few days later, an official government letter arrived.

Satsuko's voice pierced my eardrums, "Takashi. What is this?"

I grabbed the letter from her, not even remembering I had given the man in the government office my sister's address.

My heart stopped! I feared it was from Kobe, and the truth was revealed. The return address was Hiroshima City Hall. I crumpled the letter into my pocket, while Satsuko hurled daggers of accusation that I was guilty of some wrongdoing.

"Nothing! This is none of your business!" I yelled, as I escaped from the house.

The city official had written to tell me about some plan which he felt could help me. When I had left his office I had wanted to kill him. But now, strangely lured back by this letter, I found myself storming back into his office, rudely pushing aside his secretary, and shaking the letter in his face. He ignored my exasperated conduct and smiled, offering me a seat. I was stunned.

The official was totally calm as he asked his secretary to bring me a cup of tea. I was determined to give him a piece of my mind.

She politely returned with green tea for both of us, and bowed as she left, smiling reassuringly, which made me feel ashamed of the way I had treated her a few minutes before. Reluctantly, I decided to be nice. The official was the only individual who seemed concerned for my wellbeing. We exchanged courteous holiday greetings.

"Tanemori-kun." He looked straight into my eyes, with a sense of urgency in his soft voice, "Please hear what I have to tell you."

"What is it to you whether or not I go to America?" I asked. "Why would you even suggest I go to the place responsible for all my misery in life?"

"Do you understand that I despise Americans? They dropped the *pika-don* and took my Father from me!" I looked at him with defiant angry eyes as he stood.

He silently and deliberately walked around my chair to gaze out the window. It seemed theatrical, staged. Was he playing on my emotions?

I too stood, waving my hands in front of my face, clearly defining a barrier between us. He simply stood in front of the window, gazing into the distance for a long time, as if lost in his own world.

I sat back down to wait for his next dramatization. I wouldn't give him an inch. Then I noticed his eyes were filled with tears. How strange it was to see a total stranger crying. Was this, too, a theatrical performance?

He reminded me of the time, three years before, when I had seen Tamura *Sensei* standing beneath the pine tree in his garden, his body shaking with grief for me. But I couldn't believe that this stranger also had tears for me.

He seemed to recover, and he wiped his face with his open hand. He pulled a file from the cabinet.

"Tanemori-kun, there is a possibility we might be able to send you to America. I have the necessary papers here. The American government has a relocation program for the *hibakusha,* the a-bomb survivors. The American government will welcome you to their country."

My thoughts turned immediately to when the Japanese government had evacuated my sisters Satsuko and Chisako. They were relocated because they were standing in the way of progress. I became furious. My body began shaking uncontrollably.

"Relocation? What do you mean by that? Don't you know what I've gone through? Do you know who I am? I am the Number One Son of Tanemori who needs no relocation!"

He smiled. "I understand that America is a Christian nation and the people there welcome all survivors of Hiroshima with open arms."

"What do you mean that America is *Kiristan,* Christian nation? How do they justify killing my parents and causing so much suffering? How do they justify taking everything from me? Tell them to give me my Father back!" I was startled by my own rage-filled voice.

He looked out the window. "I understand the streets of America are paved with gold, and money trees are planted in every corner."

"If America is a Christian nation," I scowled, "then why did they drop the bomb on Hiroshima, killing tens of thousands of children and leaving more, like me, to suffer? Tell me more. Tell me again."

"Killing the children of Hiroshima wasn't enough for the American people. No! That is why they had to drop a second bomb on Nagasaki, to kill tens of thousands of children there."

I raged out of control, shaking and beating the air with my fists.

"No! You are crazy. I will not accept your explanation. You must have been paid off to say what you just said to me. I don't believe you at all. What do you know about America? Even Buddha has more compassion than the American god!"

"Tanemori-kun, pull your chair closer!" he said. "There is something I want you to hear which might help you better understand."

I tried to interrupt. "I don't think you heard what I just said."

I sensed great waves of emotion overwhelming him. He was openly weeping now, tears running down his cheeks. He wiped his nose with a trembling hand.

He told me his son would have been about my age if he had survived the bombing. Seeing me before him reminded him so much of his son. He couldn't shake the image from his mind.

I learned that he had also lost his two daughters. He looked at me squarely, asking me to open my heart to listen to him.

No! I would not accept his story. I could trust no one, especially anyone who would try so hard to sell such a deceitful scheme. I would not be tricked. I restrained myself.

Perhaps he was a weak man, and had sold his conscience to some American propaganda. If indeed he had lost his son and daughters, why did he want me to go to America?

I thought he might have made a deal to sell me to the Americans. Otherwise, why would he work so hard to persuade me to go? He was trying to betray me, just like Buddha. The green tea served to me was prepared like a drink of *maccha*, the bitter herb tea served at last rites.

"No Sir! I will never sell my soul!" I tearfully retorted as I stormed out. I had almost fallen into his trap.

Instead, I found a job in a small Papa- and Mama-san restaurant in the city of Kure, fulfilling my promise to Satsuko.

Kure, like Hiroshima, had been a Naval Shipyard during the war, and still had the vestiges of shipbuilding and military factories, a sorrowful reminder of Japan's defeat. The place was crawling with American Occupied Forces, and GI's—Government Issues—were spending money like it was going out of style. I was flabbergasted to watch them burn their dough. When I asked where all their money came from, I was told it grows on trees in America and all one has to do is find the right tree.

As a "utility boy," sweeping floors, peeling vegetables and washing dishes, I began making about fifty cents a day, plus room and board. My job was mostly miserable, especially when I had to deliver food in February in my "holey" rubber boots.

The one thing I looked forward to was the daily arrival of the mailman. I simply loved to see his smiling face. He reminded me of *Ebisu-san,* one of seven Gods in a fable. He had a large face, big eyes, and the biggest of all possible smiles, bringing blessing and joy. When he saw me, his encouraging words were like honey to a bear.

One day, to my surprise, he had a letter for me. With his huge grin he handed it to me. "Aren't you going to open it?"

He waited for me to open it. He was curious because it appeared to be an official letter from the government in Hiroshima. It had been forwarded from Satsuko with "urgent" scrawled on the envelope.

I couldn't believe that it was from the same official, still pursuing my emigration to America. What was wrong with this man? Didn't he have an ounce of brains?

A personal note read, "You are too young to throw your life away. If there is anything I can do, I would like to do it for you. Please hear me out one more time."

"The first step," it continued, "however insignificant it might seem, is the most important one of a long journey. Tanemori-kun, please come see me before you make any major life decision."

To seek advice and to console my soul with his spirit, I secretly made a couple of trips, each a two-hour train ride, to my Father's gravesite. Considering my other options, and my lack of opportunity for advancement in my current job, I began to soften to the sympathetic official's tears, believing he might genuinely be holding my best interests at heart.

The stigma of being an orphan, and the potential of the truth about my failed suicide attempt surfacing, made me ever more anxious to leave the culture of Japan in the dust.

I searched my soul over and over again. Either my head needed examining or a spell had been cast on me, but finally I made the unthinkable decision to emigrate to the land of the enemy.

The only way I could exact the revenge I sought was to make sure all American children learned the suffering and loneliness of living without parents. I also wanted all American parents to experience the pain of having their children mercilessly murdered.

This was my opportunity to avenge myself on my eternal enemies, to make a million dollars, to marry a blonde-haired, blue-eyed woman, to return to Japan with my trophy, and to re-establish my honorable family name.

I paid the crazy man at Hiroshima City Hall one more visit and signed the papers. It would take a few months for the papers to be finalized. He recommended that I return to Kotachi Village for the next phase of the process. The American government wanted to verify the truth of the paperwork, and would come check on me.

Since it was planting season, the Grandparents Sakae agreed for me to stay at their house in exchange for me working in the fields. For once, it seemed I had the best of all worlds.

Grandmother begged me not to drink *sake*, which Grandfather secretly gave me every day after working in the fields. Grandmother gave me money to buy cigarettes to keep me from drinking.

Their house was much more comfortable than Satsuko's, and she didn't bother me much. I was determined to be on my best behavior, in order to keep the eyes of the *sen-gen* looking the other way.

They couldn't look the other way, however, when a huge black Cadillac drove up to stop right in front of our house. When the driver finally figured out how to park the car, it took up nearly half the width of the main dirt street.

Neighbors came like swarming flies, gathering around the house to see what was going on. Some of the villagers had never seen *Gai-jin,* a white man.

The translator and chauffeur, a small, middle-aged man, rushed to open the rear door. A tall, distinguished, curly-haired American, around 6-foot-2, emerged from the car. He looked like a giant from another planet, towering over grasshoppers!

Their naiveté made me sick. I wanted to drive them away. When the white man walked deliberately to Satsuko's door, the neighbors fled like cockroaches, hiding behind telephone poles or peeking out from behind the corners of the house.

I opened the door to discover Satsuko watching the scene from the window.

"Takashi," her voice hit the ceiling, "what is going on behind my back? I saw the smirk cross your face."

One of the Gossip Committee members approached the Japanese chauffeur with his finger pointed at the *Gai-jin*, "Young man, what is the meaning of this?"

I slid open the external *shoji* screen of the porch. Standing on the elevated porch, I was as tall as the *Gai-jin*, who was standing on the ground.

The interpreter introduced me to the *Gai-jin*, who, since he had already seen my photograph, acted as if he knew me. He bungled a formal greeting in Japanese to Satsuko.

She bowed slightly, warning, "Takashi, you had better tell me this minute what you have done behind my back! Why in the world have you brought this ... *Gai-jin* here? Have you no shame? What more disgrace are you bringing to the Tanemori home?"

She shouted to a neighbor. "Go! Bring a bowl of salt quickly!" She couldn't stomach having a *Gai-jin* desecrate her sanctuary, her home! The interpreter began to explain the purpose of the visit.

I was indignant.

"Well, let me tell you!" I said, seeing I had everyone's attention. I spoke loudly so the neighbors could clearly hear me. "You told me many times over that you want to have peace.*"

I confronted her squarely, "You tried to put me away in a boys' institution."

"And all of you," I directed my comment at the neighbors who had been severely disappointed when there hadn't been enough evidence to send me away, "here's your chance to know that I will never see your faces ever again! No more Takashi for you to kick around like a soccer ball. I'm going far away from here, once and for all, because I know most of you don't have the *kintama,* balls, to go anywhere."

The translator, perceiving my sister as the elder Tanemori, bowed to her several times. I couldn't hear everything he was saying. I wanted to be the one to tell her of my firm decision. I hoped this man wouldn't deprive me of the honor!

"*Amerika!*" She exploded! Her hatred and anger toward Americans knew no limit. In no uncertain terms, she let me know that she would never accept my decision to go to America.

"How could you!" she screamed at me. She pushed the interpreter aside. "Takashi. How could you belittle yourself to accept handouts from the American Government, the very people who killed our parents and destroyed our lives? Am I hearing right? You coward! Drop dead! Do you have brain damage? Can't you make any right decisions? Do you think our Father would allow you to behave so foolishly? You have become a *kichigai*—a madman!"

The hatred and bitter fury which had fed her soul for years finally detonated, sending shrapnel flying in every direction. It was really funny to see the tall *Gai-jin,* trying to escape her tirade, trying to shrink, as if he thought he could hide behind the tiny interpreter.

Then she screamed again at me, "I will not have you bring any further shame and disgrace to our family name. I will see to it with my own hand that we will not breathe the same air anymore!"

"How could you make such a preposterous decision when you are the heir to the family name? Let me get my hands on you!" She lunged at me as if to grab me by the neck and choke me to death.

I jumped off the porch to avoid her attack.

The neighbors chimed in, questioning my sanity. "We knew all along you were not one of us. You have always been an oddball. But this is an outrageous betrayal! How dare you bring a *Gai-jin* into our village to desecrate our ground?"

This brought me to the breaking point. I clenched my fists, ready to swing at anyone who came within arm's length. Someone brought the requested bowl of salt and scattered it on the ground, around and at the startled American. The interpreter tried to explain what was happening.

"How can think for a minute that I have betrayed you?" I exploded! "Why should you folks care whether I go to America or not? You have never accepted me as part of the community."

"When bad things happened, you automatically condemned me. You never had room in your hearts to consider my feelings, let alone to accept me."

"Did one of you offer me a cup of cold water when I was thirsty? Did anyone give me a piece of fish when our whole family was starving? Did anyone here offer me any clothing when I had none?"

"None of you! Instead, you just laughed when I wore rags instead of a uniform to school!" I cried through tears of rage. "Tell me, who among you has a pure soul? Does anyone here have the right to criticize others?"

"It was only Honda *Oba-chan* who offered my brother and me a piece of cold watermelon. It was only Mitskawa *Oba-chan* who gave me baked sweet potato in the cold of winter when we had no food."

Honda *Oba-chan* stepped forward, protectively, with sadness in her eyes.

"Taka-chan, I don't understand why you have to go so far away," she said, "but I know you will make it. Buddha will guide and protect you. Just go to America and see what you will see."

"It makes me sad because I'm such an old woman. I'm afraid by the time you come home, I may have gone to another world. But not to worry! Be strong and live a healthy life and come back soon."

The interpreter had papers with special instructions for me to sign. Satsuko slammed the *shoji* screen loudly as she disappeared into the house.

I never told her the true motives for my decision to leave the country. I didn't even attempt to request her final blessing. I avoided her at all costs.

Our Grandparents were surprisingly amenable to my plans. Grandfather Sakae gave me his blessing, as long as I returned a rich man, and Grandmother insisted that I never become part of the white man's religion. I promised them both.

In my final preparations, I worked up the courage to visit Tamura *Sensei*. He was very surprised. "Tanemori," he said, grabbing me by my shoulders and looking me straight in my eyes, "be strong and live according to your heart. No matter how difficult your life might be, never forget the teaching of your parents."

"I look forward to hearing about your adventures some day. Promise me you'll come home."

I promised him I would uphold my Father's teaching and be strong and courageous; and that I would return one day to honor my Father's spirit and restore the honorable family name.

He blessed me for my bravery. He had confidence in me.

Of course I couldn't leave Japan without saying farewell to Nakamura *Sensei*. We went to our secret secluded place next to the river.

In a small clearing, covered in soft grasses, we lay down and gazed at the white clouds floating against the deep blue summer sky. Birds sang and bees buzzed. The delicate summer breeze carried the butterflies to kiss the flowers. Two red dragonflies, tied together, unified in perfect harmony, wove acrobatically through the tall summer grass.

"I believe in you, Takashi. I know in my heart that you will live strongly and will not be defeated by your weaknesses."

"*Sensei*, I've been told all the streets in America are paved with gold. Money trees are on every corner." It sounded so fabulous it was as if I were about to become part of a *gunwa,* a fable. "When I make a million dollars, I will return to my homeland to reinstate my family name. I will try to do it in ten years."

The thought of ten long years before I would see her again was hard to bear. The summer breeze played with her silky hair. I gently brushed it from her cheek to look deep into her dark, starry eyes. I felt a warmth course through my body and noticed the rising and falling of her breasts beneath her sheer blouse.

"*Sensei* ..." My Adam's apple made a lump in my throat. I couldn't speak.

"What is it, Takashi-kun?" Her soft voice was also colored by her emotion. She took my hand and placed it gently on her excited bosom. I could feel her heartbeat traveling into my heart.

"*Sensei*, I am going to write a diary every day for you to read when I return home. I will succeed and return home with glory. Please wait for me." I kept talking to try to keep my mind from the growing arousal in my loins.

She asked me if I would be lonely and miss her.

"Of course I will miss you! No one could replace you, *Sensei.*"

It was so painful to think of the prospect of losing her. I held back my tears and could tell, by her quivering lips and breathing, that she, too, was holding back tears. How I wished to tell her how much I loved her, and how much I wanted her to come with me to America. I could no longer hold back my emotion. I buried my face in her bosom, and she held me tightly.

Her fragrance reminded me of *Okusan.* Her heart pounded, her breast surged with energy. I felt as if I had entered into the deepest chamber of her soul.

My heart was bursting with love for her. My fingers touched her lips. She moistened them, ready to accept my gentle kiss. I was in heaven. Her lips were soft, sweet and warm!

Our lips touched again! I kissed her again and again. My mind went dizzy. I lost all sense of time and space. Our hearts and minds and spirits unfurled for each other like buds on a warm spring day. Her smooth cheeks blushed crimson in the light of sunset!

We promised each other that we would always be together. No ocean could separate us!

Part Two:
"The Butterfly"– A Life in America

Chapter One: Sayonara, Mount Fuji

I JUMPED out of bed at the sound of the alarm clock—it was four-thirty and the rooster had yet to crow! Washing my face with cold water ... this would be the last time, in Kotachi. By the time the sun peeked over the familiar *Setoyama*, I looked for the last time toward the place where only yesterday I had spent moments with Nakamura *Sensei*.

Chugging through the still morning air came the sound of the *Nobori-Ressha,* the train, going uphill, toward the city of Miyoshi where we had often secretly escaped. Soon I would be riding the train to escape the Village of Kotachi—first to Hiroshima, and then on to Tokyo. I looked at the clock once more; it told me it was time to hurry.

I carefully double-checked the train tickets by patting my pocket. It was time for me to say "so long" to my younger brother, Sadoyoshi. As he conveyed very little emotion, our goodbye was more or less cordial.

At last, I would be free, not only from Satsuko, but also from the Gossip Committee. Holding small duffel bags which held all my possessions, I stood on the street, looking around the Village one last time. I didn't know whether to cry or laugh—my heart had no feeling for the villagers.

Several neighbors knew of my departure and approached Satsuko for varied reasons—mainly curiosity, or gladness that her brother would finally be gone for good. Because of the neighbors, Satsuko insisted on escorting me to Hiroshima.

"Takashi, I must accompany you. It is my last duty, as required by the Village code. You owe me this one thing—could you at least honor me before these villagers and neighbors by acknowledging me publicly, by expressing your gratitude, as a symbol of my honorable deed of accompanying you to Hiroshima?"

My mouth dropped open, wide and deep. I thought the hinges of the door had broken off. She had no shame! What more could I say about my sister. Should I be disgusted with her or should I cry for her?

The previous evening I had noticed a little gift wrapped on Satsuko's dresser, and that her nice clothes were hanging on a coat hanger. Well, it was obvious that I had no choice but to honor her, since she would be living in the village long after I left.

I now had little or no interest in my older sister. Her action would only fulfill her duty—a last "obligatory social" action before the villagers. This was indeed disingenuous. But it was the only acceptable behavior in Japanese society. And the last thing I needed from her was an eternal *urami*, a curse, for any perception that I was keeping her from fulfilling her social obligations.

This was the moment I had waited for—a final escape—as if I were a disappearing magician.

While riding the train to Hiroshima, Satsuko and I exchanged few words. Although my sister had the gift of gab, I had little patience for her nonsense. My mind was focused on memories of Nakamura *Sensei*, focused on her tender, warm and loving spirit.

Neither my sister nor I had tears for each other. Perhaps she was also overwhelmed by the fact that I might not return to Japan, my birthplace. Or was it my wishful thinking? Who knows?

Chisako, who lived on the Island of Ondo, near Hiroshima City, met me on the platform. This last meeting was overwhelmed with sadness, for I had never demonstrated my heartfelt appreciation for what she had done for me when I needed her in Kotachi Village. She was very happy that I was setting myself "free," like a bird flying away. She wished me good luck.

Satsuko and I casually said good-bye, wishing each other good health and longevity, at Hiroshima station, and I continued on to Tokyo. However, it was a very painful departure for me. I saw their shadows on the platform and their images were burned into my mind long after the train pulled out of the station.

Riding the train, staring blankly into the distance through the window, I saw the landscape as though projected onto a cinema screen. Many events since my Father's death momentarily appeared and disappeared, as if I was reliving them.

The conductor reminded us that the train was approaching the city of Kobe. For the next five minutes, memories of that fateful drama and disgrace returned to me. I could see the store, the face of my boss, the doctor, the nurses and the hospital room. I covered my face, burying myself deeply in shame.

"Sannomiya! Sannomiya!"

As the train came to a stop, I suddenly returned to reality. "Oh, thank goodness!" My entire body was covered with cold sweat! I could almost wring water out of it. My hands were wet and slimy and my knuckles had turned white.

Three hours earlier I had left my sisters at the Hiroshima train station. Satsuko's last words once again rang in my ears, her questions in regards to my decision and my self-worth, and her judgment that I had sold my pride and shamed the Tanemori name.

How true it was! My now-bitter life had been so changed by one American bomb. My sister might have been right. How often she had wished that I had died, rather than living to further shame and disgrace the family name.

On the other hand, I should have been rejoicing! After all, at last, she would finally be out of my life, probably for the next ten years, unless I contacted her before then. I let out a big sigh of relief! Going into the enemy's fortress was good for my own survival and would allow me to avenge my Father's death.

It was my final day in Japan, June 21, 1956. Clutching my two bags, I arrived at Haneda International Airport in Tokyo. In the next few hours I would be cutting myself off from my homeland. I would be boarding a four-engined DC-4 airliner.

Oh, my! How strangely people behaved. This was the first time I had been at any airport, let alone Haneda. I had never dreamed I would find myself in this place.

"Wow! I'm in Tokyo! How many people would like a chance to come to such a big city?" I couldn't count the people, and had no idea where they could be going!

Against this backdrop, the image of Nakamura *Sensei* tugged at my heart.

"No! She didn't want me to cry!" Yet as hard as I tried not to cry, tears came, and there was no way to dry up the fountain. I told myself to stop crying and shut my eyes tightly against the tears.

While I sat on the bench, it occurred to me and seemed strange that no one showed any concern for anyone else. Everyone was busy with their own affairs. I wiped my face, ears and nose, all in one motion.

An official directing traffic signaled me to follow him. My two tiny duffel bags lay beside me, *samishii-so,* very lonely.

All of a sudden, I began to cry again in self-pity.

"Yes. That's my whole world!" The bags held one cotton blanket and two sheets, some underwear and t-shirts, two pairs of long pants and one windbreaker, one pair of tennis shoes, two bars of soap, and a couple of toothbrushes.

To protect my pictures of Nakamura *Sensei* and Father, they were carefully wrapped and placed between pieces of cardboard. I could almost hear the heartbeat and feel the warmth of Nakamura *Sensei* gushing into my heart.

It was time for the last walk. I stepped outside the building and picked up a handful of dirt to smell. It had an entirely different smell than that of the Kotachi Village soil where I had toiled planting sweet potatoes. My heart started to beat faster and louder, as soon I would be escorted to a special room, then onto the plane.

When the time came to board, and I finally walked through the last door, it took me 15 minutes to reach the plane. I felt like the longest walk I had ever taken. Once on the plane, I had no difficulty tucking my duffel bags into the overhead stowage compartment. I then took a seat by the window.

How curious my behavior must have been to anyone watching me!

I touched everything within my reach, smelled and felt all around the seat. Then, I sat down and got back up, repeating this action several times. I was like a little boy. This was my first experience of an airplane, except for having seen the *B-sans* overhead ten years earlier.

Through the window, I watched a plane taxiing toward the runway in the near distance. On my airliner, stewardesses were assisting other passengers who were taking their seats, creating chaos, as some passengers struggled to fit huge pieces of luggage under seats or in overhead compartments.

"Ooi, hayaku shiro," a man grunted, displaying his impatience at having to stand in the aisle holding his bags and waiting for the passenger in front of him to be seated. He shouted again, louder this time.

It seemed I was breathing heavily and perspiring furiously. When I finally felt able to sit in my seat without thought of danger, I took out a pencil and notebook.

Staring into the distance, I entered my internal world. In my mind I saw my last day with Nakamura *Sensei.* Her sweet memories rushed at me like mighty tides against rocks.

The warmth of her breast and her strong, erratic heartbeats mixed with the soft mid-summer breeze rustling her black hair. Her warmth and heartbeats, my head resting against her bosom! I felt like a seed bursting its outer shell to go rocketing into endless orbit.

Then a wave of fear came over me, for I would not see her for the next ten long years. *"Sensei,"* I cried, "No! No! I don't want to leave you!"

"Takashi-kun," I could still hear her tender words, *"Sensei mo samishiku naru wayo. Demo, anata ga wa America ni itte rippani natte kaette korareru made Sensei mo samishi sani makenai de Takshi-san mo Sensei to isshoni ganbari masho ne!* I, too, shall be lonely. But we are going to be strong and we are going to overcome our loneliness."

Her voice filled with strength. "Remember to follow your heart!" Her energy came from deep within her like *aranami,* wild ocean waves. I felt I could last our long years of separation!

"Moshi, moshi! Moshi, moshi!" the voice of a stewardess brought me back to reality.

"Hai." I looked at her face in a daze. Wiping my face with an open hand, I awakened myself, *"Nani ka?*

What is it?" My inquiry shot into a vast vacuum. My eyes focused, but could not see her beauty.

"*Moshi, moshi. Okyaku-san, Shiito beruto o onegai shimasu.*" As she urged me to put on my seatbelt, I noticed the sound of the four engines, and felt the vibrations of the engines and propellers shaking and rattling the entire DC-4.

As I looked out through my tiny window, the midsummer sun was glittering on the wing of the plane. My pencil moved again, slowly but deliberately, adding to the diary I promised Nakamura *Sensei* I would write until I returned to her—as if it would be an eternity!

I cried again, thinking I had succumbed to Japanese social pressures and that, in a few minutes, I would bid a final goodbye to my country. When would I be able to return to my homeland? Must I not return to Japan to reclaim the honorable family name of Tanemori? But there was no assurance of fulfilling my promise of taking revenge on Americans.

I broke the pencil in half, my hands shaking, then dropped the pencil and notebook.

It finally sunk in that I was free from the power of Japanese tradition, my "enemy" in postwar Japan. I had finally escaped the sneers of the Gossip Committee, and, above all, I was no longer under the control of my sister, Satsuko! Perhaps she, too, felt freedom.

No matter how I felt, she would be better off not to live with that Kuroki, a man without spine and without spirit. I was reminded of the saying, "A room without books is like a man without spirit and life." Nevertheless, she could do whatever she wanted with that slimy slug!

Where I was going was not, by any stretch of the imagination, a land where people opened their arms an *Oyanashigo*, a fatherless child, lost in the waves of a human ocean. Although I had been told by a Japanese interpreter that America was a Christian nation where many immigrants had found a haven and had made it their home, finding prosperity, like a boxer I put my guard high, swearing never to trust anyone.

Suddenly reality struck me—I was on the way to America! Watching several American GIs taking their seats,

I recalled seeing how two GIs had abused a Japanese woman in Kobe during the spring of 1954. I could hear the woman's screams for help drowned out by the soldiers' laughter as they made "sport" of the incident.

I clenched my fists when I saw them, even though they were big and tall and could have squashed me like a fly. Consequently, I found it hard to believe that all Americans would be "helpful friends" in time of need.

I wanted to believe America would be better for me than my remaining behind in Japan without an education or a respectable name. I wondered about my chance for "survival," a big enough challenge without the burdens of finding a fortune and fulfilling my vows of vengeance.

The plane started taxiing. My head snapped to the window, which seemed to have fogged from the humidity, blurring the view. I tried, without success, to wipe the glass clean. Momentarily, I would say *"so long"* to Japan, and I wanted a last glimpse of my homeland, no matter how hostile it had been to me as I was growing up. I wanted the image of Mt. Fuji burned into my memory!

But it was not the window, but my tears, running uncontrollably, which distorted my view.

"Why am I crying?" I asked myself over and over.

Fear returned, sending chills down my spine. I was only 18 years old and utterly alone, with no one to lean on.

Some passengers shouted for joy as the plane taxied and gained speed. The airliner shook and it seemed the wings would come off. Then the nose of the plane lifted, forcing my body back into the seat. Anxiety over the realization that there was no turning back melted into a sense of relief.

The sky was blue as far as I could see, and my vision seemed endless! The airliner circled widely over the city, and for the last time I saw a snowcapped Mt. Fuji standing majestically—a symbol of grace, of beauty, and of the strength of Japan.

"Sayonara, Fuji-san! Ju-nen shitara kanarazu kaette kurukara sore made Nakamura Sensei o yoroshiku mamotte kudasai. Sayonara! Good-bye Mt. Fuji! I shall

return after ten long years! Be sure to take good care of Nakamura *Sensei* for me. So long!" I shouted as loud as I could.

I did not care what other people thought of me. Soon, the entire island of Japan, floating like a cluster of emeralds, drowned in the ocean, disappearing from sight.

I took a pencil once again and I wrote a poem, *"Nishiki o Kazatte Kaeru made Makeru na.* However often I falter, I shall rise again and again; no matter what, until I return to my birth place with glory!"

In my giant leap into an unknown world, I had burned all my bridges, except for my memories of my Father and his gravesite, and my dear love of Nakamura *Sensei.*

Then I recorded the last word in my diary of my life in Japan: *"Revenge!"* It took the entire page.

I closed this chapter of my life, and started a new chapter. I closed my eyes, the image of Mt. Fuji lingering on.

"Moshi, Moshi."

I was awakened by the persistent voice of a stewardess, who grabbed my shoulder.

"Moshi, moshi okyaku-san," she repeated, insisting I put my seat belt on again.

Stretching and yawning, I inquired, *"Ah, Gomen nasai. Honto ni yoku nemashita. Mo-o Amerika desuka?* Was I a sleepy head? Where am I? Am I in America?"

"We are preparing to land in the Aleutian Islands," explained the stewardess. "You might say we are in America."

The stewardess' cynical tone of voice amused me.

"Why are we landing here?" I asked.

"We will be here for a short while, just enough time to refuel before we fly to Alaska."

"Alaska?" My boisterous voice startled the stewardess and the passenger next to me. "You mean A—A—Alaska, that place of white giant polar bears?"

She smiled, checked my seatbelt, and then retreated behind the curtain.

I quickly picked up my pencil and diary and recorded my impressions of the Aleutian Islands. All I saw was flat, brown land, and no living thing. Except for a few distant smokestacks rising from buildings, the entire landscape seemed frozen, dead. I could almost hear the cutting cold gusts of wind, whipping down the airfield.

Half a dozen workers wearing heavy parkas and gloves approached the plane. On my left, I saw a fuel truck rolling nearer.

I wrote down more of my impressions while the plane was refueling, noting even images in the clouds—animals, birds, and human faces.

Shortly after taking off from the Aleutians, the frozen brownish-gray landscape disappeared, replaced by dark ocean.

Hours seemed to tick by slowly as my eyes returned to a normal shape and size—little, tiny, sliver-like shapes, no longer conveying what was in my heart.

The sound of the four prop-engines intermittently drowned out the snores of the passenger next to me. I looked at him frequently, between snores. His mouth was wide open; and I could almost see his throat. I wondered how he could be so relaxed, to find such deep sleep. Or was he drowning himself from the fear of high flight?

Hours passed, and when we landed at Anchorage, Alaska, we were surrounded by inky darkness. Countless twinkling stars conveyed an incomprehensible depth and space. The runway was outlined by streams of lights like strings of pearls.

While our giant bird rested her wings, passengers were allowed to roam the confines of the airport for an hour. Then we left Anchorage just as we had come in—like a thief in the night.

I continued writing about my journey, wondering where all the white polar bears were hiding from sight!

A new day dawned as we approached the city of Seattle, Washington. My eyes lit up at its magnificent colors. Oh, how beautiful the rainbow was! No! It couldn't be? I rubbed my eyes again.

How could it be so? I had never seen such an intensity of color. I must have been dreaming. All the rainbows I had seen before were half-moon shapes. Looking from the window, the brilliant sun reflected in the blue sky, painting a complete rainbow circle. Nobody had ever told me of this magical occurrence!

I quickly jotted down notes and drawings. The seven colors perfectly complemented each other, blending to represent "harmony," "peace," "circle"—just as in the written Japanese language character *heiwa*.

On the next leg of our flight, we landed at, then left the Portland, Oregon airport. The sun was huge, reddish-orange, reflected in the ocean below. Massive white clouds seemed like a cotton blanket, making me feel as if I was floating.

My heart was overwhelmed when I heard the Captain announce that the next stop would be San Francisco. I recall that he added—"We will be there in no time at all."

Leaving Portland, I glued my eyes to the window, searching for the Golden Gate Bridge. The hour seemed so long.

"Oh, that's *Kinmon-kyo!*" The Golden Gate Bridge was in sight, spanning two points, stretching out with mighty arms, as if welcoming me!

"But why isn't it a gold bridge, instead of a reddish color?" I murmured to myself.

The same stewardess approached once more. I patted my stomach, showing her I was wearing the seat belt. We landed at San Francisco International Airport.

Was I a tiny midget?

Everyone I saw, men and women, seemed extra-large, like mighty giants. They stood tall, as though every ceiling of every room was built for them. Their hair was blonde and kinky, like giant balls of cobweb, untidily plopped on top of their heads.

Their hands were large forklifts capable of holding the world, with bony fingers so long that they didn't need a bamboo spear to catch fish. As for their arms, did someone stretch them? They could surely reach between west and east, wrapping around the earth.

"Watch out!" I shouted. "Look at the size of their shoes. Stupendous!" I would be crushed to powder, buried in the crust of the earth, with no identifiable bones, if they stepped on me.

Out of their mouths came the most incoherent and irrational sounds I had heard since the day I met that giant American government official at Kotachi Village.

And there were not just one or two of them. They numbered in the hundreds and were everywhere! As I tried to avoid one, I found another standing before me, looking down at me.

I felt as if I was surrounded by ferocious giants, who all looked the same to me. Thinking about the *Gai-jin,* Americans, I quickly rationalized that their peculiar language and enigmatic culture had been created by the Devil solely to confuse me and frustrate me from fulfilling the vow I had made to my Father. I had indeed landed in the midst of my true "enemy."

My *Seiko* watch, on my right wrist, told me it was shortly after noon. I was informed through an interpreter that there would be a two-and-a-half-hour layover before we left for our final destination, Fresno.

"Two and one half hours to 'kill' at San Francisco Airport before flying to another airport?" I murmured. I couldn't afford to sit around here. "It is not for me to 'kill' time—time certainly would kill me, if I didn't watch out!"

I had never had the luxury of "time" while growing up, let alone, to sit in an airport, doing nothing. Every minute, every second had counted, just to survive in the atomic ashes of my homeland.

There was no time to allow my heart to relax. I felt as if I was sitting on a lookout point, watching every movement and listening to the many "babblings" of a foreign tongue. Nor could I allow anyone to come closer to me, lest I fall in my weakness. I had to put up high and thick walls around myself. And I felt that I should be walking backward, peeking over my shoulder, just to be aware of any enemy who might be sneaking up on me from behind.

Ha! I chuckled, envisioning myself walking backward.

"Why do so many of you look at me as if I have a dirty face? Or haven't you ever seen a young Japanese man?" I said loudly in Japanese.

As I was anxious to reach the streets paved with gold, and the money trees planted at every corner, I looked at my wristwatch again. I put it to my ear, hearing its tick-tock.

"How slowly time is ticking!" I thought.

I pulled the picture of Nakamura *Sensei* from my pocket, imagining I was talking to her, as if she was beside me! My voice suddenly quivered with loneliness.

"No! She is not here. I am all alone in this strange place. She is not here for me to lean my head against her bosom. I am the only one, and I must stand strong," I cried out, wiping my wet nose and tears in one motion.

"*Sensei! Koko wa San Francisco desu yo. Yo-o ku mite kudasai ne.*" I swung her picture around for her to see San Francisco.

"*Mo shibaraku desu. Kyo no go-go niwa kanarazu mokuteki chi ni tsuki masu.*" I told her we were where the streets were paved with gold, and where money trees were planted at every street corner.

How strange it was that everyone seemed preoccupied with themselves. Some people just sat on the benches; some were standing and talking; many were going or coming. Yet one thing was clear—no one seemed concerned for another. I was a Japanese man, all alone in this strange place, and no one said "hello," cast warm eyes on me, or offered me a smile.

Suddenly, I felt an urge within my body. I looked at my wristwatch to find that I still had more than an hour before the plane would board.

"No, I don't think I can wait that long." I decided to venture out. "Of course, I am confident. All I have to do is find it."

I walked straight down the corridor and came to the end of the hallway, where a stairway led down to the first floor. I bent over to look down the stairway and wasn't sure what I was looking at.

I retraced my steps until I passed where I had been standing.

"No!" I didn't see what I was looking for. "All right!" I said to myself, "I am going to find it!"

I walked back to the stairway, then awkwardly down to the first floor. I looked at every door on the first floor to see what I was looking for. I looked anxiously down both sides of the corridor.

"Maybe I missed it as I passed by?" Climbing the stairway once again, I started "dribbling" between my legs.

"Hold it tight! Tighten up muscle," I shouted to myself. By this time, I was walking down the corridor pressing my legs together. Feeling ready to burst, I held my abdomen, walking slowly and deliberately, to keep control.

"Why are you looking at me like that?" I shouted in Japanese to a boy who was pointing his bony finger at me and looking up to his father, jabbering in an unknown tongue. Suddenly, I noticed several other people were also watching me. Two women, covering their mouths with one hand and pointing at me with the other, shook their heads with disapproval.

"Doshita to yuno ka omae tachi no baka mono?"

Had anybody any concern for others, or had they understood my Japanese, they would have known my anguish. My misery increased by the minute, turning to excruciating pain. I felt my face turning reddish, getting hot.

"Please someone show me where I need to go—I need go to *benjo!*" I shouted in Japanese.

How pitiful it was to find myself unable to get what I wanted, unable even to ask for it. I crossed my legs a different way, started down the corridor again, and felt a warm sensation running down my legs as I made one last turn down another corridor.

"Oya, Okashii na?" I scratched my head. Suddenly I noticed something strange.

"Did I miss it before?" I wondered. "What's going on there?"

I saw many men and boys disappearing through a door, while others came out through the same door. I looked in the other direction to another door and saw a parade of women and girls doing likewise.

I inched my way to the closest door, and a whiff of air unmistakably told me I had found the right place.

"*Hayaku, hayaku!* Hurry, please, please!" I pleaded, waiting my turn.

"*Ouuh!*" I let out a great sigh of relief. Then the pain subsided as I stood, one hand against the wall, releasing fluid like a fireman's hose. I almost crumpled to the floor when emptied.

I'd never experienced such relief in my life.

"You! Americans!" I shouted. "How stupid could you be? Why can't you do like the English people and put a sign on the door, WC, for "Water Closet!"

I didn't understand Americans plastering "Men" or "Women" or "Ladies" or "Gentlemen" signs on restroom doors. No one had ever told me about them.

A cynical smile crossed my face, as I remembered how I had cheated to get a passing grade in English class during Junior High, without learning anything. Who said the most important thing was to do whatever necessary to get what you want? Did I not graduate?

Later that afternoon we finally reached the Fresno airport. There excitement was in the air because we were on solid ground. And I was expecting the answer to my quest for gold-paved streets and money trees. My *Seiko* wristwatch had kept its record—we arrived 38 long hours after leaving Haneda, Tokyo.

I saw a dark-complexioned man, whose looks revealed that he was of Japanese descent. He was running around like a headless chicken, and definitely seemed to be a farmer. Acting as though he was a leader, he was instructing others. Every instruction received a response of "*Shooo, bozu*" ("Sure, Boss," I thought.)

Suddenly, a middle-aged man who had also flown from Haneda emerged as though he, too, was someone of importance. I thought him to be nothing but obnoxious in his appearance and high-minded behavior.

If he was not stupid, he certainly displayed his ignorance of English. All I knew of English consisted of a few words, such as *"I uum loost."* (I am lost.) *"Hai, Ai connot speeek Enguliesh."* (I cannot speak English.) *"Ai don no Enlguliesh."* (I don't know English.) *"Ai NO! I no understand Enguliesh."* (I have no understanding of English.) *"Sankyu you"* (Thank you.) *"Ai uum hunglee."* (I am hungry.) *"Mee, Japaneeze."* (I am Japanese.) and *"My neimu izu Tanemori."* (My name is Tanemori). Everything else was "Greek" to me!

Every unintelligent sound came out of this man's mouth and was repeated several times. He made some long introductory speech, which I cared nothing to hear. My concern was my destination.

"Doko e tsure te ikuno desu ka?" I boldly shouted. "Where are you taking me?"

At last we were led with our belongings outside the airport. A short distance away were three old trucks covered with tattered canvas. I looked around to find the "end" of earth, and all I could see was flat distance.

"Where am I?" I wondered.

There was nothing to indicate I had arrived at the place where I would accomplish the goals I had set in Japan.

Then I chuckled, for the dark brown farmer, who I learned later was "Mr." Kawasaki, the camp director, began to speak to us in English. Except for a few recognizable but antiquated Japanese phrases here and there, he revealed himself as an educated man.

With him were several men, two of them elderly, Japanese-like men, and one who was obviously what I called a Yankee. He was a white man who stood head and shoulders taller than the rest.

They all had one common denominator—forced smiles on their faces. I instinctively erected large walls around myself, for their looks told me I had better not trust them at all.

Whether or not this was a conscious effort, I was already building resentment against people who acted like they were "somebody."

"Am I forced to subject myself to these people? It looks like I started on the wrong foot!" I chuckled. I was getting a stomach ache, an unsettled feeling toward them. We were told we were in Fresno, the heart of California.

"Is this America?" My mental response was very negative.

"Sah, hayaku nimotsu o torack ni motte ike, Hey, you, take your stuff to that truck," one of the men shouted at me.

One man on the truck and another on the ground were waiting, and they quickly took my two duffel bags and threw them onto the truck.

"Where are you taking my duffel bags? Those are all my possessions!" I shouted in Japanese.

Whether or not they understood, the man on the ground motioned me to get out of his way and to get on the next truck, while continuing to throw the suitcases and boxes of the man behind me onto the truck.

I couldn't help but sense the exuberant energy the others were displaying. I questioned why I was not as willing as they were to submit to the directions.

"Do they care to know what is really happening?" I wondered. "No one has told us where they are taking us."

When all the luggage was finally loaded, Mr. Kawasaki gave a signal to his men. We were hurriedly led like sheep to the second and third trucks.

"Oh, what a welcome sight!" I uttered, disgustedly. I was directed, like the others, to get in the back of the canvas-covered truck, and to sit on the wooden benches fastened to the bed of the truck. "Why this canvas, covering the truck? Are they trying to hide us from someone?"

The sun overhead seemed twice as big as the one I was used to seeing in Japan. It glared down beastly hot, and I felt as though my eyes were being seared when I tried to look at it.

The air was dry and dusty. I noticed that my breathing was faster and shallower, as I tried to get all the air I needed. I felt as if my throat was cracking from its outer walls.

Suddenly, undeniably, the sensation of August 6, 1945, returned. I was under debris, gasping for air. I felt I was choking with each breath as the word "Revenge" became focused in my mind and heart.

Not a moment too soon, the last person got on the truck, and a man pulled down the canvas, like a door, closing the back of the truck. The only light came from two small windows in the canvas, one on each side.

An unthinkable thought flashed by.

"Are these people trying to smuggle us somewhere? Are we being hurled onto the truck like cattle, to be taken some place where no one would ever know we had been sold? Or are we like sheep being sent to a slaughterhouse?"

These were the questions that raced through my mind as the truck continued set out for an unknown destination.

"Where are we going?" I asked a man in Japanese.

He just smiled at me as though resigned to his doom.

We rode and rode on a seemingly endless straight road. I smelled dusty air and couldn't see anything from where I sat on the dirty bench. Although several people were sitting by the tiny windows, peeking out, they said nothing about what they saw.

By the light sneaking through a tear in the canvas, it appeared we were heading southward on a road which I would later come to know as Highway 99. After some time, we turned off the main highway and headed east.

It seemed several hours had passed when the truck finally came to a stop. Two men came around to pull open the canvas on all sides. What I saw from the flatbed of the truck was beyond words to describe—groves of grapes and grapes and more grapes.

We climbed down and the trucks moved on. I was in awe of kilometer after kilometer of vineyards, on both sides of the road, all so neatly parceled, and the sun reflecting brightly off the leaves and the ground. It was an awesome sight!

Even if I had known the superlatives of every language, I don't think I could have used them to adequately describe the hugeness of the earth, *Tai-riku*, continental, through which we were driving.

America! My mind and heart were captivated by the greatness of the land! It was inconceivable that the earth should stretch forever, disappearing beyond the endless edge.

I was totally awed and my heart momentarily forgot the reason I had come to America, the land of "my enemy." How could my eyes see the landscape so innocently?

When I rediscovered myself, a pencil was in my hand and my spirit was documenting its first impressions of the land of America:

Iridescent Green Carpet

How long had we been riding this old, rickety-split
                                                  truck,
Covered with brown tarp to keep the sun from
                                            looking upon us;
How fast was the truck rickety-splitting
In the midst of a waveless ocean of green
By the disappearing of telephone poles
Standing alongside the road?

How strange it seemed, the earth being held
                                          motionless,
In the midst of a green ocean,
Or spinning its own axle like a "kaze-guruma"
                                    (wind mill/pinwheel),
Seeming "ever-green."
We seemed to stand still in the midst of a seamless
                                          and endless
Iridescent Green Carpet.

Chapter Two: A Migrant Labor Camp

I am like a tadpole in the ocean,
Enclosed by the deepest blue water.
Where does all the water come from?
Where is it going--the endless journey?
Will it ever find a resting-place?

I look around and see no one to reach out to.
My constant companion is but blue water,
Going in one direction and returning another way.
I never saw and I never felt the same water again.
"Take me," I cried out, only to hear my voice echo
                                                    "lost."

I look to the blue sky yonder, mirroring the Ocean
                                                    below,
As if they were twins, merging into oneness in the
                                                    distance,
Where I cannot go, or reach out to them.
Suddenly, I am caught up in the fear of the unknown,
As I find myself alone in this Migrant Labor Camp.

T HE HOT wind whipped dust-laden air in front of a
migrant labor camp. The place was barren, except for a
hillside where tall trees hid several white rectangular
structures, painted, but worn and ghostlike.

I hadn't the foggiest idea what was unfolding, but as
I began to size things up, I felt like I would have dry heaves.
My stomach knotted with fear and sensed a sort of
impending doom. I felt like a fish caught in a net and
thrown on dry ground.

"Oh my God! What had I done to deserve this?"

In the *Samurai* code, a son could avenge his father;
and while this was my duty and obligatory honor, I quickly
had to search my soul.

I cried out. "Why, Buddha, have you failed so far to
help me when I needed you? Have I been so stupid and
hardheaded I didn't hear the whispering voices? Perhaps,
my sister Satsuko was right? No! I shall not give her the

pleasure of thinking, even for one-hundredth of a second, that she was right with that nonsense!"

The other men around me seemed happy to be arriving at the camp. My heart was pained to see my two duffel bags being thrown onto the dirt, along with other luggage. At least Nakamura *Sensei*'s pictures were safe with me. They had never left my sight, remaining close to my heart. I double-checked them by patting my chest.

I still couldn't believe or accept that, instead of landing in a place with life's conveniences and luxuries, we were in the midst of what looked like a graveyard stacked with dirty white crypts.

"Where are all those promises of the American Government?" I asked, beginning to feel like a fish attracted by glittering bait, only to fall "hook, line and sinker" to a Japanese-American now revealed as a "go-betweener."

Later I learned he was known as a broker who sold and bought modern slaves for migrant labor camps. Had I sold my soul for thirty pieces of silver to this man and his scheme?

"Is this the land of dreams and opportunity for which millions of immigrants, uprooting themselves from the four corners of earth, had risked their lives in search of new horizons?" I asked myself.

After being transported to a migrant labor camp in Delano, why should I hold any expectation of fulfilling my vows? As far as I was concerned, I was now "dead" to a Japanese society in which my family once had preeminence. My coming to America was like water spilled over the "dam," beyond the point of no return!

"Nani o guzu guze shite iruno ka?"

A familiar phrase I had heard many times in the fields of Kotachi was directed at me.

My head was spinning like a top, as I felt heat beating down from the sun and rising up from the ground, through my thin tennis shoes. In front of me were newly painted white railroad boxcars, a new "home" for me after having been home to countless immigrants before me.

"Ohy! Omaeda! Hey, you!" a billy-goat-gruff voice barked as I felt a hand grab my shoulder.

"*Itai!* Ouch!" I screamed as I turned, looking up to a man who towered over me. This giant, with his reddish-brown skin and hairy arms, was obviously not one of us! Where did he learn such Japanese?

"*Omae wa Tanemori ka?* Hey, are you Tanemori?" asked another man my own height. He shook a bony finger in my face. He was older, grubby, his face and hands cooked by the sun and weathered. His skin reminded me of the bottom of a dry lake baked hard by summer heat. His voice indicated that he was taller than I was!

I followed his orders for several of us to go to one of the ghostly railroad boxcars.

"Oh boy, we're in America!" someone shouted in Japanese.

How I pitied him. I didn't join in with the cackling voices of the others. I hadn't sacrificed my life to come to a dust bowl camp paved with American fool's gold.

Yet I was like an ant that had fallen into the hole of a giant anteater. No matter how hard I tried to climb up the shifting soil of the hole, I would be unsuccessful in escaping. I was doomed forever!

"What is this?" I asked one worker in Japanese as I looked around the boxcar.

"That is your new American home." he replied dryly.

"No! It can't be. This has to be temporary." I said. "Surely we will arrive tomorrow at our destination."

I could hear a silent cry deep down in my soul, "Takashi, be strong! Don't ever forget who you are, let alone why you left Japan!"

I was shocked by the bleak surroundings and what appeared to be several older Japanese men sitting outside in rocking chairs, men who should have retired many years before to take care of grandchildren in a peaceful place.

My legs were shaking as I approached one old man. Speaking in Japanese he said, "You look like another sucker who was allured by the smooth talk of a blankety-blank man."

"Excuse me, sir," I asked, "could you tell me where I am?"

"Where are you?" He burst into laughter. "Young man ..." He sat up in his rocking chair, as though stretching his crooked *sebona*, spine, "... you mean to tell me you don't know where you are?"

As if I was deaf, he shouted, "You are in America! Ha, ha, ha! Yes, sir! You came to the right place. This is what we call America, the land of the hopeless and dreamless!"

I saw unspoken pain and loneliness in his anguished face. Looking beneath his wrinkles and brown baked skin, I searched for words to comfort him, but I couldn't speak to relieve his pain.

I asked the man about the streets paved with gold, about the money trees planted on every corner.

Other workers standing nearby burst into laughter.

"Oh, how many times we've heard that story, over and over again. Once you find yourself in this place, there is no hope of escape. It's like a death camp without hope. There is no outside beyond the unseen walls around you. We pick fruit for Americans. That's how we've survived."

This man led me to one of the boxcars where I saw eight migrant workers inside. Each of us would claim an area. As I was the last to claim his space, I had no choice but the final bunk-bed, by the entrance and covered in dust. Two tiny orange-crate-like boxes served as a dresser by the foot of each bed. The dust was so thick it clung like glue to the wire springs of the bed.

"These are army bunk-beds. Once, GIs slept in them," someone spluttered contemptuously.

As I looked at the others, I scratched my head. They seemed to have accepted the fact they were here to start a new life.

I went to my "space" to sit quietly on the edge of the bunk-bed, where my heart rehearsed the last fleeting moment when I made my promise to Nakamura *Sensei*, "No matter what, and however many times I may falter, I shall rise again until I return to my birthplace with glory!"

These words had become a sharp, double-edged sword!

My co-workers were already making their assigned spaces "home." Some plastered pictures on the wall. One man in his mid-thirties turned an orange-crate into a "shrine" to worship his "sun-goddess." Yet another put a statute of Buddha on the box and lit *senko*, incense, filling the boxcar with the aroma. Although I didn't understand his chanting, it was obvious he was expressing gratitude for his safe arrival in America.

Smoke from the incense and cigarettes soon filled the boxcar, and I quickly grabbed a notebook and ran outside. Rounding the corner of a boxcar, I saw a line of workers. I assumed they had just returned from the field and were, for some reason, stretching single-file from the pump towards a dilapidated house a short distance away.

"*Konnichi wa,*" I asked a grubby man who walked by. "What are those lines for?"

He turned to me, as if annoyed by my question, wiped his face with a white towel now gray with dust, and answered, "They are all lining up for their turn."

"What do you mean, for their turn?"

"They're all waiting for the modern convenience!" he responded. Then he added sarcastically, "Don't you know anything about an outhouse?"

Someone yelled at me, "Out-howzuu?"

I had never heard the word before, so I asked, "What do you mean by Out-howzuu?"

"Hey!" He shouted to several people standing in the line, "This little boy has never heard of an outhouse!"

"Out-howzuu?" someone else mimicked, causing workers to explode into laughter.

"What's so funny about what I asked?" I challenged the grubby old man, then turned towards several cackling men who were equally as grubby.

"Well, it looks like we've got our job cut out for us. We need to initiate him. He needs a crash course on the lifestyle here in this camp. Ha, ha, ha, ha!"

I returned to my boxcar, shaking my head—"Out-howzuu?"

"Clang! Clang! Clang!" Startling sounds suddenly sparked commotion in my boxcar and the others, sending all the workers stampeding outside. Sitting on the edge of my bed by the doorway, I barely escaped being trampled.

"Hold your horses!" I shouted, getting up and rushing out to see what was going on.

Workers were forming a line and shuffling toward a long building in the center of the campsite. To my surprise, some of the newcomers were already in the line. The clanging started again.

"It's chow time!" someone shouted.

"Chow time, Whhat's zaat?"

I gathered we were heading toward what is known as a mess hall.

The sight triggered memories of Hiroshima, as if a movie reel had started—stark images of thousands of people fleeing the inferno, accompanied by the smell of smoke and burning flesh and the buzzing of black flies. I remembered the long line of people who had reached a small village where they were offered rice balls and cups of tea.

I heard despairing remarks from workers heading to the mess hall. "Well, I hope we have better things to eat tonight!" someone snickered with disgust in Japanese. "We've been eating pancakes, pancakes and more pancakes. And potatoes, potatoes, and more potatoes. And there wasn't enough butter either."

"Oh, well!" said one worker to a man who seemed very frail, "We better get in line before someone else gets our share."

"I heard from the field foreman that we're having something special for the newcomers' sake!" said the frail man.

"What special?" someone wanted to know.

"That's right! Yeah. I bet the foreman was teasing me. Or, who knows, he might be telling the truth. Maybe we're having steak because of the new workers from Japan."

"A steak? That must be mis-steak? Ha, ha, ha!" came a cynical laugh.

"What you don't know won't hurt you!" said another. "I feel sorry for these new workers. They are getting a steak all right."

"Oh, boy! What bait 'Mr.' Kawasaki puts out for these innocent workers!" one of the old, worn-out workers blurted.

"*Shiranu ga Hotoke da.* Not even Buddha knows what's going on here!" someone shouted with sarcasm.

When I reached the hall, I saw long tables lined up wall-to-wall. Each table was accented with salt and pepper shakers, and tall glasses which held used chopsticks. But most of the workers were using forks and knifes.

Each table was also set with two large bowls filled with cooked vegetables. This looked like a "boarding room" style of eating, where one's share of food was determined by one's reach. I hoped it wouldn't be a conflict of manners and courtesy versus starvation.

Suddenly, I saw myself as a *Samurai*. I would not conduct myself like a pig, "digging in" as the others were, even though I might be starving. I wondered how long I would last with such a high-minded approach.

While cautiously reaching out for food, I carefully sipped an iced tea, touching it to the tip of my tongue to make sure there was no "foreign" taste that caused my tongue to "tingle." I wanted to make sure I wasn't being poisoned.

I kept my eyes peeled as a piece of meat was flopped onto my plate by a server. I cautiously waited until others started indulging in the steak, watching their expressions to make sure the food was safe.

Noise and more noise! Inexplicable excitement had been created in the mess hall. Yet I couldn't share the mood.

Someone called for a toast—"*kampai!*" I supposed there was no reason for me not to join in. After all, there were many of us who, for one reason or another, had left home to start a new life in the strange land. I had to believe these people had also given up their roots to seek a better life in America. They too had emigrated here for the gold-paved streets and money trees!

Whatever our reason for emigrating, we shared a common courage to have uprooted ourselves from our homeland. And yet I felt different, in that my heart was filled with the spirit of REVENGE!

As the evening slipped into the wee hours of morning, the drinking seemed to get out of hand. Some people moved from table to table, their voices growing louder and louder until they seemed to be shouting. While the *kampai* was started as celebration of the first night, I surmised the real celebration was over the steak.

"*Shizukani shinasai!*"

I heard clanging. It was "Mr." Kawasaki banging on an empty canteen to get our attention. He then told us to shut up.

"What an ugly-looking face!" I said to myself. Something about his shifty eyes told me I would be getting into trouble with him, if and when we met face-to-face. I felt, even before I got to know him, that he couldn't be trusted.

"Mr." Kawasaki got our attention, but not before I had seen through him as a man who was self-righteous, arrogant, haughty, and conceited. He tried to hide it all behind a smile. I wondered if I was the only one who saw him this way. But deciding I should give him the benefit of the doubt, I silently dared him to be a nice guy, to knock me dead with kindness.

He tried to introduce a *Gai-jin* to us, a man I supposed was important and who wanted to extend a greeting.

This welcoming speech seemed aimed at giving us great hope of prosperity. It was received irritably by the older workers, who seemed to know what would take place tonight, minute by minute, without a script. Most of the workers had an attitude of "Here it goes again. We might wait a thousand years before all these promises come true."

I considered the talk nothing but stand-up-comedy. "Mr." Kawasaki, trying to interpret for us, sounded as if he was from the Tower of Babel. There was a confusion of tongues as he spoke half English, half heavily-accented Japanese. I had trouble understanding what he was saying and had no idea whether he was translating accurately, since I had no understanding of what the *Gai-jin* was saying. I just wished he would stop his gibberish so that I wouldn't need to find a gracious way to leave before I made a fool of myself.

"All we want from you is your faithful commitment to work: an honest day's work for an honest day's pay."

Some workers mimicked and parroted, without rehearsal, "Mr." Kawasaki's message. I had no problem with an honest day's work, but I wondered how far he would be willing to go to help us realize all we had been promised in exchange for our hard labor under the beastly hot summer sun.

I forced myself to applaud when he finished his talk. I felt like a slave who had been sold to the highest bidder, and questioned the sanity of the others who had arrived with me. How could they be happy with the events of the evening? Many toasts—*kampai*—had been meaningless. What price would I have to pay to retain my soul?

"Say, *chibi*, little shrimp," a voice gravely called to me.

"Is someone calling me a *chibi*?" I asked myself.

A reddish-brown giant suddenly appeared.

"*Kimi wa dare ka?*" This huge sun-roasted American stood tall, looking down at me.

If he wanted me, I thought, he should have had the courtesy to sit down beside or in front of me. What kind of fool demonstrated his stupidity by talking down, figuratively and literally, in such funny Japanese? I pretended I didn't see or hear him.

After he repeated his Japanese, he grabbed my shoulder and asked, "*Omae wa dare ka?*"

The contact didn't go well with me. Instinctively, I brushed away his hand.

"Don't you ever touch me! And get your blankety-blank hands off!" is what I really wanted to shout at him in Japanese. I formed saliva in my mouth, ready to spit at him!

Instead, cowardly, all I mastered up in Japanese was, "What do you want?"

"*Kisama wa namaiki-dazo!* You punk—saucy!" was his angry response. He obviously didn't like my brush-off.

The man reminded me of my *nomisuke*, drunken uncle. He lacked graciousness; he should have introduced himself before barging in on me; most importantly, he seemed to demand respect from me.

"As a first impression is usually right, I bet a wooden nickel he isn't worthy of my respect, regardless of who he is in this camp!" I thought to myself.

I didn't know until just before the evening was over that this man was the field foreman, who could be an obnoxious bully over the workers if he so decided.

Darkness encircled me with an eerie feeling that first night at the migrant labor camp. I returned to my boxcar, picked up pencil and notebook, and began to write the first day's entry of the diary I had promised to Nakamura *Sensei*. I had a long cry of loneliness and mixed emotions, over which I had no control, and tears spilled onto the pages. I finally managed to close my eyes and sleep.

I was awakened by pain throughout my entire body, from my back and neck, to my arms and legs. I had never felt such pain before, as if someone had hit me with a two-hundred-pound sledgehammer

I grabbed my head and held it between my legs, then ran outside, disoriented, my equilibrium out of kilter. The brilliant sun, larger than any I had ever seen, was already beating down on the ground of the camp. Once again I recalled the heat blasting the City of Hiroshima, engulfing me. Heat waves rose from the roofs of the boxcars.

As I gazed around, my stomach felt unfathomed, and my hands were sweating from fears of the unknown. An awesome feeling of being lost gushed from deep inside my soul, darkening the brilliant sun.

Gazing beyond the campsite I could see only waves and more waves of green, distorted by the heat of mid-morning sun. I was an insignificant insect in the midst of this green ocean.

"*Omae wa nani o shite iru noka?* What are you doing here?" I turned toward the voice to find out who was speaking to me. Seeing "Mr." Kawasaki, I showed some pretense of respect for the sake of his position as camp director.

He glanced at me, inquiring what I was doing here. "What do you mean, what am I doing here?" I responded angrily but silently. "I'd like to know myself! I'm here because I was transported here."

I had already concluded that many of the migrant workers were nothing but a flock of turkeys, following the one who dropped the bread crumbs.

The moment I saw "Mr." Kawasaki's eyes I knew that he was not to be trusted, that he was not a man of great integrity. He was just effective at "pulling the wool" over the eyes of others.

Another thought crossed my mind. Either these people were like rats, following a mystical melody I couldn't hear, or perhaps they had mastered the principle of *yowatari,* how to "live" by what was perceived, as practiced by my former colleagues at Maruhachi Company in Kobe.

"Young man," another older worker shouted, "We have the first meeting, down at the mess hall." I understood his Japanese clearly as he spoke to me.

"Dare ka shiran keredo, kimi wa genki ga nasa soda no?"

He seemed to express genuine concern when he observed my obvious look of disgust. *"Ah, Oji-san, shinsetsu ni arigato."*

I bowed slightly to display respect, expressing my heart for the concern he had shown me. His baked-brown, weather-beaten face smiled. Deep facial wrinkles indicated his maturity, his wiry hands many years of hard labor in the field. His dark brown deep-set eyes were still bivalent.

"Shitsurei shimashita. Boku wa Tanemori desu. Korekara wa dozo yoroshiku onegai itashimasu."

I introduced myself, requesting *amae,* favoritism, from him. Then, I bowed again, deeply, to display my sincerity.

"Ah! Tanemori ka!"

He too bowed in a formal Japanese greeting, filling the void of my hesitation to shake his hand. That struck my fancy.

"Ojisan wa ...?"

"Oh, washi no namae wa no 'Kazutoshi' ja." The man told me he was known as *"Oyaji-san"* (an *oyaji* is an aged man who has earned respect due to his wisdom). I was impressed that this man spoke the dialect of the people of Hiroshima. I sensed a smile in his voice.

Hurriedly taking my hand, he urged me to accompany him to the meeting.

I was awakened the next morning by a clanging akin to cowbells. The sound jolted the labor camp, even as the sun remained in slumber.

As I rubbed my eyes and tried to orient myself, through the screen door I saw the weathered face of Oji-san, as he meandered towards what I now knew was the outhouse. A soiled and worn towel was draped over his shoulder. I wondered how many years he had risen to the clang of cowbells.

Most of the newcomers, oddly, were already up. They seemed ready to go anywhere and to do anything, as if ready to jump off a cliff or be led without resistance to a slaughterhouse.

"Atarazu soshite sawaraze. . . ka!"

It might be safer for me to ride the waves until I saw a clear turning of the tide! There was excitement among the newly-arrived migrant workers; they chatted with each other like chicken hatchlings. But I was very apprehensive about what the day might bring.

After finishing breakfast, we were given instructions. Groups of workers were to ride on the trucks. Directed to the third truck, I sensed that I was being silently herded onboard as a prisoner. Looking around to see if anyone felt the same way, I suspected nobody did.

The trucks left the camp obscured in swirling dust. The dust turned the rising sun a deep, reddish-orange color, making it reminiscent of the *hino-maru*, Japanese flag, although it was much larger.

The road disappeared into the dust as the truck traveled to an unknown destination. When it came to a halt, we were in the midst of a never-ending iridescent green carpet. I wondered if we had been driven in a circle only to return to where we had started.

"Everybody get off!"

I carefully climbed down, making sure of my footing.

Someone yelled, "Hey, you. Jump off ..."

Startled, I shouted back, just as someone grabbed my short legs, trying to pull me down.

"Jump, you short-legged Jap!" one of the workers ribbed me as others laughed.

The ground was way, way down. I couldn't tell whether the foreman had grabbed my legs as his way of helping me, but I didn't at all appreciate the gesture. I made a flash decision to always keep one eye on the foreman when he was around.

We gathered around the foreman, whose name I learned was Joel, while "Mr." Kawasaki tried his best to interpret and describe what we would be doing.

I almost laughed at Joel's demonstration. Here was a man more than six feet tall and weighing about 200 pounds, bending over to clutch the root of a vine. He then used a special knife to cut a ring in the bark about five inches from the ground. It was important how deep and how wide the cut was made.

I faintly recalled that villagers near Kotachi who had *budo-en*, vineyards, had done similarly with table grapes before farmers picked them. The ring prevented the grapes' sugar from returning to the ground, keeping the grapes sweeter and hastening their ripening.

Foreman Joel had made some older workers mimic the vine cut he was showing us. Then he noticed my inattentive look, as I recalled my homeland grape experience.

"Hey, you!" Joel shouted toward me.

"Don't you know how to call someone without saying 'Hey you'?" I shouted back in Japanese, showing my contempt. "I have a name. You certainly should call me by it!" I said this loud enough to be heard by all the workers.

I continued, "So you have to use someone else to show what you are trying to teach us, because what you are doing is not good enough, is it?"

I thought to myself, "Twice is fine, but the third and fourth demonstrations, I took as an insult! We certainly are not stupid, and didn't deserve being shown how *not* to perform the work!"

"Just do it right the first time. That's all you need to do!" I shouted in Japanese, loud enough to disrupt the foreman's performance.

"Tanemori!"

"Mr." Kawasaki cautioned me about my bad manners, especially toward the foreman.

I had only questioned the leadership of the foreman. Yet "Mr." Kawasaki acted like a puppet, responding to every tug of the string by the foreman. I felt like vomiting. I detested any man who acted without a spine like a *namako*, slug. I pitied "Mr." Kawasaki.

Now it was time to work the field. As I was short, I had no difficulty getting low to the ground and doing the work. As a matter of fact, I was the smallest worker in the migrant labor camp, and I'd bet you a nickel I was the fastest and best worker in that group, having needed my hands to survive in postwar Japan.

"Hey, shrimp!" the foreman soon called.

I believe that, because of my speed, he was checking to see if I was doing sloppy work. I gave him a dirty look as he went away to check somebody else's work.

The first hour seemed to last a day! It was one thing to work at something new, but another to do the same work constantly. This was especially true if you were nearly on your hands and knees, moving from one vine to the next. I looked at my next row, then behind me. By my count I was about fifteen vines ahead of most of my fellow workers.

I said to myself, "I am going to stand up, stretch and rest until they catch up to me." Considering that reasonable, I plopped down to the ground, stretching my legs while I leaned against a vine. I was practically hidden by the green grape leaves.

"*Ooon! Itai!* Ouch!"

My hands, arms and shoulders ached. As I tried to rub my shoulders I suddenly heard, "Get up lazy hound-dog!" yelled into my ears. Foreman Joel kicked my legs, asking what I thought I was doing.

"You, blankety-blank Jap!" he chided, posturing over me with the authority of muscle.

For safety, I rolled out on the other side of the vine, making sure he couldn't easily grab me.

"You ... shrimp! Sleeping on the job?" he screamed at me.

"Look!" I yelled back, pointing to other workers, who were mostly just catching up to me. "I am not lazy, nor am I a slow worker. Look at my work."

Then the thought dawned on me—were we nothing but prisoners-of-war? If we tried to escape, where would we go but into a vast strange land where we might soon find ourselves carcasses.

I decided not to explain why I was resting, ignoring his agitation except for sending him a smirk. I returned to the back-breaking work of cutting rings.

The rest of the day was precarious. The foreman continued to sneak up on me, trying to catch me goofing off. I lost track of how many times he tried, but I was too smart for him.

I was sometimes working two dozen vines ahead of the others. Then I would very slowly move to the next vine and partially cut a ring, positioning myself comfortably, yet as if I was working hard. I learned how to avoid the foreman's harassment in the first three hours of my first working day in America.

"How about that for a great accomplishment?" I couldn't help my ugly grin. The foreman and I had played a game only to my advantage.

Several weeks later, my first back-breaking job had come to an end. I carefully counted how much I had made toward my first million dollars. How gullible I had been!

Instead of harvesting money trees, I was "picking fruit for my enemy." At this rate, I needed to work for two hundred forty-one years, depositing all my earnings with daily compounded interest, without spending a penny, before I would reach that fabled figure!

I cried out in despair. Uncontrollable feelings of hopelessness had overtaken me.

The bright morning sun no longer boosted my energy; the moon's reflection faded. Muggy breezes wrestling the leaves on the vines no longer carried a scent of hope.

And the face of Nakamura *Sensei*, an image I tried to erase from my heart, appeared and reappeared more often than I could bear.

"Nakamura *Sensei*," I muffled my voice in tears. How I wished for the howling wind of the North, coming down from Rokko-zan, as I realized the hopelessness of my predicament in this strange land.

Irritation and anger grew over the next ten days. We sat around the labor camp without work because the grapes were not quite ready for picking. We were at the mercy of the sun to ripen the grapes on the vine. Each day in the camp without work kept me from making my million dollars, while putting me deeper in debt for food and shelter, because we migrant workers had to pay for room and board whether we could work or not.

I had great trouble understanding the rest of the workers, who seemed carefree. They all appeared to be "having a good time," drinking beer, smoking, telling stories and playing Japanese card games to idle away the days and nights.

The longer I was around them, the more I realized that I didn't belong there. At day's end, I found myself all alone by the edge of camp. The soft, brilliant full moon cast down its shadows. The summer breeze pulled at my lonely, empty heart.

"*Oh, Tanamori-ka! Nande sonnani kurushii kao o shite iruno ka?*" sounded the familiar voice of old Oji-san.

He looked into my face, and asked why I was crying. I looked into his eyes, and said nothing. But my eyes betrayed my inner turmoil.

"Tanemori," he started gruffly, but then gently continued, "*Kono Oji-san wa no okina kata o motte iruzo.*"

He patted his shoulder and said, "Go ahead and cry. It's okay to lean on my shoulder."

"*Oji-san mo no, kimi no yoni wakai toki ga ichido atta-keno.*"

He cast his eyes toward the distance momentarily, remarking that he was once a young man like me. After a deep breath he went on.

"*Iron na samishi hibi mo soshsite kanashi, hibi mo takusan atta-keno ... Ore mo okina yume o motte issho kenmei ganbatte yatta kedo no ...*"

His eyes were teary as he continued, "*Ano goro wa taihen kurushi katta keno. Oji-san jishin mo yoku naitazo. Ima koshite furikaette miruto yoku yatta to omouzo!*"

I realized I was listening with my heart to his past, to the dreams and hopes he once had. I asked myself why he wanted to share dreams which were now shattered into pieces. It was like the story of Humpty-Dumpty, broken, without a kinsman to attend to him with tender hands and heart.

Oji-san had struggled in this strange land; he had faltered without hope of anyone reaching down to lift him up and help him stand on solid ground. And now, facing his own twilight, what could he do? What could I do for him?

For the next several days, it was impossible to maintain order amongst a boiling mix of disgruntled white, Hispanic and Asian migrant workers. We were merely existing like animals, in a place where dust and dirt filled empty bellies.

Fear of going into debt, my inability to communicate in English, and false promises added to my fury. The false promises were from the interpreter who had welcomed me through a broker into the United States, and from Americans intent on acquiring migrant workers. What Oji-san explained added to my hatred for Americans. I was frustrated beyond reason and also enraged that my "road to revenge" was not going as planned.

Sitting idly in the camp, it occurred to me that the stigma of being a "Jap" in America would ring in my ears until one day I could no longer tolerate the insult. My inner struggle for revenge and my sense of isolation grew dangerously in this strange land, where some workers blamed me for the Pearl Harbor attack, although I was only four years old at the time! A series of fights and violent eruptions were the only steam valves I could find to resolve my inner conflicts.

"Tanemori," Oji-san would caution me about getting in fights, *"Oboete irukai. Oji-san wa okina katao motte iruto ittadaro?"*

He reminded me that he still had big, strong shoulders for me to lean on.

Finally a day came when I found myself in the field picking grapes with the others. Exhausted from laboring in the heat, I carried a full crate of grapes, setting it on the back of a wagon behind a tractor. In doing so I accidentally knocked into a worker I had fought with several times.

He yelled at me in Spanish and pushed me to the ground. All hell broke loose when I pushed him back, yelling in Japanese. Punches were thrown and I lost control. When another worker restrained me to stop the fight, I punched him instead of walking away.

"Why don't you restrain that blankety-blank instead of me?" I raged.

"You … blanking Jap!" The foreman berated me, having done nothing to the other fighter. He then took a bunch of grapes from my crate and threw them in my face, ordering me to work, not pick on his Spanish worker.

"Don't you ever do that again," I angrily responded in Japanese to his hateful behavior. I took a crate full of grapes and threw it at his feet.

I kept on in Japanese, condemning him for his racial prejudice. He was obviously enraged as I walked away.

"Kisama wa ore o dareka to shitte iruno ka?"

I was shocked when the foreman answered me back in pidgin Japanese and began to chase me. Somehow I dodged him the rest of day, avoiding being beaten up.

Returning to the camp that afternoon, I sat in the outhouse and recorded the events of the day. I was angry and disgusted with myself for having given the foreman a perfect opportunity to insult me in public.

A knock on the door told me someone wanted to use the facility. In my anger, I quickly arose, trying to put the notebook in my pocket, but it slipped from my fingers and fell into the hole.

"@#$%&~@$<%&**!" I exclaimed. Pinching my nose, I peered into the dark hole, but couldn't see anything in the abyss. Realizing my diary was lost, I pounded the wall in rage and cussed the foreman again and again.

That night Oji-san told me the foreman had learned Japanese in the army during the Occupation.

It was about four o'clock one Sunday afternoon when all the migrant workers in the campground had no work and were wasting the time away, that I discovered a "canteen" where we could get candy and other personal items like toothpaste. It seemed this was the place for the workers to gather for "busy-body" purposes—talking, eating and drinking.

Licking my chops, I asked a clerk in my halting English for a candy bar. He looked at me as if at a blank wall.

"Hey, we don't talk Chinese here, boy!" he finally responded. "Come back when you learn to talk good English."

I didn't like the clerk and he knew it. It was my unfortunate luck that another Japanese worker was nearby to translate.

After some angry words, the clerk declared, "All right! All right!" He then waved his hands toward the Japanese man and went to the back room, returning with a small package of what looked like two halves of a tennis ball, capped with a pink and white rubbery substance. He called it a "Hostess Snowball."

Blowing dust off the wrapper, then practically throwing the package at me, he said, "Here! This is really good if you're hungry. Go ahead. Eat it. It's free ..."

"Free?" I didn't know what to make of it. I examined the package, slowly unwrapping it. I ate the thing, first licking it and then taking a small bite, wondering why the clerk was suddenly so kind.

About eight o'clock that evening I started sweating and writhing with a pain in my abdomen. Then I started vomiting. By the time some co-workers noticed, I was spitting blood and gasping for air. I soon became delirious.

I vaguely remember riding in the back of a station wagon that "Mr." Kawasaki was driving ...

Chapter Three: An American Snake Pit

I AWOKE in a hospital in Delano, my head spinning like a kite without its tail. The ceiling rolled. Or was I the one that was rotating? Everything seemed to move without any sense of direction.

"*Kurushii!*"

Unbearable pain ran from the top of my head to the tip of my toes, back-and-forth. I had no energy, as if someone had pulled a plug, draining my gas tank. Suddenly, fear overwhelmed me. I couldn't hear my own voice. Although I was screaming, I heard only loud scratchy sounds, as if someone was ripping sandpaper.

"*Tasukete!*"

Pleading for help, my voice echoed in a forest where there was no one to hear.

"Someone! Is anybody there?"

I felt as if I was lying in thick fog, until it seemed that someone had turned on mercury lights which, ever so slowly, chased away the darkness. I was in a strange place. Then shadows appeared, becoming two human figures standing beyond my reach. They quickly came to my bedside.

When fully awakened by the two doctors (male nurses, as I later learned) roughly shaking me, the midday sun was already scorching the San Joaquin Valley. I had no knowledge of how long I had been confined to the bed.

"No, No, No. PLEEEZU. Tell me. Where am I? No! What did you do to me? Who are you, and what are you doing to me?" I was shouting in Japanese, a totally foreign language to the men at my side. I only wanted to know where I was and what they were doing, but the men probably took my outburst as a threat, leading them to react for their own safety.

They quickly called for help, bringing several doctors and nurses rushing in, crowding me and shouting to each other.

"*Itai ...*"

Almost without blinking, they stuck me with a needle. It immobilized me and allowed them to strap me to the iron bed. My head, arms, legs and abdomen were tightly compressed by leather straps. Did they think I would harm them? I didn't know where I was, or even who I was, at that moment.

The last thing I could recall was eating a "snowball" cupcake, and later vomiting blood. I couldn't remember exactly what had happened when the camp director came after the laborers, in panic or curiosity, got his attention.

Now I found myself confined in a strange room, strapped to an iron bed. The pain I felt brought back memories of my suicide attempt in Kobe, of a struggle in another hospital bed, of another fight for my life. Now "Hell" had broken wide open and unfathomable trouble flooded out.

Because we spoke different languages, I couldn't tell the doctors what had happened. Failing to determine the cause of my vomiting blood, and discovering that I was a Hiroshima survivor, the doctors concluded that my illness was either caused by, or related to, radiation exposure.

I was told later that the doctors at Delano Hospital thought I should be treated via additional medical procedures or exploratory experiments. They felt treatment should come quickly, to avoid risking their own health. After giving me a shot, they transferred me that afternoon to another hospital.

When I came to, I was immovably bound to an iron bed by leather straps, in a naval hospital in Bakersfield (as I learned later). Like all the subsequent hospitals that treated me, this was a maximum security facility, like a prison.

I must have been viewed as a criminal or a crazed, dangerous animal, to have required such a cage.

As the morning sun peeked through a tiny window, I considered how difficult it must be for the light to get through the window. Although I couldn't see my surroundings very well, I sensed there was nothing here to make me any better off than I was at the last hospital.

How much time had passed since I was moved from the first hospital, I had no way to know, but I felt I had lost many hours, if not days.

There was a vast vacuum in my head, as if someone had banged it between two giant cymbals, leaving it reverberating. Whether I was coming down from the effect of drugs or not, I only knew the ceiling was rotating irrationally, and that I was on a roller coaster. Being strapped down, I could only shift my eyes to find clues as to what had happened, what was going on, and where I was. I had no idea that I was under the scrutiny of doctors taking turns to watch me struggle to free myself.

Due to the hospital staff's fear of radiation contamination, I later learned, I had been taken to a locked room and held in seclusion. This increased my feelings of being thrown into a bottomless abyss, and falling, falling without ending. At times, I felt I was flying in a restless circle against a dark canvas devoid of twinkling stars or any moonlight to cast shadows. The darkness was so deep I couldn't even see my own hands before my eyes.

In my pain and isolation I was aware of countless doctors (interns) who came, one after another, in protective white jackets, hats, gloves and masks revealing only their "deadened" eyes, who took notes as they looked me over.

I had become a "guinea pig," an experiment in the hands of doctors acting in the name of radiation research. They gave me shots, forced me to take "horse pills" and gave me other treatments in an attempt to "cure" me.

Day-in and day-out, even under the night's darkness, they continued to subject me to painful tests and exploited me with experiments. The worst treatment came when two male nurses, a female nurse and several doctors came to do spinal taps. Each insertion of a long steel needle into my spinal canal caused unbearable, excruciating pain that lasted for days. After every procedure, I tried to stand upright by leaning on the iron bed bolted to the floor. I couldn't. There was no way I could keep my balance.

I reacted to spinal taps like an intoxicated brute. I instinctively grew violent, verbalizing my anger and refusal to undergo such torture. I quickly realized my physical reactions and verbal responses in Japanese had no affect.

There was no one to prevent these monsters from torturing me with a needle, or from strangling my throat to snatch my last breath. I could only scream and scream again, incoherently, as if I was a madman.

I soon became like one of "Pavlov's dogs," screaming as I heard them coming down the hall, well before they reached me to start their work.

Despite my cries, and with little effort, they subdued me. They drained fluid twice, if not three times a week. After each spinal tap, I spiraled into a bottomless abyss. Then they made me get up and stand on my feet.

Having a sensation as if someone was pumping the blood out of my brain, I sometimes held my breath. At other times, I banged my head against the wall, creating new pain to defuse their torture. These were the only choices I had to deal with the brutal physical torment I underwent. But there was no way for me to deal with the emotional scars in my heart, or with the experiences that clawed at my soul. All I could do was close my eyes for the sake of my wounded soul.

By doing these things, I probably confirmed their perception of me as a dangerous, crazed animal to be kept in a cage.

In addition to the probing spinal taps, the doctors subjected me to needles for drawing blood samples, and they observed and observed me and observed me. I started to notice that at certain hours of the day, and even under the darkness of night, always in groups, doctors were stealthily entering my room to watch me and "compare notes."

"No! You get away from me. Don't you ever touch me!" I would plead. I even spat in their faces to keep them away. But no matter how hard I resisted, they suppressed me without effort, like a little bug.

Often, two male nurses would grab my arms tightly, as if I were shackled in chains, my feet dangling off the floor virtually the whole way. Then I would bury my head in shame as they took me down a long corridor to a special room, with several doctors following distantly.

The sharp sound of the steel door closing shut behind us would ring through my entire body, driving excruciating pain into my brain and chills down every bone of my body.

I knew I had no way of escaping from the electric shock treatment. Like a lamb in a slaughterhouse, I was doomed! They would turn on the switch, jolting my body several times. My hands and body would get slimy with sweat. A sharp tingling pain would run up and down, across and through my body.

I tried to hold on to my soul. I can vaguely remember hearing my own words faintly, "No! No, no, pleeeazu ... no, no, no, no ..."

When they brought me back to my room, it was as if I was dead.

I lost all sense of time, and would find myself lying in my room, sometimes on my bed, at other times on the cart or on the floor, like a zombie.

Countless doctors, taking turns, watched me for hours, notebooks in hand, recording anything I incoherently responded to after a shock treatment, until I came to my senses. Usually I reacted violently to the treatment, not knowing this was what the doctors anticipated.

The repeated treatments, week after week, were taking their toll. I was breaking down; my behavior had become predictable. I was programmed to be defiant for my own survival.

"No! Get away," I shouted. "You are not going to put me in that contraption. I am not a *kichigai*. I know what you are thinking. I am not a demon, nor am I possessed by demonic power!"

An alternative to being strapped in an iron bed was a straight-jacket. Once jacketed, they would leave me in the room like a mummy for hours, sometimes for an entire night.

The walls of my throat became dry, as if collapsing. My lips were chapped, and I begged for water. I sometimes found myself totally exhausted by the morning, biting my tongue, wishing I might never waken.

I often fell asleep from sheer exhaustion. At times, doctors gave me shots or drugged me. Some nights, they turned a bright light on me, which reminded me of the pure flash that had ripped the sky of Hiroshima so long before.

I would close my eyes to avoid being blinded by the unexpected piercing light. No one could escape the scrutiny of the eyes searching my tiny room. And then I found it very difficult to fall back to sleep.

My behavior, carefully recorded in their charts, became the basis for further experiments, all administered without anyone knowing how they might affect me.

It seemed the medical staffs in a series of hospitals during a six month period of time were determined to accomplish a single objective—discovering the effects of radiation exposure on humans. While the doctors didn't know my "normal" behavior and thus had no basis for comparison, my emotional outbursts must have provided a harvest field for them.

Because of my poor English, I was not understood. Had I been able to communicate with a doctor who spoke Japanese, I could have explained what was happening in my heart.

Instead, I was lonely, completely isolated, terrified, and confused. I was almost insane. I longed for death.

The agony of spinal taps, blood samples, and electric shock treatments were nothing compared with the shame and disgrace I experienced in my heart before my Father. As the proud Number One Son of Tanemori and heir to the honorable family name, I couldn't bear to further shame my family. I had already debased myself by failing to take my life by my own hand when I was 16 years old.

In my shame, I felt as if the claws of wild animals had pierced my chest. The pain had impaled my heart. No longer able to bear my soul, I had to do something to deter the doctors from further experiments and tests.

"I hate you," I shouted to the sun. "Go away, and leave me alone. I don't want to be seen by others in daylight. Please. Please, go away and give me darkness so I don't have to shame myself, covering my face with my hands. Oh, please. Let me have the night back. Go away!"

During the daytime, hiding under a sheet or a blanket, I believed that my Father would never find me. There was no way I could allow him to discover that I was being treated as a *kichigai*, a mental patient, a dangerous beast. I would rather die than face my Father's broken heart. I often shut my eyes tight, but daylight still filtered through my closed eyes, revealing my soul.

I shouted still louder to the sun, "I cannot bear to see myself in this place of shame. You are the one who reveals everything openly that lay in darkness. I don't need you. How could you do this to me? I cannot bear this place of shame!"

Exposed to daylight and driven toward insanity, how I wished to fall asleep and never wake up. How peaceful that might be to my soul. I couldn't breathe without feeling my heart tearing into two.

Ripping a blanket from the iron bed, I would bury myself under it during daylight hours, sticking its corner into my mouth to prevent the shrieking that welled up from my soul. I couldn't bear to hear my own weeping, and so I muffled my cries, lest they might reach heaven and enter my Father's ears. While under the covers I sometimes sat for hours in the corner of the room.

As much as I could, I kept a watchful eye on the doctors, who were in turn watching me like hawks through the observation window in the door. Sometimes I reacted, running toward them, beating on the door and covering it with a sheet or blanket. I screamed for them to leave me alone. They were like evil spirits spilled over me, holding me in a stranglehold. It was like dying slowly.

Darkness was my friend and my comfort! There, I felt safe. Only under the darkness of night did I come out from under the covers. For a fleeting moment, thinking my Father could not see me, I let the mercy of the night's darkness embrace me. I found a moment of relief.

But I was terrified when dawn's light began to steal the darkness that had shielded me from shame. I was not at all certain my heartrending goal, "Revenge on Americans," would ever find fulfillment. For I held little hope that I would be set free from this American "snake-pit."

My deepest anxiety was the thought of my Father turning his back on me. I could no longer bear my own soul. I had no alternative but to seek his face and ask for his compassionate understanding.

"Daddy!" I said, covering my face. "I am very sorry for dishonoring you. But daddy please understand. I didn't mean to bring further shame and disgrace to our family name. You know I tried everything I could to explain how I got sick.

"You know it was the snowball cupcake that caused me to vomit blood. I had no idea how it should have tasted. I didn't know it was spoiled."

I couldn't shake off what had happened that afternoon when the canteen clerk gave me the cupcake. It was so vivid in my mind—I saw him dust it off and say, "It's good for you ..." I saw myself reaching to take it from his hands and eat it.

"Daddy, I'm sorry I was so gullible to accept a handout. I should have conducted myself as a son of a *Samurai*, following the *Samurai Code*, as you instructed me."

"Daddy, please don't turn your back on me. I need your understanding. Please accept my heart as it is, and extend your pity to me. Yes, daddy. I am true to my own heart. I have been trying to hold on to your teachings and spirit. But I'm afraid that I'm losing the strength which holds me together, and allows me to overcome my own weakness. Please give me inner peace so that I know in my heart you're not angry with me. Daddy, please, please. Am I not still a proud son of Tanemori?"

> *Having a need to endure the darkness,*
> *at last, I struggled out of the ashes*
> *and ruin of postwar Japan,*
> *the sprouting of a new blade of grass*
> *through the healing power of earth.*
>
> *Falling into the "snake-pit" of America in the 60's,*
> *hope of ever getting out vaporized like a dream;*
>
> *The vice of the hands of savage doctors ever so*
> *   strong;*
> *Oh, would a long-awaited spring*
> *ever emerge to salvage my soul?*

I nearly fainted when I saw my disfigurement, even as reflected in shadow. My eyes had lost their power and were hollow, driven deep into their sockets. My cheekbones protruded. My ribcage had dried up, as if a wild animal had ravaged my flesh. There was no beauty I could recognize in myself—either of who I had been, or of who I was supposed to be. I was a ghost, standing in darkness. Somehow, my soul was not dead. The inferno of revenge was keeping it alive. Revenge, my friend, and comforter!

Following their agenda, the doctors were entering the next stage of experiments on me. Preparations for my transfer started early one morning. Shortly after breakfast, a half dozen doctors and nurses, charts in hand, paraded through my room. I had not eaten, as smelling unpleasant food made me gag, and left me without the energy to eat.

Around ten o'clock, two police officers entered to confer with the doctors. A nurse then gave me a shot and I was escorted by a doctor and the officers out of the hospital to an ambulance. A police car carrying the officers followed us to an airport.

All I remember is that I stood with my head throbbing with pain while a tiny plane circled in the air. I have no idea what airport we took off from, or how long we were in the air.

The policemen, both with stony faces, wore their hats low over their eyes—eyes which never seemed to blink. As they made me sit down in the plane, I could only avoid eye contact with them by closing mine. But, unable to trust them, I kept one eye open.

Sitting in front of them, I felt like prey unable to escape a predator. I was at their mercy; only a few people knew that I was thousands of feet above, high in the air.

A middle-aged white man, hand-cuffed to the seat beside me, kept his eyes closed during the entire flight, as if he was resigned to whatever fate might bring. The doctor sat in silence away from us, on a seat by the door. Periodically, he would glance toward us.

My teeth chattered and my knees knocked. Above all, my heart pounded. From time to time, I held my chest, to calm my heart from erupting like a volcano.

We finally arrived at a remote airport obscured by tall dry weeds. A short distance away, a police car was waiting behind a dilapidated building. We were hustled to the car, the driver slammed the door, and off we went. With the midday sun directly above us, I had no way of knowing the direction we were traveling.

A large sign soon ended the mystery of our location.

As the police car approached the main security gate, I saw the sign "Modesto County Mental Hospital." I wondered if the tall fence was to keep outsiders out, or to keep insiders in, and was amazed at the blocky, massive white buildings, arranged row after row like a fort, standing defiantly against the blue sky.

I don't know what they said, but one policeman patted my head. The doctor who had ridden silently with us on the plane grabbed my right arm tightly, and we walked to a door where he was greeted by several nurses and doctors.

Another hospital? I had no idea why I was here, nor why the doctors still feared I was dangerous, nor why I was being used as a "guinea pig." I was fearful of how long I would be kept, of how I would be watched, and whether I would be isolated in this psychiatric institution. What new treatments would they administer without any hope of the answers they so desperately sought? Or would new tests simply help offset their guilt and ease their consciences?

I was impressed by the "welcome wagon" that greeted our arrival. There was a huge gathering of towering doctors and scores of female nurses. The nurses seemed to have lost the tenderness of womanhood, as they were big-boned, harsh-looking women. I didn't want to run into any of them alone at night!

I rubbed my eyes. Although some of the men, whom I presumed from their white uniforms to be doctors, appeared to be normal, the rest of the men and a number of the women had faces like skulls, without the warmth of human flesh. Some were dressed in long, dark robes, standing in readiness, with sharp sickles in their hands.

Either my mind or my eyes were playing tricks on me, or I truly could see the "Grim Reapers" who were waiting for us. I heard the eerie sound of a blade being sharpened, as if demons were waiting for a command to start gathering heads as trophies.

In front of me, thick documents were signed and turned over, and the policemen and doctor who had delivered us to these "harvesters" turned and headed toward the main gate.

Two muscular men, nearly three times my size and wearing white uniforms, converged on the handcuffed man. He quickly disappeared into the building, with several doctors following.

Would they take me to a nameless place where I would disappear without a trace? Apprehension and fear enveloped me again as a small knot of doctors encircled me like poachers. A stout, bald-headed bully-like man approached us and looked me up and down, as if examining a shipment of new merchandise. I could tell that he (I learned later his name was Dr. Henry Gallop) was the boss.

I had to smile.

The other doctors and nurses, all acting and obeying the boss like robots, were there for my "grand reception," since I was to be the important subject of a battery of tests and treatments.

How strange a place it was! People were dressed so strangely, wearing masks and gowns. I noticed a man wearing a skeleton costume. He reminded me of a man cremated in Kotachi Village shortly after the Hiroshima bombing. Another person wore a grotesque mask reminiscent of the Hunchback of Notre Dame. Glancing around, I saw a witch, a tin man, a scarecrow and a lion. I cast a smile at a woman dressed as a deep-orange-colored pumpkin.

So, this was an American mental hospital! The day was October 31, 1956. I would later learn that Americans celebrate Halloween on this day.

I burst into cynical laughter, a cackling that caught the attention of the bald-headed doctor. In response, he sent the two muscular men to grab my arms behind my back, hold me like a twig, then quickly walk me down corridors and through so many double-doors that I lost track of their number. At each portal that we came to, either these men used their keys, or someone waited to swing the door open. It was an entrance of epic grandeur.

At the final set of double doors, another document was signed. My escorts wished me "good luck" and turned me over to white-uniformed men and nurses.

Before I could catch my breath, two men and a nurse quickly took me into a tiny room that looked eerily like the inside of a furnace, being reddish-orange in color. What little furniture it held was fastened to the floor. They turned a bright light on me and quickly stripped me, while a nurse checked and catalogued the contents of my little bag.

I was rushed into a shower room and scrubbed until my skin turned red. The hot water was hot! I felt like I was in the *Goemon-buro*, a Japanese hot bath for death-row inmates, part of a last rite before execution.

I came out of the shower feeling like a boiled octopus. They gave me a gown with nothing underneath. I felt naked. A nurse forced me to take some "horse pills."

Then I was marched into another bright room, once again reminding me of the flash in Hiroshima's sky. While I rubbed my eyes and covered them, blinded, I heard voices coming from outside the room. Focusing, I could make out the face of a man watching me through a small window.

A parade of doctors began—doctors of all different shapes and sizes, yet with faces like graven stone. I couldn't imagine why so many doctors had to look me over. The parade seemed to last several hours, exhausting me to the point that I wanted to scream. The bald-headed doctor was in the room the entire time, keeping his distance from me. I wanted to use his face for target practice with a bow and arrow, or a double-barreled shotgun. I liked the shotgun idea, for it would be impossible to miss such a big target. The thought of using an ancestral Japanese *Samurai* sword brought me a cynical smile.

Days and nights became indistinguishable. I could only crudely mark time by counting the needle marks on my body. At times I felt I was in a pressure-cooker, steadily boiling and building pressure until I would explode.

About a month later, I was moved to another wing of the hospital, with a change of supervision to an older woman named Mrs. Mary Furr. She was the head nurse of the psychiatric ward to which I was transferred.

I was still in isolation under the eyes of Dr. Henry Gallop, the bald-headed man, who directed his tests upon the Hiroshima survivor, who, he thought, might be suffering from radiation exposure.

Given the season, my latest preoccupation had become the sound of dashing horses, and jingling bells were strangely attuned to my ears.

"Jingle bells, jingle bells … Silent night, holy Night … Joy to the world, the Savior comes …" the tunes floated from the public address system.

Are you crazy? How could I rejoice "to repeat the sounding joy"?

But "Dashing through the snow," though an unfamiliar melody, seemed to have a magical effect on me, even in an asylum.

As strange as the songs were, how truly shocking it was for me one day to find myself face-to-face with Mary Furr, as she entered my room all alone, with empty hands. I didn't know if she was naïve, or crazy, as I was perceived to be by the staff. She showed no sign of being afraid of me, nor of trying to intimidate me. No one had ever come into my room alone before. Under the strict orders of Dr. Gallop, no professional staff—doctor, nurse, or anyone in any official capacity—would ever visit me alone.

This unexpected intruder, especially being a woman, caused my heart additional turbulence. I literally grabbed my chest and held my breath!

"No. Get away from me!" I repeatedly screamed at her in Japanese. What was going on? I panicked. "No! No! No!" All I could say was "No" and try to fend her off by wildly shaking my hands and covering my face.

The contrast of this head nurse's actions to the stated instructions of Dr. Henry Gallop spun my head. What kind of man was he, the way he strutted? As a man, it seemed he lacked the *kintama*-ball, testicles—a sign of manhood in Japanese culture—because he never once entered my room alone.

I don't remember whether she said anything, or what she said if she spoke. Neither do I recall how long she stayed. I do remember her leaving an indelible impression on my heart. Her tender smiles and big blue eyes seemed incapable of harming anyone, and certainly not me! After she left the room, I realized my mind was already revisiting her, and I was unsure whether that was wise.

Her first visit, though, proved to be the tip of an iceberg. Mary's visits became more frequent, and longer, although there remained a distance between us. She always stood in front of the opened door. I wondered whether the door was left open for her to run if I reacted dangerously, or for me to escape.

As the days and nights passed, I began to notice a different attitude from her staff—almost as if they were reaching out to me. This change of attitude became apparent as I found myself standing at the open door.

Sometime during the day, either Mary or her staff had left my door unlocked. The next thing I knew, my door was swinging open into the hallway. How scary! I peeked out and looked down the hall to see if anyone was there, secretly watching.

I began to notice a male nurse who worked for Mary, whom I later learned was called Mr. Greg (or Mr. G.). He was often with other patients in the hallway. But I never felt as if his eyes were on me.

My puzzlement grew as I began to see "outside" my confined world. I had yet to venture out into the hall for fear of what might happen. Of course, I didn't want to be surprised by the face of Dr. Gallop.

I detested him with all my passion. The only reason I didn't get in greater trouble with him was that I restrained myself. I wanted so much to stop in front of him and spit in his face, a display of extreme contempt in Japan. But I couldn't be sure what he might do in retaliation. In his rage, he might exercise his authority and subject me to further experiments, which I could not afford. It was safest for me to avoid him when I was alone.

Meanwhile, with the passage of days, Mary would stay longer and longer, without saying much. I didn't know what to make of this, although I realized something was happening in my heart. I began to feel less and less internal energy was needed for me to hold my heart on guard.

I quite distinctly remember a day when she seemed to act differently. She came in and locked the door behind her, putting the key in her white uniform pocket. What a chance she was taking, if anything happened in a split-second!

My heart started pounding as she sat silently at the edge of my bed, while I sat at the other end. Momentarily, she reached out for my hand, but I quickly moved away from her. She moved toward me. Again she tried to touch my hand.

I didn't know what to make of it. Why was she taking a risk, subjecting herself to danger? Why? What was there for her to gain?

I began to ponder her sanity, which in turn marked an apparent change taking place in my heart. What was wrong with me? Was I taking a moment to think about someone else's feelings?

I had been totally occupied with myself, and there had been no time for anything else, much less to soften my attitude toward another person.

We played the game for about a week. Then one day she succeeded in taking one of my hands between hers. At once, I felt her warmth surge through my hand, my arm, my body, until it found its way to my heart. I found myself alone with Mary, at last. This was the beginning of my journey outside my confined, locked room.

After she left my room, I felt as if I was waking from a deep nightmare. There was a mystical feeling, like a pleasant dream of escape from bewildering experiences. I was dazed and sought perspective. I questioned whether I was feeling a diabolic energy working on me. But my internalized voices warned, "No! Help Me!"

I had to ask myself many questions for which I found no answers. There was somehow still an emptiness, as I was petrified by what was going on in my heart concerning this new experience with Mary, a woman I considered my "enemy." I could feel the lingering warmth of her hands, as if they were still at the door, trying to enter my heart.

My mind took me back to the secret "hiding place" in the Village of Kotachi, where Nakamura *Sensei* and I had found ourselves alone. It was the last place where my heart had been so touched by a tender, warm and loving spirit.

Now, as I had felt Mary's heartbeat, my heart, long frozen by hatred and revenge, began to be affected. I tried to deny this as a freak incident, but my frozen heart and soul had shown signs of melting.

I was totally bewildered by Mary's actions, and at the same time was helplessly drawn to her, as though she were a magician. My tiny heart began fluttering.

As I had often forced myself to be safe in my own solitude, I felt I had to resist anyone who even attempted to come close. Although I couldn't prevent anyone from trying to destroy my body and mind, no one dared attempt to destroy my soul!

There was no light where I had been thrown, no heart where I had been kept, and no life where I was existing. There was only a feeling of death all around me. Yet an inexplicable desire was surfacing from the depth of my heart, like a sprout, traveling through the darkness by instinct, at last reaching toward a faint light in the distance.

How could my frozen heart, raging with hatred, ever have a chance to feel any warmth, let alone be touched from without? It had been so long since anyone had come close to touching and cuddling me. I was starving for the warmth of human contact.

I lost no time focusing on Mary's love, hoping for at least a glance of her when she arrived at her nursing station at 7:45 a.m. How desperately I listened for her voice in the hallway each day! Just hearing her sweet voice brought some comfort that, even though tests were still being administered by Dr. Henry Gallop, she was there for me.

And, of course, I wanted to see her, even when she left for home at 3:30 p.m. The long weekends became almost unbearable, as I would wait for her to return to work on Monday morning. As a sign of change, I now had a reason to beg that the night's darkness would depart before the roosters crowed. Mary's unexpected, unfamiliar love somehow began to penetrate a heart that had been protected by rage and a longing for revenge. Her love was like a piercing light reaching into the inner chamber of darkness within my soul.

I had no idea what day it was, or what was about to happen. Shortly after 2:00 p.m., Mr. Gregory approached me with a very serious face. He asked me to clean up the nurses' lounge, where someone had made a mess. Given the serious look on his face, I didn't trust him. Although I didn't understand clearly, this is how I believe the conversation went.

"Mr. G.," I said, "I don' wanna come wiz you!"

"Tommy, Mrs. Furr asked me to see if you could help her clean up the mess somebody made."

"Mizess Farrr wanna mee to heluop har to kleen?"

"Yes, Tommy, Mrs. Furr would like you to help her."

"Hai! I go wiz you!"

I was reluctant, but I didn't want to disappoint Mrs. Furr. I had cleaned the nurses' lounge one hour earlier, and couldn't imagine why anyone would make a mess and ask for somebody else to clean it up.

Mr. Gregory took me by my hand as we entered the pitch-black lounge. The lights were off and the shades pulled down, so I couldn't see anything. Suddenly, from the darkness, came a song I had never heard before:

Happy birthday to you; happy birthday to you;
Happy birthday Dear Tommy! Happy birthday to
you!
We love you, Tommy; we love you, Tommy;
We love you, Dear Tommy; we all love you!

Years later I learned that "A Happy Birthday" was composed by two sisters, Mildred and Patty Hills, of Kentucky, in 1823, and that Americans young and old have been singing it ever since.

From out of the dark, someone lit the candles. As my eyes adjusted to the light, I saw the beaming smile of Mary Furr, the one throwing this birthday party for me. I had never been at an occasion where people lit candles, sang and smiled at the same time. From my experiences in Japan, burning candles were always associated with pain and mourning for the dead!

The candles brought back my Father's funeral, representing darkness. This was not light but hopelessness for me. The impression of my Father lying in a pine box was so deep, so indelible, I would relive the event again and again. The smell of burning candles also triggered my memory of the bomb shelter the night of August 6, 1945, before the bombing of Hiroshima—the screaming of children, the responses of their panicked parents. It remained overwhelming.

How deranged these Americans were! The presentation of candles and happy singing was like mixing fire and ice. This was a total culture shock.

Mary, her nurses and Mr. G. must have been crazy! Didn't they realize the candles were burning neither on *toro*, candlestands, nor in a lantern, but on top of some obscene object? All my life, the proper burning of candles had been either at a *Butsudan*, Buddha Temple, at a *Korimbo*, gravesite, during the Obon season, or in candle lanterns floating in the river.

It seemed the nurses' lounge had turned into a place of spiritual mockery! I could not take part in this obscene ridicule! Surely, Buddha's curse would fall upon them harshly!

They plopped me right in the front of the "obscene object," a birthday cake with the words "We love you, Tommy! Happy Birthday!" written in icing. They handed me a white envelope, reminding me of the envelope Mr. Ueda handed me when I was forced to leave Kobe.

One nurse, seeing me unable to open the envelope, grabbed it and quickly opened it. I couldn't read the card, and wondering what message they were sending to my Father gripped my chest in fear. I believed these Americans were making a mockery of me, and I couldn't take part in making fun of my parents' spirits!

I was further confused when one nurse said, loudly, something like, "Tommy, don't you like what we've done for you?"

"Why should I participate in the farce?" I said to myself. I didn't understand at all why Mary was making fun of the most solemn rite of lighting candles!

They all waited for my reaction. This expected joyous occasion might turn out to be the worst disaster of all! This would have finalized my direction—the road to revenge—if no one was to explain these actions.

Although I didn't want to hurt Mary Furr, she had better give me an explanation for this unpardonable behavior!

"Tommy, this is for you! Today is your birthday. We want you to know we all love you! This is all for you. Look, this is your birthday cake; and this is your birthday card; and these are your birthday presents from all of us. And of course, this ice cream goes with your birthday cake."

"Fo all zeeese fo mee?" I asked.

"Yes, these are all for you!" Mary said, gesturing across the table.

"Why?" I asked. The softening of my facial expression relieved the nurses.

Mr. G. hurriedly urged me to blow out the candles. A nurse named Hazel told me to make a big wish, holding her hands together as if praying. She claimed my wish would come true.

"Hurry, blow out the candles!" someone else said.

Everyone made a face like a blowfish, and demonstrated the motion of blowing out the candles. They all waited eagerly.

Mary was as excited as a child having her own birthday party. She came around and her soft hand touched my shoulders.

I was startled! I wasn't sure what to make of the lit candles and the singing. Now, they asked me to blow out the candles. This was taboo in Japan. We always fanned our hand to extinguish candles, for using our dirty breath was disrespectful, and desecrated the ritual of burning candles!

"No! You all are *kichigai*, mad!" I said in Japanese. Then in my fractured English, "Me no like you ... Me no blo kandles!"

The flame of candles represents life. I was being asked to fulfill their request to snuff out life with my dirty breath.

No! I had failed suicide once, which had forced me to come to America for revenge, in the hope I might redeem my life. I would not participate in this unpardonable sin with these Americans!

I ran from the lounge. I knew there was one place I could be protected. I returned to my asylum and closed the door behind me. In my confusion, I began to cry.

"No! No! No! I cannot do it." I was beating the door. "No! Whatever it was they were trying ... I cannot allow them to touch my heart! How can I betray my vow I made at my parent's grave ... my vow of REVENGE."

I was totally perplexed by the actions of Mary and her staff. I wanted so much to think that what they were doing was out of their kind hearts. But I could only see this as a deed of blasphemy.

"How could they say they love me?" I cried in silent protest.

I sensed that right outside the door Mary was holding back Mr. G., allowing me the release of crying my heart out.

"Why have you tormented me with your kindness?" I cried, becoming a crazy person caught between my opinions and their energies, both tugging at me with equal force. Finally, with no more energy to cry, I crumpled onto the floor.

Mary quietly entered and stood by my side, waiting for the right moment to touch me with her soft hand. As I looked up, she reached down and pulled me to herself, hugging me. She held me in silence like a hen gathering a chick under its wings.

My body shook. So, too, Mary was shaking. That was all I needed.

It was like the sun warming a traveler on a long, treacherous winter journey across a desolate plain, the warmth causing him to take off his overcoat. I was clothed in hatred, but feeling her irregular heartbeats started a thaw. The warmth of her love caused me to take off my coat momentarily.

I gave my "enemy" a split second to enter my fortified camp. I made a miscalculation and irreversible error. How could I have this moment of weakness, as my heart was Japanese and hers American?

By opening the door of my heart, however small the opening, the stirrings of an avalanche started. It began like a snowball rolling down a slope.

I was hoping to see Mary more than anyone else, and my heart began to forget what it was like to be under the power of Dr. Gallop and his pack of doctors, who were attempting to destroy my body, my spirit and my will. Just hearing her voice in the hallway somehow brought comfort and held my soul against Dr. Gallop's continued experiments.

And now we had embraced!

Later that afternoon, at about three o'clock, Mary said with her usual smile, "Tommy, I will be home during Christmas vacation. I will be gone for one week."

"I don't see you any more, Mary?" I shot back.

"No! No! I will be back one week from Monday." Mary reassured me, taking my hands into hers. "Tommy, no need to cry!"

"OK, Mary." Then, I promised her, "I would be a good boy. OK."

My first Christmas in America had no meaning for me. I didn't see Mary's face, and that was enough for me to retreat back into my shell. Even though the winter sun was warmer than expected, my asylum became an icebox without Mary and her smile.

Mr. G. was ever-present and very helpful, but the more he tried to help, the more my heart pushed him away. I felt the place was turning into a graveyard. It was dead. How could I survive for a week without seeing her face, let alone hearing her voice?

The week moved like a thick marmalade flowing downhill. How glad I was when Mary returned to work. She had a little Christmas gift for me.

I was like a chatterbox, unwinding, or like a spring-powered toy that had lost its hold, talking on and on and on. Even though I wasn't sure what I was saying, there was no stopping until I told her everything I wanted to say.

"Tommy! Hold your horses. You need to catch your breath," Mary cautioned.

After several fumbling tries, I finally blurted out, "Mary, I went to a chaarch with Mr. G.," as I stuck my chest out like a robin that had snared a worm.

"Did you go to church?" She smiled quizzically.

Seeing her smile, I knew that I had pleased her. "Yes," I said, so very proud of myself that she had understood what I said.

As Mary took my hands, she shouted, "Good! Good! Oh, Tommy. Good for you." She hugged me. "Tell me, what church did you go to?"

I shook my shoulders. She saw my facial expression.

"Do you know the name of the church?"

"Me, no name ..."

Though she was glad Greg had taken me, she still wanted to know what kind of church we went to during her Christmas vacation.

"Me no go to church. Was going to church bad?" I had to ask.

"No! No. No. I'm glad you and Greg went to church." She smiled. "Where did you go? Did he drive the car?" She motioned as if her hands held a steering wheel. "What did you do?"

"Oh. Mary, I went to chaaarch. I put my fingers in the water ... water in the bowl." I gestured. "I crossed my heart with wet fingers, right to left and up and down."

"Oh no! Tommy! That ... was a wrong church!" She shouted with a surprising look on her face.

Sometime later I learned she belonged to the First Baptist Church in Modesto, a very conservative, strict, Bible-based Baptist church. I had been to a Catholic church without understanding any of the differences between the two denominations.

How little I realized at the time that my birthday party would be the beginning of irreversible changes in my heart. I began to realize that my struggle was not because of Americans, but was within my own heart.

I alone could see inside my heart. It was gutted and crawling with millions of worms, as if someone had opened the hatch of a silo that contained years of misfortunes, failures and negative thoughts. No one would want to smell or see such an ugly, powerful collection of enraged energy.

Mary succeeded in communicating with me, even though we couldn't communicate with spoken words. In solitary confinement, I was alone with Mary—her heart and mine.

Although gradual, the change I noticed in my attitude and behavior toward Mary was unbelievable. But I was still under the scrutiny of the "thousand eyes" of the doctors, and was thus afraid to be alone each afternoon when Mary had gone home.

Yet I began to see a shift in my own heart and in my surroundings. I had my doubts as to what had happened. Prior dark events had so deeply contrasted with my awakening, and things had so brightened so suddenly and so strangely that I questioned my sanity.

Dr. Gallop showed denial of my changes in attitude and heart, but my start at transformation was noticed by others, including Miss Jean White, my social worker. These changes showed up in my facial expressions, and I now believe that only those who were blind or callous of heart could have missed the symptoms of what was taking place in me.

One sunny afternoon Mary came in with the biggest smile on her face, took my hand, and walked me to a door that led outside to an open space. She motioned, as if pushing me out.

I stood like a frightened kitten, shivering with fear. My feet froze in the doorway! The sun was so bright I was blinded, and instinctively I covered my eyes with my hands. The sun's rays penetrated my brain through my covered eyes. It was painful. This was the first time in a long time that I had felt the sun.

"No, no, Mary!" I was afraid to move.

She took my hands and led me to the first step, then to a second and a third step—into an open area enclosed by a high wire fence. Through this fence I saw the sky, uninhibited! I was confused. I wanted her to help me crawl on my hands and knees.

Then, taking a few steps, I began walking, then running. As Mary took my hands, I discovered a new strength in this open space. And with this strength I felt I might be able to withstand Dr. Gallop and his followers.

Suddenly, I became like a butterfly, soaring from one flower to the next, as my mind drifted back to my early days in Hiroshima. A song I learned from my Mother returned to my lips.

"*Cho-o-cho, cho-o-cho, nano hani tomare; nano hani aitara sakura ni tomare, hana kara hanae, tomare yo asobe you, tomare yo asobe* ... Fly, butterfly fly, from one flower to the next, and the next; then fly to the cherry blossom until you get tired; then fly again from flower to flower ...*"

I was free. My soul was liberated like a spirited horse. I gathered wildflowers and I gave them to Mary. How strangely my days and nights had changed!

When I came to my senses, I felt as if I had returned from a nightmare. I noticed that I was not afraid of myself, even in the daylight hours; neither was I begging the darkness of night to linger. Nor did I need to hide under the covers. I almost forgot what my Father might think of me.

One day, Mr. G. took me to a meeting room at the end of the psychiatric wing. Slowly, with trepidation, I made my way. In the room local newspapers, books and magazines were available for patients who had the "freedom" to leave their rooms for supervised exploring and visiting.

Under the supervision of Mr. G., I was allowed to mingle with other patients. I soon became an object of curiosity among them, receiving so much attention I didn't know how to act or react. This proved to be a positive experience and I grew to enjoy "visitation hour," looking forward each afternoon to being with the others.

Although it had taken about one week for me to learn, or mimic, some English words the other patients had taught me, it had been fun. I had no idea what I was saying or learning. But I was very excited when they got big kicks out of my efforts, laughing out loud, encouraging me to mimic them again and again. I was very proud of my accomplishment.

So, the day came ...

After practicing and practicing, I could say it now without stumbling. I was so proud of myself—of my newly learned speaking ability. I ran to the nurses' station.

"Mary, Mary. Are you there?" My high-pitched voice echoed down the hallway.

"What is it, Tommy? I'm here." She looked at my face from behind the door.

"I larrned to speeek Enguliesh." I smiled.

She seemed pleased. Undoubtedly she thought I had learned something from the Children's Bible stories Mr. G. often read (sometimes he just told me the stories). Mary seemed as eager to hear as I was anxious to tell her.

"What is it?" She asked me.

"Oh, I larrrned the Enguliesh."

"Oh, tell me, Tommy." She acted like a little girl waiting to see the gift she was about to receive.

"#$%#^&@#&^%@#+ZX#$! That's what I larrrned today."

"What did you say?" she snapped, in a raised voice.

It seemed Mary didn't understand me the first time. So I repeated it, with the biggest smile on my face.

"#$%#^&@#&^%@#+ZX#$!"

"Tommy!" Her disturbed voice pierced my ears. I immediately knew that she disapproved. Her face changed several different shades. She shook her hand in front of her face.

"No. No, no, no! Tommy," she scolded, covering my mouth with her hand. Don't you ever say those bad words."

"Maarrrry, why are you angry at me?" I looked into her face. "No goood Enguliesh? Me no understand. Why you don't like me anymore?"

"Tommy, those are naughty words. Who taught you to say those things?" She continued. "Of course, I have a sneaking idea. Those patients are bad, Tommy. I will talk to them …"

Mary grabbed the nape of my neck, rushed me into a bathroom and washed my mouth with bar soap. How strangely she demonstrated her love and caring. It somehow reminded me of my Mother disciplining me in unconventional ways.

Yet this incident paled with what my Mother had done to me when I was in the second grade. As a "left-handed-boy," I was looked down upon by Japanese society, as if I had no brain.

On a beautiful day, when mid-summer's heat gently cradled the entire city of Hiroshima, I had been with a group of boys playing "war-games" on the way home from school.

My Father had strictly forbidden me to play these games, and although he had given his reasons, I didn't accept them, and secretly continued to play.

As the firstborn son of a proud *Samurai* family, I recall being astonished to learn that I was heir to a family name said to have descended from the Tokugawa Shogunate. Tangible evidence of my lineage was the family crest, an ancient heraldic insignia bearing the coat of arms of the Tokugawa.

I had every reason to be proud, and to hope that one day when I came of the age, the highest honor bestowed by the Emperor himself—the spirit of *kamikaze*, the winds of the Gods—would flow through my veins.

For Japanese parents, ultimate fulfillment of parental duties meant seeing their sons become proud Japanese soldiers; for a male child, there was no greater honor than to serve and, if necessary, to sacrifice one's life for one's country, and for the Emperor.

Too weak to resist, I fell to the temptation of social expectations, thinking of myself, of my pride and honor to serve the Emperor as a greater duty. I played the game, dishonoring my Father's wishes.

And so, on a beautiful afternoon with the sun high in a blue sky, I was chosen by my peers to be "it"—the Japanese Imperial Military General to lead warriors into battle and eventually win the war. I was to crush the power of the Imperial United States Military, to prevent it from ever threatening global peace.

On the battlefield, after each conflict, "American soldiers" killed under my command made "pools of blood." I was having victory after victory. Oh, how we played! One war-game became two, and two became four. When I came home to do my homework, my Mother anxiously wanted to know why I was so late. I had an answer prepared, telling her I had been held back by my teacher to finish an arithmetic assignment. Math was my weakest subject and I thought Mother would accept my explanation without question.

I proved unsuccessful, and Mother told me it had been folly to lie in the first place. I was severely punished for playing the forbidden war-game, but the discipline for my lying seemed unduly heavy to me.

Besides lengthy lectures and preventative instructions, she tied my hands behind my back and to a post, so that I had to watch my sisters and brother have dinner with our parents. Mother tried to explain that her duties as the Mother of the Number One Son of Tanemori demanded such action. Her lot in life was to bring up her son as a worthy heir to the family name, to perpetuate the family without end.

My Father kept his silence, while two of my older sisters, Chisako and Satsuko, took great joy in seeing their younger brother, the Tanemori heir, being punished. They finished supper to their content, while I was tied to the post without food, licking my dry chops.

I greatly resented my Mother, as I was extremely disturbed by her explanation and her depriving me of dinner. Neither did my humiliation before my older sisters go down well with me.

I felt there was a code of honor and respect that my Mother spoke of which should have been carefully guarded for her proud Number One Son.

I wasn't willing to give my *tamashii*, my soul, to obey my Mother. Whether she didn't tell me the real "heart" reason for which she disciplined me, or whether I was too young to understand the teaching behind her actions, I do not know. Nevertheless, she was as alarmed by my lying as she was by my disobeying, and doing something clearly "wrong."

While my siblings found their bedtime comfort, my Mother sat with me and kept me awake. She hoped I would soon come to my senses instead of continuing to fume with anger.

It was then that my Father whispered to her, and came over to whisper into my ear. With a quivering yet strong and warm voice, he looked squarely into my eyes and said, "These may be the only moments we have to spend together, closely, as father and son."

I felt an element of urgency and anxiety in his spirit. He spoke to me to reenforce the *Bushido,* the way of *Samurai*, the code of honor and the principles of *Jita-Kyoei*. These instructions were not new to me. Having been under his tutelage for nearly eight years, I could now recite them in my dreams.

However, I had a little difficulty following him at first, seeing that he, too, was struggling with his heart.

I cannot recall my Father reinforcing my Mother's teachings, defending her methods, as he did that night. Why did he have to tell me that I should have accepted and given the understanding to my heart to my Mother? How could I not conceive that she did what she did because of her love, which drove her to say what she did?

Then he quickly tried to impress certain things upon my heart by reiterating his simple instructions and teaching, which he had previously tried to instill within me. I vaguely remembered:

"*Jibun ni makeru hod kno yo de kowai mono wa nai.* The greatest fear in the world is to be self-defeated by one's own fear, weakness. The greatest enemy is oneself."

"*Jubin ni katsu hodo kno yo de yuuki no irumono wa nai.* The greatest demand upon our courage in the world is to overcome oneself. Having victory over oneself is the greatest honor and accomplishment."

The code of *Bushido* and the principles of *Jita-Kyoei* should be the foundation and mortar of the building blocks for your life. "Remember who you are and try to honor your spirit and follow your own heart, even when the time comes to go against the norms of society."

My Father thought the most important goal of life was to maintain loyalty to whom it belongs: he was to stand true to himself. In many respects he was misunderstood, for his conduct and often his character were equated with selfishness by the norm of Japanese society in his day, a norm by which one's life must be dedicated and committed only for the sake of the whole. Individual achievement and success were identified and subordinated to group achievement.

Thus my Father was seemingly caught in the horns of a dilemma. As a Japanese man, he undoubtedly held allegiance to the Emperor, but as an individual man and a father, his duty was to prepare his son—building his character, guiding his person—to be a worthy heir to the family name.

I never had a chance to tell my Mother how sorry I was to lie to her. I never asked for her forgiveness. I wondered what my Mother thought of a son whose heart and stubborn will were still unbroken?

Then I heard again my Father's instruction, "Takashi, remember always who you are and follow the light of your heart. Never forget you are responsible for all your judgments and actions. Be true to yourself, regardless of consequences."

I really did not understand the impact of my Father's last instruction. Except that he told me he loved me and was proud of me as his son.

At the time, I did not know that this was to be the last supper my Mother would ever prepare for us; three days later, August 6, 1945, Hiroshima was reduced to ashes.

Somehow, Mary's caring love came across as if she was supplying me with the motherly love that I was robbed of in my formative years, as I struggled out of the ruins of postwar Japan.

"Mary," I was in earnest, "me no mooore saze thozu baaad things ..."

As she hugged me again I felt her tears drop on my face. She said, "Tommy, there is someone bigger than I who loves you very much."

"Whooo is that bigger man? And who thaat beeg person louves mee? Whaaat his name is? Do youu know him, Mary? Is he bigger than Mr. G.?" I said, all in one breath. Mary was in tears for my innocence.

There were still greater struggles and conflicts plaguing my soul—between the vow I had made to avenge my Father's death, my revenge on Americans, and the inexplicable love I had begun to feel from Mary, to be released from revenge.

My heart remained caught in a whirlwind which had subsided only to regain energy and again leap forth with energy beyond my control.

However hard I tried to shake it, even to deny the experience of Mary's tender love—I could not. What was it that I had to do, to be true to myself? I began to find my frozen heart thawing by the energy of Mary's love without boundaries.

The decision I was about to make would have a lasting impact upon my life and the destiny of the Tanemori family. My duty to restore the honorable family name and to perpetuate the "seed" of Tanemori rested heavily on my shoulders. But now, I found myself teeter-tottering between loyalty and duty. I simply felt it was too late for me to retreat or abandon her love.

One day, two doctors escorted me from my room down a long corridor, then ushered me into a conference room which immediately made me shiver, due to an unexpected drop in temperature. The room was as cold as a freezer! All my senses told me that I was surrounded by lifelessness and death.

A man in a black gown (I later learned he was a judge from Stanislus County) was surrounded by seven doctors.

"What kind of doctor is he, wearing a black robe?" I asked myself. Wasn't a black robe a symbol of evil and death? It became apparent that he would preside over the special meeting about to be convened.

The judge sat at the center of a horseshoe-shaped table. The doctors took their seats. Mary was standing beside another table, directly in front of the Judge. Miss Jean White, my blonde-haired, blue-eyed social worker, entered the room and sat down at Mary's table. Why? What was going on?

Although I was made to sit at the far end of Mary's table, two doctors guarded me closely, as if they intended to control my breathing. Was I a criminal?

Before Mary took her seat, she walked over to take my hand firmly in hers, held it warmly, and whispered, "Tommy, don't worry. I'm with you."

I sensed urgency in her eyes. What was she trying to tell me? Her big blue eyes filled with morning dew, reflected by the midday sun. Her concern for me reassured me and would help me keep my sanity during the meeting.

As the roll call began, I recognized one doctor: the bald-headed Dr. Henry Gallop. He was wearing a white gown, as if representing purity and honesty—a physician who administered mercy. Ha!

My suppressed rage returned, full-flared. I recalled an image from a fable: an "evil devil," a man in a field wearing a long black robe, harvesting skulls with a wickedly sharp sickle. Dr. Gallop should have been the one wearing a long black robe! He had everything to do with my physical and mental sufferings and tortures. He was the one who exercised his power to keep me in "HELL."

These men were gathered in the name of medical research, in the hope of discovering answers to the effects of radiation on human beings, if there were any, especially on me. They could have destroyed me, literally—physically, emotionally and mentally—if not for the daring of Mary, who had taken me under her professional and personal care.

I had no idea why I was in this room, before the judge and doctors, nor did I understand what was going on when the meeting started. But through confusing discussions and heated exchanges, I gathered that they were deciding what to do with me.

Each doctor, in turn, presented his evaluation and judgment. Dr. Gallop begged the other doctors to support his cause. I saw his face redden as he spoke and responded to other doctors. He said that his "ideal" experiments would work if he had more time—something like that.

They had each spoken a second, and some a third time, expressing opinions and counter-opinions, in regard to the additional tests Dr. Gallop was asking for. Alll the while, the judge sat quietly, presumably taking notes.

I noticed that some doctors seemed to have an influence on his judgment, perhaps stirring his empathy through their own empathy toward me as they glanced and pointed at me several times during their heated arguments.

My social worker was allowed to speak briefly. Then, finally, the time came for Mary to speak. Although I didn't understand all she said, I heard my name mentioned several times, through her tears. Then they all exited to another room, except for Mary, who remained in her seat. Who was on trial, I wondered.

The moments we spent waiting for their return seemed like an eternity. Even in those anxious moments, Mary cast her eyes on me. I felt as if the distance between us might never be bridged again, that our paths might never cross again. Suddenly, fear overwhelmed me. I was gasping for air. After all, everything she had done for me was clearly against the leadership and authority of Dr. Gallop. I could well imagine his spitefulness toward Mary, thinking she had caused him to miss the opportunity to become an "expert" on the effect of radiation exposure on humans.

My thoughts ran wildly—from the day I was taken to the Delano hospital, then to Bakersfield, then to other hospitals, and finally here to Modesto. Darkness and pain overwhelmed me and I became frightened, petrified.

How could I allow my heart to go through that again, even for a moment? I felt like a candle about to be extinguished, like a flame soon to be snuffed out, leaving ever-total darkness.

"NO! I won't let you take my life," I screamed silently. "NO! Whatever you are going to do to me, I won't let you!"

How can I allow this bald-headed doctor to destroy my life? Then, suddenly, a thought flashed into existence: what would happen if Dr. Gallop didn't get his way? Would they send me back where I came from? How could I go back to Japan, where my relatives and countrymen had rejected me, thinking my emigration to America was the selling of my soul? I would become a laughingstock without having fulfilled my goal!

My goal of revenge must be accomplished at any cost. If not, I would rather remain a crazed monkey in this hospital. Let Dr. Gallop have his way! This would be far better—or any other alternative—than to be crucified again by the hands of my own relatives and countrymen.

In the land of the enemy,
as an outcast with slanted eyes,

I fell before the indifference of strangers;
sightlessly, they trampled upon my dignity.
This life of anguish seemed to be my destiny.
Oh, Hiroshima take me back
to my "hiding" place.

Would my six long months of despair and loneliness come to an end? Would there be the sound of a jubilant trumpet, or a wailing from the abyss? The moment was a windstorm, the very air fraught with fear and anxiety.

The seven doctors returned to their seats and waited for the judge to return. Mary came over to sit next to me. She held my hand tightly, her eyes showing her capacity for caring. How could anyone miss her compassionate eyes?

The moment finally came. I never had seen a person as solemn as the judge had been during the often-heated arguments of the hearing. Nor anyone as solemn as the judge when he returned to announce his decision.

Suddenly, the entire conference room became filled with a mystified air. Mary squeezed my hand again. I waited impatiently, expecting the judge to speak right away. Instead, he sat quietly, flipping the pages of his notes. I could hear the breathing of the doctors, who were anxiously awaiting his decision.

Then, in a deep but soft voice, the judge began to elaborate the grounds of his decision. Although I didn't understand much of what he said, I was able to gather that he spoke of Delano and Bakersfield as two of the hospitals in which I had been treated.

I also heard the names of my social worker and Mary Furr. Mary's hands were sweaty, and she began to breathe erratically. It was some time before the judge ordered me to stand, and Mary as well. I looked over at Dr. Gallop. His facial muscles were so tight, it seemed he might break into pieces.

There was the austere pause, then the judge announced his decision. Cheers rang from several doctors as the judge granted Mary's wish on my behalf. She had successfully intervened. In my eyes she was a true angel, sent by Whitman's God, a God I did not know! I was discharged from the hospital into the care of Mary, my new Guardian Angel.

That Friday, Mary and I walked out of the main entrance of the hospital together, into the outside world, and I felt my spirit become a white butterfly, soaring and dancing freely in the wind. I never turned to look back.

My heart was restored. My eyes, filled with gratitude, were set forward. How little I had known of the power of love, and of the compassionate heart of Mary, who was the instrument of my heart's freedom. Her life was a demonstration of Divine Love that would later help me to learn and define the Divine, and the essence of human relationships.

At last, I was found! How precious was the life given back to me! My enemy never had the power to take it from me. I believed the healing power of Mary's love and the tenacity of human life had combined to create an unconquerable power within my soul.

Budding leaves renew this tired soul;
gently the rain was embraced by her love,
comforting this salvaged heart
as if I were a blade of grass
emerging from the ashes of death,
and my heart connected to heaven.
The hope for the future,
this would be my new destiny.

Mary—an older American nurse I had once considered my enemy—had made the difference in my behavior and my attitude toward doctors and psychiatric wards. They were no longer my burden. I had relearned how to trust and to be trusted. I had regained knowledge of how to be loved. My experience with Mary was like finding myself in my Mother's cradling arms. Although I had great reservations about Mary's love, this new experience gave me the one thing my life sorely lacked—LOVE. It saved my life and sanity. This would be the beginning of my long personal journey "from revenge to forgiveness, and on to peace." Mary had shown me how to heal my heart and how to forgive. And above all, how to be loved.

Through her actions, she had introduced me to Jesus and His teachings about God's love and forgiveness: a message that fell on my parched heart like a gentle rain. This allowed me to move forward and explore new paths. For the first time I felt hope!

Chapter Four: College Life

A Man without Spirit
is like a room without books,
learning knowledge and
never gaining the wisdom—
a truly foolish man.

I LEFT Mary Furr and her husband in 1959, and began seeking my new life in America. While attending fashion design school, I found a job as a "houseboy" for the Steiners, a well-to-do Jewish business family in the Presidio District of San Francisco. In that enchanting city of fog and light, of wind, western history and tourism, I began to enjoy the lifestyle of the community. I learned to get around by riding buses, street-cars and the famous cable-cars in a world that attracted tourists from the four corners of earth.

I enjoyed seeing all sorts of people, especially those parading through the downtown financial district and Fisherman's Wharf. I amused myself by just sitting and watching people, and by trying to learn something from the experience! I could spend hours and hours just watching stupid people do stupid things!

You could say I became one of them. Should I have been congratulated for having become as "normal" as any American, except for my inability to speak good English? I had learned fast by mimicking Americans: "Monkey see, monkey do!"

Nearly ten months of my new duties and my new life had passed, before it occurred to me that I had done nothing to fulfill my promise of revenge. It struck me as almost a "crime" to enjoy a life of leisure, conveniences and luxuries, after having struggled to rise from the atomic ashes of Hiroshima. The more I lived a comfortable life with the Steiners, the more I began to feel a great storm brewing within my heart.

I couldn't bear to see the face of Mary, who had risked herself, her care, and her social-standing, to salvage my soul. What I had promised her was not getting done, and

I knew I wouldn't be following my heart by continuing to meet the wishes of the Steiners.

Out of my gratitude to Mary for having become my "guardian" and for charting my footsteps a new course in America, I had promised to commit myself to a new life. When I begged Mr. Steiner to let me return to Fresno's agricultural fields in order to make money, I was doing what I needed to do to prepare for the future.

I told Steiner I would spend the entire summer of 1960 earning money towards an education. Of course the Steiners were happy for me! Mr. Steiner had said loud and clear, "Young man, you need to learn English, and American culture, if you are to survive in this country."

Thick fog had recently rolled in, blanketing the entire Golden Gate Bridge. I had just returned from doing "piece-work" at a migrant labor camp in Fresno, where I had earned the first installment payment on my latest adventure: attending a private Baptist College in the fall. Three months off from my obligation to the Steiners had allowed me to make the money I needed to start school. No one in Fresno had guessed that I clutched $300.00 in one hand as I waved goodbye with the other, saying, "So long until next summer," after which I had dragged my worn, beaten body from the beastly hot Central Valley to "cool" San Francisco. The money represented my promise to become like Mary, "reaching out my hand to strangers, giving hope, pointing the way to a brighter future."

Just as soon as I had cleaned up and made myself presentable, Mr. and Mrs. Steiner, for whom I had been working as a houseboy for more than two years, asked me to meet with them in their living room. The white, furry-carpeted living room had been normally been off limits to me, except when I was serving in my "official capacity."

"Why, of all places, in the living room?" I asked myself with apprehension. The only times it hadn't mattered to them whether someone walked into the living room in dirty street shoes was when their friends had come over for wild parties. At such times, Miss Burnice, her crew members and I would serve their "honorable guests," and I would invariably be disgusted to see so many haughty-minded people in one place. Otherwise, I had only been allowed to enter the living room shoeless, in clean socks, to dust and clean.

While Mrs. Irene Steiner tried unsuccessfully to console my heart, her husband, Mr. Richard "Tommy" Steiner, the master of the house, boisterously demanded my attention. His appearance conveyed inner turmoil and anger.

"When you asked us to give you time off during the summer to go to Fresno to make money, it made us happy to think you were following our guidance and the advice we had given you for the last two years."

"Yes, Zarr. Mr. Steiner," I responded, fumbling, my heart beating like a *taiko*-drum. I held my heart with my tiny hands to stop it from bursting from the inexplicable excitement I had somehow stirred.

"You, of all people," his voice quivered, "deliberately lied to us." His thunder and lightning crashed down on me over and over again. Blood vessels protruded on his face, adding several years to an already aged visage. He tightened his fists, threatening, I thought, to pounce on me like prey.

Mr. Steiner was six-foot-two and 280 pounds, whereas I was five-foot-three and 125 pounds soaking wet. I sat there like a skinny alley cat caught by a saliva-dripping bulldog.

"I just don't see how you can sit here with a straight face; I'd like to know what kind of Christian you are, as you profess to be?"

I swallowed heavily! If I wasn't eaten by the time he finished, my head would soon be rolling off a chopping block, for sure!

Mrs. Steiner looked at me, and spoke softly, reassuringly, "I'm trying to understand how you want to repay the kindness of an American nurse. I think that's what you've told us. That's wonderful."

She inched toward me, asking, "But how can you throw away two years of design school, with only one more year to finish? And how are you going to pay all those school expenses? I'm sure whatever Bible School you're planning to attend won't be so kind as to let you in for free. Who are those people who think they know you better than us, and have led you to enter the ministry, in *Minnesota*? Such a strange place, with unbearably cold winters."

"After all," she continued with her soft, yet ever-sharp tongue, "Mr. Steiner built a studio for you in the basement and we have provided many things just to make a workable situation for you. We'd like to see you get a fashion designer certificate. Who knows where it would take you? Can't you see what we're trying to do for you?"

She took a deep breath. "You haven't forgotten, have you? When we took you in, you were a strange Japanese who couldn't speak English. No one was willing to take you in, and you had no identity. Haven't we risked ourselves to bring you into our home? Haven't we provided you with a roof over your head? Haven't we given you freedom, even allowed you to raid our refrigerator? As a matter of fact, we encouraged you to bring your friends here, making this truly your home." What a mouthful she spoke in one breath!

"Have you forgotten the many embarrassments and irreversible troubles you got into with your poor English?" She persisted. "How humiliated we were when we had to cover mistakes and blunders you made during the entertainment of our important business and social guests! And I won't let you forget that we had to hire Bernice to help you, so that our friends wouldn't be embarrassed again. She cost us a great deal of money. She didn't work for free, you know!"

"Yiezu, Maaaam, Mrs. Steiner." I dropped my head even lower. I didn't remember so many blunders. As Mrs. Steiner refreshed my stinging memories, I felt I should defend myself because many of these mistakes were innocent, unintentional. They were honest mistakes, almost entirely owing to the unkind, impatient rudeness of their friends and guests when I was trying to accommodate their needs. I had tolerated them with my Japanese *heart,* while they had acted stupid, like drunken sailors.

Mrs. Steiner looked at her husband, as if seeking his support, then back at me. "You haven't forgotten, have you?

We managed to pay you in full at the end of the month (twenty dollars a month) as we agreed when we hired you."

Her voice sounded odd as she continued, "Remember how many times you bowed and thanked us for our kindness and generosity. Let me remind you that you promised then to stay with us to attend Continuation (Adult) School to learn English while you finished design school."

Every word she uttered, every incident she resurrected, was like a grinding millstone crushing me into powder.

"Tommy. Listen to me. It's impossible to get ahead or do anything without speaking good English. You simply need to learn good English. That's the only way you can become a real American someday. If you want to go to a Bible School, why don't you go here to the theological school in Berkeley? Do you have any idea how far away Minnesota is? I know Mr. Steiner is totally against you going. You have a home here, and friends. Wouldn't you miss us all?"

"Yiezu, Mezzezue Steiner," I nodded my head.

Then, all of sudden, Mr. Steiner barked at me again, "Tommy Boy, Mrs. Steiner is right. How many times have we told you there are no money trees growing on every corner! Neither are American streets paved with gold! Look at our hands!" He thrust forward his big hands, as if they were shovels, somewhat worn and callused.

"Nobody gave us what we have. We worked and worked, day-in, day-out, with these hands." He almost burst into laughter, perhaps trying to hide his own pain and disappointment.

"Hey! my boy! You've certainly been sucked into believing the propaganda of the American government, coming over to work at a migrant labor camp."

I had to take his sermon as castigation, mocking me. Momentarily, I lost sense of where I was, until he continued, "I think you have a great and noble idea to honor that nurse, but what do you think of us?"

Their words weighed heavily on me, like massive, ponderous sledgehammers striking my heart. I felt a heavy pain rush into my bowels, gutting my insides.

After the heated one-way discourse, I realized they had the upper hand over me, the houseboy, unable to speak English, to convey my heart.

Through the Steiners' eyes, I saw that staying with them was an attractive option with great benefits—provision for daily needs, security in a familiar environment—and that I simply needed to do what they advised and continue to work for them.

But if I were to honor my heart, they would certainly see me as an ungrateful, disturbed, misled Japanese boy who had found "new faith" in Christianity. That was contrary to their beliefs, a mockery of the Steiners! My decision to go to Minnesota would be nothing short of betrayal, of denying everything they had done for me.

So far, I had utterly failed to convey my appreciation for their investment in my life. I needed to try one last time to move their hearts, even if the effort was to be in vain.

In my mind, giving my life to the gospel ministry and serving humanity was nothing short of honoring their hearts. How noble! I had hoped they would understand and give me their blessing, because this was the best way for me to manifest my gratitude and demonstrate it in action.

But even as they were unable to consider my heart, my heart was now unable to consider the advice of the Steiners. The unconditional love of Mary Furr, the love that had rescued my soul from the "snake-pit," tipped the scales against the Steiners' requests.

In subjecting myself to the will of the Steiners, however attractive their offers might be, I would be like a bird whose wings have been cropped, which is kept in a cage with an iron padlock on its door. I could not consign my soul into their hands to be "played with" at their will!

I set my eyes toward Minnesota, without the foggiest idea how far away it was, nor of what lay between San Francisco and Minnesota. All I knew was that I held my future in my own hands!

Here I was, caught between two opinions' powerful energies welling within my soul. I could hear the internalized voice of my Father, who had said so often in my first eight years, "Son, remember who you are and try to follow your heart, no matter what, even sometimes against the opinions and ideas of others. Remember, you are responsible for your own judgment and actions."

My decision followed my heart and the "Three-Fold-Principles" my Father had instilled in me!

The day came when, having said a painful goodbye to the Steiners, I left San Francisco, literally without turning back to look at them. I had burnt a "bridge" and there could be no turning back. I wondered if I had broken their hearts.

I set my face toward the unknown waters of the future, as I was determined to affirm my faith in God's Word: *"... but my God shall supply all your needs according to His riches in glory by Christ Jesus."* [Philippines 4:19]

I had $300.00 in my palm, my entire earnings from that summer. I let God do His wonders, keeping His promise as the test of my faith and my heart!

My friend Gilbert Manning, one of the young people from our home church, left San Francisco for Minnesota, an unknown territory. Gilbert was a white man, six-foot-five and 250 pounds. His fellow traveler was Japanese, five-foot-three and 125 pounds. It took four long days of driving in a 1953 Ford (Fix Or Repair Daily) jalopy for our trip across the vast, beautiful expanse of America from the coast of California to Minnesota. On September 4, 1960, we finally arrived at our destination: Owatonna, Minnesota. We were 70 miles south of Minneapolis, at the campus of Pillsbury Baptist College, a private institution.

As the only Japanese in the midst of many "white" students, all gathered together by the same God who had called us to the ministry, I would soon learn more harsh lessons about being a survivor of Hiroshima and a Japanese immigrant. The culture in which I was raised, enigmatic values, my poor English, and my misunderstanding of Christianity (including its perceptions and misconceptions of the Japanese), would all play major roles in building the "character" of this ministerial student in the American Midwest.

My reception by the students, faculty and town people was amusing, as they had never seen a "live and kicking" Japanese man before. They looked at me as if I was a representative of the Japanese race—the "Little Brown Artisans"—who had stolen the brains of the whites.

The grotesque & unpleasant Japanese "heathen" ...
they perceived me so poignantly.
I had to chuckle to myself under my breath.
Their attitude toward me—of a non-occidental race,
like a monkey in a circus ring—was most amusing;
and some questioned my blood—was it red or
*   yellow or green?*
My buckteeth protruded from my mouth,
my eyes were slanted and narrow enough,
like a single stroke of the brush;
and my goggle-eyed glasses were "made-in Japan,"
considered antique—"cheap-junk" of the Postwar-
*   era.*
My small, chubby nose conspicuously needed,
underneath, no need for shaving of "peach-fuzz."

They recognized me for what I was supposed to be,
but I was, to most of the people in the community,
even less realistic—for there was no one to compare
*   me to.*
There may have been grains of truth in such images,
but I thought they were still misled
by their own ignorance, by their own perceptions
and suspicions, not conducive to understanding
who I was—a Japanese—and who I was not,
accepted into their circle as a part of them.
To see me as a ministerial student,
Is it possible for God to make mistake?
Oh, heavens, no!

I waited in the long registration line in the hallway. Finally my turn came and I was bewildered by a grumpy voice. "Your name?" the man sitting behind the long table asked me, without looking at me. I remembered how often my Father had said that, as a Japanese custom and show of respect, I should always look into the eyes of the person to whom I was speaking. I gave him the benefit of the doubt. Since he had been dealing with so many students before me, perhaps his eyes were tired.

"I know who you are. You are a Japanese."

"A JAP-anese?" A high-pitched exclamation from one of the students standing right behind me created some commotion. Immediately, more than half a dozen students huddled together, whispering among themselves.

"Yeah! He doesn't look like us," someone muttered under their breath. "Of course, what do you expect? He has slanted eyes," someone else said.

I wanted to ask the man behind the table, loudly, "If you knew who I was, why did you ask my name?" But I internalized my feeling with a silent comment to myself in Japanese.

"How much are you going to put down?"

While I was computing what "how much … put down?" meant, it must have appeared I was displaying slowness of mind, or aloofness. I was looking at the man as if peering into a dark hole.

"I need to know how much money you want to pay!" he impatiently demanded. If he had only looked at me, I might have been able to understand him better.

"The MONEY!" he said, raising his voice.

"Aaa! M aa N EE Y!" I smiled at him. "Hee-re!" I gave him all three hundred dollars. He took it without raising an eyebrow, and gave me back a few coins.

Coins in hand, I was proud to see myself paying off my entire school expenses—tuition, room and board—for the entire year.

"See, Mr. & Mezzesu Steiner," I said to myself. "I have enough money, and a little extra change. You really needn't worry for me now."

From day one at Pillsbury Baptist College, I conducted myself in a circumspect manner. It was as if I walked everywhere backward, sweeping my eyes from right to left, making sure no one would sneak up from behind and jump me. I behaved patiently, not giving emotional responses to people staring or being rude as I passed them.

But one student, David Sailor, constantly called me a shrimp, sometimes shouting at me to stand up. I had given him plenty of warnings that I didn't appreciate his picking on me. The time finally came for me to stand tall and let him know that I was not going to take his "blankety-blank" attitude any more.

"David," I stood right in front of his face, pointing my finger upward toward his nose. "If you call me that name one more time, you'll be wiping the hallway on your back." I surprised myself with my commanding voice.

"David. I'm getting frightened. I better pull my tail between my legs ... Look! I'm shaking," Thom Ridder, who weighed about 225 pounds, spoke mockingly.

"Enough is enough. I'm warning you, David. You better behave yourself before it's too late."

"Hey, David! This shrimp speaks good English," another student jibed. "At least we understand half of what he's saying. That's not bad, not bad at all!"

David voiced his response, "What did you say, shrimp?"

Just as he finished saying "shrimp," I struck, like lightning. I used the skill—*seoi nage,* judo—that I had learned growing up. I swiftly rolled underneath him and threw him over my shoulder. As I expected, he lay flat on his back, having no idea what had hit him.

Wiping my hands as I stood over his body, I glared at the rest of the students, then walked away, slowly and deliberately, without looking back.

Over the next three-and-a-half years, David Sailor became, as it were, my "bodyguard." He looked after me when other students tried my patience, my faith and my Japanese heart.

I held probationary student status since I had no high school diploma and couldn't speak good English; I was told that I had to take "bonehead English." I found great consolation in the fact that I wasn't the only one who had to take "bonehead English," for at least a dozen or so *genuine* white American students occupied the same boat with me.

My head spun as I attended class after class, as most of the professors eloquently expounded their "knowledge" through their lips. In their lectures, I was only able to recognize a few frequently repeated words or short sentences. I felt as if I was sitting in the shadow of the *yagura,* the Tower of Babel. I thought these professors were just reading from notes they had taken from their own professors many years before.

I needed either a special kind of machine to record and slow down their speeches, and then translate them into Japanese, or else an extra brain. I wondered if my brain had been damaged by the atomic blast so long ago.

Using a Japanese-to-American dictionary, the harder and longer I studied, the further behind I got. How I longed to take time off, like many of the other students, to enjoy the early autumn season.

I would have been even worse off if it wasn't for the kind help of Miss Hazel Wilcox, a "white" female classmate who was old enough to be my big sister, and who secretly helped me.

Miss Wilcox was in all of my classes, except for the "bonehead" English class. She was blue-eyed and blonde and stood tall among the female students. She was what I called a true *Kin-patsu Gaaru,* a blonde American girl, one I would often see in my dreams.

Simple and natural in her beauty, her white skin reminded me of *sui-mitsu,* a white Japanese peach, both in pigment and in the aromatic air that teased my nostrils.

One afternoon, she came to me and said, "I once knew a missionary who struggled to study the Japanese language." There was a pause. "You, being a Japanese student, I know how hard and difficult it must be for you to study in English. I want to help make your study easier." I looked at her with my narrow-slanted eyes opened wide under goggle-eyed glasses.

Each evening at dinner hour Hazel and I rushed to the "Big Dipper," the campus dining room. There, quietly and inconspicuously, avoiding the "all-seeing-eyes" of students and professors, she slipped her neatly-typed lectures of the day into my hands. One day she explained her method, "I take every lecture by short-hand, and I have no problem at all typing them."

I had no idea what "short-hand" meant, seeing that my arms were much shorter than anyone else's!

If I wasn't in town looking for a job, I was buried in the library or in my room with my Japanese-to-American dictionary. I frequently banged my head against the wall in frustration and anger for failing to meet class deadlines. I had no special dispensation from my professors—they punished me all-around for my inability to complete assignments on time. I was stacking up demerit after demerit for turning in work late.

I searched for answers to my study problems. The only thing I could do was "steal" from my night hours, cracking the books while other students were deep in slumber.

School rules clearly stated that all lights were to be off at 10:00 p.m. during the school week. No one was allowed even a whisper after that hour, and if a monitor caught you, the offense was punishable by demerits.

I had two dormitory roommates on the other side of a curtain that divided our big room into two smaller areas, of which I had the smaller space. One night, I noticed that a streetlight outside the window cast its light faintly into my room. I moved my bed around to the window, and discovered that I could study by its dim illumination.

For the next few nights, studying by streetlight, I gained very little understanding of the lectures, but a pair of very red, bloodshot eyes.

Then I remembered my fourth grade teacher Ms. Takahashi *Sensei* letting me use her small mirror to catch sunlight. Her mirror had such power to send light deep into a dark school storage room!

Several days after my "vision," I found a jagged mirror in a dumpster. After several discouraging attempts, I managed to hang it inside the window frame. It was out of view from the room door, hidden by the window drapes.

I was rather pleased with my cleverness, until the monitor caught me one night while I was studying.

"Tonnaamoori." The boisterous voice of the Monitor shattered the tranquillity of the night. He had sneaked like a thief into my room, catching me unawares.

"I caught you, didn't I? Ha, ha, ha!" Carrying a twisted smile and waving a thick demerit book, his voice was enough to make me sick. "You sure are a sneaky blankety-blank!"

He took great pleasure in confiscating the broken mirror and bringing me before the Discipline Committee, where I was given a whopping 25 demerits for my "sin" of studying after "lights out."

Must I not settle the score with this monitor, even if it meant additional demerits? Trying to outwit him for extra study time, I took refuge in the bathroom, after-hours.

"Oh, my! Why didn't I think of this long before?" I smiled with contempt. I was confident that the ugly monitor would never find me.

I sat on the commode, behind the closed door, attending to my business. It seemed, since I had become an orphan, that I was always alone. And yet in solitude, in shutting the world out, I found peace with myself.

The bathroom offered me a safe haven until one night when mice, running every way above the ceiling, attracted the same monitor, who caught me in the act of studying.

"I am taking all these," he sneered, grabbing my notes. "This will be perfect evidence before the Discipline Committee of the transgression of school laws."

The next day I stood before the Discipline Committee for my "blatantly-committed sin." I was without remorse. I questioned why was I being punished for extra studying and preparing myself to do the work of the Lord?

Multi-prismatic autumn leaves had long since danced and disappeared, and the landscape had evolved into a snow-covered graveyard, swept by the piercing north wind. All the trees stood like skeletons, reminding me of the few mangled steel and concrete buildings that had stood over Hiroshima's ashes so long ago.

My heart, too, was frozen. I had no money to spend, not even for a cup of hot chocolate. I felt like the "Ugly Duckling" of the children's fable. Most of the students had already headed home for Christmas vacation.

There were a number of students like me who had no home to go to, and others who stayed on campus while they worked jobs in town. My two roommates, whose homes were within three hours of the school, left without saying a word to me.

Suddenly, inexplicable feelings welled up, as I saw the faces of Susan, Mary, Brenda, Mike, Kenny and Jennifer—the church youth group in San Francisco—seemingly a million miles away. How I longed to see them!

With Christmas vacation over, the students geared up for the end of first semester. It was now January the 10th. The north wind whistled through my thin pants.

A summons came from the Registrar. Now what had I done? The Registrar also carried the title of Business Director. Had I met him before?

"Tanemori."

I stepped into his office. The man sitting behind the desk with an open book was none other than the man I had first dealt with at the registration line. It seemed so long ago. His left hand conspicuously guarded a small black box.

He pointed to a folding chair, and I sat down. The oakwood desk separating us demonstrated the obvious difference in our respective positions. He then pointed at the ledger. "It's time for you to pay for your tuition, room and board for the second semester, if you want to stay in school. It was due last week."

I was dumbfounded! He was talking about "money" again. The few coins I had left from the $300 were already long spent.

"Yeizu. Waaat do you mean if I want to stay second semester?" I protruded my mouth, questioning him. "Did I not give you all the money I had? And you thanked me."

This was the first time I learned that the three hundred-dollars paid for registration covered only the first semester and not a full year. He wanted more money from me. I was totally confused and bewildered by the predicament in which I found myself.

"Yiezu. I haave no moore maaa neey. Mee go baack to Fresno again next Saammar. I waark haard and I waark haard again for long time. I meiku Maach Maa NEEY for schooool. I come baack next September to gieve youu maaneey. OK?"

"No! You don't understand, do you, Tanemori?" The Registrar was short-fused, and it was obvious he didn't understand my mixed tongue.

He quickly resorted to his authority, edging his upper body toward me. "You need to come up with the money for the down payment. Or we need to have someone guarantee you for financial support by February 1st, or else you're out. You have three weeks to give us an answer."

"Caan yuu gieve mee a jaab on campus?" I asked in desperation.

"What can you do?" he blurted.

"Yiezue, Saaar. I caaan duu any things." I tried to convince him that I was a fast learner. That I was also not afraid to get my hands dirty.

"There is no work for someone who doesn't understand and can't speak good English. But you have until February 1st to come up with the money," he repeated, pointing me out the door.

I guessed by his smile that he must have pleased himself with his decision.

So many questions were unanswered. Unless I came up with the $300 in three weeks, I would be forced to leave Pillsbury Baptist College, shattering my dream of becoming a Christian minister.

I couldn't afford that austere man's pleasure of cutting short my decision to give my life for Christian service; neither could I afford to destroy my heart. It was awesome to realize the power of money.

Instead of returning directly to my room, I made my way downtown. The streets, sidewalks and storefronts were very familiar, and by this time I recognized the voices of some of the storeowners and managers. As a matter of fact, I could almost repeat their rejections of me, word for word. I likened my job search to that of a little monkey amusing children by performing acts in a three-ring-circus.

"Here he comes again."

"Yeah, sure. He's the same one."

What I was asking for was for a job: sweeping a storefront, washing dirty dishes at a restaurant, scrubbing toilets, or taking out garbage. I simply begged for work.

As I was passing by, a little boy pulled his mother's hand, calling her attention to me. This became a regular scene for me.

"Shhhh!" The mothers' hushing of their children did nothing to prevent their taunting of me. Little children called me names and pointed their fingers, even long after I had passed them.

"Look Mommy, there goes a China-man!"

"Didn't I tell you that we don't talk to Chinese here!" another store owner shouted.

So my search for work continued to the next establishment. I begged the owner of Webber's Printing Shop, "Sar, mai naime izu Tanemori, aaa...stoodant of a BAPUUTESTO Kallagie. I neeed a jaab."

"You're back again?" He turned his back on me.

I began to speak a little more clearly, tried showing a genuine smile, although given the responses, it was very difficult to be cheerful.

The owner of Kelly's Mama and Papa restaurant said sharply into my ear, "You listen! I know *all* Japanese are sneaky, just like when they attacked Pearl Harbor ..."

Was I to be blamed for war crimes, I wondered? I had been just four years old. I wondered why the people of this town had difficulty trusting me. Either they didn't want to, or they didn't know how to deal with Japanese.

"You come back after you learn to speak GOOD English," said a manager of the Jameson Hardware Store. He too had told me there was no job, even though he hired my white classmate, Steve Johnson, who came to the store right after I left.

I passed Jake's Café, a local hangout. I peeped inside, envious of the students inside who were laughing, eating, drinking and enjoying themselves. My empty stomach was like a frozen tundra-box, discarded in the field. I smelled an aroma! "Aaaah, a cup of hot chocolate ..."

I needed more than that to thaw my frozen heart. I needed money to buy a pair of shoes, boots, a heavy winter overcoat, good furry gloves. These necessities would make my life a little more tolerable, a little more able to withstand the icy unwillingness of the community.

Trudging along with frozen feet, I was determined to make one more stop before returning to campus.

"Bang, bang, bang." I knocked repeatedly and called out loudly. "Pleeeezu. Saaar! Lit me ien. I aaam luuking for jaab."

It seemed the door had been locked just a split second before I arrived. The "closed" sign was still swinging. I watched a man's back fade and disappear into a back room.

"No!" Wailing, I cried out in disbelief and anger, then crumpled to the frozen sidewalk.

"Hey, Japanese boy, anybody in town trusted you yet?" a college student who lived next door yelled at me.

I returned to the campus and bumped right into the Business Administrator, under a street light. He was bundled up in his heavy overcoat, heading home after finishing his hot dinner at the "Big Dipper."

"Sir!" I stopped him. Shivering, my teeth chattering, I could hardly see his face, but I sensed he was disturbed.

"What do you want?"

"What do I want from him?" I asked myself. And then, silently, "Can't you for once have a warm thought or concern for me?"

"Hurry, Taanemorie. I am on my way home to take these hot meals to my family. They will get cold."

I told him how I had failed to find a job in town and that I wished that, perhaps, he might help me find one. He stood there, mute. Then he disappeared in the darkness toward his home.

"Chikusho! You wait and see! Like it or not, I will see to it that one day you'll be eating your own worm—half worm," I raged.

It was already January the 24th. Only one more week remained. Either I came up with the money, or else. How many times I rehearsed, over and over again, to the point that I could say it without stuttering, exactly what I would say when I faced up to the Registrar one last time.

My method-to-my-madness approach to confronting him was based on my being a "probaaaaa-cionary" student, one who didn't get all the benefits of the "white" students.

"Taanemorie, I don't have all day. Besides, there are other students waiting at the door," he said, pointing his bony finger to show me the door by which I should leave.

"If I'm a probationary student and don't have the same rights and benefits as the white students, why should I pay the full tuition, for less?" I looked straight into his eyes. "It's not fair if I pay the same and get less!"

"Tanemorie," he could no longer take my gibberish, "Just remember your deadline ... "

My first Midwest winter seemed far colder now. The merciless Minnesota wind was unbearable. It howled through my thin cotton clothes. My teeth chattered and my whole body shivered with the piercing cold. My hands, chapped and bleeding, seemed to have forgotten how to touch others' heartbeats, let alone to receive. But the pain of my hands was nothing compared to the aching of my heart.

The language barrier grew. I was unable to communicate with others. My world seemed darker as my hope of becoming a minister dimmed. The reality of life seemed to be harsher and harsher as I was forced to search for an answer.

I was like a wildflower, uprooted without soil to grow. In the harsh Midwest winter, I felt as though I had been thrown back into the ashes of Hiroshima.

With no hope of a job, and no hope of getting one, the tuition deadline was approaching fast—too fast. Time had no mercy. Feeling utterly defeated, I began to argue with God—the God I trusted with all my soul, who seemed to be turning His back on me when I needed Him most!

In my last desperate attempt to find an answer, I retreated to the basement of the dormitory. There, alone with my thoughts, I prayed and searched for His guidance. It seemed my prayers went no farther than outside my lips, never traveling beyond the dark storage area in which I sat. Only scurrying mice listened to my heartbeats.

The promises the Steiners had offered now seemed very attractive. Yet they were *"ato no omatsuri."* It was too late for me to cry over spilled milk, wasn't it?

Even the internalized voice of my Father, a voice I had heard so often in my childhood, failed me. Even his voice failed to comfort my aching heart. Seeing myself standing at the *kegon-no-taki,* a famous spot of suicide in Japan, I was again at a crossroads.

After long prayers, my mail slot remained empty. I still hoped to hear from my Baptist youth group in San Francisco. They had promised to send $30 a month for my personal expenses, and I had received one check from them in early October. But since then, I hadn't heard from the young people at the church.

My Bible studies did offer some relief from my despair. I felt my heart jostled as if it were waking from a deep nightmare. An inner voice spoke, *"Hath thou faith? Had it to thyself before God? Happy was he that condemneth not himself in that thing which he alloweth ..."* [Romans 14:22]

For the next three days I chose to fast, seeking God's face and begging to see His Faithfulness to His Words and His Promise. Was I putting Him on the spot, seeking so blatantly to know whether or not He is real? I stood on my feet! I dared Him! Would this be the last desperate act of one who was drowning?

With tearful eyes I looked at the calendar. The blurry numbers indicated it was now the 30th of January. I had one more day to go. I started to gather my few belongings. There would be room to spare in my suitcase and duffel bag. I had no clear plans beyond tomorrow, only my faith, and even that was shaky.

I tossed fitfully most of the night. I was like a tiny potato, its skin being peeled off as it's washed in a large bamboo basket. I awakened to the banging of storm windows by a piercing wind and jumped out of bed to stand on the cold floor. Dawn's light was yet to reveal itself.

Determined not to show the sadness within, I attended what I thought were my final classes. In my daily ritual of checking the mail slot after chapel hour, I found undisturbed dust.

I had my answer; there were no options available. Tomorrow would be the deadline and I must inform the Business Office that I could not stay. I saw in my mind the face of the austere man, the Registrar, smiling victorious.

The day passed without additional commotion. After dinner my roommates Richard and Donald offered to take me to the campus soda fountain known as the "Little Dipper." In the past, they would close the drapes that separated our rooms to eat the cookies their families had sent, as if behind a curtain, without offering me a crumb.

"Let's celebrate your leaving. This gives someone a chance to take your place. Who knows, the next roommate might be a China-man."

Reluctantly, I agreed to join them. As we passed the mail boxes, Richard said, "Hey, Tanemori, come back. There's something in your mail box."

Having seen the mailman leave after his four o'clock delivery, I replied, "There could be nothing for me."

"Well, it won't hurt you to check and see," Donald agreed with Richard. I thought them cruel for teasing me.

"Here, Tanemori," Richard handed me the letter he had pulled from my box. "See, I told you you had mail."

Believing my roommates might have been unethical by checking my mailbox without permission, I was reluctant to listen to them. I suspected I was being set up. Yet as a drowning person will grab the straw that floats by, I took an envelope from Richard's hand.

I couldn't believe my eyes. The letter from Fresno was stamped VIA AIR MAIL - SPECIAL DELIVERY.

Suddenly my head spun and my heart pounded. The mail was from Mr. Leonard Hotchins, whom I had met while doing "piece-work" at the migrant labor camp.

How well I remembered the day he had driven up to the camp in a white Cadillac to meet me for the first time. He wore a white Panama suit with sharply pressed pants, a white Panama hat, and an unusual pair of white shoes, the heels of which clicked as he came to the screen door of the meal hall. He must have looked like an Immigration Officer to most of the migrant workers.

Only a few remained eating their dinner, as most of them shot off like bullets in every direction. When Hotchins entered the meal hall, it was as if someone had stuck a long stick into a yellowjacket hive. The workers seemed to know exactly where to hide from the eyes of "authority."

After he completed his grand entry, Hotchins spoke softly to the camp director, "I'm looking for Tommy Tanemori."

Hotchins had subsequently taken me to his church and invited me into his home several times that summer. My mind drifted away with warm thoughts.

"Hurry up. Open and read it," Richard said.

My hands were trembling. The letter was dated January 29th, 1961, and had been sent by special delivery. I would be gone by tomorrow and there would be no forwarding address. The letter read:

Dear Son in the Lord:

The Lord has indeed been so faithful to His children! We were blessed by Him as He sent you to us during the summer. Although it was a short and unusual circumstance in which we met, He gave us another "son" in the Lord. You were one of a dozen college students that He has allowed us to enjoy as part of His abundant blessings.

I imagine that you were surprised to receive this letter from us, seeing that we have not spoken to you since your phone call last summer to say you were leaving for Minnesota.

God had multiplied our business and we had been praying for the last three weeks, seeking His direction and guidance as to how we could share His blessings.

After many prayers, my wife and I were confident that God had laid your name upon our hearts. We felt the need to send this to you as quickly as possible.

Although we had no way of knowing what or how much to send:

(1) The first check for $300.00 is for your school needs (if you need more, please let us know immediately)

(2) The second check for $25.00 is for your personal needs.

After all, Minnesota is a very cold country, I think you may have enough to buy yourself, perhaps, a nice cup of hot chocolate for yourself and your "girl" friend?

As the Lord has prospered us, we are confident that He wants us to support you for the next three years until you finish your college education.

We thank the Lord for giving you to us in His Caring Love.

Sincerely,

Your Mother and Daddy in the Lord
(signed by Leonard Hotchins)

Wasn't that a Miracle? The next thing I remembered I was sitting in the *"Little Dipper,"* surrounded by Richard, Donald, and dozens of other students. At the same time I felt I was alone, sitting with my God, renewing and recommitting my tested heart to Him, for He had said: *"...They that wait upon the Lord shall renew their strength; they shall mount up with wings as eagles; they shall run, and not be weary; and they shall walk, and not faint."* [Isaiah 40:31]

I ordered my first hot chocolate, savoring its sweetness. It was so warm. It was so smooth. It was so creamy as it touched my lips. The aroma of chocolate, like roasted chestnuts, teased my nostrils. The richness of its taste filled my mouth. It reminded me of the only Japanese "creamy" milk I ever had. My fourth grade teacher, Ms. Takahashi *Sensei*, had given it to me secretly when I was very sick. Suddenly, I was back in the fourth grade classroom, burying my head against her bosom.

With my hands encircling the mug of hot chocolate, I felt warmth soothing my chapped hands. I was filled with gratitude, my broken heart mended, and my faith restored. I thanked my roommates for celebrating my departure, and then walked from the "Little Dipper," leaving them behind.

As I realized I was all alone under the black sky, I heard the distant howl of a dog. I couldn't see any yard lights. Rubbing my eyes again and again, I looked up and saw nothing.

Then I rubbed my eyes again and saw a street light casting its shadow as if in thick fog. I looked back up to the sky. I didn't know countless stars were already joined with me to celebrate the "miracle" of God, as they sparkled high above.

I had withstood the mid-western climate, but even more, I had stood against "unthinkable" odds at school!

How proud I was to realize that I, the scion of a proud *Samurai* family, had been tested by these Midwest experiences to where I could begin to grasp the significance of my family name, *TANEMORI*. It means: "The life within a Seed had its own volition and would bloom at its own time, independently."

> *Regaining Spirit of God,*
> *come to me...whatever lies ahead!*
> *I shall not be afraid, nor will I ever be fainted-heart;*
> *Here I stand*
> *as a Japanese Black Pine Tree!*

Time flew, and although it seemed impossible I had already endured two years at college. Many thanks were due to Hazel Wilcox, who had touched my life since the beginning of my first year.

While several dozen students dropped out for one reason or another, I survived and was promoted from my probationary status.

One day, I decided to try something completely different. I tried out for a pitcher position on the intercollegiate baseball team. With much effort, I made the team as a "bench-warmer." I always took schoolbooks and materials to the dugout (I preferred to call it the "doghouse"), where I studied while others played ball.

It was a rare situation when the coach shouted, *"Tanemori!* Stop studying and get over here!" I often ignored his blustering voice, and would wait until teammates teased me.

"Hey, rock head! Coach is calling you. Show your hard head!"

Even an opposing team aware of my "status" from a previous game or two shouted in sarcasm, "Please, please. Stay on the bench and gain wisdom and knowledge." They quoted the Scripture: *"A wise man is strong; yea, a man of knowledge increaseth strength ..."* [Proverbs 24:5]

In one game, I was called onto the field as a pinch hitter since I was the only player with a five-inch strike zone! It was the top of the 9th inning and the situation was almost picture perfect! We needed one run to force the opposing team to bat in the bottom of 9th. The bases were loaded and there I stood—no, crouched—in the batter's box.

Having already lost the first game of a doubleheader, the coach didn't want to see us riding the bus home "shut-out." Meanwhile, I was trying to avoid becoming like *minchi,* the shredded ground meat thrown into an animal pen at feeding time. I couldn't let the pitcher have the pleasure of striking me out! There I stood, the hunchback of Notre Dame, with a bat in my hands.

"Three balls and no strikes!" said the umpire.

I had the biggest smile as I turned to the catcher and said, "Go ahead, cuss me!"

"Oh no!" I shouted, when the next pitch smoked by like lightning. I hadn't seen it coming.

The umpire bawled out, *"Strike!"*

I argued but, to no avail! My comment was taken as a joke.

I clumsily tried to avoid the next pitch, a fast ball, coming at me. The ball whacked me, somehow hit my bat and looped over the giant first baseman, rolling into right field.

Of course none of the players on the other team were prepared for such drama. Neither were my teammates, at first. My short legs seemingly couldn't run fast enough, but I reached first base, painfully short of breath.

All of a sudden I became a "miracle" worker. I became "it," the man of the hour. Our old beat-up school bus carried us back to campus, its "rickety-clock, rickety-clock" rattling-on now a lighter, happier note, music to our ears.

Unfortunately, I never saw another miracle for the rest of the season! Neither was I asked to pinch-hit, which gave me the opportunity as a "bench-warmer" in the "doghouse" to study as I had before!

I dreaded each week when the time came for Physical Education. No team captain wanted me. The coach often smiled and said, "You're left out, again!"

If only I could have used my "head" to play basketball, I thought, I might have helped my team to victory. Whenever I had a chance to play, I never got the ball in my hands, much less had a chance to shoot a hoop.

While thinking "what simpletons, morons and ignoramuses these Americans are," I had to admit that I couldn't keep up with the others.

I was five-foot-three inches short, even in "elevator" shoes. I couldn't see myself holding onto a basketball, bouncing it while running down court, nor shooting the ball into a basket hoisted high in the sky. And I couldn't figure out the minds of Americans. Why did they make the basket-net bottomless? How could you catch fish with it?

However, I had an achievement which made many students envious. I was the first Japanese in the state of Minnesota, I was told, to earn an official badge as an American Red Cross Water Safety Instructor. In retrospect I believe there may have been an exaggeration involved, but I never pursued the point.

My services as a Water Safety Instructor, not merely a lifeguard, put me in an elite class. My voice and judgment made me an "authority" during the summer camps that kept me busy.

Furthermore, with American Red Cross approval, Fairview Hospital of Minneapolis opened the door for me to volunteer my services to help rehabilitate multiple sclerosis victims.

Working with disabled children, I saw the full spectrum of pain endured by children and their parents. At first, I wondered whether it was a blessing or a curse for parents to have a child whose body was so maimed by an incurable disease. I often flashed back to the crippled children I had seen at Kotachi Train Station the day we fled from Hiroshima.

Before long, I began to realize that working with these children was the greatest thing that could have happened to my soul! My service to physically challenged children taught me about human frailty and the tenacity of the human spirit. And I began to see "life" with compassion.

Another event also indelibly marked my soul, much as a mason etches his artwork in granite.

Ray Pope, a senior student who lived in St. Peter, a city two hours southwest of Minneapolis, ministered to a congregation. He voluntarily became my prayer partner, and I called him by the nickname "Holy Pope."

After we had spent several weeks together, he invited me to speak to his church. I became suspicious of the invitation. Even though I was in my third year of college, not once had the school administrator or anyone else asked me to speak for even five minutes at daily chapel hour. So what was the catch? What did the "Holy Pope" have up his sleeves?

Still, I was persuaded to speak, and for the next two weeks I managed my studies and prepared my "red-hot" sermon. I told myself, "I'm going to let them have it! Hit them so hard and fast they won't know what hit them!"

Carefully guarded in my conversation with Ray as he and I drove to St. Peter, I wondered how people would react when they saw me, a Japanese, face-to-face?

"Tom, I didn't tell you this before, for fear of a misunderstanding," Ray said as we rolled down the highway, "but you'll be staying this weekend with Ken and Maple Peterson's family. They're in good standing in our church." "What! Ken was a Japanese war prisoner during World War II. Why didn't you tell me this when we first talked about speaking at your church?" I was furious, and it showed in my voice. "No! You betrayed me!" I shouted, not considering Ray's feelings. Well! This could be the beginning of World War III. But this time no one could accuse *me* of a "sneak attack."

We arrived and I was introduced to the Petersons. After the introduction, the *"Holy Pope"* tarried just long enough for cookies and a cup of coffee. Then Ken showed me my room for the weekend, on the second floor at the end of the hallway, the farthest room from any exit. I felt trapped that night as I went to sleep.

I was awakened by knocking on the door. I must have been sleeping deeply. I noted the chair I had placed against the door for my safety before crawling into bed had not moved even an inch.

As the day progressed, I faced seemingly endless introductions to other residents of St. Peter. With each one, I asked myself if I would be openly attacked by the congregation when I stepped up to the pulpit. Or would they be courteous enough to allow me to preach?

I wondered whether these white people would receive me with open arms, as a trophy of God's grace. I was reminded how a former Japanese Navy Captain was received when he preached at a church in Hayward, California.

Captain Mitsuo Fuchida, aerial leader of the Pearl Harbor attack, was invited to give a sermon at Highland Baptist Church in early 1960. As he spoke, tears streamed down the faces of the all-white church members in a demonstration of their love and forgiveness.

Now the stage, with all its backdrops for drama, was set here in Minnesota. I waited for the curtain to be drawn.

After Sunday dinner, Ken took me to his study. I saw several photo albums on his desk which contained gruesome pictures of Ken and other American soldiers as prisoners of war. There was no beauty portrayed, nor any warmth of human dignity.

I couldn't believe how cruel the Japanese soldiers had been—barbarians, merciless!

Every photo depicted the hideousness of war. Ken had been starved until he weighed about 85 pounds, and was little more than skin and bone. There were many such unexpected photos.

And yet in the eyes of every American prisoner I saw an indestructible human spirit housed in a body of mortal clay. Though the clay melted away, the spirit burned on, if only to be extinguished for some by a death that, at worst, would be release from painful torture.

After the service, we sat at the table. Looking at Ken, who sat opposite me, I internalized what I felt deep in my heart. Having Sunday dinner with Ken and his family was an extraordinary event.

It was a totally different experience than the dinner I had with Captain Fuchida and our host, the Reverend Clarence Bennett of Highland Baptist Church. I reflected on that occasion.

That Sunday in Hayward was different than any other Sunday because of the presence of Mitsuo Fuchida. While he was preaching I stood alone, the only Japanese person in the congregation. No one in the sanctuary seemed to consider the feelings of a Japanese victim of the war. Perhaps many didn't even realize I was there.

The church had hailed the appearance of Mitsuo Fuchida as the biggest event ever to come to Highland Baptist Church. For Captain Fuchida, the leader of the Pearl Harbor attack, had received Jesus Christ as his personal Savior, an experience that changed his life. He came to America with the message of love in Christ, realizing the awful cost of the war to his country and the United States.

Captain Fuchida was in great demand all over the country. People wanted to see him and listen to his message. There was still hatred for the Pearl Harbor raid, mixed with sympathy for Fuchida's personal burden.

There was no doubt in my mind that Captain Fuchida made restitution through his appearances and that Christians in America were touched by his sincerity and love for Jesus Christ.

And yet I had reservations. In Captain Fuchida I had seen a man frozen with hatred and revenge, overwhelmed by his memories.

The congregation's tears, as well as Captain Fuchida's, symbolized nothing more than a scene from the Japanese art of *Kabuki*, for his message was "waxed" with his indifference!

I didn't verbalize my feelings of resentment to the Captain. The services that day will long be remembered in my heart and in the hearts of all those who heard him. But the story didn't end there.

As a young man, I had met a pastor at the Baptist summer camp at Clear Lake, California. During this time I became involved in the lessons of salvation through Evangelist Merril Booth, who had lost his right arm during a Japanese attack on a battlefield in the South Pacific.

One evening, I gave my life and heart to Christ. I was thrilled by the two years following my conversion, as I was adopted by the preacher, who became my spiritual father and I his spiritual son.

We had a precious relationship. I saw him practically every weekend, riding a Greyhound bus from Turlock, California to Hayward to study the word of God with him. I stayed the day and went back to Turlock in the evening. God truly blessed our relationship.

No one knew that day when Captain Fuchida was sitting at one end of the table, dining with us, reminiscing of his years prior to Pearl Harbor ... that sitting at the other end of the table was a victim of the final chapter of the war which had begun at Pearl Harbor. The uniqueness of my experience suddenly dawned on me.

The host pastor was caught up in the feelings of Fuchida, but paid little attention to the person at the other end of the table who had indirectly become a victim of Fuchida's actions. The two men continued to recall events about World War II in the South Pacific.

I never verbalized my heart's resentment toward Captain Fuchida. Although Captain Fuchida may have felt something toward me, he never expressed it. Two countrymen, both born-again Christians rejoicing in a blessed event that had changed their lives, sat at opposite ends of a table—the Captain, embraced by love; and myself—forgotten, lonely and confused.

Unable to contain my emotions any longer, I rose from the table, went to the bathroom, and lost my Sunday dinner. Had I told the host pastor that such resentment existed, I wonder if he would have made other arrangements. Though the agony that afternoon would never be forgotten, I am sure it has been forgiven!

We received Swedish hospitality and heartfelt love from the hands of the Maples. There was an enormous spread of food, a banquet truly "fit for an Emperor." Sitting at the opposite end of the table, watching Ken, a former war prisoner of the Japanese, I truly enjoyed the homemade pie and ice cream that topped off our Sunday dinner.

By the time the Sunday evening service was over, Ken and I both felt as though we knew each other from another life. We embraced until we felt our blood pass into each other's veins, no longer distinguishable as Japanese or American blood.

No one knew it then, but this was the moment when the "seed" began to germinate deep in my soul for concrete steps toward reconciliation and healing, toward making peace between former enemies—Japan, my birthplace, and the United States, my "adopted" nation.

There was another person who played a major role during my last year in college, as well as for the rest of my life. This woman would shape the life of a young Japanese man whose faith and heart had been tested and tempered. She was a second generation Chinese-American who arrived at the campus from Tucson, Arizona, committed to pursuing a career as a missionary to Taiwan.

I met her the afternoon of September 4, 1962, under an oak tree. An unusually warm sun peeked through the clouds, reflecting off multi-colored leaves as they danced in the wind, a sign of an early autumn.

Could it be love at first sight? I wondered if she was the one God had sent in answer to my prayers. I had prayed for two years that God would send me an Oriental girl. Perhaps I should have specified a Japanese girl with a Japanese heart. But I didn't want to trouble God about finding that particular girl.

"Would you like to go to the "Little Dipper" for an ice cream cone?" I asked. "It's on me."

"No thank you! I have money if I want to have an ice cream."

"No! No! I didn't mean that," I rebounded. "I just like to have company. Ice cream tastes great if someone will have it with me. I just wanted to share it with you."

After some persuasion, she reluctantly accepted my offer. Then I asked, "How about two scoops?"

"No. Just one scoop will be fine," she replied, holding her ground.

With ice cream cones in hand, we sat down again under the same oak tree. I was somewhat intimidated by all her fuss over ice cream. Why couldn't she be gracious? At ten cents a scoop, there was no great financial burden on anybody's part. My only motive was to share the "treat" with her.

Somehow she read my facial expression. After a bite of her ice cream, she sat up straight and looked right into my eyes.

"Let me tell you why I came to this College and why I consider eating an ice cream cone very foolish. I actually consider it offensive, especially when every dime toward my tuition counts."

I seemed to have offended her. I had merely wanted to share a small token of my heart.

"Tom, go ahead, finish your ice cream before you waste it."

I quickly finished it, licking my chops, savoring the last taste. Who knows if I would ever have ice cream with her again?

Then she opened her heart, slowly and deliberately.

"I would like you to know I have only three older brothers and that I ventured out to Minnesota from Arizona. My parents vehemently opposed my coming here, far from home, especially to attend a private Baptist College. They said it was deplorable when two of my brothers earned Masters Degrees in electronic engineering, and the oldest brother received his Ph.D. in civil engineering from the University of Arizona. My parents considered coming to this non-accredited college, this Christian college, a betrayal of their teachings and upbringing."

She took a deep breath. "My family couldn't see me throwing my life away by becoming a missionary to Taiwan. My parents came from mainland China. They wanted me to attend the University of Arizona and offered to pay for my education."

"Tom," she continued in her fervency. "Do you understand I had to follow my 'calling' to become a missionary, turning my back against my parents and the wishes of my brothers? I paid a high price to come to this Baptist College. As far as I'm concerned, it's a matter of life or death. I'm not here for fun. My future life is dependent upon my earnest desire to pay my way through school. Even if they sent me a thousand dollars without any difficulty, I would not accept their gifts."

I asked for that, didn't I?

She took another deep breath and launched again. "Do you think for a moment that I am such a fool and ungrateful daughter? Of course, they would not send me one dime even if I asked them to do so."

She smiled.

I thought I had never seen such a pained smile.

After an "official" date, a Valentines Sweetheart Party in February, Joyce and I and three other couples became entangled by the web of the "six-inch rule," the School Discipline Code. We had danced as couples, our bodies apparently perceived as being closer than six inches apart during this activity.

Joyce and I were summoned, along with Bob Sinclear, Jerry Johnston, Max Forrest and their girlfriends, to appear before the Discipline Committee. We were accused of touching the girls' thighs in an inappropriate way, as observed by the school monitor, on the dance floor. "Young men," said Mr. Douglas Duffey, the committee chairman, waving his finger as he looked at each of us, "I am horrified to learn that you have misbehaved in a manner I consider hideous and sinful."

He gave us a dirty look, continuing, "You must learn to keep your hands to yourself and never, never allow your hands to commit such an immoral act. Do you know why you have been summoned here today? You are here to be disciplined; and, more importantly, to learn of God's holiness and His punishment of sin."

Mrs. Creek, the Dean of Women, sitting as committee vice-chair, launched her thoughts, "I have been the Dean of Women for the last 10 years. I never thought the day would come that we couldn't tell between the conduct of Christian women and non-Christian women. It's shocking to see the looseness of our young ladies nowadays. I wonder whether I should even address you as 'ladies,' I am so horrified as to your influence and how it may affect the rest of our 'unsoiled' students."

She continued, "How is it that you allowed these young man to defile your most sacred ...?" She choked on the emotions created in her mind. "We must make you understand and 'pay' for your un-Christian-like conduct."

We were attending the most conservative Baptist College in the land. The school took great pride in being what it believed to be "theologically" correct and in setting both spiritual and moral standards. There was no room for compromise with the "sins" of the world, as the outside world and its influence were a "Hollywood cesspool."

We were charged with violating Section II of the School Conduct Code, accused of desecrating the code by the alleged immoral sin of "touching" the thighs of young women while we were dancing.

Mr. Duffey turned to the four girls, saying "I am deeply ashamed to learn you lured them to committing such a sin. You have caused them to err from the path of 'righteousness.'"

"And," he continued, "you young men! How can you claim to be Christians? Intimate acts must be kept to yourselves until marriage. I have never touched my wife's thigh, and I've been married now for twenty years!"

Bob Sinclear blurted, "Oh, Mr. Duffey, tell us. How did you manage to have three children if you didn't even touch the thighs of your wife, seeing your children were not adopted?"

"Oh, that's Immaculate Conception," Max Forrest responded, as if his answer had been comically scripted.

"This is serious. We didn't know we were in the presence of a professor who performs miracles," added Jerry Johnston.

I sat there amazed at how innocent dancing had been convoluted into an ugly incident and how ridiculous this matter had become. What had we done? How preposterous for the Chairman to think that he and his Discipline Committee members had the "right" to teach us the Holiness of God.

"Sir. Mr. Duffy," I said, moving closer to the Chairman. "You need to consider the informer. I think she is what I call *Ure-nokor,* left-over, a flower having lost its fragrance and no longer attracting even a bee, a jealous woman never asked for a date.

"Whosoever is without sin," I cried, "let him cast the first stone!"

His face turning red, the Chairman of the Discipline Committee stood up from his chair. I stepped back in line with the rest of the young men, waiting for the judgment, the condemnation.

The Committee gave each of us 50 demerits for our immoral sin. Then we received an additional 25 demerits for "vulgarity" and a bad attitude.

Seeing Mrs. Creek nod her head, my Japanese blood again reached its boiling point. The Chairman must have been gratified for his judgment and for punishing our sins.

Shortly thereafter was an event on November 23, 1963 that irrevocably changed not only my theological beliefs—the conservative, fundamental "Baptist" frame of reference of my future ministry—but also my life.

Our studies were disrupted when we learned in disbelief of a national tragedy. One of the students ran quickly back to his room and brought a radio so that we could hear for ourselves that "President John F. Kennedy was shot by an assassin's bullet ..."

I was outraged that anyone could commit such a hideous crime against the national leader. I was devastated. However, it was not so much the news that shattered my heart, as I faced two tremendous extremes of experiences that afternoon.

"Whoopee!" George Madison, self-claimed leader of the post-graduate class, shouted for joy. "Hey, President Kennedy got shot." Practically every student in my Biblical Hebrew class jumped out of their seats for joy.

"That's the best news that we've had for a long time!" one student shouted.

"Yeah! That Catholic President got what he deserved. You know. He was a Catholic Pres ..."

Yet another student grinned from ear to ear.

"Whaaat...?" I shouted at them. *"Baka mono!"*

My *Samurai* blood surged through my veins, my anger flashed to their faces. I stood alone, the only non-Occidental theology student.

I had no understanding of the significance of John F. Kennedy as a Catholic President and how that could affect these students. I couldn't believe what I was hearing and witnessing. The students' behavior shocked and infuriated me. What possessed them?

While my soul was still consumed with obtaining revenge on America, I couldn't allow the white theological students to rejoice over the news. I rose with righteous indignation.

"How could you ..." I choked on my own words as I stood before George Madison, the loud mouth.

"You, of all folks, should be ashamed of your conduct. How dare you rejoice at the President's assassination? We all need to pray to God that He might intervene to spare his life."

Richard Gilbert hissed at me, "He's Catholic, an Irish Catholic. And we're Baptist, with a big "B." Don't you understand? You're a JAP, born on the other side of the world, you're Buddhist, and an immigrant. There you are, three strikes against you from the beginning!"

As he continued, everyone seemed to get a big kick out of that remark. They all laughed at me.

"What do you know about our politics, let alone of the differences between Baptists and Catholics like Kennedy?" Dan Washington interjected, shaking his bony finger, as he splattered all over my face.

"It doesn't matter whether I understand what you Baptists are, or what Catholics believe. What kind of heart do you have to rejoice over the assassination of a President? What does his being an Irish Catholic have to do with it?"

"See, that's what we mean," jabbed Mike Wells.

"Oh, boy! How dense you are," added Martin Houser, revealing his intellect. "I had great doubts as to your brains when we started the semester. You just don't have the intellectual capacity to understand the political and theological world of Baptists, guardians of the TRUTH! We are the 'light of the world!'"

Sam Montgomery, who always sat in the back row and kept to himself during classes, quickly came over and stood in front of me. I was alarmed by his angry face, which resembled a mad gorilla's.

"Hey, you, Japanese immigrant!"

He stuck his face close to me, his breath almost knocking me out. "You just don't know anything. Kennedy's assassination is not just an accident. We've been waiting. Matter of fact, we've been praying for it. Don't you think for a moment you've earned the 'right' to tell us what we should or should not do! Just because you're doing graduate work doesn't give you any more 'intelligence' about what's going on. What audacity you have to criticize us, when you were raised in Buddha's faith and in a JAPanese culture that eats raw fish!"

He pinched his nose to make a funny face, which he didn't need to make any worse than it already was. He also spoke a mouthful, revealing his stupidity. "Raw fish?" What a simpleton he was!

"What kind of teaching did you get from Buddha? Ha, ha, ha!" Steve Green sneered. "I thought so ..."

I was outraged. I wondered how the "blood" of Christ could have transformed the souls of these students. I couldn't believe my ears—Baptists condoning the murder of the President because he was Catholic. We were the ones who needed to cover ourselves with sackcloth, to mourn, to ask for forgiveness and cleanse our souls.

I could never have dreamed of finding myself standing alone, outside the mainstream "Baptist" theological camp. These students had demonstrated bigotry and hateful hearts, obvious differences that caused me to repudiate their standing and their Baptist "faith."

Four long, struggling years in Midwest had come to an end, but not before my "Japanese heart" was tested. Whoever would have thought that this immigrant, marooned by the ghosts of war and lambasted by racial prejudice, who could not speak good English, who was without a high school diploma, would graduate from college?

I was the only member of the Tanemori family to attend, and to reach the moment of "COMMENCEMENT," with a sheepskin, of a new life! Stepping onto this higher plateau forced me to terms with the essence of who I was—the first Son of a *Samurai* family—Tanemori.

I had conquered many icy storms and *Tsunami* during my four years of college, and not by accident. After God brought me to the place of testing, I had to face Him to see if my faith could stand "trials by fire." I believe my faith was tempered like steel into becoming a Japanese sword.

It was a miracle I had survived, physically, emotionally and spiritually, while keeping intact part of my Japanese heart!

Chapter Five: Two Become One

Union of two—one "flesh":
who or what could separate
that which is girded by love?

THE long-awaited spring came. This was, indeed, America, the land of opportunity and dreams! The realization of my first dream was something all American young men in the 1960s wanted to experience—having their hands on the wheel of their own automobile.

I saved $250.00 to buy my first automobile, a 1955 Ford Sedan, from my neighbor. To cover lots of rusty spots, I painted it with garish shades of yellow, black, white, and green. It was an exotic paint job!

My first road trip was to Owatonna, seventy miles due south of Minneapolis, and twenty miles due west of Rochester, Minnesota, where Joyce still attended Baptist College. As it was the weekend, I picked her up. This was my first official date "on wheels."

I recalled having watched Bill Young, whom I had met in Turlock, California, and his technique for sidling up to his girlfriend at a drive-in theater. Although it seemed awkward, I tried putting my arm around Joyce as I drove her back to Minneapolis.

She told me she'd schemed to get her weekend pass by telling a half-truth. I couldn't help wiping a smirk from my face when I learned that Mrs. Creek, the Dean of Women whose Discipline Committee had given us our fat demerits, had been the one to give Joyce her pass. I figured Mrs. Creek must have been affected by "spring fever."

We couldn't have asked for a nicer day for my first date since college. My mind was wandering like white cotton clouds, drifting aimlessly in the wind. By the time we drove into downtown Minneapolis, I was a little more comfortable. I had my right arm around Joyce's shoulder and my left hand on the wheel.

Waiting for a traffic signal, I suddenly heard "Hey, taxi!" as someone tried to flag us down. My car had been mistaken for a Checker cab!

Welcoming the spring sun, Minnesota's thousand lakes were thawing from their winter freeze. I planned to make the most of the warmth by proposing to Joyce on the bank of the Mississippi River. I admit I had a very difficult time keeping my hands off her.

Secretly, I had saved money to buy Joyce her first "star." This was truly American lifestyle. The diamond I had bought was ever so small—requiring a magnifying glass to even be seen. But it was a symbol of my manhood. I wondered, coming from a Japanese man, if she would accept it.

Did she!!!

With the return of Minnesota's prismatic autumn, in Joyce's final year at college, her father suddenly showed up at the school. Whether or not this was his response to my honorable request for consent to marry his daughter, wasn't clear. On a Saturday afternoon I drove down to Owatonna to meet him.

By his formality in exchanging greetings with me, I suspected he was very annoyed about something. After some fashion of introduction by Joyce, he insisted that he had come to see his daughter and not me or anyone else. Furthermore, he said he really wasn't interested in taking time to talk with me. He displayed no cultural grace in the way he revealed his feelings. He simply told me that he refused to grant consent to the marriage of his daughter. I sensed an unquenchable fire burning within him.

"You are Japanese," he said, his voice quivering. "You should bear the sins of the Japanese Imperial Military Government for atrocities perpetrated on the Chinese in the 1930's. We suffered untold ..."

As his voice trailed off, he gazed toward the horizon. Perhaps horrible memories were flooding his heart and mind.

"There is no way that I would allow my daughter to marry you. You symbolize and remind us of every abhorrence we endured." His entire body shook.

"Sir! Mr. Dea. Would you give me just five minutes? That's all I ask, please."

Finally consenting to listen, he turned sideways and stared at his wristwatch while I poured my heart out to him.

"Five minutes is up." He reminded me he'd come all the way from Globe, Arizona to visit his daughter.

How little I understood the effect a painful past had on this man and how it would influence our lives if we allowed him his way. I didn't want to become another victim of a heart raging with hatred and retribution. I left him alone with Joyce.

Although he vehemently refused consent for me to marry her, Joyce and I believed we could overcome his cultural suspicion and enmity. My fiancé and I eagerly cemented our spiritual commitment with a shared desire to bring the message of God's love to all whose hearts were frozen with hatred and distrust.

My marrying a Chinese woman was something daring. After all, it was cross-cultural, a mixed marriage. I knew Nakamura *Sensei* would understand and rejoice with me for this occasion. Returning to Minneapolis, I informed Minister Dr. Springwater of my desire for him to perform our wedding ceremony.

"Tommy, congratulations. I understand you're going to get your marriage license at the County Office."

"Yes, Sir! I just want to start early to get everything ready."

"You don't need to worry about getting a marriage license. It's very cheap. You'll get it with a snap of your fingers."

"Oh, is that so? How much do I need to get married?"

He smiled at me, explaining, "It will cost only five dollars. All you need is one picture of Abraham Lincoln ... plus the rest of your life!"

The next day at the county clerk's office, I strutted like a peacock, my chest in the air, to stand behind a couple getting their marriage license.

"Aaaah, you are Mr. Taa-nemor-rie?" An attractive lady in her thirties approached me.

"Yes, Maaam!" I responded crisply.

"I think we need more information about you before we issue a marriage license."

I had to think a long time before I answered, "Maaam. Would you kind enough to speak slooowly so I could understand whaaat you are saying ..."

"Seeing you are a graduate student, you should have understood what I said. We need more information about you."

"Yes Maam. But, you need to understand that I never have had any experience getting married. It is all new to me. You know what I mean?"

"We want to make sure," she replied, "that your children would not have any ill effects, because of the bomb."

It finally hit me. The county clerk was afraid my children might be affected by the radiation I was exposed to so long ago.

"What do you mean by 'ill effects,' Maam?"

She swallowed her saliva. "Aaah! What I mean is ... deformed. Do you understand? We want you to get an affidavit from a doctor, a specialist on radiation, and come back with that document to prove you're a safe, normal person who can marry."

I was furious. "What do you know about radiation? Look at me. I'm as normal as you!"

I took a step toward her, while she backed away from the counter. It was good the counter stood between us.

"Maam! Do you have any idea that the American Government has already put me through all sorts of tests, by Japanese as well as American doctors, before I immigrated here? I got a clean bill of health! What more do you want? What reason do you have to know more about radiation than those specialists?"

I took a deep breath, realizing that several people nearby were listening and watching. My raised voice, echoing through the large office, had attracted some county employees, who also stood watching.

She waved her hands and yelled at me, "No one knows what kinds of diseases you might pass on!"

I was irate. I stood at the counter, waiting another twenty minutes to see an official who might talk with me a little more intelligently. No one came.

"Are you still here?" she grunted at me. "There is nothing I can do for you. Just go home, get your affidavit and come back. We'll talk then."

I stormed from the office, cussing her in Japanese. How I wanted, if I could, to use her as target practice! I returned to the office several times for a marriage license but was unable to get one without providing an affidavit from a doctor.

Two months later, after receiving an affidavit from Dr. Marvin Johnson of North Minneapolis, I finally had my license. By then I could only chuckle at the idea that a county clerk wanted to make sure I was "normal" enough to get married.

With the preacher's heavy schedule, the Thomas/Joyce wedding date was set for Saturday, January 29th, at 6:30 p.m., just six weeks away. I smiled to myself.

"Say, Tommy." The preacher's smile told me he was up to mischief. He called me to a window and said, "I remember that you wanted to marry a blue-eyed blonde. Do you still want to marry her?"

I fumbled my response.

"I am not a miracle worker, but I can help you. At least there's something I can do for you." He told me to look down the street from where we were on North Broadway. "Do you see the Rexall Drug Store? If you want Joyce to be a blonde, that's the place."

"What do you mean, that's the place?" I wondered aloud.

"She's one bottle away from the blonde you wanted. Well, it may take two bottles." He laughed, "Joyce is a good girl. Be sure to take good care of her. And if there's anything you need or if you have questions, please tell my secretary, Donna Johnson. She'll let you through this door."

He put his hand on my shoulder and sent me off "with Godspeed." My heart filled with new energy and a sense of direction as I said goodbye. I was finally a man!

With a promise from Joyce's big brother, Stan, that he would give her away, we began our wedding preparations.

"I want you to know," Joyce shouted at me, "that this is my wedding. I don't want any handouts from my family. My father refused to bless my wedding."

"Joyce," my voice was shaking, "I never had any experience in getting marry ..."

"I hope you haven't!" Then, she smiled. "Of course not! This is my first one!"

"But Joyce ..."

"You still don't understand, do you?" She chided me, and then breathed deeply. "Honey, look at me. We have been through so much by being Oriental. No! You are JAPanese and my father rejected you. You know why, don't you?"

She continued. "My father couldn't stomach even seeing you in the distance, much less committing his daughter to you for the rest of her life. As far as he's concerned, you're nothing but a war criminal and I don't think he'd have any problem seeing you executed for atrocities by Japanese soldiers against the Chinese."

"Tell me then," I countered, "why are your mother and Stan willing to come to our wedding?"

"They consented to the marriage because of Dr. Johnson's statement that our offspring will not be affected by your being a Hiroshima survivor."

She seemed relieved as she took a deep breath. A deep sigh followed, which I interpreted as dissatisfaction with me. It told me I was perceived as insensitive to her feelings, perhaps due to my misunderstanding of the willingness of her mother and brother to attend the wedding. At least Stan would act as her father, giving her the protection, honor and respect she deserved.

"The reason I turned down their financial offer was to protect you from their sharp tongues and claws. They will, sure as I am standing and talking here, come after you for lack of 'manhood' if we accept even one dime. I don't want our wedding to be poisoned by their superficial generosity. I'm proud of you, proud of who you are. I despise anyone, including my own family, who thinks of you as 'less than normal' just because you're pursuing a gospel ministry, or just because you're Japanese!" The die had been cast. We knew we needed a plan for the reception after our wedding. We carefully selected special friends for the wedding; Joyce chose her bridesmaids and flower-bearer, and I chose Dan Kirby, a college roommate from California, as my best man, making sure he understood I was the "best" man in the wedding! Selecting 100 honorable guests to be invited and to honor us was quite a task, rather like completing a 500-piece jigsaw puzzle. Some pieces didn't quite seem to fit. Arguments continued for several days as to which friends were more likely to be in harmony with our lifestyle and would honor our inter-cultural marriage between Chinese and Japanese.

"You are not including your sister from Hiroshima, are you?" Joyce shouted at me almost contemptuously. I had mentioned my wish-list of guests from Japan without naming names. Looking into Joyce's eyes, I saw unquenchable fire.

Of course, I wanted so much for Nakamura *Sensei* to be here. No! My mind had drifted to a fantasy of having her, instead of Joyce, in the wedding gown.

"Your sister is not welcome at our wedding. After all, she has yet to respond to any of your repeated requests. How many times have you written her?"

She was right. My sister responded with silence. I wondered if Joyce was deeply disturbed by her father's strong refusal for consent and by my sister's disapproval, marked by her hushed silence. Of course I knew full well my sister would never allow herself to be included in the marriage of her brother to a Chinese woman.

After some struggle, we finally agreed to a list of guests. I had limited choices from my list to appease Joyce after she said, "This is my wedding!" I guessed I was just "accompanying her" as her husband in this wedding ceremony!

Given that we had five hundred dollars to our names, we knew our wedding could never be as extravagant as the weddings of some wealthy friends we had attended.

My desire was to make our wedding ceremony as beautiful as it was meaningful. I had never prayed so hard for selfish reasons. How delighted I was to run into a man from our church who owned a printing shop. Promising to donate his time to design and print our invitation, he told me our cost would only be for materials.

We were also blessed by a florist who gave us special arrangements more expensive than we could ever have afforded. He provided a candlestand for free, and asked us to pay only for his helpers' three hours of labor.

"This is good advertisement for our shop," he smiled with a sense of pride.

So far, having spent 125 dollars, we still faced one of our greatest financial challenges: making reception arrangements for 100 guests and as many as another 100 members of our church.

"Joyce," my voice shook, "I don't think we have enough money to invite all the guests to a respectable reception."

"Well," she said, coming closer, "that depends on who you call respectable. We need to provide for all the guests to exchange a greeting. It's okay with me to just have coffee, tea and wedding cake."

I conceded that Joyce's idea had greater value than I was willing to admit. But I also wanted much more for her than coffee and tea. We continued to pursue options for the reception, trying several caterers to see if one would meet our needs for a total of 375 dollars. We were just one week from exchanging vows when the telephone rang one night, waking me from my slumber.

"Hello. Is this Mr. Taanamori?" The voice of the woman was upbeat!

"Yes? This is he." My voice undoubtedly showed my annoyance. The wall clock, ticking silently, read nearly 11:30 p.m., and I had just managed to nod off.

"I know I'm disturbing your sleep. But I just got back from a business trip and found two messages from friends regarding your wedding. My friends are very interested in helping if I will do this reception for you."

"I'm still looking for someone to cater our reception. But why did you call at this hour?"

She quickly apologized, then said, "Mr. Taanamori. When my friends told me about you and your bride to be, I wanted to make sure nobody would make an offer before I had a chance to speak with you first."

"Bu-but ... why?"

"I wonder if I can get together with you first thing in the morning? I'll explain to you why I'd like the opportunity of doing the catering."

Before I could respond, she said "good night" in her upbeat voice and hung up. I didn't recall whether she had ever mentioned her name.

I wondered who in the world could feel such urgency about our reception that she had to wake me up. I mumbled to myself before I curled my legs in my cold bed to go back to sleep. I remember the clock striking one o'clock, then the alarm being exceptionally loud a few hours later. I felt groggy and had a pounding headache as I reached the campus.

"Hey, Tanemori," a professor prodded me, "what's wrong with you? Getting cold feet?"

It drew a laugh from my classmates.

Trying to think of the name of the woman who had called the previous night, all I could remember was her upbeat voice. But that voice gave me a hunch. I ran to the back of the building, and the entrance facing the parking lot. As I ran, I thought there was no way I would recognize her, even if I met her face to face.

"Aaaaa, Mr. Taanamori? Yes. You are ..." The voice came from behind me.

I turned to see a woman who might be in her early sixties. Her facial lines clearly radiated beauty and elegance.

"I was anxiously waiting to meet you," she smiled.

Her voice was definitely the one on the phone the previous night. She possessed such energy!

"Yeeesss. I am Tanemori."

She took my hand in hers, conveying her warmth. "I'm so glad to meet you, and I'm excited by what my friends told me about you. I slept little last night after we talked. I'm so excited about what we can do to make your wedding so special. I hope you don't mind this old lady, this 'busy-body,' taking such interest?"

"May I ask who you are?"

"Oh, I'm sorry. I'm Sue Olson. My family has owned a catering service in North Minneapolis for the last 25 years."

Sitting in the chapel, as we talked, I was very curious as to why she wanted to help us.

"Do you know we have little money for catering? I know it's not enough to adequately accommodate our guests after the wedding ceremony."

Determined to offer her services, Mrs. Olson said, "Well, two of my employees are donating their time and labor, and I'm willing to donate my energy to make the reception truly memorable. We want to give all we can to make your reception elegant and exquisite for all your guests."

I asked Mrs. Olson why she was so willing to sacrifice all the food, time and her profit for our event.

"Mr. Taanamori," she answered, "Let's not worry! Can we shake hands on that?"

"I am extremely overwhelmed by your generosity. But please, why?"

She told me that, during the fall of 1953, her son, a soldier in the occupation of Japan, was serving at Tachikawa Base, near Tokyo. He and a couple of buddies were on weekend passes out in the country, away from Tokyo. While sightseeing in the hills and watching colorful maple leaves dance in the wind, her son lost his footing and fell into a deep gorge. His buddies rescued him and carried him down the mountain to a humble farm.

The Japanese farmer and his family attended to him and called a local doctor. That doctor examined the young man, and then contacted a colleague from a nearby city, who came to offer his own diagnosis. Although the family could not speak English, their kindness and compassion was felt by all.

Besides scraped elbows and knees and a few bruises, the soldier had no apparent broken bones, nor head injuries. But without x-rays, internal injuries could not be ruled out. The doctor recommended that the soldier rest quietly for a few days in the care of the farmer's family. He did, and when the local doctor returned, Mrs. Olson's son was deemed healthy enough to return to base late Monday night.

She wiped away tears as she finished her story.

"Mr. Taanamori. I don't know much about you. It was the kindness of the Japanese farmer and his family, who took care of my son, a total stranger whom they might have thought a threat. Unable to communicate verbally, they spoke to my son with their heart and spirit. Even though my son failed to keep in touch with the family, he has always been grateful to them."

"Mr. Taanamori. This is the moment I feel God has given us an opportunity to repay our debt of gratitude for what the Japanese family did for our son, by allowing us to help one of their countrymen on his wedding night."

I didn't know what to say.

"More importantly," she added, "It's not so much to repay their kindness, but that I feel they taught us how to extend our hearts to others, even total strangers. I hope you will accept our heart and desire to express our appreciation. Yes, there is something money can't buy."

I was stunned. I thanked Mrs. Olson for her generosity, but above all, for her tender heart and willingness to help others. She deeply touched my heart.

Church members heard our wedding announcement for January 29, 1966 from the pulpit during Sunday services and they saw it printed in church newsletters, all heightening their curiosity during the week before our union. This was the first time the congregation's white preacher had tied the knot for a non-white couple.

A piercing north wind never let up as the temperature dipped below zero. Drifting snow blanketed the entire city.

"Today is the day!" I shouted with glee. I quickly finished a cup of hot coffee, wiped my unfathomed smiles, and felt my heart beat with a new passion.

By the time I had bundled up and checked my car, parked in the street, the "snow-bird" had been by, piling five to six feet of snow on my car. It took me nearly an hour to clear the snow and attempt to start the car.

I cussed and cussed again, in Japanese. My car was frozen metal. It made no sound as I turned the ignition switch. The battery had been sapped by the howling north wind during the night. I looked under the hood, neither understanding the problem, nor knowing what to look for.

"What the ?$~#&$?" I muttered unintelligently to myself.

Suddenly uncontrollable thoughts overcame me. "Don't I need the car for our honeymoon?" I looked to the dark, gray sky for an answer. The only response was a shrieking of the wind whipping from the clouds.

How bleak and disheartening things seemed as I stared at my dead car, after it once again refused several attempts to start it. Instead, the merciless north wind continued its onslaught. I admitted to myself that I had few options. I couldn't dip into the money set aside for our honeymoon to call a tow-truck to start the car. I stood by the frozen vehicle, feeling helpless. I cried out. My runny nose quickly froze as soon as a drip left my nostril. Around 10:30 that morning one of my friends, who was helping in my wedding ceremony, came over.

"I've been trying to get hold of you," he said. "I rang your phone over and over the last two hours. I decided to come over to see if there was a problem."

"Oh, thanks." I wiped my nose with my gloved hand.

"You were crying," he said, looking at me with a cocked head.

"No! I wasn't crying. It was cold, and my nose was running. That's all."

"Well, it looks like you're in a pickle. Should you or should you not go on a honeymoon is the question, isn't it?"

"Don't be so philosophical. My car is dead for good. It won't even budge."

My friend ran upstairs and called his friend, George, a handyman and jack-of-all-trades. Around noon, George brought his half-ton truck equipped with a tow-rig to my rescue. The car disappeared, and I later heard he spent almost half the day getting the car started, replacing several parts along the way. By five o'clock, my car finally responded to his tender, loving care.

While George was working his mechanical miracle, people were in and out of the church, decorating and preparing for the ceremony. All the flower arrangements were done by four o'clock. Three white candles firmly grounded in a single candlestand stood at the forefront of the altar. I had never seen an altar so beautiful and serene. It reminded me of a tiny shrine nestled in a Japanese garden where Nakamura *Sensei* and I had often escaped the reality of village life.

Following my nose, I made my way downstairs to where the reception would be. Before I entered the banquet room, I noticed aromas already filling the hallway.

As I stepped in, elegant table settings captured my eyes, sending tingling sensations through my entire body. Ornate centerpieces and shiny silver dishes glittered under the lights. Sparkling coffee- and tea-pots dignified one table, and the smell of gracefully arrayed delicacies tempted the guests to indulge themselves.

Near the entrance, a long table held a few wedding gifts, boosting the sense of excitement … and there, finishing their last touches before returning home to clean up for the wedding, were Mrs. Olson and her employees.

"Mrs. Olson," my voice was choked with gratitude.

She took my hand in hers and said, "We're delighted that you included us for the blessings. I hope the arrangement is acceptable to you and your bride."

She looked at her watch and said, "Oh. Mr. Taanamori. You'd better get ready!"

I wanted to linger, to be filled with their warmth and kind-heartedness.

The church auditorium was filled with honorable guests and "curious Georges"—casual friends from church. From a glance, I surmised that more than 150 guests on the main floor and about 20 on the balcony had honored us by their presence. Distinguished ushers seated the guests.

The Bride was gathered with her bridesmaids just outside the auditorium's rear door.

"Tom," said the preacher, placing his hand on my shoulder, "you still have time to change your mind, if you want to call it off." He shot me a wry smile.

"Hmm. I think I've come out too far out on the limb. I've passed the 'redemption point,' haven't I, preacher?"

"Well, I wouldn't be a bit surprised if Joyce is thinking the same thing." He laughed. "I'll make sure the knot we're tying is so tight no one can unravel it." He looked at his wristwatch and let us into the side room.

Patting my back, my best man said, "It's time for us to go over the cliff. There's no turning back now, Tom."

With final instructions from the minister, we marched into the altar area to music from the pipe organ. Each note, energized by the organist, lightened my steps. The mood of our guests was jubilant, for our life's journey about to begin.

Our special honorable guests had already been escorted by the ushers. Mr. & Mrs. Stanley Westlund honored me by acting as my parents. They couldn't conceal the joy of seeing their "son" take this extraordinary step.

Mrs. Lily Dea, Joyce's mother, sat alone. In her modest apparel, I saw her beauty and the elegance of her past. She was wearing a corsage created by our florist.

Just as the organist was about to hit the last major note of the prelude, before my bride's grand entrance, there was a subtle mood change. I felt cold air, and a hush fell over the auditorium, as if someone had deflated a helium balloon.

Among the guests a collection of whispers rose, growing louder and louder. Then I clearly heard, "Oh no! The altar boys have forgotten to light the center candle. What a shame to make such a mistake."

In that pause, while waiting for the first note of "Here Comes the Bride," my heart beat erratically with thoughts of the unknown territory I was entering. The guests rose and turned to face the back of the auditorium. My face beamed as my bride Joyce entered the "gate," escorted by her brother, Stan. The momentous event was unfolding. I waited for her to walk down the aisle, wondering if she would ever reach the preacher and altar.

"Who gives her away?" the preacher's voice echoed throughout the auditorium. In the strongest and most confident voice of any man I had ever heard speak, Stan answered, "I and her mother do!"

I walked up to Joyce and Stan and thanked him for standing with her, granting my wish to take his only sister as my wife. Then I took Joyce's hand and brought her before the minister.

You could have heard a pin drop. The entire auditorium filled with an inexplicable loftiness, seemingly in anticipation of our next move. Except for the unlit center candle on the altar, everything seemed in order.

The eyes of the guests followed our moves. Joyce and I held each other's hands, gazing at each other face-to-face, while we exchanged our vows with the preacher, promising to cherish each other *"until death do us part ... "* I saw such innocent beauty in my bride—she was glowing from within—this woman who would be my wife.

I still sensed the unanswered whisperings from our guests about the unlit candle.

As I thought about the absence of Joyce's father, my heart momentarily turned to my parents. How I wished they were here in place of the Westlunds. Surely Stanley and Irene could join with my parents, sitting with the other guests of honor.

There was an air of unfilled expectation when we departed from the traditional ceremony at *"with this ring I betroth ... "* Most of the guests seemed a bit bewildered. Instead, Joyce and I, at this glorious moment of our lives, held hands and walked up to the candlestand. My bride took the burning candle on the right, while I took the candle on the left. Together, we lit the center candle. We joined our flames, uniting them in one "everlasting flame," a symbolic joining by God that no man will ever sunder! With this flame we joined our hearts and souls ...

Then we extinguished the individual candles and placed them back on the stand. We felt this part of the ceremony was a beautiful, graceful symbol of our two lives becoming "one." The audience erupted with joy, for they had never seen this metaphor in matrimony. Later that month, another couple would use the same lighting of candles in their wedding.

At the reception line, the Westlunds stood with me, as family. At the end of the line, one of the seminary students said to Mrs. Westlund, "I didn't know you were Tommy's mommy?"

"Joe," I quickly responded. "Don't I look like her? Look closely. We both have two eyes, two ears, one mouth and ... we even have ten fingers. Should I take off my shoes, too?" I smiled at him.

As you might imagine, the wedding reception was out of this world. No money could buy such beauty, elegance and the abundance of God's blessings—in food, or in the gracious service featuring the professionalism and personal warmth of Mrs. Sue Olson, her two employees, her son, Steve, and the many volunteers from our church.

By the time the reception was over, the temperature outside had plummeted to 59 degrees below zero—before the wind chill was factored in. George, the mechanic who had worked on my car all afternoon, was waiting for us. The car's engine was running. Many church members and guests sent us off on our honeymoon with their blessings. We stopped at the Howard Johnson Hotel in Edina, Minnesota, about 30 miles south of Minneapolis, on our honeymoon night. Inexplicable joy filled our minds and spirits, hearts and bodies.

My hands shook as I signed the register book "Mr. & Mrs. Takashi Thomas Tanemori." I had never dreamed that this day would ever come, that I would find someone to join me on my life's journey. This could be the "redemption" of my life, and ultimately of my family's. The honorable Tanemori name might finally be restored!

The clerk at the desk smiled at me when he saw my hands shaking. Noticing Joyce, my new wife, blushing beside me, suitcase and bag in hand, he said, "May I congratulate you folks? You are Mr. & Mrs. Taaaanamorie." He butchered our name, but I didn't mind at all. Just hearing the name "Tanemori" brought a wave of pride and sweet music to my ears!

We were escorted to room 216, the "honeymoon suite," with the bellhop carrying our baggage. He opened the door, turned on the light, and held the door as we walked in. He then put our luggage in the closet, checked the thermostat, and surveyed the bathroom to ensure that all was as it should be.

"Here's the key, sir." He smiled again.

I shook his hand, and in my shaking hand were two "George Washingtons" as a token of my appreciation. He treated us royally and made us feel we were special!

Showered by a day full of thoughtfulness and kindness, I found myself in a rarefied atmosphere. I should have married a long time ago!

We quickly dimmed the light. It was too bright!

I smiled with inexplicable joy.

The next morning, as I tried to start our car to continue our honeymoon, it refused to cooperate. It was dead again, frozen dead! Because it was Sunday, there were no mechanics available to resurrect the car, so we had to change our plans.

By midday Tuesday the car was repaired, at the cost of an arm and a leg, leaving us little choice but to return to our apartment. Without fulfilling our original honeymoon plans, we were back between the paper-thin walls that separated us from our neighbors.

Somehow I managed to sneak our car into the garage. We walked softly, holding our breath, up the ever-squeaky stairways. Avoiding the last step, which always made a loud noise, we stepped aside and turned the key as quietly as possible, to avoid giving ourselves away.

We found everything in our familiar, humble abode as we had left it three days before, except for the multitude of wedding gifts scattered all over the tiny living room. We looked at each other and hugged. Such a short-lived honeymoon!

I had to make sure that I covered my mouth when I sneezed, and that we took precautions to avoid making any unexpected noises, for fear of upsetting the world we had known before our marriage.

Chapter Six: Theological Seminary Training

How I dreaded to see the summer come to an end! Returning to the college campus to seek the advice of Mr. Wealth regarding my postgraduate work, I felt as if I had stepped right into a ghostly cemetery.

"Mr. Wealth," I sheepishly asked, "I have a troubled heart. I'm not sure whether I should go into ministry, or return to San Francisco to pick up design school where I left off …"

"Well, he began, "I've watched your attitude change since the events surrounding the death of President Kennedy."

He knew of the irrevocable change that had taken place in my heart. He grabbed my shoulders, looked into my eyes, and said, "Let's go get some fresh air."

As we drove, a soft breeze helped me endure the muggy Sunday afternoon. We stopped by the banks of the mighty Mississippi River.

"I hope you're not here to have me recommend a secular university! Are you, Tanemori?" he asked in a serious tone. "Of course, you know I supported you in your college work for the last four years, but not without conflict with my superiors and peers."

He cast understanding eyes upon me. "The reason I backed you was because I simply believed in you. I still do. But I can't go against my own beliefs to sanction your attending a secular university. An ungodly university … is against everything we teach and stand for."

"Mr. Wealth," I responded, "what I went through the last four years was like a nightmare and my newfound 'faith' was poisoned. It came very close to being destroyed. The reason I'm standing here with you is because Mr. Lester Hotchins demonstrated his true Christianity, offering to support my Christian training."

"And yet most of the students and professors here, except for you, Hazel Wilcox and Joyce Dea, have been more like 'foes' than friends to me."

I continued, "My greatest concern is that I might not be strong enough to guard my heart from becoming like those of white American students doing graduate work. When it comes to being assimilated, I won't have any part of it!"

"Tanemori, I'd do anything to prevent your attending a secular school. Those schools are like Hollywood cesspools. Don't be deluded by secular education. You'd not only be poisoned, but killed."

"How could I be more poisoned?" I asked myself. "I'd rather eat food with knowing it's poisoned than take sugar-coated poison pills." How I wished I could tell him how I really felt about my experiences of so-called 'Christian faith and Christian people' during my four years at Baptist College. The face of the registrar came to mind.

"All right! Why don't you test your 'faith' once more? Prove it to God. But more importantly," he dared me, "prove to yourself how strong a 'Japanese black pine tree' would stand against northern Minnesota's raging weather."

"Mr. Wealth," I told myself, "I'm going to prove you wrong by showing that those 'blankety-blank' white Americans are nothing but deluded, self-deceived, duped theological students who would lead our nation to doom!"

I took his challenge—as a challenge to myself of who I was and what I was made of—thus proving I was a Tanemori! My decision was perhaps self-serving, but at the same time I decided to enter the seminary with a firm commitment to serve Christ. I renewed my decision as fervently as I had when I had left San Francisco four summers before. Knowing I must guard my Japanese heart from becoming *shu-ni magiware ba akaku naru*, I could not be "soiled" by pseudo-Christianity.

Central Theological Seminary in the heart of Minneapolis was known as the citadel of "extreme" conservative Baptist theological isolationism. Either one stood with its teachings, as a friend, or stood outside its teachings, as a foe. There was no middle ground.

To survive spiritually, emotionally and physically, any student who attended the school must put his or her life on the line. This would mean demonstrating total faith and blind obedience to the institution, and unquestioning loyalty to the professors and spiritual leaders of the institution. This was the school that I would be attending.

What was I trying to prove myself, or to whom? Should I have my head examined, or have it put on a chopping board? What would my Father think of my rationale?

In my early life in Japan, growing up as an *oyanashigo*, an orphan, I had been involved in constant struggles against "authorities" who displayed no mercy to subordinates or to the needy. They had great influence on who I am today, because I always fought against leaders who behaved and thrived according to the Japanese "pecking order." The traditions of this order made a clear distinction between the "rights" and "duties" that applied to the leaders of the order, and to those below.

I had often heard from preachers, "Do what I preach ..." But more often than not they were silent on "Do what I do," failing to practice what they preached. My ears had already become like *mimi ga tako-ni naru*, a boiled octopus—I had heard enough; I was up to my gills in hypocrisy.

For me, it was not so much a matter of contrary or conflicting theological positions, but of "politics" revolving around an attitude that God had deposited His Truth with them only, making them the guardians of Christianity. In this atmosphere, there could be no truth learned or taught apart from the institution, and its professors had at their will the "key" to Divine Truth.

From the beginning, I was perplexed by the only two alternatives I could see. Either I would learn quickly not to cross these leaders, developing "blind" faith in their leadership. Or I would take a stand based on my heart's interpretations, jeopardizing the possibility that I might become a star theologian accepted by this ultra-conservative Baptist denomination.

Perhaps surprising me most in the midst of this all-white theological camp was a Korean professor. He was seated as Chairman of the Church History Department, and I wondered why. As I was the only Japanese theology student, I couldn't think of anything positive to come from an encounter with him.

Historically, Koreans and Japanese were like cats and dogs, with as bad a relationship as between Chinese and Japanese. Koreans were our perennial enemies, going back several centuries to the Tokugawa Shogunate. As I saw it, the school's motive for having Dr. Daniel C. Kim Sung, a Korean Professor, was spiritual "egotism," a long feather in Sung's cap as well as in the institution's.

"Tanemori!" Dr. Warren Van Dustrum, the Academic Dean, shouted over my disagreement with his teaching of the meaning of the "letter of the law" versus the "spirit of the law" before the entire class. The students upheld the tenured position and spirit of their professor. Standing alone, I questioned his understanding of the "truth" and its application. I challenged his demand that I subject myself to his authority, as his other students meekly rendered their will.

"I cannot believe my eyes and my ears," said the Professor, moving towards intimidation. "I can only say to you, Tanemori ... that what you need is a true conversion experience like that of all these students." He pleased himself, grinning, seeing the rest of the students nodding their heads with cynical smiles.

How could I allow him to fashion my soul as if he were the potter? According to him, I had become like dried clay, no longer pliable in the hands of a potter. But what I needed was a blacksmith with the heart and the know-how to temper steel and forge it into a Japanese *Samurai* sword.

Before long, word of this incident spread throughout the entire school and to many local ministers. From professors to students, everyone heard the warning—"Watch out! We have a heretic in our camp!"

Suddenly, what had been a sympathetic relationship with the Korean Professor turned ugly. Dr. Sung called me into his office, expressing his disapproval of my "non-converted" Christian behavior. He condemned what he considered my Japanese "spirit," and my frequent challenges of the village authority in postwar Japan.

Right then and there, I made a decision. I would no longer give my heart, mind and soul to him. Dr. Sung had called me aloof. And he had questioned my family reputation the moment he touched upon my Father. I had to remain true to my family, true to myself.

During the Christmas season I had an opportunity to test my character. Rather than considering this a coincidence, I believed it to be a personal challenge of my understanding of "right" and "wrong," of "proper" and "improper," and a test of the values and judgments by which I conducted myself.

Having been recently hired as a maintenance engineer (a janitor who cleaned toilets, swept dust, polished copper pipes and emptied wastebaskets), I had no idea I was about to challenge the authorities of the Dayton/Hudson department store in Minneapolis.

The spirit of Christmas was running high. Every store on the street, including the Dayton/Hudson store, was decked with stunning decorations. Although I normally worked the graveyard shift, my boss, Mr. George Elliott, had asked me to work daytimes for two weeks until the Christmas rush was over. I had no problem changing my schedule, since we were on winter break.

One morning he assigned me to guard the employees' entrance. Unfortunately, this particular morning the temperature had dipped to 15 below zero with the wind-chill factor. My strict order was to allow no one to enter the building before 7:30 a.m. As I stood inside the door, I watched people standing outside, their breaths turning into icicles. The contrast between the cold outdoors and the warmth inside was extraordinary. I was almost sweating.

Bang! Bang! Bang! A distinguished-looking man shouted, "Open the door; let me in!" He stuck his face close to the glass door, distorting his appearance. Or perhaps that was merely what I saw through my thick glasses.

"I aaaam soooory. I caan't let you inside!" I pointed at my wristwatch, telling him it was not quite seven-thirty. He banged the door again, and told me he was Donald

Dayton, the owner of the department store. I frowned, questioning his credibility.

"Saar," I shouted, "I don't know who you are. I have a strict order from my boss not to not anyone to enter the building before seven-thirty."

It was mouthful for me. I hoped the man understood. I stuck three fingers against the door, to show that he must wait three more minutes like the rest of the people.

He banged the door again, pointing a finger on me.

I mumbled in my heart, "If you are Mr. Donald Dayton, then I must be the famous George Washington who crossed the Delaware!"

My boss hadn't said anything about letting Mr. Donald Dayton in, or anyone else who might have a title. As I smiled to myself for my conduct, some employees who had arrived reacted comically to my response to the man.

Later that morning, I was picking up trash from station to station on the fourth floor, when suddenly a boisterous voice called from behind me, "Tanemori!" It was Sam Carter, my supervisor.

"A big boss, George, wants you to come into his office."

"What time is it?" I asked Sam.

"What time is it? What kind of question is that?" Sam looked at me quizzically. "I told you George wants to see you!"

It had nothing to do with time, as my big boss wanted to see me. I could see his face, behind the desk. Momentarily, an austere man, the face of the Business Administrator of my College days came to me. I could almost recall his exact words and the tone when he said, "No job for you. What can you do without speaking good English ... It doesn't matter; the deadline is February one ..." I tried to erase the smirk that appeared on my face.

"Sam. Do you know why your boss wanted me?"

"Well, Tanemori," Sam turned and looked at me with a serious face, "what did you do that George told me to find you so quickly?" I wasn't sure whether he was teasing me, or not.

I was somewhat intimidated by this special attention; it was the first time he'd demanded my presence since I had interviewed for the job two summers ago.

"Just follow me," he grunted. We took a shortcut to the second floor, where Sam told me to wait while he walked into the inner office.

Mr. Elliott called me in and Sam said "Good luck," then slapped my back as he disappeared into the corridor.

I was a "scared cat." Mr. Elliott sat behind his polished oak desk, reclining in his chair, his arms supporting his head.

"Good morning, Tanemori. Have a seat." I sensed a smile in his voice.

"Haaa … hai." My voice was as strong as a mosquito's buzzing. "Yes, Saaar. Mr. Elliott. What do you want from me?"

"How is your schoolwork coming along?" asked Mr. Elliott, instead of asking about my job. "I imagine you're doing very well."

I was flabbergasted that he was showing a personal interest in my seminary studies. Although he had five other seminary students besides me working for him, none were really my friends; nor were we ever really together, save when we were called to a general meeting, or happened to run into each other at lunch in the lounge.

"Would you like a cup of coffee? Do you use cream or sugar?" asked Mr. Elliott.

It was hard to get a "yes" out of my mouth. Mr. Elliott's warmth stunned me.

"Tanemori," began Mr. Elliott. "I received a call directly from Mr. Donald Dayton himself, upstairs on the 8th floor, this morning."

Suddenly, I flashed back to a distinguished man banging at the door on the main floor, telling me he was *the* Donald Dayton. I surmised it hadn't been a ruse, after all!

I was ready to defend myself, for what I had done was right and no one, not even the owner, had a "right" to break company policy. "Yes, Mr. Elliott." I suddenly felt strong. I sat up in the chair.

"The first thing Mr. Dayton wanted to know was ... who was the young man that refused to let him in?"

"I see, Mr. Elliott. You told him who the young man was, didn't you?"

"Secondly, he wanted to know whether or not you recognized him as your employer, Donald Dayton."

"That's interesting, sir. Should I have let him in if I knew he was Donald Dayton?" I suppressed an unsettled feeling.

"Mr. Elliott. Did you get in trouble because I didn't let him in, obeying your order? Wasn't I right? If you get in trouble with him on my account, I'd have him court-martialed!" I joked.

Before he had time to catch his breath, I continued, "Well, if Mr. Dayton has a problem with my holding a 'gun' at him by upholding the company policy that he instituted, then I don't think he should be the one who sits upstairs ..." I said all this in a fumbling way, but with an earnest heart.

"No one had ever refused to let him in when he identified himself as Donald Dayton," said Mr. Elliott, "until this morning."

I noticed a sense of pride in his voice that finally one of his subordinates had carried out a strict rule and instruction given in the line of duty.

"It looks like you're the first one to stand up to the responsibilities of his job." Mr. Elliott continued with a lighter spirit. "Donald Dayton felt that, being the owner of the Dayton/Hudson Department Store, most people are intimidated by him and often react so that he simply gets his way."

Mr. Elliott finally came out with it, "You've made quite an impression on Mr. Dayton and, of course, you've made me proud as your boss. He gave you a commendation for a job well done."

Several years later, I had the privilege of inviting Mr. Elliott to my humble dwelling to enjoy a Japanese dinner. My relationship with him, both professional and personal, grew.

The last two years of seminary, my status at work contrasted with my first three years, when I had swept and mopped floors and the like. Because of the incident with Mr. Donald Dayton, Mr. Elliott gave me a job I enjoyed immensely at one of Dayton's warehouses, six blocks from the main store in the heart of downtown Minneapolis.

The warehouse was where all shipments came before delivery to the main store. It was also where discarded cardboard boxes came for recycling. Besides cleaning a few offices and restrooms, my main job was to use a gigantic compressor to crush cardboard boxes into neat packages, like bales of hay, for recycling.

The boss at the warehouse was Mr. G. Voggs, who usually had plenty of work for me. But when things were slow he, unofficially, let me study on the job. Once I had completed all my work, I could discreetly use the remainder of four working hours for personal study. This provided me with additional incentive to do my job quickly, neatly and perfectly, creating as much as one hour to study before punching my time card.

Sometimes I was so engrossed in my studies I forgot what time it was. The next day, I had to go to Mr. Voggs for a special OK on my card, to avoid any apparent discrepancy. No one else knew this creative time had become an essential toward my finishing my seminary training and becoming a bonafide gospel minister.

After our marriage, Joyce thought it would be appropriate for her to take theological training in order to keep up with me and help me in my ministry. She became the first full-time woman student attending this all-male theological institution, and this brought new challenges.

Joyce was looked upon as "poison in the well." Many students were unable to tolerate her simply because she was a woman.

The school year was 1967-68 and students from Korea flooded the halls of the school, sheltered under the protective wings of Professor Daniel C. Kim Sung. This would prove to influence our lives so radically as to create nearly fatal scars on my soul.

Nine long years of schooling were coming to an end, and I already had two "sheepskins" to show for my work. For the last two years, my work had been toward a third degree—a Master of Theology—which would give me a Japanese title of *Sensei*, a master of theological dogma, with all the honor and dignity such a title carries. I soon would be thrust into the field, as a minister of the Gospel, upon the completion of my dissertation: "The Final Restoration of the Nation of Israel to the Promised Land of Palestine."

One major concern was that my work had to follow a prescribed format in perfect English, and required acceptable intellectual values. No one was more qualified to help my English than my wife, Joyce. Yet she needed to devote time and energy to her own work, finishing her Master of Religious Education.

Since the incident with the Academic Dean several years before, I had regrettably received little support from outside. It seemed the Japanese blood running through my veins was too strong and unacceptable. As the only Japanese student, I had to sink or swim, alone.

With winter break over, I returned eagerly to my routine, sitting down in front of the typewriter to craft my thesis. The typewriter was to get a workout, as my wife was finishing her dissertation. Whoever got there first each day had control.

This theological institution was "far-right-wing Baptist," fostering male chauvinism; therefore, it had seemed far-fetched and contradictory that Joyce should make history there. Against all odds, she would not only complete her work, but would graduate Summa Cum laude, should her final dissertation be accepted with an A.

After conferring with my advisor, I was ecstatic to find he was pleased with my progress. He noted my ability to wade through an enormous volume of Old Testament material and careful interpretations thereof, in both Biblical

Hebrew and Aramaic, while also citing secular historical data whenever required and possible.

I felt I had one "friend." I carefully noted in my calendar the times I would come see him for the next five months before I would again wear a cap and gown.

As I stepped out of his office, grinning ear-to-ear, I replayed in my mind what he had said to me:

"Tanemori, I too am a new faculty member here. I shall see to it that you graduate with the kind of work that reflects your accomplishments here. It will be a feather in my hat."

His beaming smile was itself a reward.

"Thank you, Sir!" I could hear the pride in my voice. This was a great shot in the arm for me! I could see my second Masters Degree within reach. All I needed now was to be faithful like a donkey at a millstone, executing my schedules without delay or deviation. Nothing could be allowed to deter me from my goal.

The Dean called me, with a smile in his voice, just as I stepped out of my Advisor's office. It was as if he had been listening in or watching for me, I surmised cynically. I turned to look at him before answering, suspecting he had something up his sleeve.

"Do you have a minute or two?" he asked softly, causing me to put up my guard. I knew he could talk "sweetly," but I felt his sweetness was chemically produced—an artificial substance like "Sweet'n Low," which I never used.

"I have a very important proposal to present to your wife." His tone of voice almost made me sick.

"Oh? Sir, I suggest you talk to her directly." I looked squarely at him. "Besides, sir, if you have an important matter to discuss, I recommend that we go into your office."

The Dean responded without emotion, "I understand that your wife, who is Chinese, is very proficient in English."

I didn't like his tone. He seemed to have not heard what I'd just said.

"I would like to ask a big favor of your wife …"

"Dr. Van Dusen. You still don't understand me, do you, SIR?"

I was chafing at his manner. I was not a child, and he had no right to speak to me like one. Still, he insisted, and continued to talk in the common hallway. He began speaking louder, which I took as indignance.

"I understand that your wife has not yet responded to Dr. Kim Sung's request," he said. "I thought I would ask you a big favor—to persuade your wife to help Dr. Sung for the sake of his Korean students and his academic position."

It took a moment to put two and two together. Then I recalled my wife telling me the week before that the Korean professor had tried to persuade her to help three of his Korean students. They were here in America for only their second year and were also working on Masters Degrees. Like me, they needed to be sure their dissertations were written in good English.

The expectation was that my wife could help them with their English. I knew she hadn't made a decision whether, or how much, she could be of help to them. Besides assisting me, she had to work on her own dissertation. I felt that she shouldn't be pressured, and that even if she declined, no one should blame her.

Dr. Van Dusen quickly took a deep breath, then rushed on, "By the way, you could also help them in cultural understanding, seeing that you are Japanese and seem to have a great understanding of both Oriental and American cultures."

It was clear he wasn't much of an Orientalist, invariably confusing the vast differences between the cultures of Korea and Japan. Either he had just displayed his ignorance, or he had intended to insult me.

"Yes. Of course! She has a good command of English. If you need a favor from my wife, why don't you ask her?" Although I heard the resentment in my own voice, I felt I couldn't let my heart be lost.

"Tanemori … knowing Japanese culture, I thought it only proper to show my personal respect to ask you first and to see …" He almost choked his own words.

"Hypocrite, hypocrite, hypocrite! Why can't he be honest?" I muttered to myself. I certainly felt unflattered by his attempt to show respect for my culture. He knew nothing of me and I was flabbergasted that he thought he was using the proper "channel" of the husband-and-wife relationship when he had never been married!

What was critical here was the issue of burdening my wife with extra obligations, with asking her to sacrifice energy and time for the Korean students. Above and beyond our schoolwork, she was also working as a clerk at the Hinnepin County Office in Minneapolis. She was already devoted to her own work and to my dissertation, which was not an easy task due to the nature and the length of the paper, which required her to work closely with me. As my wife, she had no other option, and the task required special grace and infinite patience of her.

How would the Dean react if I decided not to honor his wish? Would he take it as defiance? Would he use his authority to the extreme? Would he destroy me with his academic power? Most importantly, would I go against the teachings of my Father?

It seemed I was in an indefensible position, as he insisted on talking to me in the hallway. Geographically, he held the advantage. This was his domain.

"Tanemori," said the Dean, playing his trump card, "can you live with your decision to refuse to save your countrymen? How can they face their countrymen, without those sheepskins? Won't you allow Dr. Sung to save face?"

If Korea's culture had any similarity to Japan's, it was as a society "be-ers," not "do-ers" like the United States. A Master of Theology degree from an American institution would carry almost unlimited weight and influence when these students returned home. Their achievement was for the "good of the whole nation" and they would be looked upon as "unselfish" people who had sacrificed for the community, and the nation. They would be revered in word if not always in deed.

Could I afford to sacrifice my coveted Master of Theology degree? I, too, must honor my dignity, and what about my own "save of face?"

I was trapped. I knew that my refusal to allow Joyce to help would be interpreted as defiance to his authority. And if the Korean students failed to get their degrees, they would be looked upon as having failed their communities. Then, quite peculiarly, a story I had heard while struggling to survive in the ashes of the atomic bomb came back to me. I found myself again a *gaki*, one of the dead in the Hell of Starvation, in Kotachi Village. I was in the fourth grade, with an empty stomach, wearing rags. On a muggy summer mid-afternoon Honda-no Obaa-chan gave me a piece of ice-cold watermelon to share equally with my brother. I now heard her voice again as I faced a predicament:

"Taka-chan," she asked, watching my quizzical eyes, "do you have any idea what heaven and hell are like? I once thought them to be different, but they are actually exactly alike!"

"No! No! Obaa-chan," I protested, "Obosan (a local Buddha priest) told me many times they're as different as day and night. In fact, they're located in different places."

I looked up to the blue sky and said, "That's where heaven is, where my Father is." Then I pointed down at the ground and said, "That's where hell is. Deep in the center of the earth, burning with fire and full of people screaming."

This was the teaching of Buddha and I had no way of disputing it, except that I knew in my heart that my Father was in heaven, not because of some "mercy" of Buddha, but due to my Father's own righteousness, the kind of life he had lived before his children!

"Oh, Taka-chan. *Soka, soka.*" She patted my back with a tender smile. She seemed to tolerate my childlike understanding. "I tell you they are both very similar to this world where you and I live. Let me tell you the secret of what's different about hell and heaven … are you ready? Oh, by the way, did you like the piece of watermelon?"

"*Ooon. Taihen oishi kata yo. Obaa-chan arigato.*" I told her how sweet the watermelon was, and thanked her for her kindness.

"Taka-chan, listen carefully to what I'm going to tell you," she began her tale. Her tender eyes were ever-cast upon me. "In hell, people try to eat *gohan*, steamed rice, from the arm's length *hashi* God gave them. With those *hashi*, one might scoop *gohan*, but it's difficult to get it to one's mouth. The *gohan* keeps falling. Fights break out as everyone tries to keep others from stealing their *gohan*. And *gaki*, with demonic facial expressions, fight among themselves on empty stomachs."

With a smile she asked me, "Taka-chan. Did you fight over a piece of watermelon with your brother?"

"Well, you told me to share it with my brother. You know Obaa-chan, I am much bigger than my brother." I rationalized, "I should get a bigger piece. Shouldn't I?"

"Did I not tell you to share it equally between you?"

"Yes. My brother and I fought about who was going to cut it and get the first piece. I told him that since I'm the older brother, and the knife is dangerous, I should cut it. And, of course, I should get first choice of the pieces. But by the time we'd settled our problem, the watermelon had ceased to be an icy-cold one for us to enjoy."

"What did you do, Taka-chan?"

"Obaa-chan, he is too young to tell me what to do," I complained."

She smiled in response as I continued, "Can you believe what my brother said to me? 'Big brother, if you want to cut the watermelon, go ahead. Then I will pick my piece first. Or, if you prefer, I will cut it. Then you can be first to pick whichever piece you want.'"

I had been angry, fuming at his suggestion. He had shown no respect to his older brother. But why hadn't I thought of this solution, instead of him?"

She continued with her story.

"In heaven, people use exactly the same length of *hashi*, and follow the same instructions, but they don't spill a grain of rice; they fill their stomachs with *gohan* and live happily together."

"No!" I argued. "I bet they use different *hashi*. How can they use the same length of *hashi*, yet not spill a grain?"

"In heaven," she paused, smiling, "people feed each other. If they try to feed themselves, the *gohan* will fall. But if they feed each other, the *hashi* are very handy and people find themselves with full stomachs."

"Taka-chan," her eyes filled with tears, "you get back what you dish out. And remember: what you receive, you can give out. This way other people benefit, and so do you! Let's use *hashi* to benefit others, and in turn we all benefit."

"Taka-chan wa Otosan kara oshierareta koto o kesshite wasure naide, kesshit hazukashi ku nai yoni genki yoku ganbatte iki te yuke yo. Obaa-chan ga inotte irukara no!" She made me promise her I would never forget my Father's teaching of the Three-Fold Principles. "Be true to his upbringing and never bring shame or disgrace to his name. Be strong and live upright, follow your heart. I will continue to pray for you."

"Tanemori! Tanemori!" I shook my head several times, as if to clear it. The Dean was standing so close to me that his stale breath almost knocked me out, but at least it had brought me back to reality!

I wondered how the Korean students would feel towards Dr. Kim Sung in this strange land. Out of concern for them, I accepted the Dean's challenge. Yet I felt I had little latitude about "honoring" Dr. Kim Sung. Ahhh! The story of long *hashi*! I raised my eyes toward heaven.

How time had flown! It had been two years since our marriage. The only word from my wife's father was by mail, all his letters addressed to Mrs. Joyce D. Tanemori, as if she had become a widow. Never once did he address a letter to me, or to the two of us.

As we returned from winter vacation in January 1968, Minnesota's coldest winter lay ahead. The "cozy" home we had so enjoyed was turning into a hive of "yellow-jackets." We lost our privacy, and our relationship as husband and wife did not keep us as warm as it should have. How irritable I became, hating to see the Korean students disrupting my routine, my lifestyle.

A huge pile of snow made the garage inaccessible for several days, and I was forced to find places on the street to park my car. On an unusually cold night a howling north wind pierced my thin pants. Climbing to the top of the stairways of our four-plex apartment, I could almost taste the hot chocolate waiting inside.

"Honey, I'm home."

Before Joyce greeted me, I saw the three Korean students she was helping; they were having a good-old time while she kept her nose to the grindstone. They seemed confident her editing would help make masterpieces of their work.

"Aaah, Mr. Tannemoori." In perfect harmony, the Koreans extended their greeting. My wife had not yet noticed me.

"Mr. Tannemoori," began one student who spoke better English than the other two. Not at all bashful, and without giving me a moment to myself, he pointed to the papers in his hand, saying, "we need you to explain to us."

"Yes," said another student, trying to hand me his paper, "we don't understand that what we say in Korean is not quite the same as in English."

"Give me space!" I shouted silently.

This was my home. I had just returned from work to be bombarded by students whom I had little desire to be with, especially this late at night. Feeling like telling them to leave at once, I stormed into the kitchen. Joyce was typing away. Manila folders, reams of paper, and loose papers covered the tiny kitchen table. There was no room for me to sit, let alone put down a cup of hot chocolate.

I went into the bathroom and flushed the toilet time and time again, to cover my screams! The students, like rats, were taking over my domain. It was Friday night and Joyce seemed as anxious as them to see their work progress.

"Mr. Tannemoori," another student shouted from the living room, "I made room for you. You come. I ask a question, OK?"

"Oh, you're home." Joyce noticed I was annoyed at my chair being taken.

"After you catch your breath, I have several questions before I make the final changes." She grabbed a pile of papers. Each page bore a number of notations showing areas requiring my attention.

I felt these outsiders had stolen my space, my time and my energy, which I had intended for my own dissertation.

By the time the students left, the kitchen clock's "frozen" needles pointed nearly to midnight. At last, I found breathing space. I quickly popped a Banquet TV dinner (bought at a special discount price of 19 cents instead of the regular 25 cents) into the oven for a midnight snack as Joyce and I worked on our own dissertations for the next two hours.

Before I fully realized it, springtime had arrived, with its unbearable mess of melting snow. I had denied myself any snowbird activities during the entire winter, due to our obligations to the Korean students.

Joyce and I had spent no recreational time together, since when we momentarily escaped the Korean students, we devoted all our energies to our own schoolwork. The only consolation I could see was the final success of the students' dissertations as our reward.

May's calendar was nearly filled to the brim. There were only two weeks left before I would strut, proud as a peacock, parading in cap and gown, across the graduation platform.

"Honey," Joyce called, running up to me, "I just heard that all three Korean students met their requirements. They'll be graduating with honors."

We shared a great sigh of relief. I was somewhat content over the good news for the Koreans, and was very proud of my wife's contribution to their recognition. Now, surely, I would be hearing good news about my work. Joyce shared my optimism, as she had sacrificed her work to see all of us get to the day of graduation. For all of us, our hopes and dreams were wrapped up in this very hour.

Then … a bump in the road.

"What is this?" I questioned, momentarily confused.

A note from the Dean, Dr. Warren Van Dusen, was in my mail-slot. The note simply stated, "You have a meeting with the Academic Committee at 1:15 p.m. on May 16, 1968."

I was stunned.

The Academic Committee was composed of the Dean, the Chairman, Dr. Sung, Dr. Richard Snider and Dr. James McDonald, my academic counselor.

"What do you think?" I gave the note to my wife.

"I suppose," she stated optimistically, "they are considering a special award for your achievements. That's no small matter. Besides, the subject of your dissertation must have impacted the Academic Committee members, don't you think? You have come a long way and made an invaluable contribution to those Korean students."

However, rather than welcoming smiles, when I walked into the meeting I sensed a cold, suspicious air in the tiny room where the Academic Committee members sat stoically. Even the arrangement of the room could be clearly read as indicative of a caste system.

"Can't anyone talk to me?" I mumbled to myself. I quickly realized that the Dean held my finished dissertation, which I had given to my Advisor. The work was 280 pages, including seven pages of cross-references. Although I couldn't tell what the other members held in their hands, they seemed to have before them several pages of my work, along with their own scribbled notepads.

My dissertation represented two years of diligent research. I was proud of it, as it foresaw the hope that the Nation of Israel would be fulfilled one day, with a return to the Promised Land. This would be a culmination of the Davidic Covenant in which the Messiah would sit on the Throne of King David. Chills ran up and down my spine as I thought of such an event unfolding, seen through the eyes of the Prophets of old.

At the moment, though, I felt ambivalent about our having helped the Korean students. I wasn't quite sure whether or not I should express joy for their success. I expected the Committee members, especially Dr. Sung, would express gratitude to my wife and me on the students' behalf. Was I expecting too much, or should I not have entertained such selfish thoughts?

The Dean broke the silence as he picked up my dissertation and dropped it on the table.

"I am shocked at your interpretation," he thundered. "I cannot see why you failed to reflect our theological point of view in your dissertation."

I listened with an open mouth, wondering what in the world I had gotten into.

Instead of responding to the Dean, I calmly said with a smile in my voice, "Dr. Kim Sung, I'm so glad to hear the good news about your Korean students. You must be proud of your 'sons' being able to return to their homeland with honor and dignity." Dr. Sung's incoherent response was amusing. While he struggled to say something, I sensed irritation in the Dean's voice.

"Tanemori, we are taking our valuable time to discuss your unacceptable work. It's clear you havn't honored any aspect of our theological position. We interpret the position you've taken as defying our theological beliefs. You have deliberately gone against our teaching. You have smeared our position as defenders and depositors of the 'truth.' We conclude that you cannot graduate from the sacred halls of our institution."

I resolved not to waste my breath on the Dean.

"Dr. McDonald, do you recall, sir? I came to you with my interpretation practically every day for the last three months. More importantly, have I not sought your intellectual and spiritual guidance for my dissertation?"

He couldn't deny that I had faithfully followed his guidelines and intellectual input, and above all, that I had demonstrated the Word of God as the final authority, rather than the Dean. I threw my calendar with proof of my scheduled Advisor meetings on the table, in evidence.

I waited … then spoke in an irritated voice.

"Do you remember, sir? You repeatedly told me how good and faithful a student I was. As a matter of fact, you even told me you had never seen a theological student with such a sweet spirit, strong conviction, belief and individual integrity."

"TTTTanemori," the Dean interrupted.

"Sir, with all due respect, I feel my Advisor has a right to defend himself or to comment. Please allow him to respond. Otherwise, I would take your action as intellectually dishonest."

"Tanemori, it is I who have the final say. It is I who makes the final decision on academic matters. I have observed you since you entered this institution. We take this very seriously. It is my moral and sacred duty to correct any student who errs from the truth."

He glanced through the corners of his eyes to the rest of the Committee for support.

I thought, "And, more importantly, it is my judgment that we cannot afford to let you pass through this sacred institution to represent our theological position. You are very defiant. We must guard our reputation and will do everything we can to maintain it."

I read him like an open book. What a simpleton, what a small man, he was!

"Sir, I believe Dr. McDonald needs to respond to you, in my place. He's the one who guided me to maintain my theological position in accordance with the Bible. If there was any contradiction, or any defiance to your authority, he should have dealt with me severely long before. Don't you agree?"

"TTTTanemori," the Dean burst out. His face was red, indicating that his Dutch blood was at the boiling point. "You must understand that Dr. McDonald has not been groomed under our tutoring. He came from different theological institution ... and he ..."

I detected his cunning, foxy heart.

"Let me say again, sir," I addressed the Dean, "do I understand it was you that contacted Grace Theological Seminary in Wynona, Indiana and persuaded Dr. McDonald to join this seminary as the Chairman of the Old Testament Department?"

I looked at my Advisor for his acknowledgment, then continued, "It is also true that because of his academic training and doctrinal position, irrefutably grounded in the Word of God, you thought him in accordance with the theological position of this institution, and you hired him."

Dr. Sung stepped in. "Tanemori ..." His voice reflected what one might call a stereotypical Oriental expression of disgust. "I'm ashamed of your disrespect for the Dean's authority. How can you challenge him this way? Don't you know your place, seeing you have grown up in Japanese culture? Don't you have any shame left in you?"

Silence settled on the room.

"Maybe you don't have what it takes to be a gentleman," Dr. Sung continued in his folly. "We are taught to obey authority with due respect and honor, without question. After all, the Dean is the man God ordained to oversee this place of higher learning."

"Dr. Sung, with all due respect ..."

"Tanemori ... See! That's exactly what I mean. You have no respect, even for me. Why do you interrupt me? I am not yet finished, and I am baffled by your haughty attitude. I never expected to see anyone, especially you, supposedly raised under the *Samurai Code,* act this way. Let me tell you what your Father should have taught you ..."

"Dr. Sung. Don't you ever, ever speak of my Father!" My voice filled the chamber. "Who do you think you are? Your doctor's degree does little to impress me. And I am appalled by your unprofessional conduct defending the Dean. Neither you nor he has yet to express any appreciation to my wife for the investment she made to see your Korean students fulfill their dreams. Talk about my attitude; pardon me, sir! You owe an apology to my wife ..."

My voice could be heard down the hallway as I led them back to the core issue. "Where do you think my dissertation is off target? Show me exactly where I have erred in interpreting the Prophets, where I have failed to reflect the theological position of this institution?"

I glanced at my Advisor. He had yet to open his mouth to defend me, or himself.

"Tanemori," the Dean interjected, trying to cut me off.

"Let me, please ... finish what I need to say. If all you say is true, then why have you rejected my thesis when my Advisor approved it?"

My vigorous protest against the Dean ended in vain.

While the Korean students we helped graduated with honors, my graduation was denied. Furthermore, I had to confront the Academic Board as to why my wife, with her 4.0 grade point average, was forced to graduate Magna Cum Laude instead of Suma Cum Laude.

The Dean gave a reason I couldn't accept. "Tanemori ... she is a woman and we could not allow a woman to graduate with honors above or equal to men who are called to the ministry of the Gospel."

I realized their actions revealed the way they looked at women: "... *women adorn themselves in modest apparel, with shamefacedness and sobriety ... let them learn in silence with all subjection ... suffer not a woman to teach, nor to usurp authority over the men, but to be in silence ...*" (I Timothy 2:9-12) and "... *let your women keep silence in the churches, for it is not permitted unto them to speak; but they are commanded to be under obedience ... and if they will learn any thing, let them ask their husbands at home ...*" (I Corinthians 14:34-35).

I was more determined than ever to become a Gospel minister, serving white men's churches, against my gut feelings and in spite of the advice of Dr. Clifford Parker, who had warned me that an American congregation would not accept my leadership because I was Japanese. Sooner or later they would reject me as their spiritual leader.

I asked how I could refuse to serve white men's congregations. I felt that ministering to white men's churches would be my reward and would fulfill the vow I had made over my Father's grave to avenge his death.

Chapter Seven: The Purple Robe

No one can measure a "Heart"
by a yardstick or by a scale;
nor can it be touched like a tender petal,
or inhaled like the fragrance of a rose.
But your "Heart" can be demonstrated,
like a flowing river,
by sharing it with others.

MOST of my life as a postwar Japanese immigrant in America, I was marooned by a dark and bitter past. While I wrestled with the ghosts of history I learned the importance of healing the human heart. It was the test of my heart and my faith to serve white men's congregations—"exacting revenge through love and service."

The day we said goodbye to some old friends, we left Minneapolis shortly after midnight. I was determined never to look back to the city in which we had spent our last five years. I had to burn that bridge! Our new destination was Hillsboro, Indiana, about 15 miles west of Indianapolis.

I was soon standing at the threshold of my first ministry, the tiny country church called Hillsboro Bible Church. The senior minister there, Buffer Davis, had been in the class ahead of me during seminary. While I was being groomed into a bonafide ministerial student, I considered him an extraordinary comrade, especially during the last two years of our schooling together.

When he became a senior minister, he immediately asked me to become his associate. He promised me we'd serve together, no matter what "high water came our way."

My first responsibility, as an Associate Minister serving the white men's congregation, was to conduct a Vacation Bible School. The goal of the school was to reach children and their parents in Hillsboro and its surroundings, proclaiming God's love with a theme of "A Fisher of Men."

We borrowed a pickup truck from a church member, and decorated it like a ship sailing through mighty oceans. Wearing a white jacket with gold buttons, and draped with medals and insignia, I stood at the helm of this "ship." A naval captain's cap made me look six feet tall. I presumed I would be looked upon much like a modern day Commodore Matthew Calbraith Perry, with a mission of opening the hearts of children to Jesus.

I was ecstatic to see children following me as if I were "Tom the Piper's Son." By the time we finished our canvassing, we had gathered the names of nearly two hundred children. My wife was kept busy making signs and pictures to be used with songs for Vacation Bible School. All the preparation created an atmosphere akin to a carnival.

Six days before we were to open the school, we were ready, but didn't have enough space at the church to handle such a large crowd. On Wednesday morning, I had a strange call from a man who wanted to donate a large tent for our use.

"That's wonderful. God answered our prayers to resolve the space crunch. Hallelujah!" I jumped out of my seat. I was feeling God could perform any miracle He wished if we were willing to accept.

Of course, I wanted to know more about this stranger. He was probably equally curious to find out why a minister was dressed up like a fool ship's captain! Our meeting should answer these questions.

"You know, Reverend Tanemori," said Jimmy Carlson, "I came to last Sunday's service to find out what kind of a church this crazy preacher belonged to."

I learned that Mr. Carlson owned and operated a tent business in Indianapolis, and that his offer was genuine. There was no bait dangling on a fishing line.

"I don't know what you did to my son, but he's excited about this "Fisher of Men" thing. I haven't seen my son smile like this in a long time."

Jimmy Carlson was the father of a boy in the second grade who was confined to a wheelchair. On Saturday afternoon Mr. Carlson and his crew came and set up a 40-by-60 foot tent in the church parking lot. He was excited beyond words when I invited seven teenagers to guard the tent overnight.

Vacation Bible School was a success. We reeled in many "little fish" for Jesus as well as their "big fish" parents, many of whom started to attend our church on a somewhat regular basis. Their untainted excitement was contagious, inspiring some regular church members, who seemed, spiritually, to have been "dead-fish" for years. The tiny country church had never experienced such a blazing flame as the one now sweeping the cornfields of Indiana.

The Senior Minister was grateful and Joyce and I were thrilled. Our apparent success gave us confidence and assurance that our decision to come to Indiana, to serve a white men's congregation, had met with God's approval.

Dirty handprints of children, along with their artwork, were all over the walls. Yet we didn't mind at all. We were glad we had enough wall space for them to do their artwork, and we kept busy washing walls every week for their fresh paintings.

With children running around, there was an unruliness to our school, but at the same time, their laughter became medicine to most of our church members. Still, despite the apparent joy in this fellowship, the church's Chairman of the Board and his followers expressed concerns that the spirituality of church services was being disrupted. They vocalized their contempt, questioning my sanity and my ministry.

Only four weeks after Vacation Bible School ended, Buffer Davis resigned, reappearing practically overnight at Grace Baptist Church in Michigan City, Indiana. He apparently had been planning to go there for some time. I felt he had pulled the rug out from under my feet. My heart was gutted, having dropped into a bottomless black abyss.

When practically every minister I knew, as well as the ministerial students I knew at school, had questioned my becoming a minister for a white congregation, I had taken Davis' invitation as nothing short of God's "Calling." How else could I have interpreted such a willing, open commitment as he had given me?

If there were any "dirty hands" involved, those at play in the Senior Pastor's exit were worse than those of the kids marking walls and disrupting services. I detested learning that the Chairman of the Board and Mike Ridder had agreed I needed "proper, hands-on" training in the field, and that they had been called by God to administer that service. And instead of upholding the promise he had made to me when he made me his associate, Rev. Davis accepted the assessment and recommendation of the two elders.

Working together with my comrade from the seminary had proved to be short-lived!

For the next five Sundays, the Chairman of the Board brought guest speakers to the pulpit, but none satisfied him. On the last Sunday of September I noticed the Chairman seemed panicky, as he whispered to Mike Ridder, who led congregational singing. While the Chairman asked the congregation for greater financial support and to pray harder in the search for a new minister, Mike approached me sheepishly.

"Pastor Tom," he said, "the Chairman needs you to step up to the pulpit to talk … just talk about anything to offer hope to the congregation. When the guest speaker arrives, he'll take over. Would you be willing?"

Selfishly, I wanted to tell him off and let the Chairman sweat this out. On the other hand, I was looking for an opportunity. This was not a time for modesty, neither was it one for me to tend to my feelings!

There was a sigh of relief as the Chairman and Mike descended from the platform to their seats in the front pew where I was sitting.

I had no way of measuring how my message—more or less my first Sunday sermon—sounded to the congregation. Except that I noticed a heartfelt surge of energy as I knelt with those few who came to the altar to pray together. It was like a parchment of rain that fell on a hillside, refreshing our souls.

Senior Pastor James' parsonage, owned by the church, was located in the town's newest suburb, where the community's elite families lived. The three bedroom parsonage had a den, living and family rooms, a spacious dining room, pantry, utility room, a one-and-a-half-car garage and a large back yard. Magnolia trees surrounded a home epitomizing the luxury and modern conveniences of affluent America. What more could any minister ask for?

In comparison, the Associate Minister's dwelling was a tiny, dilapidated trailer, about 10 feet wide by 36 feet long, in the midst of an iridescent green cornfield. As the Church Treasurer handed us the keys, he said, "It's my duty to see the church doesn't go further into the red. I expect you folks to live within the means we provide."

Hearing this, Joyce was very calm, and I wondered how she was able to control her emotions so well. I detested the assumption that a minister must learn to live humbly. Tears, whether born of self-pity or of anger, ran down my cheeks, through my hands, and onto the ground.

Late on the afternoon of October 3, 1969, while I was visiting a church member, Beverly, the church secretary, tracked me down. She said Joyce was in pain and had been taken to the hospital. By the time I arrived there, she was in the delivery room, having contractions. Suddenly I reflected on my Aunt Takae telling me long ago about my Father's irrationality when his first child was born.

A nurse came to me with the message, "Rev. Tanemori, your wife delivered a healthy son half an hour ago. She's resting comfortably in the recovery room."

"See, Daddy … it's BOY!" I beamed, nodding toward heaven.

We already had a name for a baby boy—Jonathan Takashi Tanemori. The moment Joyce and I brought him home, we placed him on the couch, knelt beside him, and prayed, as if offering Jonathan, "A True Friend of God," as a "sacrificial" lamb.

We beseech Thee, O Lord,
to make us faithful guardians of this gift of new life.
Knowing we are all clay in the Hands of the Potter,
may we help him to be both pliable and strong,
always tempered by the light of your heart.

Grant us, O Lord,
Guidance from Heaven above.

To lead him to know the Truth—the Truth of God,
and to know the difference between right and wrong.
We implore Thee to direct his path to Thyself.

Help our son, O Lord,
as he takes each breath to hear the heartbeats of
                                                    others.
And to be strong enough to know when he is weak,
And humble enough to know his great strength.
Thy servants are here, hear our prayers.

Guide him, O Lord,
not only to enjoy the beauty of the world, but also
to stand firm in times of hardship, stress and
                                                    affliction.
May he always remember his humble beginnings
And have compassion for those who are weak and
                                                    frail.

Aid him, O Lord,
to find courage when he is afraid,
and to accept honest defeat with dignity.
Let him be humble and gracious in victory.
As he learns to be true to his heart

Lead him, O Lord,
in the path that is "right" for him.
May he not shirk from the truth and consequences of
                                                    his decisions.
Nor abandon what is right for the sake of ease.
And may he always stand for the Truth even if others
                                                    forsake him.
Fashion him, O Lord,
with character and a pure heart.
May he always follow your lead,
Learning to laugh, yet never forgetting how to weep,
reaching into the future, yet never forgetting the
                                                    past.

Endow him, O Lord,

with humility so that he may always remember who
he is,
and help him not to be misled by his own cleverness
or ingenuity,
or to become dependent on earthly wealth and fame.
Help him to understand that true greatness and true
strength
lie in the shadow of Thy grace and mercy.

At last, O Lord,
when his long journey has come to an end,
and he looks back on the road he has traveled,
may he be able to see how his stumbling, crooked
steps
have become a straight path, and how on this lonely
road,
he has never been alone.

By the Parents of Jonathan, Our First Son,
on October 3, 1969

While we were immersed in his arrival, several church members visited us during Christmas and New Year, wishing us the best year for our ministry.

Since we had experienced many winters in Minnesota, I felt we could take any kind of winter in Indiana. How wrong I was. I was to learn a harsh lesson as penetrating cold and blizzards whipped through Indiana's once-iridescent green fields.

In the first week of February virtually all main arteries of the town were buried by snow. Without a skirt around the bottom of the trailer, the frozen air turned our "home" into a freezer-box on the open tundra.

The single tiny oil heater failed to keep the trailer warm, much less cozy, and we could see our own breath as it tried to rise to the ceiling. My main concern was for the safety and health of our son, for he needed protection from the cold.

We taped layers of old newspapers on every window and placed old towels against the bottom of the door, to keep cold air from blasting in. It was a losing battle. We also faced a shortage of diapers. We kept washing diapers but when we tried to dry them by hanging them inside our trailer, they turned to icicles!

At least we had set aside food for the winter: 10-pound bags of rice and a few canned goods.

As the gusty wind whipped by one evening, the trailer shook so much I was afraid it might turn over. Just before three in the morning, we heard a big "kaboom." Something had snapped and fallen to the frozen ground. My wife shouted, "Honey, I want you to check the heater." There was no flame, and the pilot light was out.

Shivering, I went outside, to discover the oil tank lying on the ground. The pipe from the tank to the trailer was broken in half, and I had no idea how much oil had been spilled. We wrapped our son with more newspaper and further insulated the windows.

Early the next morning I called Ed Johnson, one of the faithful church members, for help. His wife, Ann, responded a couple hours later with great news.

"Pastor Tom. I called a number of people, and I got enough Green Stamps from them for you to get a small space heater for your son's room. I already checked with the store manager, who said she would keep one for you."

Their generosity was overwhelming, but I didn't have the three dollars I needed at the Green Stamp Redemption store for the heater.

"Oh, don't worry," said Ann. "It's important you get a heater as quickly you can. I want you to get here for the Green Stamps, and I have that money for you."

A treacherous icy road, covered by snowdrifts, made driving risky. Taking my life in my frozen hands, I returned home two hours later with a space heater.

"Honey, look!" I was ecstatic! I knelt with Joyce by our son, praying for Ann and our friends who gave us "Redemption Stamps" to meet our needs. We felt their genuine warmth and caring hearts. And as the air finally thawed, we took the extra newspaper out of our son's room.

"Pastor Tom," Ann's voice was strong, "I'll tell Ed about the tank and I know he'll check with Charles about fixing it. You'll be back in business in no time!"

Our rejoicing was short-lived.

"Honey."

I sensed something was wrong in her voice. Joyce had seen Charles Baggman, the church Treasurer, coming toward our trailer.

"Look out! The way he's coming ..." She was cleaning the last few dishes from our early dinner.

I tried to defuse any tension by thanking him for coming to rescue us. Charles said nothing, just grunted. I followed him as he stepped outside, a big, powerful flashlight in his hand, and started to walk around the trailer, looking up-and-down, checking and searching. Then he noticed the tiny window of my son's room was free from ice, as if that was what he was looking for.

"Do you mind if I check the inside of the trailer?"

"Charles, don't you need to see the fuel tank buried in the snow over there?" I pointed into the dark.

Ignoring me, he bee-lined into my boy's room and yanked the space heater from the wall.

"What's the meaning of this, Pastor Tom? Didn't I tell you the very first day that electricity is very expensive? I didn't even allow you to use a fan during the muggy summer. Have you already forgotten, or do you think you've earned the right to go against my wishes now that you're the Interim Pastor? Do you think for a moment that I'd let you use a space heater to heat the entire trailer? You seem to have forgotten who's paying the utilities."

"Charles," my wife begged, practically holding on to him. "Please, don't take it from us. We need it to keep our son warm. Don't you understand the space heater was given to us by Ann and some of our church families?"

He brushed her off. Holding the heater under his arm like a conquering war hero, he stepped out of the trailer.

My wife held me back. I could only look into the cold, dark night where Charles had disappeared. I couldn't cry. Having lived in postwar Japan, I had survived the piercing iciness of Japanese society. I had learned to live naked, cold, hungry, deprived of the warmth of human touch. And I had survived! But now my tiny four-month-old son lay in a crib, wrapped once again in newspapers.

While the Chairman of the Board frantically looked for a minister, church attendance grew. That was in spite of my poor Japanese/English sermons and a constant struggle against evil forces. When I had come to the church, our average attendance was sixty members. We now numbered one hundred at a given Sunday morning service.

And yet the congregation's spirituality suffered, as the Chairman of the Board insisted that he ought to be at the helm until we had a "bonafide preacher" to deliver sermons in eloquent English. As time passed, the church became like a morgue, gathering the "spiritually dead." The Chairman of the Board and Charles Baggman were like a *furu-danuki*, an old raccoon, and they were as cunning as a red fox, mastering their tricks on a young preacher whose heart was innocent and pure, and willing to serve.

These things affected me emotionally as much as physically. I looked like a dark brown frog, marked with welts. I had become very critical, even of Joyce. I couldn't bear to feel her tender protective eyes. Even if she wanted to touch and comfort me, I felt I had to reject and deny her. I no longer had kind words for her, and she became an easy target for me to take out my frustrations upon.

I have often heard others say that we hurt the ones we love the most. My wife took much of the verbal abuse that I couldn't turn toward any member of the congregation.

It was easy for me to go after Joyce, for I knew her weaknesses and was able to keep control by holding onto the tiger's tail. I knew better than to cast shrapnel at church members, for there would be repercussions beyond any "damage-control" in our tiny gossip-prone community.

Instead, my wife became the target of my tirades, and this gave me a sense of conquering her. This may have been due to the fact that I was a Japanese man, but subconsciously, subjecting her to my leadership may have been my twisted notion of spiritual superiority.

In spite of our difficulties with church life, a special occasion eventually caught the attention of the community. Reaction to this event was both positive and negative. The local newspaper ran the story: "Thomas T. Tanemori, Hillsboro Bible Church was ordained into the gospel ministry at a service in the church auditorium, Saturday July 18, 1970."

After my ordination, we moved into the parsonage, where the mailbox proudly read: Rev. T. Tanemori, 317 Magnolia Drive, Hillsboro, Indiana.

"Pastor Tom," the church secretary followed one step behind my wife, vigorously shaking her shoulders. "I'm sorry I couldn't stop your wife ..."

My wife stormed into my office, practically pushing the secretary away, as if she were a bully. "What is the meaning of this?" She stuck a canceled check into my face. The check was written unmistakably in my peculiar left-handed style of penmanship.

"What did you use this money for and why this large amount? Tell me!" Joyce's voice was clear, angry.

"Honey," I was as exasperated as my wife, "I will not tolerate your behavior. You know what is right and wrong in family matters. You should never, never show your face like this here at church! I am ashamed of you."

"Hear me," She countered, "the check I wrote for groceries bounced. The money you gave the church as a special offering came from our grocery money. Why in the world would you give to the church when we've been sacrificing so much for so many months? How could you take the food from our son's mouth and give it to somebody else? You're heartless! And, there's still a little over one week before your next meager check."

I had to answer her.

"Do you remember the missionary and his family, with a little boy our son's age, who came to our service to raise support for his return to the field?"

Explaining to my wife, perhaps to justify my own irrational behavior, my mind and heart retreated to postwar Japan. In Hiroshima, how I had struggled to survive. I foraged for weeds, searched garbage cans and waste dumps for food. I remembered, in desperation, how I had begged from a few villagers. But no one had responded, except Suzuki-no-Oba-achan and Hosokawa, the barbershop lady. I believed the need of this missionary was greater than ours. I also believed my wife would understand my heartbeats for the missionary's commitment to his work.

"Can't you understand why I needed to do it? I must set a good example for others. How can I ask the congregation to sacrifice more, if we are unwilling?"

Noticing, as she left, that Joyce's shoulders were somewhat stooped, I grasped how much my wife carried heavy burdens in her responsibilities as mother to our son, and as my wife, to myself and my ministry. I felt deep regret for those burdens!

Fumarete mo
Mata fumarete mo
tae shinobe
waga me 'shiba fu' ya
Moshun no Kou!

A blade of grass,
Trampled over and over again by travelers
                              unknown,
Enduring in silence,
Bearing down with burdens,
Waiting for earth to be cradled by warmest spring
                              day.

A long-awaited spring came to the prairies of Indiana. Wishing to complete my Master of Theology, I aimed for one last chance to complete my dissertation, the only requirement remaining for my coveted degree.

I made arrangements with the church board to take my family with me for one week's vacation, so that I could bury myself in the library of the Dallas Theological Seminary. Having completed my research in Texas, I returned home to what I considered an ambush.

At the church office I found the secretary with a stoic face.

"Beverly, what's the matter?" I asked. "How were the services last Sunday?"

Instead of responding to me in her sweet voice, she handed me an envelope.

"It's all there," she responded, nearly in tears, when I asked her what was in the letter.

The letter said the Board had decided to terminate my position as Pastor of the Church. During my absence, the Chairman of the Board had called a contingency meeting. The Board had voted to fire me without explanation, except to say I must fulfill the church constitution and bylaws by ministering for the next 30 days before vacating the parsonage. In closing the letter, the Chairman stated his wish for God's guidance on our unknown future ministry.

So ended our first ministry honeymoon. I had never seen something so beautiful, tender and precious turn ugly and unlovable so quickly. And yet through all this we did find a precious "black pearl." Several wonderful families stood by us even though they, too, were rejected and ostracized by the church's "circle of leadership."

To these, we bade farewell and Godspeed!

How much just seven miles of country road can change a person's perspective. At a Sunday morning service we found ourselves before the entire congregation of Sunnyville Baptist Church.

After the service, most of the members welcomed my family and me with firm handshakes. When I came to my office, I immediately noticed a black plaque with gold lettering: "Rev. Thomas T. Tanemori, Associate Minister." Suddenly, I felt I was six feet tall and could meet any minister "eye-to-eye."

My main responsibilities would be Church Visitation and Christian Education Ministry. Before I launched my ministry, I was determined that Joyce would not be directly involved with the ministry of the church, nor would she work closely with me. Even though she had a

Master's Degree, I wanted her to be known as my wife and not a "minister's wife."

My foremost task was the selection of a personal secretary. Whether my ministry would "make or break" would largely depend on the "amiable quality" of the person filling this role. Selecting a secretary was like buying a tree from a nursery—carefully looking at the tree itself, not where it was growing or where it came from, but at how well it adapted to the local soil and climate.

What I was looking for was an unwritten qualification, the capacity to feel the "heartbeats" of others.

There was madness to my method! I purposely made a mess of my office, scattering everything here and there. I hung pictures crookedly and out of place. I put objects in such disarray that one had to walk around or move things to get to an empty chair conspicuously positioned under a window as the furthest object from the door. The stage was set for my final test in securing a secretary.

The first candidate, highly recommended by the Senior Preacher, could type and take shorthand, and was an exotic beauty, but failed my test. I considered this beautiful woman, merely a *zo-ka*, an artificial silk-flower!

I held great hope for the second candidate, a mother of three children. But I wondered if she would meet my qualifications, and if not, what I would do then.

Peggy Jones, arriving five minutes early, peeked in and asked if it was all right to enter. I took note of her facial expressions and her emotional reaction as she saw my messy room. She stood momentarily in the doorway, sweeping the room with her eyes, until invited to sit down. She moved a coat stand to the corner of the room, instead of walking around, before she took her seat.

"Pastor Tom," she smiled, "it looks like you could use a hand or two to make it easy for you to do your work. Would you like me to open the curtains and window to let in fresh air before we get down to business?"

I soon learned she couldn't take shorthand, nor type, except with her index fingers. Yet in contrast with the first candidate, Peggy's simplicity and wholesomeness reminded me of a *yuki-wari-so*, a Japanese wintry flower that only blooms in the shadows of the deep forest.

On a morning early in December, 1972, as I left home Joyce reminded me to stick around the church. She had been counting the days, and it was either today or tomorrow that she anticipated the birth of our second child. The Tanemori family was receiving blessings from the Heavenly Father beyond my dreams. Surprisingly, after only four short hours of labor, Joyce delivered our healthy Number Two Son, on December 6th. We named him Nathan Yoshio, "a friend whom one could trust, or Righteous One." A Japanese father of two sons, I was as proud as I could be!

Our ministry at Sunnyville Baptist Church had been thrilling; partly due to the great support we had from the Preacher. It began to seem as though anything I touched, personally and professionally, the Lord blessed with His approval. Our ministry suddenly took an upward swing with Sunday service attendance growing from an average of 450 parishioners to 600.

Then without warning at one Sunday service, the Preacher dropped a bomb. He announced that he would be taking one of his associates with him to Baltimore, Maryland to an established Baptist church three times bigger in membership than Sunnyville. He would also have an honorary Doctorate conferred upon him with his acceptance of the "call" to be pastor.

Many church members took the news hard. We felt as if a mass of giant locusts had ravaged our crops, leaving only a few beaten stalks standing. I also questioned whether I was a jinx ...

Dick Sutter, the Chairman of the Deacon's Board, immediately called a private meeting. There was an urgency to stabilize the situation to keep the congregation from scattering like sheep. I assumed the position of Interim Pastor to handle most of the church ministry under Dick's leadership until a new Senior Pastor was found.

Unfortunately, this created a conflict with Youth Director Chuck Carpenter and his followers. Given his seniority, he thought he should have been called in as Interim Pastor. I gave my best to resolve the conflict, but apparently that wasn't enough.

Unable to build the cooperative working relationship needed with Carpenter and his followers, my emotional and then physical condition took turns for the worse. I dreaded going to work each day, as seeing his face was more than I could handle. I felt alone, as if standing in the *sabaku*, Sahara desert. Yet even in this desolation, I found an oasis in church families the Lord had given to our care.

Sandy Crawford and her family were among the first people whose hearts touched mine. I first met her at the end of a stormy winter afternoon, when she stood in my office doorway, wearing little makeup and looking lonely.

At first I thought my eyes were playing tricks on me—her soft curves, luminous brown eyes and innocent, warm look reminded me the tenderness of Okusan. My hot coffee tasted like green tea, as I suddenly found myself sitting next to an esthetic and intrinsic beauty, in the garden where Okusan and I had created our secret world.

Sandy became a fountain of fresh water, a life-giver. Each time I visited her—or, should I say, each time we found ourselves with fleeting moments together—our relationship blossomed like a wildflower in a secret sanctuary.

As much as I saw her, she became very dear to me. Our bond grew, as our hearts were cemented by our immeasurable, unadulterated love, which a brushstroke can only start to describe:

Reflection

Kao ni deru
futari no koi wa
hito towazu
yume mo michru ya
haru takenawa ni.

[No one needs to ask what we have in our hearts toward each other; they can tell by what they see, reflected in our countenances!]

As time passed, Sandy became concerned with my emotional and physical condition. While visiting her family one afternoon, I did a poor job of hiding the sharp pains that coursed through my stomach. Covering my mouth with my bare hand, I spat blood into it. Then I passed out. When I came to, I was lying in a hospital bed.

"How are you?" asked Dr. Michael Greene, our family physician. "Reverend Tanemori, you have a bleeding ulcer. I don't think it's too serious. But you can't afford to worry and put yourself under the excessive pressure of the ministry. What you need to do is learn to relax."

I informed my secretary, Peggy, and Janet, a church secretary, about my predicament. I called my wife to tell her I would be retained overnight for precautionary care.

I dozed off; when I awoke the sun was setting. The final rays reflected through the window on the single stem of a pink rose left at my bedside. A special bow tied to it held a signature. The sight and scent of the rose teased my soul. I knew Sandy had been here.

Early the next morning, Joyce visited and told me not to worry. She then hurried home to take care of our two boys. Time seemed to tick by very slowly. While I was sipping soup for lunch, Peggy came in.

"Pastor Tom," she said, "I hope you don't mind. I'm taking a little extra time off during my lunch hour to come see you."

"Of course not, Peggy! Thanks for thinking of me."

"Oh, I see," her approving smile radiated. "A single stem pink rose with a special bow, right Pastor Tom?" Peggy knew what the single pink rose meant to me, and guarded my special feelings as a "sacred" secret love, which she never revealed to anyone.

My first task when released from the hospital was to invite two potential candidates to preach at Sunday services and to meet with the Deacon Board for an interview. As Interim Pastor, I had no vote in the choice of a new Pastor, but I was asked to give my candid (and somewhat opinionated) advice in the final selection.

One candidate took the pulpit for a Sunday service in October. His warmth, gentleness and charismatic style of preaching captured the hearts of the congregation, lifting the roof of the church. Spontaneous shouts of "Amen! Amen! Amen!" echoed in the sanctuary.

Many people responded, as it was designed that they would. Sadly, I knew this particular sermon had been polished and spit-shined several times over.

Soon thereafter, the Board met for hours to discuss a new minister, with some Board members and the Youth Director openly rejecting my spiritual guidance (especially, they said, because I was Japanese).

Against my recommendation, votes were cast to welcome Reverend Kenneth Fullerton as Senior Pastor. The scene reminded me of the famous story of Abraham Lincoln and the "five-legged" sheep. President Lincoln was facing a tough decision that would be pivotal in selecting his Cabinet members. He wanted each cabinet member to have strong self-awareness, conviction, and a political point of view that matched his. And so he tested his candidates:

"Gentlemen," Lincoln asked, "If you call a sheep's tail a leg, how many legs does that sheep have?"

To his surprise, a number of potential cabinet members replied, "Of course, Mr. President, that sheep has five legs."

Others said, "Sir, the sheep has four legs," staunchly arguing that just because a tail was called a leg did not mean a sheep has five legs. "The tail will never become leg ..."

The moral lesson was obvious. Some men failed to show convictions in their personal lives that matched those of their political lives.

The decision having been made, I promised myself that I would be faithful to my duties and responsibilities, upholding Reverend Fullerton with all the honor and respect he deserved as Senior Pastor.

Under him, the church ministries flourished like a blossoming flower, until like a cut flower they withered.

The galvanizing effect of the Reverend's arrival and early ministry fizzled, like the flame of a candle snuffing out.

Once again a conflict emerged between the Youth Director and me, and this time it sent ripples through the congregation. Some folks were loyal to me, some were loyal to the Youth Director, while some faithfully followed the Senior Pastor.

The harmonious working relationship we had enjoyed when the new Pastor arrived grew strained, and then began strangling spiritual growth and destroying our ministry. I was accused of dividing the church.

I received a call late one night from Peggy. She was in tears. "The Preacher said you were deliberately creating factions in the church, and he thought I might know something about it. He wanted to make certain this conversation wouldn't reach your ears. He said 'This conversation never took place.' I don't understand why he told me to keep my mouth shut!"

While I felt I could stand against the dark hovering clouds, I was to be proven wrong. That afternoon the excruciating pain in my stomach flared up again. It felt as if there was molten lava inside my stomach, burning and scorching everything it touched. I doubled up with pain.

I found myself lying in bed at Danville Hospital, wondering how I got there. Once again, the evening rays of sun gently illuminated my room.

Dr. Michael Greene, who had treated me for a bleeding ulcer before, told me he didn't think I had been listening to him.

"Rev. Tanemori," he warned me, "If you want your two boys to have their father while they grow up, and also want to stay in the ministry, there is a possible solution. Be like most of the preachers we both know, who wear the robe of ministry without giving it their hearts. Be like a 'professional' or 'hired' minister. That way you can stay in the ministry, but it won't kill you."

I told the doctor he sounded like he was telling a fish to live on dry land. Still, he urgently recommended that I leave the ministry if I couldn't heed his advice.

The next morning my wife visited me with teary eyes. Yet she was composed, and in her gentleness I sensed inner strength. Joyce told me I couldn't afford to ignore the warning signs. And she told me that, while she would take good care of our children, I should consider the fact that they might not have their father much longer if I disregarded the doctor's counsel. She pointed out that his professional advice to me was just as important as my spiritual advice to church families. The choice was mine.

I asked why I should hear a sermon from my wife. I despised anyone, including my wife, admonishing me for what I should or shouldn't do. And I certainly didn't need to be kicked while I was "down in the gutter!"

"You see, that's your problem," Joyce said. "You think you're the only one who has the answer to everything." With a smile, my wife squeezed my hand and left, to return to our boys.

That afternoon I stewed over what she had said. No one from the church, except for Peggy, visited me. I was upset that the Senior Preacher failed to stop to see me, especially since he lived only five blocks from the hospital.

Shortly after I had sipped a bowl of soup for supper, Sandy's soft, familiar voice filled the room with her "Hello." She stood in the doorway, waiting for permission to enter, as was her manner.

I didn't know whether to welcome her with open arms (I yearned to see her more than anyone else) or to hide my face under the covers for fear of unnecessarily burdening her.

I caught her beautiful eyes, watching me as a mother would her baby, and knew it was safe to invite her in. Our eyes conveyed our inner feelings toward each other. Her warmth, as she touched me, traveled through my body and into my heart, until it was ready to burst. I squeezed her hands and asked her to sit close to me, by the edge of bed. I could almost hear her heartbeats, riding on high waves.

"Saaa ... ndy ..."

"Shhhh!" She covered her mouth with her finger as she squeezed my hand.

I had no visitors the third day. That evening, as the moon peeked through the window, I felt a cold wind sweep through my soul. I was in solitude, as if my heart had vanished. I grabbed the phone, desperately wanting to connect with Sandy, and dialed her number. Over the background chatter of children, I heard her sweet voice, which helped ease my anxiety.

After a few moments, curiously, I could hear only sounds like the beating of a *taiko*-drum. I wondered what the sound was and where it was coming from.

"Pastor Tom," she said, her voice filled with inexplicable feelings, "can you tell what you're hearing?"

She told me that she was in her bedroom, away from her children. "Can you hear my heartbeats? They're for you." The deep drumming sounds came from her heart, for she had placed the mouthpiece of the telephone directly against her bosom. As her heartbeats traveled deep into my soul, I could see myself falling into her arms, entering the deepest, most secret place where only we belonged.

I don't remember how long we talked before a nurse walked in and said it was long past my bedtime. As the lights went out, my room returned to solitude. The next morning, I was released from the hospital.

Coming home brought me no escape, no rest from what ailed me. There were the stresses of the ministry, and now there was my awakening to Sandy's heartbeats. Although Joyce had been a pillar of my ministry, even through our Seminary years, I hadn't been able to communicate my feeling that I was always under her scrutiny, as if I was the subject of labwork.

I felt as though she expected me to be "black" or "white," "positive" or "negative"—to her, there was no "gray," no matter the circumstances. But Sandy always allowed me to have areas which I would describe as lying between the "letter" and "spirit" of the law.

With Joyce, there was another factor which preyed upon my soul. Since I was an immigrant without proper knowledge of the English language, I found myself often intimidated and feeling I would never measure up to her. Of course, she never conducted herself in a superior manner in public. But I knew in my heart that I had to take second place to her, intellectually. Even though I had a total of nine long years of schooling, and two Masters degrees to her one, my education was of an inferior quality to hers.

I found myself all alone, crying, and then going crazy because I had been unable to talk with Sandy when she called shortly after lunch. Joyce had already gone to the church with our children. Finally the phone rang, and I picked it up to hear Sandy's voice.

"Oh, it's me...!" I tried to convey that I was strong. At last, we communicated our feelings toward each other and her warmth traveled through my entire body, soothing my bleeding ulcer. How wonderful it was to know that she was medicine to me!

When Sandy told me she was about to go to the evening service, I decided to go with her. We would meet at the back of the church auditorium after the service started and I would leave quietly before the service was over. No one, I thought, especially the Preacher, would find out I came to meet her. I didn't think I could stomach seeing the Preacher! Seeing him would turn my stomach inside out, and aggravate my ulcer.

This evening service was special. The choir from Madison Baptist Bible College in Wisconsin was presenting a musical program under the leadership of the college President and his wife, our personal friends. It would be wonderful to renew our friendship, as it had been more than seven years since we had last seen each other.

When I arrived at the auditorium, all the lights were focused on the stage. The back of the auditorium was dark. Walking in, I paused momentarily to adjust my eyes.

The choir's voices blended with a small orchestra to create mystical music, filling the auditorium and rising through the roof, heavenward. I spotted the President sitting on the platform, in the background.

Finding Sandy, I sat as close to her as I could without being too ostentatious, or revealing my feelings. Touching and squeezing her hand, I felt her energy shoot through my entire body, creating a feeling of orbiting a world that belonged only to us. It may have been excitement that caused me to suddenly double up with sharp pain. I spat blood, and she quickly handed me her handkerchief.

She reacted immediately to my need, quietly and inconspicuously, so that we wouldn't disturb anyone else, practically carrying me as we left the auditorium, stopped at a restroom down the hallway, then went to my office, where I rested in her arms. Sometime before the service ended, she followed me as I drove my car erratically home.

I had never felt such pain saying good night to anyone as I did then, as if part of my heart had been ripped out and disappeared with her into the dark. Her warmth lingered while I rested on the sofa until my wife got home.

When I returned to my office the following Tuesday morning, Peggy handed me an envelope from the Deacon Board. It contained a summons to an emergency meeting requested by the Preacher on Monday night.

That Monday night I was dismissed.

Once again my ministry had been snatched from under my feet, without any warning. How could I tell my wife? I couldn't accept the accusation that I had been involved in "hanky-panky." The Preacher had said my "activity" at the evening service was grounds for dismissal.

"Oh my God! How can this be?" I cried out, burying my face in my hands. All I could say, over and over was, "Oh my God!"

There was no one who knew how to comfort my bleeding ulcer, nor to communicate with my heart, except Sandy. There had been no one near us in church to help, and if anyone had been watching us, why hadn't they offered assistance? How could the Preacher charge me with immorality? As I stewed, a blazing fire enraged my bowels!

I wondered if members of the Deacon Board had questioned the truthfulness of the accusation, or if anyone had challenged the Preacher's honesty. I tried to reach the Preacher, but was unsuccessful. My heart was crushed with this new burden.

Two days after learning of my dismissal, I stood at my office door in a daze. The "Rev. Thomas T. Tanemori, Associate Minister" plaque, displayed so proudly before, had already been removed. In its place were two tiny screwholes.

When I stopped to see the church secretary, Janet was a cold gravestone. As the days passed, never would an Indian summer bring her back to life, nor ever warm her to me. My repeated attempts to reach the Chairman of the Deacon Board at home earned only his wife's ire. "How many times do I have to tell you my husband will not accept your calls. Please do not call here any more!"

I hadn't told my wife about my dismissal, but I had no doubt she suspected something was amiss. But she merely asked me if I was physically okay.

With still no contact with the Preacher, I returned to the church before the Sunday morning service, bursting into his office while he was kneeling and praying for God's blessing on his sermon.

"Get out!" he yelled. "Don't you understand I was talking to Holy God, who demands reverence and sanctity? You, of all people: have you no shame?

"Don't worry, God hears your prayer, if He so chooses. On second thought, He doesn't need to listen to your prayer, for He knows what is in your heart."

"You have desecrated God's calling, and now you have defiled God's sanctuary. You have smeared God's name with profanity. If there is any way to strip you of your ordination, I would be first to do so ..."

"Preacher," I said, very collected, "you have violated scriptural teachings of how to resolve conflicts. I demand that, as a minister, you follow such principles before you cast a stone at me."

I saw fire in his eyes.

"I was given the power to cleanse God's House by excommunicating you, just as Jesus expelled the moneychangers from the Temple. What you have done is contemptible and we will not be defiled by your presence. Before you leave, tell me, for my own satisfaction, did you or did you not sin? Admit it. My wife said she saw everything in the darkness that night."

"Why should I dignify you by answering your question? I have nothing to say to you. I will pity you. You think you have cleansed God's House by ostracizing me and forbidding Sandy Crawford or anyone else to talk to me. Well, I have news for you! God will bring His judgment on you, by making this place desolate, and you will see His handwriting on the wall: *Iccaba,* God's Glory has departed. Your ministry will become barren."

The Preacher called two Deacons to practically carry me from his office to the parking lot. I heard his shouting behind me, "Don't you ever come back as long as I am the Pastor of this Church!"

A single pink rose with a special bow, a secret scent, the memories of which helped keep my heart intact: I was comforted by Sandy's spirit and caring heart. How often God speaks of the "Rose of Sharon!" I found solace in my sweet, sweet memories of Sandy Crawford.

Three years later I stopped by the church while driving through town. I saw only weeds growing through cracked pavement in the parking lots. The outside of the church building reminded me of a snakeskin that had been shed—desiccated and grotesque. I visualized a sign posted on the door: *Iccaba,* the glory of God has departed. The Minister was long gone!

After my ouster from Sunnyville Baptist Church, I quickly found carpentry work in Indianapolis, building government project houses.

One day I received a call from the office of Dr. James Stirring, with the Grand Lake Baptist School System. I had no idea who Dr. Stirring was, nor did I know anything about the schools. I was surprised to learn how the woman who called me, Ms. MacKinsey, Dr. Stirring's Executive Secretary, got my name, and why.

"Rev. Tanemori, it is because you are Japanese, and because he has great interest in your culture, that he thought you might be a great asset to our school system. We have ways of tracking ministers in the States. You'll learn the nature of the meeting when you get here. And to answer your question as to why Friday morning, Dr. Stirring is a very busy man, but he is anxious to meet you."

After expressing my heartfelt appreciation, I requested that our meeting be held the following Tuesday during his lunch hour. "If this is acceptable, you may call me back. If you will excuse me, please ..."

"Rev. Tanemori. I guess you don't know who he is. He is considered *The Preacher* of our country and it is a high honor and privilege for anyone, especially people like you, to see him."

And yet we had the meeting on my terms. Dr. Stirring expressed concerns about young people and asked if I was willing to give my life to "mold and build the character" of high school students. As a result of my positive response, I was hired as a high school teacher. Besides teaching academic subjects, I would have a practically free hand to inspire the lives of my students by teaching some of the Three-Fold Principles my Father had instilled in me before his death. I so wanted these young people to be pliable in the hands of "The Potter."

Joyce also gained a sixth grade teaching position in the same school system. We were committing our lives to the molding of the lives of young people.

A major life change occurred when we joined the First Baptist Church of Grand Lake, Indiana. Suddenly, I found myself an *Ido-no Kawazu*, a tadpole, in nearby Lake Michigan. The church's rolls were 5,000 strong and the church buildings covered an entire city block.

Yet instead of being lost in the shuffle, I gained instant celebrity status through a dramatic introduction to the entire congregation by Dr. Stirring one Sunday morning. I soon became known as "Mr. T" because many people couldn't pronounce my Japanese name.

The name "Dr. Stirring" quickly became synonymous with "God." It didn't take a rocket scientist to identify him as the supreme authority around the church complex. His words became law for church members and the teaching staff. It was clear Dr. Stirring's "power" rippled out to many ministers and churches across the nation.

I would learn in the course of two years that "Mr. T" would not always attract attention, admiration or appreciation. But for the present, I didn't expect conflicts regarding my Japanese amiability, my enigmatic cultural values, or the *Samurai Code*. I thought Dr. Stirring was, as he claimed, a leader with "largeness of heart."

Many folks looked at me as if I was a trophy of God's grace. They saw a survivor of Hiroshima whose life had been redeemed and would now blossom at the hand of Dr. Stirring. I was envied by many for the special attention I was getting. No one is more aware of favoritism than the one who is getting it. No doubt I was clearly seen as "it."

Early one afternoon, a call came from Mrs. MacKinsey. She said Dr. Stirring had asked me to give a talk in his absence at a nearby church the next night. I turned down the request.

I received another phone call from Mrs. MacKinsey early the next day.

"Mr. Tanemori, the Preacher will not take 'no' for an answer. You have the chance of a lifetime to speak to people who love you. I just can't see you let this kind of opportunity slip away. There are thousands of preachers who would do anything to get closer to our Preacher, let alone speak on his behalf, in his pulpit."

"Ms. MacKinsey," I said firmly, "can you please tell him that I already have a commitment I made a month ago, to speak to a missionary conference of perhaps 120 people? I can't break my promise. I'm sure he'll understand."

I had a great temptation to speak in Dr. Stirring's pulpit, but I felt that honoring my commitment was far more important. I made a sixty mile round trip to a small country church, through a driving rain, to keep my promise.

When summer vacation came, I kept busy doing odd jobs to survive since there was no income while school was out. With a combined income of less than $8,000, Joyce and I struggled to manage our finances during the summer. We became expert jugglers, exercising survival skills to persevere in maintaining an honorable family name.

We had no luxury in choosing any of the odd jobs. Though I prayed and placed my faith in God, I received no "manna" from heaven, as did the biblical Jewish people who challenged the faithfulness of Jehovah! I resented the remarks of the Preacher from his pulpit, who judged our taking the odd jobs as clear demonstration of our poor stewardship and lack of faith.

The theme and tone of his "sacrificial Thanksgiving offering" became a destructive force to me. It was like a whirlwind, typhoon, tornado, hurricane, monsoon or tempest, depending on how close I sat to the pulpit, where his thundering preaching flew at me. My internal conflict began when the Preacher challenged us to give sacrificial offerings of one month's salary to the church, as we had the previous year.

Sunday after Sunday, he used his pulpit to reach goals for the coming fiscal year. Unfortunately, these challenges no longer carried "magical" power to fill my heart to work another "miracle" as in past years.

My heart ached as I watched some of my colleagues and many church members succumb to him, surrendering one month's salary as a special Thanksgiving offering.

It was obvious to me that the Preacher and his family had no difficulty giving his month's salary many times over. Since they lived in the church parsonage, there was no monthly mortgage payment. All utilities, phone bills, gas, and insurance for his automobiles were paid for by the church.

At the other end of the spectrum, we had to add extra cans of water just to make chicken noodle soup go around. At least we filled a soup bowl for everyone in our family. But I couldn't ask Joyce to sacrifice our family needs any more than she had already done. And now she was expecting our third child. She required a great deal of attention and our family needs were increasing, but our income was the same as the previous year.

One day I had to confront Dr. Stirring. I told him that what troubled me wasn't the question of giving, but his condemnation of those unable to sacrifice an entire month's salary. He preached this was a "sign" of a "lack of faith," and he delivered this message with scathing thunder, raking hot coals over our heads. Sunday after Sunday he had railed that obeying his challenge with a willing heart was the only way for us to be redeemed from our "sins."

"We want our teachers underpaid," Dr. Stirring responded, "so they will learn to depend on the faithfulness of God. We need to keep them humble. This is the only way they can learn to follow me, as I am called by God to lead this flock. Ultimately, they will learn to follow God."

I felt I had crossed an invisible line, desecrating his holy place without invitation. He rose from his chair and stepped into his secretary's room. I waited and waited for his return. When I could wait no longer, I quietly left his office, my own heart reaffirmed.

This winter seemed much harsher than the last, as a penetrating north wind whipped across frozen Lake Michigan, penetrating my already troubled heart. I had to face reality. An immeasurable gulf had been created between some of my colleagues and the church-paid staff since I had challenged the Preacher on sacrificial giving. "Marked" by the Preacher, I had to keep my heart and my faith in what I thought was a safe place, impenetrable from coercive power, protected by my Father's spirit.

One Saturday, my wife came to me and said, "Honey, I shouldn't be wearing these." She held out a pair of maternity pants, continuing, "It's forbidden for me to wear these in public."

"Go ahead," I insisted. The pants would not only protect her legs from turning purplish-blue from the cold, but would be more modest and comfortable than a skirt, so late in her pregnancy.

My pragmatic decision led to my being called to the carpet for a blatant sin. Dr. Stirring told me that by allowing my wife to wear "men's apparel," I had deliberately challenged his authority and created a scandal, tarnishing his image and the reputation of the school. He wanted me to understand the need to make sure a woman could be clearly distinguished from a man by her attire in public.

"Tanemori, if you're concerned about the cold, we'll allow her to wear pants, as long as she wears a dress over them."

He spoke with a rationale that felt overpowering at the time. I listened with patience and an open mind.

"I see. It is not a sin, and neither does she disobey your teaching by wearing maternity pants, perceived as men's attire, as long as the pants are covered by a dress." I continued. "It sounds to me as if I could drink wine or even liquor, which we have been forbidden to touch, as long as I drink it out of a milk bottle. Thus I could avoid committing a sin. Am I right, Preacher?"

Suddenly, I saw countless veins protrude on his forehead. Shaking my head, I left his office in confusion, but ever determined to follow the light of my heart!

Grading students' work was a challenge, but usually not stressful, until one day when Bill Caesar, a senior, stormed into my classroom and stood in front of me, while I was eating my brown bag lunch at my desk.

"Mr. Tanemori, what do you mean by giving me a B on my mid-term? You are the only teacher who did not give me an A."

He told me he had been known as a "brainy student" in his three and a half years of high school, and that no teacher, especially me, would destroy his perfect reputation.

"What do you want me to do?" I queried. "You need to understand that no teacher gives a grade to a student. It is the student who earns whatever grade is given."

"Will you give me an A for the record, in exchange for extra work I might do later?"

"Oh my dear Bill Caesar, you have yet to learn anything I have been trying to teach the last two years."

"Mr. Tanemori, I assume you don't know who my parents are?"

"Oh, little brat! You and your parents do not know who I am!" Bill, you have nine weeks to make up work and improve your grade. I don't see any problems if you only learn to follow instructions and do your work. Your priority is to be a good and dependable student. I can assure you that when you are faithful to your heart, you will see that all other matters, including church youth activities, will fall into their proper place!"

"To every thing there is a season, and a time to every purpose under the heaven ..." [Ecclesiastes 3:1-11], *"Behold, to obey is better than sacrifice, and to hearken than the fat of rams."* [I Samuel 15:22] and *"To do justice and judgment is more acceptable to the Lord than sacrifice ..."* [Proverbs 21:3]

I had great empathy for him and his obsession with a perfect high school record. And while it was obvious that I might be the one to spoil his record, I wanted Bill to understand the relationship between responsibility and accountability for his actions, and how together they could lead him to graduate with highest honors. I prayerfully sent him off to reconsider not dropping the class.

Six weeks had passed since Bill and I had our discussion, and three weeks remained before graduation. One afternoon he came to tell me that, after a conference with his Youth Minister, he wanted to drop my Biblical Psychology class to avoid a possible B. It was obvious Bill had finally found someone who concurred with him.

"You are the only teacher standing in my way," he told me. "You are not going to destroy my perfect record."

I looked at him, wondering where I had failed him. He practically threw the withdrawal form at me, the Principal's signature already in place.

"Bill, I'm very sorry you had to come to this critical point, making an irreversible decision which will affect the rest of your life, marring your character."

He stormed out!

The last week of school, it seemed a yellowjacket hive had been disrupted. Excitement filled the hallways and every classroom. All grades for the seniors had been completed and were sacredly guarded in the Administrative Office. Immediately after the last class, the Principal approached me with my grade book in his hand.

"Yes Sir?" I could almost smell the rotten egg.

The Principal's soft voice gave me the willies. "You know our parents have invested their lives in their sons' and daughters' educations. They all have great hope that their children will graduate with respect and pride. And some students have earned honors for their work. Mr. Tanemori, I am here to see Bill Caesar graduate as a straight A student. We cannot have any blemish on his record. I certainly will see to it that you won't be the one standing in his way."

"No! I have given him a WF. It will stand as it is according to School Policy!" I pointed out the book and page number to him.

"Tanemori, you don't seem to understand, and I don't think you know whom you are dealing with."

"What do you mean, 'whom I am dealing with?'"

"Mr. and Mrs. Caesar are very affluent. They are great financial contributors to our School Systems.

"Oh, money does talk!" I blurted out. "What do you propose for me to do? What do you say in America? Aaah, I know! You don't want to dump the applecart. Is that it?"

"Tanemori, I will ask one last time for you to give him an A in Biblical Psychology, as it is a requirement for graduation. We simply cannot have a WF."

I wasn't shocked when I discovered that the young man graduated with highest honors, Summa Cum Laude, with a perfect record. I knew my grade had been altered.

The next morning I faced the Principal in his office.

"After conferring with the Preacher," he said, "he would be glad to give you his best recommendation to another institution of your choice."

"Sir, if you could give me such a recommendation, why may I not then stay here to continue my teaching?"

His response was that the only resolution would be my resignation.

My wife urged me to do something to regain my teaching position. She wanted to stay, for she was weary of moving. She begged me to compromise with the Preacher and asked me to reconsider my policy of "dying for principles." She reminded me that we now had three children and that I should consider putting the interests of my family first.

Our third child did bring a new facet to my fatherhood and a reawakening to me as a man. At first a bit disappointed that the child was not a boy, I was soon elated by my new daughter. My joy was a thousand-fold, as she was the *uri-futatsu*, spitting image, of my baby sister who had died in the Hiroshima blast so long ago.

We named her Roxanne Megumi Tanemori, which means "grace of God" in Japanese. She was indeed a gift from God. How little I knew that God would use her to change this *henkutsu-oyaji*, this stubborn Japanese father who was steeped in traditional Japanese culture, to appreciate her mother and see in her new life an incarnation of my baby sister. In a moment I gained new insight and new energy. A sense of fulfillment swelled in my heart, for whatever the future held for her and for her father. I began to start to live once again, honoring my heart—a brand new father, a new man!

Chapter Eight: California Ministries

"CALIFORNIA, here we come! Right back where we started from!"

After fifteen years in the Midwest, in ministerial training and serving Hoosier congregations, I returned to California, where I'd started my journey. In June of 1974, I was back in the heart of the San Joaquin Valley—the community of Turlock, to be more specific.

I could hardly contain my joy and heartfelt gratitude to see Mary Furr, the nurse who had saved me from my "snakepit" experience of the 1960s. And while her unconditional love had helped keep me whole for over a decade, another human instrument, a Japanese-American man I had met through Mary, James Yamakama, had also made an irrevocable difference in my life, helping me complete a "full-circle."

After I was released from the hospital, Yamakawa-san had pushed me beyond the safety and comfort of my environment, like an eagle pushing an eaglet from its nest. I had been a 19-year-old boy then, capable of speaking only Japanese, with neither an understanding of American culture, nor a sense of the values of my new country. I had been petrified and lonely.

Back in the fall of 1958, I had considered James Yamakama to be an instrument of the devil, if not the Devil himself, for dumping me in San Francisco's Old Japan Town and telling me to learn the English language and American culture. I had no choice but to swim or sink.

With two duffel bags, I had been dropped off in the middle of San Francisco, a foreign city buried under thick fog. I was angry then with Yamakawa-san. How things had changed over the course of a decade and a half!

Knocking on his front door now, in the heat of summer, I took two steps backward and waited for someone to answer. My heart was beating uncontrollably in anticipation of *saikai*, a second meeting, with James Yamakawa after so much elapsed time. I waited and waited.

"Oh. *Kimika*. Tommy *ka*! It's you, Tommy!"

Unfortunately, no boisterous voice boomed from Yamakawa at the moment of *saikai.*

"Yamakawa-San," I humbly extended my hand to him, a customary Japanese greeting after a long period without communication. I acknowledged my rudeness for not having kept in touch, and begged deliriously for forgiveness. At least I hadn't forgotten the Japanese manner and spirit in my deep gratitude toward him.

"Yamakawa-san, rejoice with me for my nine years of college and seminary. Now, having served several churches in Indiana, I have come back, with Rev. Jerry Hayward and Mark Johnston, to start a new church and Christian day school."

"Oh, that's good. I'm glad for you."

I felt his freezing voice. It had no spirit.

"Yamakawa-san! It's me. I have no idea where I would have gone or what I would have become if it weren't for you. You gave me your spirit and love when I needed it most. It was your Christian faith that became my 'faith' and here I am, an ordained Baptist minister."

He sat on the sofa, looking as if he were searching for blemish spots in the ceiling.

"Yamakawa-san, what is it? What God has done to me and for me because of your life, I owe to you! Please tell me if I said or did anything wrong, of which you disapprove?"

"*Onegai-desu. Onegai-desu. Doka oshiete kudasai.*"

My pleading fell on deaf ears. His face contorted. It was too painful to watch. Where was the soft and tender smile of the Yamakawa-san that I once knew? No! I would not accept his recanting of his Christian faith, only to reclaim his old Buddhist beliefs.

"Tommy, you may come back to see me if you want, but the James you see today and the James you might see again will not be the James you knew before. That James was dead a long time ago. I am a dead man! A dead man!"

With that, he showed me the door and quickly disappeared. I stood frozen in the summer heat, my heart broken.

The Rev. Jerry Hayward, a graduate of the Bible College in the Grand Lake Baptist School System, persuaded my wife and me to help him establish a new church and launch the Sierra Mountain View Christian Day School in Turlock. Another college graduate, Mark Johnston, who had a wife and two little girls, wanted to join us at the last minute. Although I had doubts about Johnston, I consented with Rev. Hayward's wish to unify our energy.

While these men focused on starting a new church, my wife and I embarked on our task of establishing a day school from the ground up. Our target for opening school was mid-September, a goal nearly impossible to achieve.

We faced insurmountable obstacles, especially given our ambition to teach Kindergarten through 12th grade. We may have been naïve, but we were definitely fearless, since we didn't know any better. At the same time, we practiced what we believed: *"... the things which are impossible with men ... are possible with God!"* [Matthew 19:26]

Trips to Sacramento, the state capital of California, became our way of life. The path Joyce and I had to weave through mountains of bureaucratic paperwork consumed us, and still we burned up the asphalt from Turlock to Sacramento. But in the end, all our hard work and perseverance paid off.

We met our goal, allowing me to wear a new hat as Administrator of a Christian Academy. Because of our apparent success at establishing our day school, I soon became an "authority" on a new frontier within the circle of Christian educators. In a short time, I was standing before a distinguished audience in Los Angeles as one of the keynote speakers at the California Christian Administrators' Conference. I challenged them with our visions and dreams, and shared our experiences: how-to or how-not-to perform the "hands on" tasks of Christian teaching!

When I returned to our school, my heart seemed to skip beats. I was counting the minutes until I would see students running from the classrooms, heading home. But as I walked into my office, there was no mistaking the sense that I had stepped into a morgue.

I plopped my briefcase on the worn oak desk and rushed into the bathroom, to refresh myself from my long trip. Feeling a bit fatigued, I sat in my chair, stretched my arms, and rubbed my eyes. In the corner of my eye I glimpsed Mark Johnston, about fifteen feet away in the hallway, and hollered at him. He either didn't hear or simply ignored me.

When I called again, louder, he reluctantly made a half turn and looked at me.

"Come in, Mark. I want to thank you for stepping in for me while I was gone. And I want you to fill me in on what transpired in the last four days." I looked at my watch. "We'll meet back here at 3:30. By that time the students should be gone ... Is everything all right with you, Mark?"

"I guess I better tell you," he started, "that I'm no longer answerable to you. The Preacher is taking over as school Principal. Didn't you know I was appointed Vice Principal as of yesterday afternoon?"

I could see his eyes flashing! How could he turn 180 degrees in such a short time? Wasn't it just four days before that he had thanked me for giving him the responsibility to oversee the school while I went to the conference?

"If you want to know why I am now the Vice Principal, assisting the Preacher, you had better talk to him directly. I can't tell you anything more," was his response.

I went to see Rev. Hayward, and he spoke first. "Pastor Tom. I terminated you as Administrator to save us from legal and moral damage. I'm taking over the school and Mark is my Assistant, answerable to me, and me only. As of yesterday, you have nothing to do with the school or the church."

"Preacher, you must tell me why you made this decision. What did I do to deserve this judgment? Whatever has prompted you, why couldn't you have talked to me first? That's the Biblical approach!"

He refused to say anything more. That evening, the Preacher came to see me at my home. With him were Sam Nickelson and Mark Johnston.

"I was told you took three boys out of the classroom and beat the 'tar' out of their hides!" said Rev. Hayward.

I affirmed disciplining three boys from the Dugan family with spankings the previous week because they had stolen money from another student. On top of that, they had agreed among themselves to lie about the theft.

"Of course, I administered 'a board-of-education' on 'the-seat-of-learning.' What was wrong with that? I had discussed the incident with their parents and they had consented to that means of discipline."

All this had been done from the beginning in the presence of Mark Johnston, who had concurred with the decision to use corporal punishment, for the Word of God was clear: *"He that spareth his rod hateth his son; but he that loveth him chasteneth him betimes ... The rod and reproof give wisdom; but a child left to him bringeth his mother to shame ... Correct thy son, and he shall give thee rest; yea, he shall give delight unto thy soul ..."* [Proverbs 13:24, 23:13, 29:15]

"Well, I was told," interjected Nickelson, "that you were so mad at them that you lost control. You couldn't restrain yourself."

Mark was sitting in a chair, staring at the floor. My anger quickly focused on him, as he had taken part, and apparently had told Sam and the Preacher that I had spanked the Dugan boys, but not how I'd done it. I explained that the boys were told they would receive harsh punishment for the severity of their transgressions—stealing money and agreeing to lie about it.

After I had administered the punishment, I had hugged them, reminding them of the reason for the discipline and how they could avoid spankings in the future. Finally, before I let them go home, I again hugged them and told them how much I loved them.

"Mark, why didn't you tell the truth to the Preacher and Sam?"

"Uh ... the Welfare people came and visited the Dugan family last Wednesday ... and they found out you spanked the boys. We were told the State would take legal action against the school. So I quickly made the decision to let you go, and by doing so, avoided being dragged into a muddy legal battle. They promised to drop any charges."

"Pastor Tom," Sam interrupted, "you know spanking is against state law. Those Welfare people don't believe in spanking."

"I see. Tell me now, Sam. Was I wrong when I got permission from you to spank your boy, George, sometime ago? How has he been since that discipline? I think he turned out to be a good boy, don't you agree?"

"Yeah, you might say so. Of course, he comes from a good family, Pastor Tom ..." Sam sneered at me.

I was crushed to learn that the boys had not been asked by the school, nor by Welfare, how they felt about my spanking them. As soon as the Rev. Hayward, Sam and Mark had left, I practically ran into the kitchen to grab a handful of salt and scatter it outside the door where they had exited my house into the darkness.

The aftermath of my firing actually brought some pleasure and relief. I was sorry for Joyce, who found herself in the uncomfortable situation of still teaching where I had been deposed. But for the moment I enjoyed my life without responsibilities, nor guilt for the challenges faced by the school and church.

After the second week had passed, I was hoping Mark would come to see me. He and I needed to bring closure to this chapter. When the doorbell rang Monday evening, I wondered if it might be Mark. Instead, my heart fluttered when I looked through the "peek-hole" in my door.

Rev. Hayward was standing alone on the doorstep. At first, I hesitated, and then I let him in. He told me the phones at the church and at his home had been ringing off the wall since people found out he fired me. Some people even went to his house to demand that I return to the school, assuming full authority as Administrator, or they would pull their children out of school. They also threatened to withhold their financial support from the church.

I wanted to tell him "See, I knew this would happen." Instead, I kept silent for the time being. He left without resolving his problem!

Thanksgiving came and went, and the streets and storefronts were decorated for Christmas. I was in my study when I heard the repeated ringing of doorbells. I sent my son, Jonathan, to respond.

"Daddy, I think Mr. Johnston is here. He is the man who taught at our Christian School when you were there. He wishes to see you."

I could only wonder why he had come. He had stood defiantly against me when I needed him the most, and had been silent since the previous spring. I wanted to tell him off, to his face!

"Daddy! Daddy! What should I tell him?"

"Go ahead. Tell him to come in and wait in the living room. Thank you, son!"

I was giving Mark room to make it "right" with me, to be reconciled for what I felt he had done wrong. Perhaps he had felt a change in heart that he wanted to communicate to me. I looked toward heaven and winked in gratitude. Suddenly, my steps became lighter.

"Son, you and your brother Nathan should go to your room or go play outside."

As I extended a heartfelt welcome to Mark, to my surprise he spoke in a voice weaker than a mosquito's buzz.

"You know what, Pastor Tom?" There was a long pause. "The Preacher called me in after the evening service last night and, without any real explanation, told me I was terminated, right on the spot."

"Come again?" I had heard him, but really wanted him to repeat it. I didn't know whether to rejoice or feel remorse for his misfortune.

"Whatever a man soweth, that shall he also reap" was the admonition of the Bible. My first impulse was to let him have it, for "what goes around. comes around." If only Mark had stood up for me when the Preacher was intent on firing me! But then my heart troubled me as in my mind I saw the faces of his two innocent little girls. My emotion should not "rule the roost" here. I would let him share his burden with me, for its weight was burying his heart.

"Mark, can you consider staying here to find another ministry?"

"No. Are you kidding? My wife is as mad as a junkyard dog. She can't stand to breathe the same air as the Preacher and the church people who turned against us."

I gave Mark the names of several church families who were my friends. I sent him home with a promise that if he contacted these folks, we would get together and talk the first thing next week.

Then I got in my car and drove and drove, until I almost ran out of gas. By the time I returned, my wife and daughter were already home with several gifts to put under the Christmas tree. I kept quiet about Mark and his predicament. It was the test of my faith and of my heart—would I let it do its work without any external influence?

When Monday morning arrived, Mark told me, "You gave me the names of church members, but I didn't see them for fear they'd reject me. I know they're your friends and I couldn't face condemnation for my own folly. There's no way to reverse what I did six months ago to save my own skin. Now I'm being hunted like I'm the prey."

Selfishly, I wanted him to know that I should be the last man to come pour out his soul to. Yet I was reminded of Scripture: *"Brethren, if a man be overtaken in a fault, ye which are spiritual, restore such an one, in the spirit of meekness, considering thyself, lest thou also be tempted. Bear ye one another's burdens, and so fulfill the law of Christ."* [Galatians 6:1-2] and *"...So that none render evil for evil unto any man; but ever follow that which is good, both among yourselves, and to all men."* [I Thessalonians 5:15]

I excused myself to the bathroom. I wanted to scream. I stuck my finger deep into my throat and gagged myself, causing myself to vomit into the commode until I could vomit no more. I flushed again and again. Then I gargled with salt water. This was symbolic of purification.

I knew what I must do for him and for his family.

My decision was rather unorthodox, and I couldn't let my wife know before I took action. I went to the bank and borrowed three hundred dollars against our credit line, as a loan for the Johnstons. It was a great amount of money,

money I didn't have for our own needs. It spelled "D-I-S-A-S-T-E-R."

While my wife and I prepared for breakfast, we argued about the Christmas spirit and our Christian duties. The argument focused on reaching out to people to share our abundance and joy.

Joyce, taken aback by my seemingly irrational activity the day before, said, "Honey, I understand that you want to help Mark and his family at their time of adversity. You spent the day yesterday helping him load the rental truck. Now they're coming for breakfast. We bought a dozen donuts for them to take on the road, not to mention that you insisted we give gifts to their girls ... What can I say? I married you for better or for worse. I just wonder if I should have my head examined!"

It was a little cuckoo. I knew my wife, who had been so patient with me, tolerated my oddity of doing things that perhaps "normal" people might not do. Or that they might do, but would first consult with their wives!

Our humble breakfast filled the Johnston's tummies, and their girls were excited by the gifts. I trusted this breakfast would be long remembered. We sent them off with Godspeed to Montgomery, Alabama, where Mark's in-laws lived. I let out a sigh of relief when their truck disappeared around the corner. *Shiranu ga Hotoke ka*, a Japanese proverb, "It is a blessing not to know anything."

So far Joyce had no inkling of my activity. Not even Buddha would ever find out, especially with a newly-created account at a local bank. Of course Mark knew the money was not a gift; it was a loan. I never set a time limit for him to pay me back; but he knew the obligation had to be fulfilled. I had no reason to think anything else. My word was just as good as his, and we simply shook hands.

I had rejoiced too soon. Returning from work one evening, no sooner than I had stepped in the front door, I knew that "Hell" had been cast wide open. Joyce stood with a bank statement in her hand, and in a split second she hammered me. I cannot repeat her description of me. I didn't know there were that many adjectives in the world.

"Tell me, what in heaven," she almost choked on her words, her body shaking as she threw the bank statement at me, "I never in my life believed you would go this far, behind my back, to do what you did for Mark. I thought I was your wife." She took a deep breath, shaking violently.

I had no choice but to let hell burn itself out. I listened to her rampage. I deserved to be hammered, or struck by lightning. It may have been less painful to be killed by a bolt of electricity than by my wife's hand. When she seemed to return to sanity, I thought the worst had passed and I could have dinner.

"May I see the paper you and Mark have drawn up for the loan?" she calmly asked. "After all, you know, when you do a business transaction, you do it professionally, with signed documents at the bank. You did sign the paper at the bank, right, Honey?"

She was totally in control! Her calm, softspoken words were like the arrows of a hunter. When she asked if I had his forwarding address, I buried my head in my hands.

I felt as if my stomach had been gutted by a dagger. It was a torture chamber. I wished she would hack off the dog's tail with one swing of the cleaver, instead of cutting it off inch-by-inch!

I finally had a chance to wash and change into a *kimono*. My stomach growled again, but there was no dinner waiting on the table. Joyce had already retired to the study, and the door was locked. I wondered what was going through her mind as I walked into the rooms of my boys and daughter to check on them.

"Daddy, you sure know how to make Mommy angry, don't you?" Jonathan said.

"What daddy did wrong was NOT telling mommy first. I kept it secret from her. I hope you don't take my part as dishonest. Sometimes daddy just forgets to tell mommy."

"Daddy," Nathan said, "I don't think she's angry because of what you did for Mr. Johnston. I think you should have told mother first. You kept her in the dark."

Nathan opened his innocent heart. He had been a young boy of few words, but he always expressed his heart, especially this night as he pitied his father's error.

Meanwhile, my daughter, my Princess, sat quietly and said nothing. She came to me with the eyes of an angel, and this saved me from my irrational contemplations.

I hugged my three children and told them I loved them as much as their mother. I prayed with them and said good night. It was after midnight when I crawled into bed, slipping quietly alongside my wife. I gave her my back as I tried to sleep. I had to sort things out.

One morning, in the second week of January, I was awakened by the phone. A strange man's voice with a Southern drawl came over the line.

He introduced himself as Rev. Lance Scott, Senior Minister of Landmark Baptist Church, the church Mrs. Johnston's parents attended. I was not shocked, but the call caught me off guard. Rev. Scott said Mark Johnston was being considered as Associate Minister, and he'd like to hear my opinion of him. It was a good thing Joyce hadn't answered the phone.

"*Konchiku sho!*" I lit out in Japanese, silently! My first reaction was to let him have it! How low would Mark sink before he hit the pit of hell, to bounce back up again? I hadn't even received a postcard, nor any word that Mark and his family had arrived safely, let alone a forwarding address. I still had to reckon with the bank, which would take an eternity. Then this call! My *Samurai* blood surged, until I remembered my daughter's tender eyes that night.

I never received any further message regarding Mark Johnston, his family, or his ministry. Of course I had to come to terms with my own heart eventually—the marker is now long buried and forgiven!

Our sweat and toil finally cleared the bank debt, closing this chapter of my life.

Choosing friends and destinations, climbing hills and crooked roads, and experiencing moments of enjoyment like the autumn-leaved mosaic of a Japanese maple, were all a part of the human tapestry being weaved about me. I was being fortified with the spirit of my Father, like a Japanese black pine tree!

Father had told his children that a tree can be known by its fruit. He said the black pine tree's tap root reached the heart of earth, its branches reached the four corners of the earth, and its upper tip reached heaven! As permanent as it was unmovable, the black pine tree would stand the test of time and the seasons.

There was more freedom in a prison than in the community where I lived. It seemed the people in Turlock knew what time the lights in my study turned off, and what time I awoke. When I happened to sneeze the wrong way at the wrong time, I created a raging windstorm. I had to walk through the town's streets carefully, like a blindfolded donkey. If I turned to look at something I wasn't supposed to see, the townspeople talked and talked until the story came back to me, with a totally different ending.

What really surprised me was hearing stories about topics I knew nothing about, and then learning I was the supposed author of the gossip. I thought it strange that a hermit could live in the middle of a city, or in the capital, and nobody would bother with him. But in the small community where I lived, a man who had been fired from his gospel ministry was making huge waves.

Two weeks after I had been whisked by a whirlwind from my last ministry, the phone rang off the wall. I finally answered, wondering who would be so persistent calling so early in the morning. Who had the nerve?!

The voice on the other end seemed surprised someone had answered the phone. There was hesitance and an apology before Dorothy Lunquest, secretary to Dr. Gordon Swanson of Mt. Zion Chapel, informed me that he would like to meet me at the church's office on Thursday.

When I asked why he wanted to meet me, she replied in confidence that she thought, knowing who I was and the kind of work that I'd been doing, that he would like to hire me as an Associate Minister.

"Since we live in a close community," she explained, "we practically know what's going on, any news, whether good or bad. You know that, don't you?" I detected cynicism in her voice, and asked if she knew I'd been fired.

"Of course! And, that's the reason our Senior Minister asked me to contact you."

How strangely the table had been turned. I somehow felt the meeting would go in my favor, and that I could always walk out if I had any reason to.

Thursday morning came with a bright dawn. As I looked into the mirror while shaving, I asked myself why I even considered meeting with this Minister and his Associates, given that they belonged to a non-denominational church and I was a staunch Baptist minister.

As I walked into the church office, I recognized Dorothy Lunquest's voice from the phone conversation. She was eagerly awaiting my arrival. I was quite taken with the plush office—each secretary's desk had a flower, which I presumed came from the garden I had just walked through.

I was introduced to Dr. Swanson, a large man, six feet two inches tall, and weighing probably 225 pounds. Dr. Swanson was different. He said little during the entire meeting. His physical movements and style of speech reminded me of a Japanese *namako*, a slimy slug, crawling, shaping and reshaping itself to fit into any hole or crevasse. No one detects its silent movement under the cover of the darkest hours of night, only to discover in the morning the white trails the slug left behind.

I have another analogy for Dr. Swanson's speech. It was like sipping lukewarm, tasteless soup. One had to swish it around in the mouth before deciding whether to shut his eyes and swallow it, or spew it out.

I constrained myself not to make a scene during the two hour meeting.

Most of the questions were asked by Dr. Gordon M. Ferguson, or "Dr. G," Mt. Zion Chapel's Senior Associate Minister. He asked about hypothetical situations and circumstances, to which I responded with hypothetical answers. How I wished he would have asked me more about my theological and doctrinal positions.

I wondered if this was what I should expect of a non-denominational church. My mind worked overtime during the meeting. As I listened to him, I felt the color of my skin was changing, as if I was a chameleon. And the other Associates conducted themselves like three monkeys—*mi-zaru, kika-zaru and iwa-zaru,* see no evil, hear no evil, speak no evil.

The Church Financial Director, Mr. Archibald Cox, had two legal pages filled with numbers, the likes of which I'd never seen before in any of my ministries. He never cracked a smile as he meticulously revealed the offer of my salary, benefits, use of telephone, church properties, and the conditions for my hiring and firing, etc. The offer was too good to be true, and yet it attracted me more for financial reasons than anything else.

That evening, while preparing the evening meal, I had songs on my lips. My wife seemed at ease when she saw me and my face of contentment. As all my children knew where I'd been, they were curious if their father would return to church work.

After dinner, I showed my wife the financial offer, the sphere of my responsibilities, and my obligations. Her eyes opened widely. We were quite amazed that my ministry could have greater freedom than if I were working at a secular company on an eight-to-five job. I accepted.

As an Associate Minister overseeing Christian Education and Evangelism, I implemented the same evangelistic program of *"Trout-Line-Fishing"* that I had used at Sunnyville Baptist Church in Indiana. This time, the fruit of our ministry was beyond expectation, as the average Sunday morning service attendance grew from 475 to 625, all within a ten-month period. This brought smiling approval from Dr. Swanson, especially as many of these newcomers became pillars of the church.

The final stretch of the Sunday School Spring Campaign was called "Reaching the Hilltop," and coming at the end of the eight week program, it aimed at having a one-time high attendance of 800.

With the entire sanctuary filled, we opened partitions to the social hall for an overflowing crowd. Hundred of extra chairs were set in the aisles, and even in the hallways.

The air of excitement grew for the final countdown on Sunday morning's service. As the counting hit key levels—750, 760, 775, 785—big cheers went up. Then the count rose to 799, 800 and was still going, 801, 802, 803, and 804. Cheers lifted the roof of the church building!

There had been nay-saying, that we couldn't reach that many new people. But I always found great pleasure in doing what people said could not be done!

Dr. Swanson's secretary was still bubbling as I walked into the office on Monday morning. She came into my office to tell me he wanted an urgent meeting with me at ten o'clock. I couldn't remember any day in the past year when he had shown up at the office on his day off. Not even to comfort a family after a church member had died. They either had to wait until Tuesday or see an Associate.

Dr. Swanson had an austere air as he led me to the "inner" conference room for our meeting. I had never been in this red-carpeted "holy place" before. I didn't even know such a room existed behind his outer office.

As I sat down, I offered my availability for whatever Dr. Swanson needed.

He finally raised his head, avoiding any eye contact. An unbearable silence draped the room, except for Dr. Swanson's deep, heavy breathing. He told his secretary via the intercom that he was not to be disturbed, and then turned toward me. "Tom," he said with hesitation, "I have been thinking a great deal, for a long time, and ..." He unloosened his necktie. "I need to let you go."

He turned his face sideways to me.

I felt as if he'd dropped a bomb on me, one which was bigger and more powerful than the Hiroshima atomic bomb! I felt as if what air was left in this inner room had all been consumed, for I was gasping for oxygen.

"I am sorry to tell you. It was not an overnight decision. I have reflected for months on how to come to terms with letting you go. For the sake of the church, my ministry, and my caring heart for my congregation."

"I see. So you have been mulling this over for months. But Preacher, was it not during yesterday morning's service, not even 24 hours ago, that you expressed heartfelt gratitude before the entire congregation for the part I played in achieving your dream?"

I breathed deeply and repeated what he had said from the pulpit, "Folks, I have been the minister of this church … and my goal was to reach 800 in attendance … I know how hard Pastor Tanemori worked for the Spring Campaign … to give me the pleasure of accomplishing this milestone. I take my hat off to him … I think he well deserves our applause."

The Preacher shifted in his seat, and then gave me his reasons for my termination.

"I have been trying to build up my ministry, but you have always stood in my way and contradicted me. Each time I compelled the congregation to sacrifice and make the financial commitment to build a new church building, you always repudiated my appeals by emphasizing evangelism and soul-winning ministry, "building" souls of people.

"You and I think differently regarding the "building" of a church. I want a new sanctuary, the biggest church building in town. It will be the monument and witness to my ministry. I can see myself standing at the pulpit preaching. But, you have done everything to prevent or discourage my congregation from making financial sacrifices for the building program."

I sneered at him. I couldn't let him have his self-gratification.

"That's right, Preacher. You emphasized a physical building and my emphasis was spiritual building."

He gave me a smirk, adding, "Can you see the mammoth building standing in this corner? I can almost see myself behind the pulpit on my 10th anniversary, preaching before the largest congregation ever assembled in Oakhill!"

"You have been the 'thorn' of my flesh. Not to mention that your poor English made us seem like a second-rate church. The truth of the matter is that most of our Elders and many church members have said they cannot have you as a spiritual leader, because you are a Japanese."

"I am already committed to the parents of a man who is graduating this spring from the seminary from which I graduated myself … to take your place."

I couldn't help but pity him.

"Pastor Tom, I really meant it yesterday when I patted your back, and told you what a good job you did. Please believe me, I meant that."

He told me that since the Caucasian minister would graduate at the end of May, he could still use me until he arrived in early June.

"That's all I have to say. I hope you understand and honor my ministry, and will let me fulfill my dream."

How should I tell my wife this unexpected news? What could I do with my numbered days? The biggest question, though, was how I could honor his wishes until the new man arrived, if our goals had been conflicting?

I had made great sacrifices for years, depriving my wife and our three children for the sake of others. And now I had come to the place and moment of the testing my faith and my heart, as I took off the "Purple Robe."

No! In my mind, the Purple Robe had been violently ripped from me after years of serving white men's congregations, of "exacting revenge in love and services" with the gospel.

I felt I had been violently raped!

The 10th Anniversary of Dr. Swanson's ministry came, and as he had so desired the opportunity, he delivered his sermon in a newly-erected church building. It was the first and the last sermon he ever delivered there. I was told "by the grapevine" that the Board of Elders ousted him, and that he moved in obscurity to an unknown small church in the country.

Chapter Nine: In Search of Salvation

I AM still baffled by the intolerance and prejudice among Christians, especially among ministers who supposedly exemplify acceptance and love! I was once a proud minister, struggling to survive, trying to feed three innocent children.

My wife posed the issue to me this way, "When are you going to stop believing that God called you to minister to Americans? Look at what they gave you. They put you out on the street without any consideration. What thanks did we get? The last preacher told you to leave town, to leave no trace of our ministry!"

I understood perfectly, accepting my wife's outrage towards me, although my inability to console her was adding to my own fury.

"How are we going to live? Will He feed your children?" my wife pleaded. "Of course, God surely provides ... I should have listened to my father when he said you would never be a provider."

Her pain-filled cry! It pierced me, like a dagger thrust deep into my soul.

"And now you are booted out of the ministry, without any skill or education to find a good-paying job to support your family. Do you have any idea when the next bowl of soup will be on the table? Do you still consider yourself a man? You could go back to 'picking fruit' and see just how long that will last!"

Perhaps her father was right in rejecting me. He had warned his daughter about marrying me, not so much because I was a Japanese man, but because I was a minister who could not support his family.

I would die before his "prediction" could become reality! I couldn't give him the satisfaction to mock me!

For several months I sank into a deep melancholy. What else could I do, for I had nothing in my hand except a wornout Bible? Even Moses had hand a staff in his hand which turned into a snake. But I felt denuded, with no skill in my hand.

In my desperate search for survival, I found an ad in the local newspaper. The Federal Government was seeking minority and bilingual employees. I knew I had to act quickly, so I did.

I passed the written examination with no difficulty at all. The examiner, quite pleased with my educational background and my test results, said, "Mr. Tanemori, you are highly over-qualified. I see you have two Masters degrees." He smiled.

My heart was bubbling, my feet were skipping and I could almost taste the food. Oh what possibilities! I could buy food with the income from the government job and put it on the table for my three children!

I internally verbalized my feelings, "See, Joyce. You asked me how God would feed our children. Here's how."

Assessing my self worth was like trying to measure steam. My personal integrity, however insubstantial it might have seemed to Joyce, was the only thing that kept my heart, body and soul together. This self-belief, the essence of who I am, allowed me to stand up against all hardships … even against the gates of hell!

When the third and final oral interview came, I was rejected.

The voice of the woman was very subdued as she explained, "When we say 'bilingual,' we aren't talking about English and Japanese. We are talking about English and Spanish."

"If that's the case, why didn't you clearly say so in your advertisement?" I responded, trying to avoid plunging into confusion and rage. "Of course, Ma'am, I'm more than willing to, and capable of, learning Spanish, just as I learned English. Just give me a little time."

I waited for her response, as I cast her a contorted look. Surely I would be qualified when it came to being a minority; I smiled internally.

"Mr. Tanemori," she looked around and dropped her voice, practically whispering into my ear, "when we say 'minority,' we don't mean Japanese. We mean black."

"What! You are a bigot! You have misled the public. If the government wants to fill a position with a black person who speaks Spanish, then you should have clearly stated those qualifications in the advertisement!" My boisterous voice bounced back against the wall.

"Oh, Mr. Tanemori, we can't say that. That's discriminatory ..."

"What did you say? You, of all people ..." my body was shaking involuntarily.

Two weeks later, I received a letter from former Senator Sam Hayakawa of California. Responding to my inquiry, he expressed his willingness to go to battle for me. Having considered the issue, I declined his offer, for I knew better than to resort to such tactics. On the other hand, my self-respect would not fill the bellies of my children.

I turned to begging for a job, any job, that might feed my three children. I nearly wore out a pair of shoes. I could put a finger through their soles. I cried bitterly, biting my lips. My search for employment continued.

Although I had no business skills, I stumbled into a job managing a new car wash, the "Kleen Machine." It wasn't much, but wasn't so bad, I told myself.

"As with my ministry, I'll still be cleaning things."

I considered this a noble and honorable occupation. What I didn't know until later was that the owner thought I was, at least, honest in my business dealings. He knew I could be trusted, that my integrity was irrevocably intact. Perhaps it was the only thing about me that was neither unmovable nor capable of being destroyed!

My new job had one immense advantage. The business establishment was just one block from my house. Often one of my children would sit on the fire hydrant in our front yard, to welcome me when I walked home.

As a manager, I also had the distinct benefit of being able to have my children help me at the work place. For the first time ever, I had the overwhelming satisfaction of having my children around me, and devoting my time and energy to them, instead of church members. I was like a little kid with new toys—being with my children was a great learning and growing process for me, and this, however momentarily, gave Joyce a sense of relief.

I almost forgot that I had been a minister and had been through a gauntlet of trials. I was simply enjoying my children, my new family lifestyle and, for the first time, being able to financially support my family!

One day in the midst of the excitement of its grand opening, the car wash offered discount coupons. Cars lined up and coupons were collected. A large Chrysler swerved in. Dr. Swanson, the minister who had dismissed me, rolled down his window and waved his coupon like a flag. As a courteous Japanese business custom, I bowed and offered my hand through the open window.

"It's nice to see you Da—da—Dr. Swanson," I stuttered. "It's a beautiful day, isn't it? Thank you. You honor us by coming today. Let us not carry the anger of the past with us any longer."

His arm hung in the air like a leafless branch. The man behind the wheel rolled up the window to prepare for rinsing and soaping.

I ran into the bathroom and locked the door. I stuck my finger deep into my throat and vomited until I could only dry heave. I flushed and flushed the toilet, as I wailed.

This incident had a powerful affect on me. For several months, I sank back into a deep melancholy. I couldn't shake the image of the Preacher, nor could I rise above the circumstances of my wife and my children.

One evening, after our children were asleep, an air of confrontation filled our living room. Suddenly Joyce stood up squarely in front of me.

"What is it you want?" she asked me, as she might ask a dying man. "You must find what is tearing you up inside … eating you up. You have to tell me! I'm your wife. I can't help you unless you tell me. Whatever it is, you're not happy here. What you're doing right now, I know, is not what you want to do the rest of your life."

"What more do I want? I've finally found a job that allows me to spend more time with my children than I did for the last ten years of ministry put together. What else could any father ask for?"

"No, that is not true," she responded, inching toward me. "For goodness sake, either shape up or ship out! I don't want our children subjected to your despair and depression. Why not just go back to Japan and find what you're looking for, or missing? Whatever it is, stay there until you find an answer that will help you know where you want to go, or what you want to do."

"What do you mean, go back to Japan? Surely you don't mean for me to leave you and the children, and return to Japan for good?"

Oh, I thought, how I wish I had married a Japanese woman, especially one like Nakamura *Sensei*, who would understand me and feel my pain.

Joyce promised that I wouldn't have to worry about our children, that she would take care of them and wait for my return.

I sat emotionlessly, my eyes focused on a "mystical" distance.

The day was December 15th, and was significant in that my children remembered my birthday. They shared their joy, telling me over and over, with a sense of pride, that they loved me.

"You're the best daddy in the whole wide world," my Princess, Roxanne, exclaimed, as she sat on my knees! It seemed an indisputable fact that I had a complete family, three children and my wife, surrounding me with their love and caring hearts. What more did I need or want? As their father, it was time for me to "shape up, shut up" and move forward!

Rather than wanting to eat cake and ice cream, my children were anxious to hand me an envelope. On it was written, "TO DADDY, BON VOYAGE!" The children's signatures were inscribed, and I could tell it had been signed with love.

Inside the envelope was a round-trip airline ticket to Japan. I was to enjoy my stay in Japan, including the *Osho-gatsu*, New Year's Holiday season. I was speechless!

Later, I learned that each child withdrew money from their savings to add to my wife's gift of the airfare.

My heart re-learned what it was to be touched by the kindness and compassionate understanding of my family.

My sister Satsuko couldn't believe that her brother, who had left Japan more than 21 years before, after betraying the honor and respect of the Tanemori family, would be returning to Kotachi Village, and doing so without giving her "proper" preparation, which meant that she couldn't receive me with open arms.

Was this not like the parable of the prodigal son, who repented of his social and cultural sins and returned home? Was I not returning to Kotachi Village, however hostile it had been to me, with "gifts" from my heart to honor my sister?

My brief message, informing Satsuko of my coming to visit her during the *Osho-gatsu*, the New Year Holiday, met with great resistance. She said she considered me a dead dog, and that she believed I would never return to Japan, except to honor her and restore the family name by buying back its "social aura." Only by my giving proper gifts to her, openly, before the eyes of the Kotachi Villagers, could I redeem myself.

December 22, 1977, two decades since I had said *sayonara* to my birthplace, I returned to Hiroshima with renewed fond memories of Nakamura *Sensei*. Winter dominated the village of Kotachi, and when I arrived at Kotachi Station, no one was there to welcome me back.

I waited and waited. Perhaps it was wishful thinking that my sister or someone would be there, demonstrating a change of heart, and openly receiving me. Perhaps I should be grateful that the ever busy-bodied Gossip Committee members weren't there. At least I didn't recognize anyone from the Committee, nor did anyone recognize me. Perhaps those "old goats" had passed away.

Standing outside the station, sweeping the *Hiroba*, square, with my eyes, I saw that great changes had taken place. Seeing both the old and the new, unrecognizable, establishments, I tried to recall the scene as I had left it 21 years before.

I visited my Father's gravesite first, and spent some time there. Only then did I deem it safe to meet Satsuko, who greeted me icily. As I stepped up to the door, she yanked my arm, saying, "Get inside quickly. I don't want anyone to see that you're home!"

"Oh, what a welcoming greeting," I murmured under my breath. She was discontented, but not only that I had returned to the Village of Kotachi.

"Now, look at yourself! After 21 years, you come home like someone from a poor house. Do you have any idea what the neighbors would say to me, having you home in the first place? Then to see you wearing a light-colored suit, which definitely is not from winter cloth ... let alone, without an overcoat! This is not socially acceptable. Don't you have enough money to at least buy appropriate dark-colored winter suits? This is not summer. Don't you get it?"

I wished she would give me time to breathe, time to allow me to honor her with an official greeting, and time for her to be enlightened before she embarrassed herself.

That night, as we sat in her one-room house, she looked over my gifts. They were the best I could afford. How could I tell Satsuko that I had lost my ministry, that I had been without the means of supporting the family she didn't even acknowledge?

"What do you call these things? Do you consider these gifts worthy of your presence?" She chided me, as if she was picking up dirty laundry between her thumb and index finger. "Don't you know that we have better things than what you have brought me? Have you done this to shame me again before the villagers and neighbors?"

Her impudence had no mercy. "I want you to know that you are not yet come home from America!" One day when you bring honorable gifts worthy to be received, I will let the whole world know my 'prodigal' brother has finally returned home. Do I need to repeat what I have just said?!"

Her contemptuous voice still lingering in my ears, she disappeared for awhile. When she returned, she had a black trenchcoat for me to wear in public, to cover my California-style suit.

In her determination not to bring any further shame to our family, Satsuko had forbidden me to visit any of my old friends without letting her know beforehand, so that she could be certain I would follow the appropriate codes of Japanese social conduct.

Meanwhile a classmate, Takumasa Yamasaki, brought good news of a class reunion party with Tamura *Sensei*, set for January 7, just because I was home.

My sister and I had great arguments about this, but the weight of Tamura *Sensei*'s persuasion tipped the scale for her to consent, however begrudgingly, for me to stay until January 7th, through the reunion party.

Satsuko took painstaking efforts to see that her brother would not bring any reproach or shame to her or the Tanemori name. She gave me strict instructions on the manner in which I should conduct my self.

Our gathering with Tamura *Sensei*, my 9th grade teacher, and a couple dozen classmates, is etched deeply upon my heart. As we reminisced about the past, I had the opportunity to ask discreetly about the whereabouts of Nakamura *Sensei*.

No one knew anything about her. Out of respect for her honor, I couldn't pursue the matter further. After I said "so long" to Tamura *Sensei* and my classmates, I took the bus to Yoshida village, Nakamura *Sensei*'s hometown. For hours, I wandered the streets searching faces, hoping I would meet her, but asking no one.

"Takashi," my sister woke me up at four o'clock in the morning. "Today is January 8th, and I want you to keep your promise. I had to honor the wish of Tamura *Sensei* to let you stay as long as I could. I couldn't, for the life of me, understand why he had to wait until yesterday to see you. Now that I have fulfilled my obligatory social code, I want you to leave this morning without stirring any dust (it was snowing outside), before the rooster wakes the neighbors. Here is the train ticket to Hiroshima."

For the next four weeks, I traveled to the city of Hiroshima, walked the sandy beach of Tenma River, returned by train to Kobe, then wandered through Kyoto and on to Tokyo, searching for the answer my wife and children wanted me to find.

I saw for the first time that even though I was born in Japan and was now a U.S. citizen, I had ceased to identify with those who wished to label me a man without a country, "a cultural amphibian." I began seeing myself as a member of the multi-racial, multi-cultural, international human family.

After six weeks of visiting my homeland, I was forced to take a look at my life through a magnifying glass. I began to feel that neither Japan nor the U.S. could provide the answer to my inner turmoil or fill the "canyon" in my heart. I began to sense that the solution to both would only come through something inside my own *heart* and through my own *will.*

That's when I decided to return to California, to my family, having resolved little in my mind, and feeling empty that I hadn't found Nakamura *Sensei.*

Chapter Ten: Reaching Americans Through Their Stomachs

THOUGH ousted from the ministry, I still wanted to reach the hearts of Americans. Responding to the old saying "the shortest way to a man's heart is through his stomach," I decided to try a new approach.

I was determined to "buy back" my social position, turn around any social stigma, and regain the all-important family honor which America had taken from me in the Hiroshima bombing. I aimed to do these things through a business I would start when I had enough money to open a restaurant. I borrowed $40,000 from a local bank and charted a new course for my life as the proprietor of a Japanese garden restaurant.

We proudly opened the restaurant's doors in Turlock on October 10, 1979. It was surely as much of a "red-letter day" as September 1965, when the McDonald's on McHenry Street in Modesto, California, sold its first 19-cent hamburger.

In the corner of a tiny L-shaped shopping center on Geer Road, in a "restaurant row" of taco joints, hamburger stands and pizza parlors, just south of Cal State Stanislaus, raw fish came to Stanislaus County with the opening of *A Touch of Japan*.

There would be no more need for gourmets to trek to Stockton, 40 miles away, to nosh on *sashimi*. Ours was the only restaurant in the San Joaquin Valley with a deep Japanese tradition, dignity and culture, all intended to enrich lives in the community and bridge my adopted nation with my native country.

For folks in this community, on the edge of California's Gold Country, there was some culture shock in regard to *sashimi*. I would liken it to ordering "steak tartar" in Germany and being served raw hamburger and egg. It would take time for the locals to learn that *sashimi* served with *wasabi* (a green mustard made from a vegetable by that name) has the cleanest, freshest taste in the world, and is anything but fishy.

The interior decor of *A Touch of Japan* was one of the most ambitious decorating schemes ever tried in the San Joaquin Valley. The moment you left the plastic hustle and bustle of the streets behind, you were welcomed by a symphonic melody—an ode to cherry blossoms, "*Sakura, Sakura*," and the chirping of birds, blended with a background of Japanese *Koto* and *fue*, flute. It was an unfathomable atmosphere, a different, enchanting garden.

Stepping past traditional Japanese art and through a *Torii*, gate, a new world opened—wooden latticework, rice paper dividers, bright paper parasols muting lights, reflecting lanterns in a pond cradled by plants and rocks and stocked with expensive *koi*, carp. A brook through the middle of the restaurant turned a wooden waterwheel, completing a tapestry of harmony and serenity.

Patrons could cross the stream by walking over the authentic Japanese half-moon wooden bridge, the symbol of my ultimate goal of "reaching out" to the community, the rest of the country, and to the world. How grand a goal!

They could sit at conventional "Yankee" tables or be seated Japanese-style, shoeless, on a padded floor. To assist "Yankees," the floor-level banquet tables had a sort of "well" for easing stocking-covered feet under the table.

Each patron was served a hot hand towel, rolled like a spring roll, for the washing of the face and hands. Then rice tea was served, its taste hinting of popcorn, then bits of *tsukemono*, pickled *nappa,* a Japanese cabbage, followed by hot broth in a fine lacquered bowl. No soup spoon for "Yankees," I declared! One picked up the bowl—two hands are *de rigueur*—and drank from it.

We then served a second salad, *sunomono*, lightly pickled cucumber. Finally the *sashimi* was served in small portions, on a bed of finely-shredded *daikon*, Japanese radish. It came with a dipping *wasabi*. Diluted with soy sauce, *wasabi* is still hot enough to clear sinuses, cure worms and make people passionate.

All service came courtesy of an authentic Japanese waitress, smiling, slightly embarrassed—she would say the cook cut his finger and you would tell her you wanted no meat—and you'd choke back a tear. Patrons loved it!

There were some eye-openers for the budding entrepreneur I had become. I was shocked to learn the State and Federal governments demanded prepaid taxes (based upon projected first year income) before we opened the business. I was overwhelmed with the financial burden, having already borrowed $40,000 for the cash flow required to operate a daily business.

Out of desperation, I went to see former US Congressman Tony Cohello, who at that time represented our district. I had great ideas to ease the entrepreneur's burden, but our urgent meetings were nothing on my part but an attempt to seek the political clout to preempt paying payroll taxes in order to get a business license.

I begged that any income tax on profits should be deferred for one or two years, in order to nurture new, small businesses. I believed the government would ultimately receive more tax revenue this way.

My plea fell on deaf ears. Therefore my plan to reach the hearts and souls of Americans through *A Touch of Japan*—as food is the language of the soul!—started on a rocky road.

Early one August morning in 1980, a stream of light flooded my bedroom, waking me a moment before the alarm clock's ring. Joyce stirred beside me as I rubbed my eyes and sat on the edge of the bed, staring through the window at the light. The phone rang, and I answered a call that came from another world! I wouldn't have guessed in a million years that I'd ever receive such a call, until I recognized her voice, a voice I'd tried to forget for decades.

My sister Satsuko informed me that she and her honorable guests were coming from Kotachi Village to visit us.

I immediately asked myself, "Why is she taking the pain to come and see me?" My reputation, in her eyes, had already been gravely damaged by an untold number of incidents of socially inappropriate behavior I had been driven to as a boy. But that was right after the war: that was hunger, that was anger.

It seemed like such a long time ago. How different everything had become! While harboring these tumultuous thoughts, I became very short-tempered with my daughter Roxanne, who had come to tell me that children at her school had taunted her with racial epithets.

"Daddy, why do they call me names? They called me 'Chink-Jap' and said I'm not American, that I'm not like them. Why do they want to hurt me?"

I could only stare painfully at my daughter as she said, "Daddy, look at me. Do these eyes look slanted?"

How could I begin to explain what it was like being Asian in America, my early life marooned by prejudice and by ghosts of the past? I knew that I must ... I would explain to her one day. But it would have to wait.

Satsuko is coming! How in the world did she hear we were celebrating the second anniversary of our business? And how did she get our business phone number? Could there have been an informer among us?

"Princess," I brushed Roxanne off, "don't you know daddy is concerned for your auntie who is coming to visit in a few days? Daddy doesn't have time for you right now. I'll talk to you after I get home tonight. I'll see you at the restaurant."

Already in final preparations for the restaurant's second anniversary, I now had to give attention to the arrival of Satsuko, my brother Sadayoshi, and his wife Sayo. How the wind could have carried the message 5,000 miles across the ocean, I never knew. But Satsuko had heard that I was a successful businessman in America, and maybe, just maybe, given one last chance, I would do something to redeem my reputation in Japan and finally bring honor to the family name.

However, all was not well with my business or my family life. After two years, the restaurant teetered on the brink of collapse. I had no choice but to buy out my business partners when I realized they wanted to milk the restaurant for profits while contributing nothing, putting the Tanemori family deeper in debt and inflicting great damage upon my already fragile marriage.

I knew the upcoming visit would be demanding both physically and financially; above all, it would be a great strain on Joyce.

My sister had not yet blessed our marriage. Moreover, I knew I was not yet capable of doing *motenashi*, satisfying my siblings beyond "duty." That fulfillment must be impeccable in every aspect. There could be no blemish tolerated in entertaining the honorable guests.

Unfortunately, disaster began the moment I arrived late at San Francisco Airport to meet our guests, due to a multiple-car accident on the Bay Bridge. This was beyond my control. No sooner did I pull up at the curb, than Satsuko's jaw opened like an *Oni*, a Japanese ogre, challenging me for being late to receive her and her guests. There was no mercy in her voice.

"Have you no shame to commit this unpardonable act? You could not wait even a moment to prove you have not changed. Don't you understand we have come a long way and paid a great deal of money. And what do we get?"

I had listened to the first of many utterances of condemnation.

While she was fuming on the way to our home, a nearly three-hour-long ride through a magnificent *Tairiku*, landscape, my old, dilapidated American car gave an impressive image and comfort they could never have expected and could not easily experience in Japan.

As they stepped from the car to the curb, my sister wanted to know why there was no welcome mat, and why my wife was not there to humbly receive them.

Our children were the "saviors" for the sins of their parents. They stretched their arms to welcome my sister and her guests and caused their father's eyes to fill with warm tears. Although they tried, all three children failed to use the Japanese greeting I taught them for this occasion.

"Taka-chan," Satsuko said sharply as she turned to me, "haven't you taught them Japanese? Perhaps, you are teaching them Chinese?"

My children tried to help carry suitcases into the house and to their rooms. As Satsuko, my brother and his wife walked in, they began snooping from one room to the next, making barely audible comments along the way. From what I gathered, they were quite surprised at the size of our house in contrast to theirs in Japan. They came through our indoor Japanese garden, walked around the *koi* pond and over a half-moon bridge, and glimpsed a separate Japanese guestroom nestled in the backyard.

That special room is where I often retreated to find solace. The intricate decor included a *sushi*-bar with a tiny waterfall on the counter. An ambrosia of white Japanese peach blossoms filled the air in the spring. It was a place of honor and admiration and I was selective about whom I shared it with. I was determined that neither my sister nor my brother would use the guestroom.

Just then, Joyce returned from teaching.

"Honey," she addressed me, before acknowledging our guests, which I knew insulted my sister "beyond recovery."

My introduction of Joyce was with deep pride. She greeted them in a Japanese manner, simply offering her greetings and best wishes to my sister, "*Hajime mashi te, Dozo yoroshiku onegai shimasu.*"

"Well, it looks like we might get tea," my sister blurted, "*So yo!*"

Sayo, my sister-in-law said, "I got you ... Joyce, a Chinese woman and, you, brother-in-law!" as she nodded her head.

Sensing her smirk, I moved everyone to the kitchen, showing Sayo where the tea and teacups were, and I even showed her how to boil water. I suggested she might serve the tea for herself and others.

"Have you not taught your Chinese wife anything?" Satsuko soon commented. "How can she insult us like this? You call yourself a Japanese man and let your Chinese wife act this way?"

Satsuko was deeply offended that I would show preference for an outsider, a Chinese woman. She said she wished she had never come to America to visit. I did my best not to be affected by my sister's taunts. I defended Joyce, and I insisted that my sister and brother should honor her because she was my wife.

My sister had brought a beautiful *kimono* for Joyce to wear to our restaurant's celebration. Given my sister's rudeness, Joyce had little problem speaking her mind.

"What do you mean 'as a Japanese woman' should wear?" Joyce asked Satsuko. "I am proud being Chinese. So be it!"

Nevertheless, Joyce reluctantly wore the *kimono* the first night of our celebration.

The Second Anniversary of *A Touch of Japan* pleased our local guests. My sister honored everyone with flawlessly performed traditional Japanese dances. This would be one of the brightest moments during their entire stay in America. I had to credit Satsuko for her effort and thoughtfulness in planning her performance before she came. It was a night to remember!

Later that night, after returning home, Joyce quickly shed the *kimono*. Internally, I smiled a "hooray" for Joyce.

"Honey, would you tell that sister of yours to take this blankety-blank *kimono* back to Japan when she goes home?" she said to me. "I really don't want to see it."

Joyce refused to wear the *kimono* the second night of celebration. Although I liked to see Joyce wear the *kimono*, she was entirely beautiful and gracious wearing her own clothes. I asked my sister to honor Joyce's wish, which brought only an eruption of Satsuko's anger, as she took this as a personal affront. I prefer not to translate what her sharp tongue directed toward Joyce.

I had planned a quiet evening, with the whole family having dinner at the restaurant. Things didn't go as planned, as I should have known in advance.

Joyce tried to please and honor our Japanese guests in every way, as she served them the meal. Satsuko took offense at being served by Joyce, requesting instead to be attended by Atsuko-san, a Japanese waitress.

Atsuko-san humbly accepted the request, saying, "Joyce, this is a Japanese woman's place and not your ..."

Realizing her place as an employee, Atsuko-san did not finish. But I heard her say to Satsuko, "Japanese food will be tastier when a Japanese woman serves you. After all, you are honorable guests all the way from Japan and deserve to be treated right. Non-Japanese don't understand what Japanese grace is ..."

My brother sipped hot *sake* after hot *sake*, as Atsuko-san poured for him, charmed him, and skillfully demonstrated the graceful service of a Japanese woman.

I felt I had no choice but to let Atsuko-san do the honors. The magical power of *motenashi*, Atsuko-san's service, provided Satsuko's "salt-in-the-wound" insult. My sister, using a Japanese waitress, successfully drove her wedge into my Chinese wife.

On the fourth day, I finally had a chance to make special sightseeing arrangements. We drove all the way to the Old West gold mining towns of Jamestown and Columbia, only to stay about 45 minutes. My guests bought gifts to take to friends and neighbors in Kotachi. For Satsuko, these gifts would determine my fate and how she would be socially reassessed when she returned to Hiroshima.

A drive to Sacramento unfortunately brought the discovery of no stores or shops to please them. They continued to compare notes, whether through unspoken words or innuendo, and already had in mind the kinds of gifts which would be "honorable."

"*Konna gifuto dareni agete kure to itte iruno?*"

Satsuko wanted to know for whom I bought gifts. I sensed her frustration and exasperation that the gifts I bought didn't confirm that her brother had finally earned good social standing in the United States, and thus demonstrated my failure to honor and compensate their sacrifices in coming to visit us in America.

The day after our shopping trip, a "knight in shining armor" appeared. Glenn Newsum, my friend, confidant and business advisor, was that knight. He was the banker who had loaned me money without requiring any collateral to start my business. All he had needed was my signature.

Glenn invited my guests to an American steak dinner at the exclusive *The Truck 29*, a famous, very expensive restaurant. Our date was the night before Satsuko, Sadayoshi and Sayo were to return to Japan.

The banker's hospitality was without limitation. We were wined and dined with thick, juicy prime rib steaks nearly covering our plates—something no Japanese would find in any restaurant at home.

Traditional Mexican musicians entertained us throughout the evening, impressing my guests. It was the first time on this trip that I'd seen Satsuko smile. How pleasantly her laughter filled my ears and heart. I was sorry I wasn't able to fill her heart.

Without Glenn's generosity, I felt my family's visit to the United States would have been total calamity! I trusted the fond memory of this positive experience would last forever, softening their hearts and their judgment of Joyce and me.

We left home at 6:30 the next morning for their plane trip at 10:45 a.m. Silence filled my big American car on our way to San Francisco airport. I had never prayed so hard and selfishly as I did behind the wheel. I prayed no accident on the road would delay us, for I couldn't consider sitting in the car with them one minute longer than I had to. The trip seemed to take forever. I wanted to scream.

When I pulled up to the airport terminal curb, Satsuko couldn't wait to let me know her feelings.

"How lucky you are to have a banker friend who showed us how rich he is by his generosity. Tell me, when will you become a rich man like him, to buy us gifts to make us proud?" She added, "I would not hold my breath lest I die for lack of air."

I was speechless!

We hurriedly said goodbye, and I wished for their safe journey and health. And how sweet the departing was! Although I had no regret they had come to visit, I knew Joyce didn't share the feeling.

On the way home, my heart was lighter, whistling on my lips. It was wonderful to see my wife and children meet me at the back door, let out a sigh of relief, and hear them say nearly in unison, "Daddy, are they gone?"

I knew my sister and brother would never, ever come back to visit. Their disappointment was so great it would take a miracle to change or heal their wounded hearts. This would be the first of many peaceful nights!

How wrong I was! That night the phone rang, waking me from my dreams. It was a collect call from Tokyo. There was to be no rest for the *"wicked"* who had failed to revere the "Honorable Guests from the Land of the Rising Sun."

"Takashi." Satsuko cursed me again for what she saw as the same disregard for the family name I had exhibited as a youth. She felt it unfair that I lived in America while she had to live in Kotachi Village without honor, and that the gifts had been unacceptable to present to her Kotachi Villagers.

I couldn't let my sister satisfy herself with such a jab. I called on Glenn Newsum for help, telling him, "You really don't need any enemies when you have a sister like mine."

He smiled at me with empathy.

Glenn arranged for a small loan to buy several gifts in order to, once and for all, shut my sister's lips. At least I hoped they would meet with her approval. These were very expensive gifts, far above my financial means, and it cost me about five times their price to have them sent by special delivery airmail.

I briefly thought I had restored peace to my life, until my wife saw the bank statement at the end of month.

"How can she have the audacity to come here when she has no respect for you and disdains our marriage?" Joyce berated me. "And what did you do? You gave in to her like a spineless jellyfish! Now the restaurant is failing, just as your ministry failed, all because of your stubbornness and your damn sacred Japanese principles! What is it about you Japanese—why did I marry you?"

Memories of our honorable guests had faded or were buried under the burden of our restaurant business. Instead of getting better, by our fourth year our business was suffering from a lack of cash flow. There had also been growing competitive, if not cultural, pressures.

My goal of reaching American hearts with Japanese food was not being met. For many people who like beef, potatoes, carrots and bread, Japanese food held nothing for their taste buds. I wondered if I was years ahead of my time.

There was one restaurant owner who took every opportunity to say blatantly to my face, "I want to see your business buried deeper than my shipmates were buried in the bottomless Pacific Ocean, never to see the sun."

As the skipper of the destroyer USS Laffey, DD-724, this man had survived one of the heaviest kamikaze airplane attacks against any single ship (about which the book *The Ship That Would Not Die* would later be written by Admiral F. Julian Becton). Her captain escaped "the gates of hell," but not before he saw many of his shipmates die as his ship was torn to pieces. This experience instilled a hatred and a desire for the total destruction of the Japanese Empire deep within his heart.

By a quirk of fate we found ourselves competitors in the restaurant business in the same town. Though our lives began quite separate from each other, a chain of events that spanned many years and milees had brought us to the same place. This was to significantly impact both our lives.

Only years later, after my restaurant had gone belly-up, as the Captain had wished, and had sunk to the depth of the ocean, did my banker friend, Glenn, bring us together in an eventual friendship. Building that relationship, however, was frequently like watching a baby learn to roll over, crawl, and then walk. Together we shared thoughts and feelings of hatred, of love and a full gamut of emotions in between. But eventually we learned to reconcile, to forgive, and to make peace with our painful pasts.

Although the Japanese garden restaurant once stood at the corner of Geary Boulevard and the main Turlock thoroughfare, there is no longer any sign of its former majesty, nor of the service that touched thousands of diners during those four years.

Although the physical structure and the enticing aroma of Japanese cuisine are no longer to be seen or smelled, the awareness of and the "essence" of the Tanemoris—our inseparable presence with the residents of

Turlock and with those who knew us near and abroad—still lingered then, and still does now. *A Touch of Japan* still lives in the hearts and minds of people, demonstrating the soul of the Tanemoris. I would like to see its continuing effects in my life's next chapter.

Keeping it secret from my wife, I made several visits to my doctor, who was not a bit surprised as I unloaded my heart. I told him I was caught in a grindstone that was turning ever slowly, yet ever finer in its milling. I recall his warnings that I had been hospitalized twice already, and that I might be crossing a bridge from where would be no return.

On an unusually restless night, our grandfather clock's tick-tock urged me to get some much-needed rest. I felt an anxious shortness of breath, and discomfort in my chest. I prayed an early dawn would dispel the darkness.

One day while in the neighboring city of Modesto, running errands for our restaurant business, a sharp pain suddenly shot through my chest—twice, then a third time. The last jolt was so sharp it doubled me up, forcing me to park along the side of the road. I gasped for air as traffic passed by, oblivious of my need.

Nearly an hour passed before I was coherent enough to drive back to the restaurant. I was cold and pale, afraid to tell my employees what had happened, and silent even with my wife. The "fear of the unknown" had its grip on me.

Dr. Girsham, a surgeon at nearby Emanuel Hospital, was enjoying dinner at his usual table. He sat by the indoor garden, watching the *koi* swim energetically through rocks and under the fire-red arched wooden bridge.

Suddenly, I silently screamed "No!" and my breath caught at my throat. Another severe attack filled my heart with terror. More sharp pain pierced my heart. I vaguely registered the urgency in Dr. Girsham's voice, as he called Joyce from the kitchen where she was finishing up for the evening. I drifted away ...

I hadn't the foggiest idea how much time had elapsed. As I became more coherent, I tried to make sense of the jungle of tubes attached through my nostrils to a machine. I discovered nyself in the cardiac intensive care unit at Emanuel Hospital. Several nurses and doctors moved around and about me.

I drifted toward a voice that was so familiar, the voice of my wife, who stood by my bedside, her eyes telling me of her love for me. She reassured me that our children were well taken care of. The restaurant was still open, and she was doing her best to run it as I would want it run.

When she left, Dr. Frank Davis stood by my bedside, a chart in his hand. The door was closed shut. We were alone.

When I asked in an annoyed voice why I was hooked to so many pipes and wires, he gently replied they were there to make sure everything was all right. His voice was soft, but penetrating.

"What do you mean ... making sure everything is all right?"

He replied, "You had a heart attack."

"Aaa, Aaaa haaart a-a-a-attack?"my quivering voice was full of disbelief.

Joyce's tender eyes were filled with fear of the unknown. Her body, overtaken by physical and emotional burdens, showed much wear and tear. With her quivering hands, she left a card created by Princess, my daughter.

"Honey, before you leave, would you read it to me?"

My voice quivered as her hands held the card. She read the message with eyes that sparkled, jewel-likeL

> *To Daddy, Get well.*
> *Daddy, I hope you feel better.*
> *I hope you know that I miss you.*
> *I love you soooo much!*
> *Princess*

How timely her card was, lifting my heart! I felt like a sinking iron warship that had taken a severe beating.

On Joyce's next visit, she pointed to the window curtain, open ever so slightly, and I glimpsed my children anxiously looking into the room where I lay, motionless.

It was the first time my mind grasped how close I had come to death. Only in my mid-forties, had I survived the atomic bomb to die of a heart attack?

I remembered the night my Father had died. How important it was for him to make sure he had correctly passed on the *Seven Codes of the Samurai* to me. It was a lesson within a lesson, as he was teaching me to repay my debts to my ancestors, by passing on to my children what I had received.

I had tried to be a good father, but deep down I was still an angry, bitter man, haunted by the ghosts of Hiroshima. I was concerned that the only thought my children carried of me was of my church ministry and, for the last four years, of my tempura-battered, sweat- and tear-stained image, as I gave my life for the restaurant, a sinking ship. How grateful I was to have had the privilege of working together with my children. Those memories were burned into my soul.

What legacy was I leaving them?

Had I passed on to my children what I had received from my Father—"Live by duty, responsibility and accountability, bonded by honor, love and principles?"

I pleaded with God to spare my life, as it suddenly became clear to me that I had to write my life story so that my children would know who I am.

I must tell them the truth, the details of my life, no matter how painful, and I must face all the pain and grief I had hidden for a lifetime. It was then that I resolved to leave my testament—"The Crane and the Butterfly, From Revenge to Forgiveness"—to my three children. It is my task! It is my promise!

As my children prepared to leave and take care of the restaurant, I asked my Princess, standing on her tiptoes looking through the glass, if she would like to stay longer, for a special time with her daddy.

A nurse plopped my daughter on the edge of the bed, as close as she was allowed. Princess burst into tears, telling me she was still having trouble in school with classmates who kept taunting her.

I understood what she was going through. I saw her tender heart broken by questions that her daddy couldn't physically remove by touching her heart.

"Daddy, look at me," she said, pointing her little index fingers at her eyes. "Tell me, Daddy, are they really slanted? Why was I born with slanted eyes?"

I held back my tears, as I realized I couldn't even move, let alone stretch out my arms to hold her. I began telling her that, as a child, I had problems in school too, that there were other students who called me names.

"But you were in Japan and you were Japanese. Why would they call you names?" she asked.

"Now, let me tell you the story. This way daddy can touch your heart and make it feel better."

"But, daddy, I don't want the story. I want you!"

"Princess, the story daddy is going to tell is special, so special that you and daddy are in the story."

Her eyes, filled with anguish, quickly transformed to sparkling jewels.

The next day my wife visited again, alone, her brow giving signs of crumbling beneath the pressure. She told me the burdens of the restaurant were taking their toll on the physical strength of our family. They were being held together by a thin thread.

"Honey, don't you understand what's going on in the restaurant? Only sheer 'gut' strength keeps the daily activity on the wheel," she sternly told me.

She revealed the purpose of her visit regarding my physical condition and future plans. She related what Dr. Davis had told her:

"Tom has been hospitalized twice in the last seven years. With the physical burdens and financial pressures of the business mounting on all sides, he can't continue in his condition for long. He is totally burnt out! I recommend that you close the restaurant and move on to something else."

I started to interrupt, but she continued in the same breath, "I took the liberty to consult with your banker friend, Glenn Newsum. He concurred with Dr. Davis and offered his assistance in dissolving the business."

"Dissolve our business?" I yelled, beginning to boil, "You have taken your liberty too far!" I didn't realize my voice was revealing my Japanese blood, and my old rage. "Are you asking me to honor your wish to give up *my* business? Are you saying that your family is more important than *my* honor and personal pride? There will be no family without the business. The future of our family is dependent on the future of the restaurant. It is the life and the future of the Tanemori bloodline. Can't you wait just a few more days before you exercise your assumed power? That's the real Chinese coming out loudly and clearly."

In my mind, obeying her wish was suicide. I would be the subject of mockery! Deep in my heart I knew the difficulties of operating the restaurant without me. Yet I couldn't afford to further endanger my family's health.

My Japanese honor won out. This was the first time I had felt the world slipping from the palms of my hands, and I insisted my wife was the start of that slippage. My anger and frustration exploded directly at her.

"Joyce, I feel I have been cheated by not marrying a Japanese! I don't ever want to see your face again. Just leave me alone!"

I thrashed the bed in despair over her thought of bringing my business to an end. It would be like pulling the plug from a life-support system. I pulled at my IV lines. A nurse rushed in, telling Joyce she thought it was time for her to go, that I would be cared for.

As Joyce ran silently from my room, tears dripping down her burdened cheeks, I felt I had conquered her by placing her where she belonged. I was a Japanese man! The beauty of a wife was to be submissive to the man she married, regardless of who was right or wrong.

How could Joyce, a Chinese woman born in America, understand what was going on in my heart? How could she understand "Japanese honor" and "saving face?" How could I tell my family in Japan that I had suffered a heart attack and lost my business? I was convinced it was far easier for "a camel to go through the eye of a needle" than for me to live the rest of my life without "social grace."

I lay gasping for air throughout the night. There was conflict with my wife, and now a decision about salvaging the business. I began to argue with God, and prayed, "Let me live, and give me back my life once again to reestablish the restaurant."

A week later I hoped I wasn't feeling sorry for myself for thinking, "Where are my Japanese employees? My chefs and waitresses? For some reason, they're keeping their distance from me. Not a flower or a card, or any apparent effort to visit me? Where are the Japanese principles of honor, respect and deference?"

While I felt betrayed by my employees, I had to chuckle for the several clergymen I knew well, none of whom visited me conspicuously.

It was ironic that, having been an ordained minister, I was now in a hospital receiving "attention." One clergyman performed a rosary, as if it were my last "rite," which I found amusing.

It seemed the critical hours had passed, when several visitors came to visit and helped me pass the day a little faster. Glenn Newsum, with his usual humor, made my hospital stay a bit more enjoyable.

The next morning, several staff members wheeled me out to an ambulance to be transferred to another hospital. I vaguely saw Doctor Davis standing by. We drove about fifteen miles north of Turlock, to North Memorial Hospital in Modesto, where several nurses waited at the emergency entrance door for my arrival.

"Tom? Can you hear me?"

"Who are you?" I responded faintly.

"It's me, Darlene Nelson." She practically placed her face over mine.

"Oh, Darlene ... what are you doing here?"

We had known each other for some time, as she had eaten at our restaurant several times. But why was she at the Emergency Room area?

"We need your help, Tom. We have a critical situation. Please come quickly."

"Get me out of this strap," I grunted, struggling with the gurney restraint.

"We have to get your signature on this transfer form," one of the ambulance attendants urged the nurse.

"We'll take care of that as soon as we get him to the second floor," she replied, directing the attendants to follow her. As we rushed into a surgery room, I met several doctors and nurses. I was told a young Japanese man and his wife had been visiting Yosemite National Park when a bus struck the man. His pelvis was broken in several places, he had internal damage, and his spinal nerve was shattered. He needed immediate surgery. His frail wife, who had escaped the accident, was sitting in the corner of the room, crying.

Doctors were trying to explain to the distraught wife that they required a signature before they could operate. As each moment slipped away, the threat to his life grew. The woman looked at me, at her husband, then back to me. *"ONEGAI ITASHI MASU; ONEGAI ITASHI MASU! DOZO WATAKUSHI TACHI O TASUKE TE KUDASAI. ONEGAI ITASHI MASU.* Please. Please, I beg of your heart ..."

His life, hanging in the balance at the moment, was in my hands! I prayed, "Oh God, grant to me a clear and precise understanding to convey what I need to ... to save his life!" I prayed fervently!

Suddenly, a sense of calm overcame me. I carefully interpreted for the doctors. I was confounded by how God had His way in the life of humankind.

Finally, the medical staff rolled me into a room on the fourth floor. In the distance, I saw the majestic Sierra Nevada Mountains in their glory. I had settled into my bed for less than five minutes when a nurse came rushing in.

"Tom, we need your help again."

"What time is it now?" I rubbed my eyes.

"There's no time to rub your eyes! It's 2:30 in the morning." A nurse put me in a wheelchair and off we went to the nurse's station, where I was handed a telephone. The human drama unfolded ...

"Moshi, moshi ... Hello." The familiar greeting was coming from overseas. It was the quivering voice of a

woman filled with fear. We exchanged the traditional greetings demanded by Japanese social codes, a first-time greeting between total strangers, even though we were in the midst of a crisis.

"*Kochira wa Okada desu ...*" The first thing that came to mind was, "How can I tell his mother of her son's true condition? He is lying in the ICU with his life in the balance, and no doctor has given any hope of quick or complete recovery."

Our conversation lasted for some time. I assured her we would give her good news. I recognized my helplessness and inability to comfort her with words. I was driven to accept human frailty.

Yet, there was consolation. I found that God, the Creator, was able to minister to her needs at this hour.

The next morning, the man's wife and I exchanged a few Japanese words at his bedside. Her eyes, swollen, and trembling with fear of the unknown, were her only means of communicating with the doctors and nurses in this strange land.

"The doctors would like you to join in a conference regarding Mr. Okada," the nurse requested of me. For the next several hours I was involved with doctors and nurses trying to make special arrangements with the hospital at the University of San Francisco. A decision was finally made to transfer him there at noon.

I was totally exhausted, having spent what I believed to be all my mental faculties. I felt nothing, and my energy was drained. Even though Mr. Okada was gone, I had no peace or relief.

"Tom, wake up," the nurse urged me, shaking me. "We have a call from Japan." I must have fallen asleep. It was 3:15 in the afternoon.

"*Moshi, moshi ...*" began the familiar telephone patter, as I told Mr. and Mrs. Okada their son was now in good hands at the University of San Francisco. I sensed relief as I told them a Japanese doctor and nurse would oversee him to full recovery.

"*Arigato gozai masu. Arigato gozai masu ...*"

I sensed they couldn't find the words to convey their hearts, to tell of their relief and gratitude. This overwhelmed me. In gratitude, I pondered the way God had put me in the path of someone whose heart needed to be touched by an unseen hand. I wished them Godspeed.

Only then did I feel relief, as if I'd been buried under tons of bricks. I had completely forgotten my own physical condition, the reason for my transfer to Memorial North Hospital. For three days and two nights I had been totally immersed in the needs Mr. Okada-san and his wife.

On my fourth morning in the hospital, the Thanksgiving spirit was high, and Darlene and the head nurse walked in.

"We have good news for you." Darlene practically grabbed my hand.

"Oh, Okada-san is all right?"

"Of course, he's in good hands." The head nurse took a step to my bedside. "I want to tell you that the doctor said he'll let you go home tomorrow."

"What do you mean? I'm discharged?" My voice raised an octave in disbelief.

"He couldn't find anything to keep you here."

"Nothing?" I shook my head. "Since I came here, you rolled me in and out of the surgery room to this room and the nurse's station. Did I get my needed rest? No! You deprived me of sleep for three nights. I had a single EKG and two X-rays after I drank icky white stuff. Now, you tell me I no longer need to be here. Are you telling me I'm discharged without knowing what was wrong?"

"Aren't you glad you really didn't have to find out?" Darlene asked, trying to ease the tension.

"Then, why in the world ..." Suddenly, I covered my mouth. Perhaps ... God had something to do with this. He has led me in so many different ways to touch and be touched by others in these years. Could it be?

"We want to know if there's any wish you have before you leave the hospital," inquired the head nurse. "You've been a great help to us and we want to thank you."

"You mean ... I could ask for anything?"

"Of course," she responded, with a bounce in her voice, reminding me of a child who had gotten her wish.

"All right ..." I smiled devilishly.

"No. Tom! You don't mean that ...?"

Darlene seemed shocked. Nevertheless, the head nurse granted me my wish.

Arrangements for my discharge were made. All required documents were signed. Now, I waited for my last meal before my ride home from the hospital.

With smiles covering theirr slight embarrassment, the head nurse and Darlene brought me a ribeye steak smothered with sautéed mushrooms, and my favorite blueberry pie and ice cream. It was almost obscene.

"Go ahead. Enjoy your gluttony, Tom. Until you get a stomachache," the head nurse laughed, her laughter echoing as she disappeared down the hallway.

While I enjoyed my steak dinner, licking a finger or two after nibbling a bone, Darlene said, "By the way, Tom, while you were busy yesterday with the Japanese man, Joyce stopped by to see you. She left a letter for you."

She handed me an envelope. I imagined it as another "dagger," another threat to my heart. I crumpled and stuck it in my pocket, deciding not to open it.

"Aren't you going to read it, Tom?"

I didn't answer.

Instead of going home directly, I persuaded Darlene and her husband, George, to put me up for the night. Darlene considered this payback for my helping out. But she did ask me why I didn't call my wife.

The next morning, finishing a traditional American breakfast, I thanked them for putting me up. Darlene then drove me home to Turlock, where I sneaked into my car and left to see friends in Fresno. The air seemed fresher and the sky bigger. The ground under me, though, moved with constant tremors like earthquake aftershocks.

I realized I was not quite physically ready to drive on the freeway. It was raining heavily and I had great difficulty keeping the car on the road. When I looked up into my review mirror, I saw a Highway Patrol officer chasing me, red light on and siren blaring. I pulled over to the shoulder of the road.

The officer asked for my license, returned to his car to use the radio, then came back to my window.

"Have you been drinking?" he asked. "You were weaving down the road for the last five miles."

I explained my medical situation, verified by the tags still on my wrist with my doctor's name, the date and medications. The officer again retreated to his car.

Finally, he escorted me about ten miles to a country shopping center in the nearest town. He was very personal and warm as we talked, and he made sure I took my pills. Then he wished me good luck and disappeared into the rain.

When I finally dragged myself to the front steps of my friend Bill's house in Fresno, it was nearly 9:00 p.m. I was shaking uncontrollably. A cup of hot homemade soup put a warm feeling in my belly, then I crashed into bed.

The next morning, as we sipped cups of coffee, Bill rebuked me for my indifference and my cold heart toward my wife.

"Bill, I didn't come here to listen to your sermon. I'm in no condition to accept your criticism kindly, if you know what I mean. I'm just recovering from a heart attack." A smirk crossed my face as continued, "If you're so interested in her, I suggest when she calls the next time you tell her I said thanks."

"Why don't you tell her yourself, Tom?" He was usually low key and sometimes irritated me with his slowness to act. He added, "Don't you owe it to her?"

I was very offended that he was defending my wife.

"Bill, you haven't any idea, do you? What I need now is somebody to hear my heartbeats—however faintly my heart is beating. I'm about to go down to the slaughterhouse with the indignity of losing my livelihood, and it seems I've passed beyond the point of buying back the honor and respectability of my family name. I can't stomach Joyce dissolving my restaurant!"

"What's the matter, Tom? To-o-o-om!" The last things I remember were feeling a sharp pain, gasping for air, grabbing my chest, and then Bill calling to his wife in the kitchen. I awoke in a room at St. Agnes Hospital in Fresno, after another heart attack or relapse. I got more medications and more instructions on how to behave myself. I would need absolute quiet and rest for the next couple of weeks.

The weekend of November 27, 1982 Joyce came to Fresno and brought our children with her. This was the second time all of our family had been together since my most recent heart attack. I saw weariness and dark shadows on Joyce's face. Yet she seemed to be holding up, displaying her dignity and inner beauty. For the first time, we were like two strangers, and said little to each other. I spent most of the day focusing on the children.

The doctor who interrupted us had a heavy accent, and his broken English amused me, reminding me of myself in my early days in America. He told me about my condition and of his talk with Dr. Davis in Turlock. I re-tuned my hearing to listen to what he had to say.

After everyone had left the room, I returned to deep thought. I couldn't reconcile myself to my wife's intention to end my business life, and the thought of divorce flashed, or perhaps resurfaced, before me.

That night, when Joyce asked if we could talk, I put up ten-foot walls before I agreed. Whatever she wanted to talk about, I knew my defense mechanisms could meet her challenge. I acted as I thought a strong man should.

"Honey, first I want you to know I'm willing to do anything," I said confidently. To myself I asked, "Hasn't she done enough already?"

"Can't you tell me what is in your heart?" she appealed. "I'm your wife. Don't I have the right to know?"

She certainly seemed to have no problem exercising her "rights" before asking me. Wouldn't I lose my business and livelihood? What more did she want, to finish me through another heart attack?

"Oh, I don't have anything to say that is important to you."

"No! It isn't true you don't have anything to tell. Perhaps you don't want to tell me. Don't treat me with silence, please!"

She was getting too close, and guarding my heart was a must! Why was I afraid to open the secret chamber of my heart to her? On the other hand, what chance did I have to measure up to her, when I was an immigrant without social status? My ministry had failed miserably, my business was sinking into the deep at a prodigious rate, and now I was in the hospital with recurring heart attacks.

"Joyce, it's obvious you and I are fundamentally incompatible. We have different cultures and philosophies that guide our lifestyles. We have more dissimilarities than similarities!" Our argument that night seemed endless.

The next morning, my daughter came to me and looked into my eyes. "Daddy, you don't need to go anywhere," she said. "I wish you would come home with us this afternoon. We know you've been sick and can't work. We'll take care of you." Bursting into tears, she hugged me with all her might. My two sons stood by my side, their silence telling me of their pained hearts. It was then that my heart finally opened to the letter I had received the day of my discharge from North Memorial Hospital. That lonely afternoon, I read:

November 11, 1992

Dear Tom,

I am truly sorry for the episode Monday night in the ICU room. I have stayed away for the last two days because I thought I would be a source of greater stress to you. I am deeply concerned for you in every way and I do care. As I have said before, you are still an important person to me. But too many issues have stood between us.

The restaurant is still open and we are doing our very best to carry on, as you would want it to be run. The children miss you, as I do. Many people are concerned for you and have asked about you.

Please accept my very basic feeling, stripped of all other entanglements, that I still care about you."

Signed, Joyce

Princess' face beamed like an angel's when I was persuaded by my children to return to Turlock.

"Daddy, you belong to us. Let's go home." All three children were anxious, and it was as if they had decided for me to go home with them.

Once again my wife had already signed the papers releasing me from the hospital.

In reality, I was tickled pink, happy as a clown, though somewhat embarrassed!

Oh, what a wretched man I am!

Chapter Eleven: The Return of the Butterfly

FOR CENTURIES the silkworm has been honored in Japan for producing the delicate fibers that result from its unique metamorphosis. It may be said that this small creature helped to weave many of the early threads in the fabric of commerce between east and west, beginning an intricate global trade relationship that continues to this day. It was the desire for silk and spices that first brought Europeans to China and Japan in the 13th century and eventually led to the discovery of the New World. The silkworm's gossamer treasure has been seen as a powerful symbol for the cultural sensibilities of the entire orient.

For me, it is the transformation of the insect itself—through its creation of something of beauty from the sacrifice of its own life—that holds special meaning and significance. As with the silkworm, is it not through self-sacrifice that, perhaps, we can go beyond the walls of our own ego, our own protective cocoon, and contribute our unique beauty to the great tapestry of humanity?

Crossing the Bay Bridge

My being ousted from the ministry has added inexhaustible fuel to my raging fire to fulfill the vow I made at my Father's gravesite—to take revenge on Americans. I am to be one of the featured speakers at the 40th Anniversary of the Hiroshima Bombing at Saint Mary's Cathedral in San Francisco, for the Anti-American War Rally. I am to give yet another "payback" speech—a speech about revenge. This may be the day I will execute my raging plan toward that revenge ... Americans must PAY! A mystical smile crosses my face.

When I left my home in Turlock, California, the midsummer sun was already dazzling the San Josequin Valley, from high over the Sierra Mountain range. Just as I was leaving, Joyce told me that I was exploiting Hiroshima, which gave me all the more reason, as if adding fuel to a raging fire, to justify my revengeful speech to myself. For what did she know about Hiroshima, this America-born

Chinese wife of mine? How I wished I had never married her! While gnashing my teeth like an angry ox, I wished I were married instead to Nakamura *Sensei*. She would have had a perfect understanding of my heartbeat.

My heart was gripped by a *tsunami*-like emotion as I condemned Americans for making peace by war! They had no idea what evil they had unleashed, killing masses of people with atomic bombs. "I pledge allegiance to the flag of the United States of America, and to the Republic ... for which it stands ... one nation, under God, indivisible with liberty and justice for all ... Give me your tired ... your poor, your hungry masses yearning to breathe free ... Send these, the homeless ... tempest-tost to me." Bah Humbug!

What liberty and justice for all? Americans will never begin to understand true peace until they have suffered like me! I was angry, trying to justify my longing for revenge for the Hiroshima bombing, wanting to avenge my Father's death.

Now exactly forty years later, my life was in shambles. No matter how hard I tried, I couldn't escape the ghosts of Hiroshima. I was marooned in a dark and bitter past. My decade-long struggle to overcome my obsession with vengeance and return home to honor my family name had become my "master." All I wanted was to destroy those who'd done this to me—the American people must suffer as I had suffered. No one had envisioned what the day might bring on August 5, 1985.

When I was about halfway across the Bay Bridge, my heart became confused and overwhelmed with thoughts as my mind focused on my message. I began to identify the Bay Bridge with the bridge that I had built, spanning the 40 years since my Father's death. Each beam shared the great weight of the bridge, as the weight of 40 years had burdened my life. As I whizzed by the angled trestles of the bridge, each one became a marker of time and space, reminding me of the chapters of my life, all consumed by the single emotion of REVENGE.

In the atomic ashes of Hiroshima, I had shamed my family name by scavenging garbage cans like a rat. My people, where once my family had preeminence, had called me an *Oyanashigo*, an outcast, and mercilessly shunned me. I had further disgraced the Tanemori name by failing at suicide when I was 16 years old. Then my vengeance plot against Americans had found me at a migrant labor camp picking fruit to feed my enemy.

Dusted with pesticide, surviving food poisoning, treated like a crazed monkey in a cage, this real live specimen of the bomb had survived the psychiatric ward! Then as a minister I had been rejected by congregations as a "Jap" who couldn't be a spiritual leader over white congregations. Later, heart attacks had stolen my restaurant, and all this time I had been unable to avenge my Father's death. Maybe my sister was right. I should never have left Japan, betraying the family name and selling my soul to live in America with the enemy that had killed my parents.

The clopping sound of my tires on sections of the Bay Bridge accompanied the reeled-off chapters of my life as I drove westward, approaching San Francisco. My eyes gazed, through 40 years of images of my life, slowly up to the horizon, and ...

The full gamut of emotions and thoughts, including feelings of hatred, love and compassion, came crashing through my head. Midway, I saw a strange mushroom-shaped cloud formation reflected by the morning sun. "Oh, God, no, not again!" I screamed. Suddenly, "How easy it is to return to Hiroshima," the *Voice* said softly. The hatred and revenge consuming my life surfaced. The thought of another atomic bomb instantly returned. I thought of that day in Hiroshima—"Judgment Day," August 6, 1945—this is the day Americans must pay!

I slammed the brakes of my car, as I was unable to continue; I pulled onto Treasure Island, parked by the side of the road and surrendered to my tears. Flashes of Hiroshima's *jii-gooo-kuuu,* hell, again flooded my mind—the smell of burning human flesh; skin dripping from arms, legs and faces; the bloody vomiting of the fleeing thousands; the shrieking cries of children. Standing alone between Heaven and Earth, "on this Spanning Bridge of Mankind," the past, present and future seemed painted across the sky in cinematic fashion. Since August 6, 1945, along with tens of thousands of other people, I had paid the awful price of the war. The last 40 years of my life flashed before my eyes.

As time elapsed ...

I wiped my bitter tears and streaming nose with one motion. Then, as I reached for the ignition, the transcendent vision of my childhood, on the night preceding The Bomb, in the dark bomb-shelter, crowded and hot with summer-steeped bodies, came flooding back. I remembered meeting the mythical white crane, *"Senba-zuru,* as Mighty as One Thousand Cranes." The *Senba-zuru* had slipped from my hands; as I was only a little boy in the second grade, I wasn't able to save the Crane from the enraged fireball and vortex. I had crumpled, in tears. When I awoke later, I saw that the fire had almost burned itself out, though embers were still swirling in the air. As I watched, these embers began to transform into orange-and-black Monarch butterflies. As they emerged, they created a symphony—an angelic chorus more beautiful than anything I had ever heard. Every fiber of my being began to sing with their glorious sound. The sky erupted with more and more butterflies, each heavenly creatures filling the sky like a magnificent multi-colored sunset. A white butterfly led the multitude of monarch butterflies, all dancing and surging in every direction. The memory of that dream was so vivid, I thought I was having it all over again.

In this returned vision, I saw many familiar faces.

I saw the face of Nakamura *Sensei* in the Kotachi village where I had survived postwar Japan. She was the one who stood for me during my adolescent years, going against traditional Japanese culture, risking her own social standing for me. She was the one who helped me experience what she called "lessons of the heart." In her arms, I learned the true meaning of *amae,* the sympathetic passion shared by a man and woman which never crosses the line, yet knows no limits. "It is sensitivity to the wonders of life," she had explained. "It connects everyone to each other; but its true meaning cannot always be easily seen. It must be experienced through living." It was as though she had transformed into *Ten-no-Shisha,* an angelic butterfly, and sang songs of compassion—swarming around, watching and protecting me.

I saw Tamura *Sensei,* who had rescued me from becoming a hooligan, steeling me to the challenge of swimming against the river's surge, while being true to myself. I saw the man whose tears were like my Father's, rekindling the *Samurai* spirit hidden deeply in my heart.

I saw the faces of my three children, "tender young shoots," when my heart was troubled as I lay in the ICU at Emmanuel Hospital. They had watched me vigilantly through the glass window separating two very different worlds, communicating with me through eyes that filled with jewels. There was no telling what society would do to them, if I committed irreconcilable and irreversible acts of revenge. What would I say to my parents' spirits if I caused my innocent children to suffer? I heard the *Voice,* "The iniquity of a father will be visited upon the children, even unto the third and fourth generations."

How could I, as a father, act irresponsibly and cause such a Judgment upon my children and their children, all innocent of guilt, for a crime they did not commit?

Then, suddenly, in the midst of my inner conflict, I saw the image of Mary Furr, the American nurse who had placed herself and her profession at risk by giving me her heart and tender love. She had salvaged my soul from the hands of Dr. Gallop, the Chief Witch-Doctor—I was nearly killed many times over—who had used me for research into the effects of radiation on the human body. It was as if he wore a black gown and carried a raised sharp sickle! Thank heaven I had been discharged into the tender care of Mary Furr. For the first time, I had felt hope!

Now I could see the seed of her unconditional compassion, which had been sown in my youth; at 19 years old, I had suddenly emerged into light with freshness of life. I could now see that hour of sudden germination, the bringing forth of new life that had lain dormant, waiting so long for spring ... to finally emerge from the deepest chamber of my soul.

As though it were a ray of glittering morning sun reemerging from a dark, thick summer cloud, piercing my ears, pricking my soul, came the voice of my Princess pleading. She appeared in this vision as a ten-year-old girl, entirely innocent.

"Daddy," she began, conveying simple, child-like understanding, "I know you have been living most of your life to get even with Americans, to deliver your REVENGE. I understand that you lost your daddy when you were younger than I am. I know it was hard for you to live without parents. But, daddy ..." Her eyes were piercing my soul. "... if you get *even* with Americans, some of them will come back and get even with us ... your children. They will hurt us, as you have hurt their children. Is that what you want? Is that how you get your satisfaction? Is that the way you want to fulfill the promise you made to your Daddy?"

She spoke a mouthful! "Oh, no, that is not what I want, for I just want American children to suffer like I ..." For the first time it dawned on me that it didn't matter whether the children suffering were American, or mine. They are all children, they are all my children. How could I, as an adult, take revenge on innocent children?

The *Voice* again came to me, "Recompense to no man evil for evil ... Avenge not yourselves, but rather give place unto wrath: for it is written, 'Vengeance is mine; I will repay, saith the Lord.' Therefore if thine enemy hungers, feed him; if he thirsts, give him drink, for in so doing thou shalt heap coals of fire on his head. Be not overcome of evil, but overcome evil with good."

"Daddy is there any other way?" my Princess asked, imploring deep into my heart and soul with teary eyes. It was the first time I realized that hatred begets hatred; anger begets anger; I was struck by the reality that revenge breeds revenge, for sure! I knew now that I would be followed by an eternal burden unless I did something to change my heart. I couldn't afford to pass down the consequences of revenge to my children. I struggled as I faced these truths. I saw myself naked, without pretense. Yet, in the deepest chamber of my soul, I was still crying out silently for revenge. Must I not fulfill the vow I had made over my Father's grave marker that I would, as the Number One Son's responsibility, avenge his death?

"Daddy is there any other way ..."
"Daddy is there any other way ..."
"Daddy is there any other way ..."
I covered my ears! Her pleading voice was piercing my heart and deep into my soul. I was at the crossroads, asking *Ishi no Ojizo-san,* which way should I turn? I cried out for the answer! "How I despair at this cursed fate of mine. As bitterness poisons these innocent children of mine, I madly waste way in this world of Revenge. Is there any Balm in the Gilead?"

I began to gain some enlightenment and human understanding. Now, the teaching of my Father became clear to me. Simply said, all actions have consequences and all action has to be taken to restore equilibrium in oneself, or life will forever be out of balance. It is wrong to act out of revenge, for an action can lead to an endless cycle of repeated actions and fruitless reactions. It is important to face the reality that another will take revenge in return.

I am literally at the crossroads ... I am at the spanning of the Bay Bridge between Oakland and San Francisco, draped with the backdrop of the Golden Gate Bridge standing as if it were opening its arms to tens of thousands of immigrants from the Far East. I ponder the reality of human drama unfolding before my eyes. I must admit that I have neither the ability nor the capacity to understand why the War was fought and to what end we sacrificed untold millions of innocent lives, both young and old, children and adults. Neither am I capable of judging whether war was ever the last human mechanism to bring a resolution between two conflicting nations.

The White Butterfly

As my soul teetered between two options, Revenge or Forgiveness, a White Butterfly flew through my open window, landed on my dashboard, and stayed there for some time, fluttering its iridescent wings, and gracing and pulsing with energy that I felt within. It was like the one I had seen in my dream 40 years before, like the one I had seen the afternoon with Mary Furr when she had allowed me freedom in the psychiatric hospital yard.

I heard the voice of the Crane, now a White Butterfly, shouting, "Takashi, remember who you are and follow your heart, no matter what!" The crane had shown me many horrors to come—loss, suffering, survival, renewal and transformation—images of a continual rebirth of life and spirit. And I also recalled the Crane's admonition that the *key* to survival was in my Father's words. "Takashi, remember the words of your Father. You are a son of a scion of a *Samurai* family; never forget who you are!" Then the White Butterfly had soared into the blue yonder against the glittering of the midmorning sun; it was like an ocean breeze, as free as a white cloud being borne away.

I returned to myself, with a sense of newness and freshness. I saw unmistakably and irrevocably that my enemies were not the Americans or Japanese society. The enemy was none other than me: the darkness of my own heart. For the first time, it all made sense to me. The dream had been waiting for me, as if it had lain dormant, deep within my soul, for four decades. The White Butterfly had become a heavenly angel that brought about my inner transformation. All my resentment, bitterness, anger and consuming desire for vengeance toward Americans and Japanese society paled against the overwhelming love I felt as the White Butterfly touched my heart with its "magical" power. It seemed as though the "energy" of the butterfly had removed the clay that had blinded my eyes for the past 40 years. It was only then that I felt, for the first time, that an immense burden had been taken away.

At last, I had found peace within myself, with Americans and with my own people, and with the "white man's" God.

I wonder to myself: how many "butterflies" are flapping their wings, desiring to touch the hearts of the children of the world?

When I was able, I continued on my way to the Rally. There, I mounted the podium. As my eyes swept the auditorium, I saw many eager faces anticipating my revengeful cry for "justice" ... But I had to share how this seemingly insignificant Butterfly had tipped the teeter-totter to the side of forgiveness. It seems beyond human capacity to fathom how my about-face could have any importance in the pages of human history, after the Event that shattered the lives of untold millions, but now I had seen that the whole world would have a chance to be healed and changed forever.

As a result of my returned dream, my message was now clear and simple. We can settle human conflicts and differences, national enmity, ethnic hatred, cultural and individual divisiveness ... without resorting to violence or war ... without the path of endless cycles of revenge. I threw away my notes and *for the first time spoke only of peace and forgiveness*. At St. Mary's Cathedral in San Francisco, at the commemoration of the 40th anniversary of the Hiroshima bombing, I finally cleansed my soul and experienced the deep transformation of inner peace. I realized that the "path" of Hiroshima, however emblematic, had brought me, at last, home to my real promise to my Father ... to a place called *Peace through Forgiveness* ... through an inner spiritual transformation. I also realized that if the human race is to survive, we all need to fight the last battle, the most difficult one of all: *learning to forgive* and making peace with our own hearts and our own pasts!

The peace for which the world is longing is only accomplished by individuals who experience what true "peace" is: what the Japanese people call experiencing *Kokoro no Yasuragi—Yutori,* the inner peace.

> *We honor this passage through darkness;*
> *we must have courage to enter*
> *the darkness of our own hearts—again and again,*
> *emerging with the gift of new life.*
> *Healing only comes through learning to forgive*
> *and making peace with our painful past.*
> *We will find the path to victory ...*
> *Then, I shall whisper, as a survivor of Hiroshima,*
> *"I have not lived in vain!"*

Postscript

In looking at my life, I have come to understand that just as the butterfly—*kaiko*, silkworm—creates something of beauty from its own sacrifice and transformation, so we can make a better world. Hiroshima remains a part of me: my body bears the scars of Hiroshima, and suffering and memories will live with me forever. My agony throughout all these years will never be forgotten, but it is forgiven!

I won't ever forget a cotton blanket I brought over from Japan when I immigrated to America for revenge. (I kept it as a visible reminder of the horrors of sufferings and sacrifices I once experienced—I still have it in my possession.) It is now old and tattered, but it has been transformed into something beautiful and warm. It covers me with the warmest heartbeats of countless Americans who helped me to rise above the bitter personal feelings I held for so long, and to keep my heart alive with compassion and understanding for the sufferings of others—turning my life "from revenge to forgiveness."

The years indeed have ways of healing wounded souls; time had its way of molding and shaping the life of this survivor of Hiroshima. Countless human dramas have unfolded; my life was being designed and prepared by the Designer for greater purposes—toward global peace. The result is like threads of many colors, adding to an iridescent tapestry of human dignity.

Chapter Twelve: Saving Humpty

THE NEXT year and a half were what I call the "silent" years of my life.

I was recovering from my heart attacks, while struggling to rise from the shame and disgrace of losing my precious restaurant business. I expected to never again feel the fresh breeze, or hear the chirping of birds, or smell the fragrance of wildflowers, or see the bright sun.

In mid-October of 1994, my friend Merv Amerine brought a whole turkey, 40 pounds worth of "America's native bird," and flopped it right down on a table, scaring the heck out of me.

Mr. Amerine, the Manager of the California Turkey Industry Board, was a favorite former client of my Japanese Garden Restaurant, where we'd spent many precious moments together. His patronage had turned into a personal friendship over the course of three years. Merv's surprising visit was a shot in my arm, as though I had rediscovered a lost black pearl of great price.

"Merv! What are you thinking? Have you gone mad? What's the meaning of this?" I sputtered in one breath, pointing to the fowl object before me.

"Slooow down, Thomas," he smiled mischievously.

"What are you going to do with that bird?" I asked.

He looked at me with a quizzical smile and said, "That's your problem! I need to pick your brain."

"Waaait a minute. What did you say?" I knew what it meant when someone said 'I have a bone to pick with you.' But, I never knew anyone wanted to pick my brain, something the size of a *suzume*, a sparrow!

As an *Itamae-san,* a Japanese master-chef, who had to learn such dishes as *fugu*—the deadly blowfish that, if not handled correctly, can poison diners—I was not a "perfect" chef. But so far I hadn't killed anyone.

As I soon discovered, Merv was wondering, perhaps facetiously, if turkey could be made a staple in the diet of the mysterious East.

In Japan, turkey is known as *shichi-men-cho*, a seven-faced bird. This is because the bird's wattle (the flesh dangling from its throat) changes colors according to its temperament and mood.

As far as I know, the Dutch or Portuguese missionaries and merchants who introduced new religions, new lifestyles and new ideas to Japan, may have also introduced the turkey. The Japanese were not opposed to the turkey itself, but they had strong feelings against the foreigners who brought it to Japan.

The Japanese thought these foreigners were "two-faced" people, deceitful and traitorous in their zeal to convert recalcitrant Japanese "heathens" to their beliefs. After all, missionaries and priests had been sent to countries that western kings wished to conquer. Japan had watched the Spanish conquest of the Philippines and had faced similar consequences when foreigners under the "mask" of missionaries, came to overtake Japan during the Tokugawa Shogunate. This resulted in the Shogun implementing the *Sakoku* Policy (seclusion from the known world) for more than 265 years, to keep foreigners from the shores of Japan. The turkey had thus come to represent the embodiment of deceit, trickery and untruthfulness.

Merv was asking me to use the turkey to create a delicacy "worthy of the Emperor."

"What an insult it would be to 'We the Japanese,'" I said to myself. I should have had my head examined before accepting such a challenge!

Many "radical" ideas of the 16th century have now been accepted in Japan, but the turkey never became part of the staple Japanese diet. I knew that to make turkey pleasing to the Japanese palette, the bird needed to be disguised as anything but turkey. This would require not only a great deal of experimention in my kitchen, but also a "miracle."

My entire house soon became filled with an unbearable stench of turkey. My children became my guinea pigs. A few days before Thanksgiving, pinching their noses, they marched into the kitchen together, wanting to know the latest. "Daddy, are you still trying to make something out of that bird?" they asked.

"Patience! Patience, my dear children! You'll be surprised to see this bird soon become *obake*, a ghost, and transform into something 'out of this world.'"

"But Daddy," my daughter pleaded, "Would you please let us have a traditional American Thanksgiving turkey instead of *obake*? This is not just for me, but for my brothers and Mommy."

"Why Mommy? I thought she liked what daddy is doing?"

"Oh daddy. She hasn't told you?" Nathan blurted out.

Finally, the day came to present 18 different dishes to the California Turkey Board's Promotional Committee. My success that day led me to my weirdest career yet, as "Turkey Tom" or the "*Samurai* Chef." I often appeared with a sword-swinging, stand-up cooking routine that landed me steady trade show and TV assignments in both America and Japan.

While doing "my thing" at an International Food Show in San Francisco, someone picked up on my creativity. An employee with the California State Secretary for Agriculture persuaded me to prepare a luncheon for Governor Deukmejian's cabinet. Using California food products, I would arrange turkey *sushi*, spelling "Duke" on the serving table.

I converted the "seven-faced" bird, disguising its "look, smell and taste," into a palatable Japanese meal, all the while amusing the Governor's cabinet by singing and dancing.

I thus became an official emissary of California goodwill and agricultural products to the Pacific Rim. My tasks included promoting and showcasing California food products, including wines, throughout the Philippines, Singapore, Hong Kong, and the Japanese cities of Kobe and Tokyo. My "Orient Tour" was sponsored by California's State Export Program.

Talk about "Turkey Tom"—I wore traditional Japanese costumes at a reception in Sacramento, in preparation for sailing to the Far East, the new frontier. I started by flying First Class on United Airlines, at government expense, to the Philippines. From the port of Cebu, I boarded the "Golden Bear," the ship of the California Maritime Academy. It had been transformed into a luxury floating restaurant and ballroom for receptions with government officials and business leaders on our tour of the East. In fourteen receptions, eight of which were in Japan, we would serve an average attendance of 500 VIPs. And Turkey Tom would work day and night, at each reception.

A large reception was organized in Kobe, the city where I had worked almost thirty years before. I had the honor of serving government and industry officials in a city where I had once been disgraced by being fired.

In Japan food speaks the language of the heart—a language of human relationships, based upon trust. I felt an ever-deepening sense of the value of food as a tool of diplomacy, and my array of food became nothing short of a tour de force, demonstrating "the language of the heart."

Before I left Japan, I paid my respects, quietly visiting my Father's grave without letting my sister, Satsuko, know that I was home.

As a result of the Golden Bear Goodwill Pacific Rim Tour, I was awarded a grant of $30,000 from the State of California, to explore and expand U.S. business in Japan. I began a two-year contractual assignment in Tokyo as a cultural consultant with a renowned Japanese company, making me the envy of some of my competitors.

As the saying goes, a picture is worth a thousand words, and a picture of me with the Governor of California, splashed about in Japan, made me an instant celebrity in my home country.

The panoramic view from the top of a mountain is great, and the freshness of the air "up there" can be clean and aromatic. But a fall from such heights, if not fatal, can cause great injury. Not unlike "Humpty-Dumpty" my climb to the mountain top was followed by a great fall. This fall proved again to be a health issue, a swift decline none of the king's men, nor any doctor, could heal.

"Today, the doctor told me I am going blind."

I wrote these words in my diary in 1987, then took out a small, faded picture of my Father. I desperately needed to look at him once more. Seeing the image of him dressed in a *kimono* emblazoned with the family crest had anchored my heart through many storms, reminding me that I was the firstborn son of the Tanemori family, heir to the family name.

My growing blindness came as a long-term consequence of the explosion on the fatal morning of August 6, 1945.

"Will I ever leave Hiroshima behind?" My faith in life was once again being tested!

In Japanese culture, I was no longer a "complete person." I was "less" than others, with shame and guilt, and bearing the "social sin" of that distinctive difference. To be disabled is a social taboo in Japan, and I couldn't escape from judgments that my incipient blindness was nothing but my "sins" finally catching up with me. The unspoken Japanese social code was swiftly imposed to keep me out of the eyes of the public.

I had become an eternal embarrassment on three counts—for becoming an American, then a Christian, and now disabled.

The world quickly closed in, like the shutter of a camera, leaving an ever-narrowing tunnel of light that would eventually shrink to a pinhole. Over time, less and less light would penetrate the dark and reach the film. I had no way to defend myself from the change, and could only succumb to fate. As a result, a brief one-way message from the Japanese company terminated my contract, and, as the only way available to "save" their honorable face, I found myself at Narita International Airport.

While wiping the clouds from my eyes, just before boarding the plane back to California, I thought I saw Nakamura *Sensei* in the form of elderly woman. She was waving goodbye to someone walking through the boarding gate. I saw tranquility in her soft jade eyes, as her lips parted and seemed to form the words *"Takashi-kun."*

On the long flight back home, sitting deep in my seat, I couldn't shake the vision of that woman. Whether I had seen her with my eyes or my heart made no difference. All I felt was pain in my past and all I saw was darkness in my future. I looked at my Father's photo again and again with my diminishing vision.

The freedom of personal mobility that most Americans take for granted is denied to the blind. And a person with a sight disability who is not mobile also faces a loss of economic independence.

The American lifestyle is largely dependent on automobile accessibility. As my sight worsened, I eventually had to abandon driving—first at night, and then later during the day. More often than not, my life was dependent on a "sighted person." Frequently, I felt I was at the mercy of "sighted" people, like a leaf caught in a whirlwind, twirling aimlessly, never finding a resting place.

"Is there any way or anyone who could make the sun stand still!" I cried out. My world became darker and darker, causing me to bump into street signs, fire hydrants, telephone poles, newspaper vending machines, and trash cans, on streets everywhere. I also began stumbling into potholes and curbs, groping through a maze of twilight-becoming-night, unable even to freely and safely ride unfriendly public transportation. My personal esteem and sense of self-worth also suffered.

Then, one day, like a flash through the sky, I felt as if I had emerged from a dark cave into sunlight, nearly blinding me again. I was ecstatic with hope about changes in the American Disability Act (ADA). Yet the main thrust of the ADA was to create a more friendly environment for "wheel-chair-bound" people.

In America, it's said that the squeaky wheel gets the greas. But I detest the notion that those who are sight-impaired have to "squeak" to get attention! I thought there was more compassion in the world than that! And blind people are very much left "in the dark."

I soon experienced the shock of discrimination because of my disability. It started with exclusion from many normal activities, but grew to include harassment and cold rejection. The life of the visually impaired is a life of frustration and anger, and can also be one of isolation, alienation and loneliness.

I was devastated when I lost gainful employment and suffered the humiliation of having to depend on meager Social Security disability payments for mere existence. Having human dignity denied, while receiving "assistance" from the hands of Government workers who think *they* are the ones extending a merciful hand when it is clearly the kindness of countless taxpayers ... I swallowed my pride even though I wanted to vomit on them!

Having been called in many times, for argument after argument, I was once again called into the local Social Security office for reassessment of my financial status. I really didn't think much of this. After all, how could anyone live "high on the hog" on $600.00 per month?

Mr. Paine, the assigned caseworker, sat looking at me over narrow glasses resting at the end of his nose. I could see a thick paper-clipped file on his desk.

"I understand we are giving you extra support in terms of food stamps, Mr. Tanemori?"

"Yes, Sir. You know that I have been getting them and you have something right there in your file telling you that I do. Why did you have to ask me?" Maybe I shouldn't have said that—I felt a cold air quickly sweep his tiny cubicle, oppressing me.

"How have you been using them?"

"What do you mean, how I have been using them?" I asked indignantly. "Of course, I took them to a local grocery store. Do you think I went to a ball game?"

"What did you buy ...?" His inquiring voice was like an icicle dripping from a crypt.

"Mr. Paine! Do I have to answer your question?"

"You haven't bought anything forbidden by law?"

I stared at him.

"Mr. Tanemori. Please ... I want you to answer me."

He looked even worse than he sounded. What do we say in America? A dog's bark is worse than his bite? There is no question that I had either hit the central nerve of this government worker, injuring his self-acclaimed "pride," or that it appeared to him that I disdained his authority.

"Well, the food stamps I received were mine and at my disposal. I exercised my good judgment to buy ... whatever I could buy with those stamps. For example, vegetables, fruits and meats ... and ... daily neccess ..."

"Mr. Tanemori," he interrupted intolerantly, "What kind of meat did you buy?"

Oh boy! He was really anxious to know! Or, maybe, just maybe, he was genuinely interested in my affairs.

How I wished I had an unused package of food stamps in my hand to throw into his face! Then and there I decided what to say, for my own self-respect was far more important than dignifying his "authority." Although I welcomed any assistance for my survival, after only three short months, it was just too long for my sanity!

"Mr. Paine," I said, "you can have your blankety-blank program back!"

My steps toward the door, then out of his office, were very deliberate, leaving his voice, beckoning me to come back, bouncing off his office walls. So the life of a "blind"—disabled person goes on!

Whether or not my ill behavior to Mr. Paine got back to the Office of the Executive Social Security Service Department or not, several weeks later I was summoned to meet Mrs. Ganzalouz, the Regional Director. As I walked in, an aged, austere-looking woman, in a chair behind a massive desk, waited for me.

"Mr. Tanemori," Mrs. Ganzalouz didn't even take a moment to return my greeting, instead zeroing in on me. "How much money do you have?"

"Mrs. Ganzalouz. Do you mind if I sit down and catch my breath? I also would like to situate *Michi*, my guide dog."

I felt her impatience to get to the "bottom" of whatever she was after.

"Ma'am. How much money do I have? Is that what you asked me?" I stared at her as she flipped through my file, not even bothering to look at me.

"You know better than to ask me. You know exactly how much I get from Social Security each month. It's a miracle I still exist!"

"What I mean, Mr. Tanemori, is how much money do you have in your pockets right now?"

"It doesn't matter how much I have in my pockets! It's not your business, Ma'am!"

"Mr. Tanemori. I want you to cooperate with us. We have the power to terminate tha ..."

"Wait a moment. What do you mean, 'we'? Who is this 'we' that has power to terminate the payments?"

She shook her pencil as if to challenge me.

"I have a couple of dollars and some odd change, I think." I stuck my hand into my pocket and jingled the few coins there.

"Would you take them out and put them here on the desk so that I can verify them?"

I yanked at *Michi* as I stormed out of the office. Then I sat at the curbside and wept bitterly.

For me, it was more than constrained physical movement or the ill affect on my financial and economical independence. I could not and I would not allow these "powers that be" to take away my personal pride and human dignity. After eight long months of rage, depression, dissolution, and then denial, I had to ask myself: how long would I allow myself to wallow in shame, disgrace and guilt which I didn't bring upon myself?

Then I recalled seeing, as a nine-year-old boy, a single blade of grass emerging from the ruins of Hiroshima, an image which has helped hold my heart together, inspiring me to live through the postwar era. The memory of that single blade of grass would again help me move forward. I became determined to treat my "disability" as a spur to positive achievement. I also became mindful of the fact that I might have been knocked down, but I was not defeated! I would not allow public indifference and labyrinthine bureaucracy to deny me living my life to the fullest.

I knew then, having survived Hiroshima, that going blind wasn't the end of the world. There wasn't any reason I couldn't get through this. I remembered the words of my

Father, who instilled his truths in my heart, "The greatest victory is conquering your own weakness! Learn to use *tekii-akugyaku*—use misfortune to create good."

My attitude began to shift to a positive approach to life when I learned about the Russian Winter Food and Medicine Relief Campaign. Without a second thought, I joined this campaign to Karafuto in the Sakhalin Islands. This experience gave me the opportunity to find ways to heal the hearts and minds of Russian people. I tried to guide myself with a white cane through the vastness of Siberia and onto Karafuto in the Sakhalins.

It was painful to witness the Russians' dark memories of suffering at the hand of the Japanese Imperial Military. I heard gruesome testimonies of physical inhumanity indelibly marked in their hearts.

In one building, converted into a museum, I saw exhibits depicting the horrors of war. I wanted so much to mend the past and look to the future. I reached out to many children, clothed in tatters and hungry, in the streets and in parks, seeing myself in their place. I relived searching for food like a rat, prowling dumpsites in the aftermath of Hiroshima.

Unable to communicate with language, we tried to share our hearts by distributing food and medicine to various hospitals and institutions. I was overwhelmed by the generosity and graciousness of many Russians, in spite of the fact that I am Japanese.

I came home with a full spirit for the good the relief program was accomplishing, but physically battered. During my efforts, I often stumbled and fell flat on the streets, and was often unable to maneuver in the vast, unfamiliar environment to successfully complete my expected tasks.

Coming home, I faced the reality of life for those inflicted with vision loss. One day, I witnessed with my dimming vision a middle-aged woman bumping into a pole and falling. She quickly rose up, brushed herself off, then stumbled into some trash cans and fell flat on her face on a platform. Many passengers walked by, but nobody lent a compassionate hand to her, nor asked if she was alright.

I don't think it was her physical pain, but injury to her personal pride that made her right herself, and without brushing off, disappear down the stairway.

I felt overwhelmed by a need for people to be delivered from social crimes against the blind. We need to live with dignity and nobility and a purpose in life. I wanted to return to the mainstream of society, making contributions as I had done in the past, as sighted people do.

If there was to be any hope of living a "normal" life, two factors presented themselves. First, how could I mobilize myself and safely navigate the streets of our nation, as comfortably as sighted people do? Secondly, how could I use public transportation, *unassisted,* with confidence and a sense of freedom? My hope was to be less dependent on others for assistance, so that I could concentrate on becoming a productive member of society.

My challenge from visual impairment became less—at first, due to a white cane, and then later because of my guide dog, Michi.

It took Michi, a white Labrador, and me nearly three months of learning each other's moods and temperaments before we became bound by spirit and love. I am quite aware that Michi went through the greater adjustment in learning to deal with me. If she could only have verbalized her feelings, she would have told me many things. For my sanity, it's probably better for me not to know!

Michi had now become my great companion and partner. She knew when to avoid me, still keeping her eyes on me from a distance. We each felt the other's need for TLC, tender loving care, and this became expressed by my calling and petting her, and by Mishi's tail-wagging and hand-licking. Of course, all this came with great responsibilities and liabilities.

How wonderfully my life changed with Michi! I had a new gift of independence, as I required far less assistance from sighted people in most daily activities. But unfortunately, Michi couldn't always successfully help me cross difficult intersections, easily use public transit, or navigate new, unfamiliar routes unless I give her a command to go from point "A" to point "B," and then from point "B" to point "C."

It became clear to me that "mechanical eyes," or some device that would give me specific details and feedback about my route, public conveyances and possible obstructions, would be of great help.

This information would not only boost my safety, but would give me a degree of self-confidence and a sense of freedom. I knew there had to be some kind of device to help visually impaired and blind people get around. My specific needs were: (1) Navigation: knowing where I was and how to get to where I needed to go. (2) Public Transportation Identification: the ability to quickly and accurately identify public transportation vehicles. (3) Collision Avoidance: detecting and avoiding physical obstacles. (4) Emergency summons: for personal safety and confidence, linking and transmitting distress calls to emergency services.

One day, I saw the "light." After all, we have enormous capabilities, demonstrated by landing men on the moon, by sending space shuttles thousands of miles away and bringing them back safely, and by navigating submarines successfully through the vast, unknown depths of the ocean.

How wonderful it would be if we could apply our enormous communications knowledge and technology to help blind people navigate their smaller but equally mysterious dark environment.

With renewed zeal, I proposed a system I called the "SmartCity" Guidance System. It would be similar to self-guided tours at many museums, using radio frequencies to guide visitors up and down corridors. I imagined the possibility of an *"environment"* actually talking to us, telling us what lies ahead, and how to get to where we need to go, and letting us know where we are at any given point! My conceptualized guidance device could be installed in the handle of a cane or a guide dog's harness.

I was convinced such a system would allow people with disabilities to return to mainstream society, contributing once again, with human dignity.

However, I was plagued by my lack of engineering knowledge and the financial resources required to fund such a project. I realized I could not move forward unless a miracle took place.

Such a miracle occurred! On February 17, 1994, I was directed to meet US Congressman Bill Baker, representing the 10th District of California, to discuss my proposed guidance system. He arranged a meeting with engineers, scientists and the Deputy Associate Director of the Lawrence Livermore National Laboratory (LLNL).

I was determined to move forward with the project, clutching to my heart the words of Mr. Anthony K. Chargin, the Deputy Associate Director of LLNL. He had addressed the House Committee on Public Works and Transportation, Subcommittee on Investigations and Oversight of "Intelligent Vehicle-Highway System' (IVHS) on July 21, 1994, saying in part:

"The Cold War having ended, the mission of Lawrence Livermore National Laboratory has changed. LLNL is addressing a host of urgent issues, among which are economic competitiveness, energy security and environmental cleanup, as well as science education. Transportation plays a major role in these areas and LLNL is motivated to help solve some of the problems using its broad arrange of resources and technical core competencies. The Lab has been working for Caltrans in developing and bringing solutions to transportation-related problems."

"Inspired by ideas from Mr. Thomas Tanemori, requested by Congressman Baker, and the passage of the Americans with Disabilities Act (ADA), passed in 1990, the Lab has studied the proposal and has made some changes and improvements to the approach. It is quite do-able. LLNL is investigating various techniques and technologies that could be applied to assist the visually impaired ... Putting intelligence into public transit systems presents an opportunity to assist the disabled and visually impaired. LLNL is very happy to participate in this socially and economically important activity."

What was both ironic and incredible was that I had found hope from such an unlikely source. Lawrence

Livermore National Laboratory, a forefather of the Manhattan Project, was one of the pre-eminent Cold War bomb factories. The Lab was working to develop an electronic Targeted Advanced Guidance System, with the acronym TAGS. The Lab renamed it *SmartCity* to reflect the peaceful use of military technology.

As proposed, *SmartCity* had universal usability—the system would operate indoors, underground, and in any urban geographical setting. *SmartCity* also had global usability—the same system could be standardized to operate in any country in the world, and in any language.

"If it takes off, it's going to be akin to cell phones," said Tom Moore, the Lab's Senior System Engineer. It could help millions of blind and visually-impaired people, allowing them to ride a bus or train, visit a doctor, go shopping, or take in a ball game.

What a great drama this was for me, to be part of a military-peace conversion project. It seemed nothing short of a triumphant experience in the life of a *Hibakusha*.

In search of funds for the proposed project, Congressman Baker invited Anthony Chargin, Tom Moore, who had been working as a volunteer on the project, and myself to Washington D.C. to testify before the US Congressional Subcommittee on July 21, 1994.

We then waited for the next four years, all the while seeking possible interest in the project by the Transportation Committee. We appealed to the heart of the President of the United States, and to California's legislators. Yet, in spite of all our efforts, the funds never materialized and LLNL decided to discontinue work on the project.

So I was back in "darkness." Was I disappointed? Of course I was! Was I discouraged? Of course I was! Have I been defeated? Of course not! This was only a challenge.

If one door closes, there must be a window. Losing my sight was a blessing in disguise. People often complain about disabilities, then use them as a crutch. But I am blessed, because I have an opportunity to be touched by others. And in turn, I'm able to touch and reach them.

More importantly, after years of dealing with suffering, emotional darkness and, now, a crippling physical disability, I finally understand that "the way" can only be found by moving beyond our own pain and the walls of our differences, our own cocoons, to help others.

Only by looking with "a vision of the heart" was I, at last, truly able to "see." There is another world of mine, and how different it seems, for its wonder, to have been discovered.

My Partner, on My Left

This world of mine, however brightly,
I thought, once my eyes caught it,
with all its glitter and beauty,
reflected by the morning sun.

For the moments of time,
I feared, I'd lost them all.
When my eyes refused to behold the sunset,
a promised dream for tomorrow.

But now, I see another world of mine,
and how different it seems
for its wonder to be discovered,
with "my partner on my left."

Chapter Thirteen: From Ikebana to Bonsai

CONVENTIONAL wisdom told me that what happened in my "yesterdays," stumbling and floundering in the darkness from my loss of eyesight, would keep happening in my "tomorrows." My mobility, my personal and financial independence would all be affected. I faced the reality that my world was getting darker and smaller. Moving to Lafayette, California was my exasperating attempt to seek out a new direction for myself.

My struggles and fear of the future seemed unnoticed by the grinding wheels of the world. Summer had passed and dancing leaves told me the deep fall season would soon be over. The thought of white blankets covering the Sierra Nevada mountains chilled my spine!

One afternoon, I received a letter from Mr. Sam Goldstein, owner of Eureka Northwest Lumber Company. In part it said:

Thank you for your time on the phone this week. It was a pleasure to learn of your interesting (and varied) background. I look forward to exploring the possibility of being a part of your future.

It is the company's intention to sell [the products] as directly as possible ... to the Japanese. And it is felt that this direct contact with them will increase company profits and improve communication channels ... And it is at this point, Mr. Tanemori, that [my company] will present an opportunity for an individual who can speak Japanese, communicate well, and sell [the products] to Japanese manufacturers.

Signed, Sam Goldstein

While contemplating his offer, the differences between the business cultures of Japan and America became obvious to me! Having marketed California agricultural products in the Pacific Rim, I had invaluable experience, especially in Japan. I was acutely aware that lasting business relationships were entirely dependent on understanding Japan's people, their enigmatic culture, and their business principles. In a nutshell, a business relationship was built on friendship and mutual trust, elements valued more than pricing or profit margins.

I seized this opportunity as a Godsend. However dimming my vision, for my own survival, I needed to keep practicing my cultural business consulting.

Was I crazy? What did I know about the lumber business? I may have exceeded my modesty, but I was confident I could optimize my educational and dual-culture business background to develop a lasting market for Eureka Northwest Lumber Company.

But would the lumber company owner understand the madness to my method, especially when the bottom line was king?

After a cup of coffee, I left home with my briefcase at eight o'clock in the morning for my first meeting with Mr. Goldstein in Sacramento. My briefcase was brimming with corporate letters, newspaper clippings and documents, verifying at a glance who I was and the work I had done as a cultural consultant for U.S./Japan Business Development.

Entering the main lobby of the downtown Holiday Inn, I saw a couple dozen white American businessmen, several businesswomen, and a half dozen Asians, whom I suspected were neither tourists nor Japanese, for they lacked cameras around their necks.

Seeking Mr. Goldstein, I presumed that he was Jewish, and from the deep-voiced proprietor I had heard on the phone, I surmised he might be in his mid-fifties, large, well-built and rugged: a typical American lumberjack.

I waited anxiously for a man matching this image, walked around the lobby, to the main entrance, the returned to the front desk to check for messages. We should have met 15 minutes before, and I despised anyone treating an appointment so lightly!

On the other hand, I wondered whether Mr. Goldstein was fuming, looking for a Japanese man who hadn't shown up at the appointed time. Although I was fifty-one, I could pass as younger than forty.

Finally, I wrote "Mr. Goldstein" on a yellow legal pad, parading it around the lobby, until a man at the front desk, in the process of asking a clerk to page me, raised his eyebrows in confirmation. We both apologized for our mistaken perceptions of each other!

Mr. Goldstein and I seemed to hit it off, each being impressed with the other enough for a working relationship, and I began consulting for Eureka Northwest Lumber.

My work in the "lumber trade" started with building a database for the company's target market. I created the list by poring through a two-inch-thick volume of Japanese manufacturers, provided by the Japanese External Trade Organization (JETRO), an arm of Japan's Commerce Department. My plan was to send an "official" introduction of myself to these companies.

At first, I spent much effort guarding my heart, as well as keeping my impending loss of vision secret. Meanwhile, Sam Goldstein kept reminding me that I was a liability and financial burden to the company. He said, "Do you have any idea how hard I had to work to get to where I am today; and how hard I worked to get you here against the judgment of Jeff (Jergenstein), my Vice President?"

"Yes! Yes!" I replied. "Money does not grow on trees! The bottom line is PROFIT!" I said this half-jokingly.

I began to see Sam's face turn a slightly darker shade of pink, then red, as we traded similar comments each day, creating volatility in our relationship.

"*Urusai na! Wakkate iru! Damatte dokokani itte kure yo. Omae tachi no kao wa mitaku nai!* I've had enough of your jabbing. I don't want to see your face right now. Just go away, please!"

My comments in Japanese were delivered with a smile and gentle physical gestures that he surely took as my appreciation of him. I felt I needed to impress Sam with my business knowledge, without insulting his intelligence.

"All right Mr. Goldstein," I pleaded earnestly, "I have no intention of putting a premium on myself. You are so right that I know nothing about the lumber business. But one thing you should know is that I do know how to deal with the Japanese. I know who they are, as I am!"

"Thomas! It's no longer Mr. Tanemori!"

"Sam," I recognized that he wanted us to be on a first-name basis, "I'm happy to make thousands of calls for you. But cracking the Japanese market is dependent on understanding and closely following the practices of Japan's business hierarchy. No foreign company will enter or survive, much less succeed, otherwise."

I explained the principles I thought would build business in Japan to Sam:

(1) We need see ourselves as the Japanese see us. We need to decide whether or not we are willing to be seen as the Japanese see us.

(2) We must understand who the Japanese are: their enigmatic business culture and ethics, the codes integral to life in Japan. One key example: the Japanese operate by group approval. No one dares to be different.

(3) By and large, the Japanese are more sensitive than Americans to personal criticism. The Japanese may experience a high degree of shame from face-to-face criticism and will do almost anything to "save face." In extreme cases, Japanese reaction could be as severe as suicide or a lifetime devoted to seeking revenge.

(4) In order to honor the Japanese, we must follow the proper business protocol. That is to say, the company President should "officially" introduce me to his Japanese employees. This introduction should include my title, rank and a sign of "authority" that I represent my company. This serves as a portfolio, as much as a business card, showing my authority to handle any business transaction.

I explained to Sam that a "cold approach" to Japanese business was absolutely taboo, or suicide! Though I may have sounded rebellious, I told Sam I wouldn't make any calls until my four business principles were honored.

Everything in the office seemed to fly in every direction when Sam screamed, "Mr. Tanemori, do you have any idea what you're saying? Don't you know Americans do not meekly submit ourselves and let blankety-blank Japanese walk all over us? Who do you think you are? I should have known that you are blankety-blank Japanese more than you think. I should have known!" Sam said all this while gesturing as if pulling out his thin hair.

"Ah, Soooo, my Highness! I knew it! Oh, I knew it!" teased Vice President Jeff Jergenstein, as he entered the office. "You want a title? You want to be a big shot! What title do you want?"

"That's right, Jeff!" I responded. "I want you to present me as the big shot. Make me as big as you can, for the sake of your company. If it's done in accordance with Japan's business culture, the rest will come as easy as pie. I guarantee the results you seek, with a bottom line of profit."

I realized that neither Sam nor Jeff, as they both laughed, had any idea what I meant. And Sam again drove home his point, "What must we do to convince you that making money is the only reason we're in this business? Let me say it again, I want you to make these calls tonight!"

"Sam, if you want to make money by dealing with blankety-blanks, as you call them, I will do that for you after I am officially introduced."

Sam rose from his chair, "Thomas, you're testing my patience. I did not hire you to just sit on your buttocks!"

"All I ask is an introduction, like presenting a gift. It's not so much the content as the wrapper in which the gift is presented, that's most important to the Japanese. For Americans, this may seem foolish and simplistic, but this is the essence of Japan's business culture."

"Tell me more ..." Jeff requested.

"The Japanese have a great sense of appreciation for a wrapped gift. For example, something gift-wrapped from Gucci is better than the same item with K-Mart gift-wrap."

I asked Sam if he had read two books in his personal library: "Japanese Business Etiquette" and "From Bonsai to Levi's." I was surprised to find he hadn't.

These books are simplifications of how Americans should behave in business dealings with Japan. They tell how American companies must adopt an attitude that the Japanese "buyer" has the upper hand, the "power" to control or influence a "seller" at will, in a deal. In Japan, this upper hand is called *Kami-sama*, Gods.

"You better think twice about this, before you find yourself crawling in to beg me." I tried not to sound too threatening. "And, by that point, I hope for your sake it won't be too late!"

Three days passed after they walked out, slamming the office door. When I returned to my office on a Thursday morning, Sam and Jeff were waiting for me, striking dominant poses to try to humble me. It was Exhibit A in a demonstration that, for self-protection, employees must subjugate themselves to the boss if they want to survive.

This gave me another chance to explain how important it was to follow the spirit of Japanese culture.

The Japanese have endless patience and endurance to give of themselves, as in nurturing *bonsai* trees. Patience and time are required before one can enjoy the beauty of these rugged plants. Americans, on the other hand, tend to seek the beauty of *Ikebana*, cut-flower arrangements, as if seeking instant gratification for apparent beauty, Japanese see Americans pursuing business dealings in a similar way.

I wondered what Jeff had done with the lists of Japanese companies I gave him? I had carefully classified each corporate category by geography, size, annual sales volume, types of products, contact person(s), telephone and FAX numbers, mailing addresses, and the like.

The list also included information from existing office files. Some files were active, some inactive, and others were considered "dead." My strategy was to target all these companies for my official introduction.

"Have you given any thought to what happened the other day?" Jeff asked. "Have you decided whether you're going to do exactly what we demand? We're here to let you know what we've decided to do with you!"

"How so?" I asked, making a deep bow to Jeff, as the spokesperson. I was getting under his skin. "Say Mr. Jeff. When were you promoted to the spokesman position? May I congratulate you?" I looked to Sam, who sat deep in his chair, waiting for my response.

"Yes, Sam. I have an answer for you." I gave him back his books, "Japanese Business Etiquette" and "From Bonsai to Levis."

If I could only convince Sam Goldstein of the relationship between short-term and long-term goals when dealing with the Japanese national market, he would undoubtedly be a success there. The question was *how* to make him understand when, to him, money was everything. And to make money he would do anything, even betray the trust of others, without blushing or even blinking an eye!

It would have been a great disservice to claim that Japanese culture was superior to Sam's or Jeff's, but at the same time I believed some cultures were better suited than others to certain activities. Although the Japanese self-image is that of *sekkachis*–a nation of impatience–Japanese business demands patience from impatient foreigners.

"Sam, at the risk of sounding redundant, I insist you send off my official introduction to Japan before the weekend is over. I want you to trust that it will work."

"Trust you? Ha!"

It seemed I had hit his giggle box. After I promised Sam that he would have the first purchase order on his desk thirty days after we sent out the introduction, he finally came around. Pointing his bony finger at me, he said, "I hold you to it ..."

I had felt for several weeks as if someone was kicking me in the stomach. Now waiting for a response from Japan was like tumbling in the mixer of a cement truck. Then one Monday morning, somewhat embarrassed, Sam walked into my office with several faxes from Japan.

"Thomas, it looks like it paid off, even with the fuss we made and the gamble I took on you! You have no idea what it took to convince Jeff I was doing the right thing."

I wondered what he meant by the gamble he took on me? I felt I had already aged two years in the last two months. As responses returned from Japan, the importance of my consulting seemed to have registered. My heartbeats sounded like a *taiko*-drum, throbbing with excitement.

I was thrilled at how kindly Japan received me. In spite of any shortcomings so far, the faxes indicated that "honor-bound" business relationships had been established.

Dealings with Mr. Iwate, the Director of Import for Nichiren Corporation of Tokyo, were noteworthy examples.

He and I exchanged proper greetings and self-introductions, after which he told me of special products he desperately needed to "save face" for a client. I made it clear to him that my strong personal desire to meet his needs was not motivated by making money for my company or myself. My personal desire was to honor him, representing his company to his client.

This spirit struck a key chord. We both understood and trusted our hearts even though we had never met face-to-face. This was the beginning of a great relationship.

I gave Sam my first purchase order, for $35,200.00, as he walked into his office, then swallowed his own words.

Needless to say, I was greatly indebted to Mr. Iwate. He made several more purchases.

I couldn't contain myself for days. Then, as weeks passed, other great deals sprang from my efforts. I would like to think that Mr. Iwate was so pleased he spread the "good word." My desktop became cluttered with inquiries about our company and products, and with purchase orders from Japanese companies.

As word got around about my activities, a number of civic and business leaders started catering to me, escorting me around. I was riding the crest of waves of the Pacific Ocean. I was asked to be a guest at local business gatherings, Rotary luncheons, radio talk shows, workshops, professional groups and conferences, to offer my expertise on Japanese business management and trade secrecy. I was twice invited to speak at the University of California, Chico, about International Strategic Pacific Rim Marketing.

"Our sales have tripled since Mr. Tanemori arrived!" Sam exclaimed on a television interview I arranged for him at NBC Channel 24. For me, seeing Sam's beaming face, I couldn't help but be overjoyed for Sam.

How little I understood the influential power of television interviews–instant changes and far-reaching affects that money could not buy were brought to the local community. Some people looked upon me as though I was the "man behind the curtain" in "The Wizard of Oz."

But to others, I was the "Wicked Witch of the West." Such reactions came from near and far when people found out I was a survivor of Hiroshima. Such knowledge triggered painful memories of Pearl Harbor and the Bataan Death March of World War II, for some people.

Although I wasn't able to identify many people by name or by association, I knew some had served in the fiercest battles of the Pacific War. Undoubtedly, some of these men had lost comrades they had fought alongside, shattering deep bonds of brotherhood.

At the same time, I must admit that not all gave me "the finger," nor pointed at me, as had happened on one occasion.

While I was speaking at the University of Chico on the subject of "Japanese Management In Business: Never Cold Turkey," I met a gentleman and his Japanese wife. He was very sympathetic about the loss of my family. I later learned he was wounded in battle and cared for by a Japanese family.

By contrast, another businessman who had attended all my workshops and seminars was publicly very vocal about whatever bugged him. He always spoke out, questioning my "motives" or the sincerity of my efforts.

He castigated me as a "member" of "the sneak attack," the preemptive strike on Pearl Harbor, as one who couldn't be trusted. He thought I had a hidden agenda and wanted do everything in his power to prove it. He openly challenged practically every point that I made.

In general, I was very pleased that public sentiment was mostly in my favor, as I was the only Japanese in the community. My most apparent success was my "Japanese Business Ethics (How To or Not To Do)" presentation, which struck the fancy of audiences. At least my presentation was unique and fresh!

One day, Sam walked up to my desk with a plate of my favorite blueberry pie and ice cream, and a cup of coffee. "What's the occasion? Not even a coffee break?" he asked. "Say, Tom," he grinned from ear-to-ear, "I saved a piece of pie for you." He then handed me a letter from Japan, written in English and Japanese, a response to one of my official introductions.

I quickly skimmed through it, commenting, "It seems obvious what we have to do. It's in plain English that even Jeff can understand. Why don't you let Jeff entertain this honorable guest? After all, he certainly knows how to spend your money, just like he blew it the last time with the Okazaki Lumber Company."

Oh, for a camera to capture his hangdog smile!

"That's the reason I came to you. We 'round-eye' Americans have little understanding of Japan's business protocols and rituals. The Japanese have a great appreciation of the various forms of entertaining guests, as individual corporations. And as a nation, Japan spends more money on entertainment than on defense or education. The average Japanese knows how to entertain; their corporate 'hospitality' is second to none!"

I watched Sam squirm as he admitted his newfound knowledge and set me up for a major introduction with Ishizaki Seizai Lumber. I considered this opportunity as God's vindication. Perhaps now Sam and Jeff could grasp how "honor" should be extended to potential Japanese buyers.

As far as my upcoming performance, I had no room for error! Any blunder I made while receiving the company's officials would be virtually inexcusable, the commitment of a social "sin" in the eyes of my countrymen. Arrangements were made at a local Holiday Inn. A bouquet of flowers, a basket of California fruits, cheese, and a choice bottle of wine would extend our heartfelt welcoming.

I couldn't conceal my inexplicable joy, nor my apprehension, when the honorable guests came through the municipal airport gate. I had no difficulty identifying them: living up to America's stereotypes of Japanese travelers, they had camera straps slung over each shoulder!

Our greetings were simple but familiar with the "art of the Japanese touch." All was sweet, like orchestrated symphonic music to my ears. Although handshakes were more common, especially when greeting someone in the States, I followed Japanese custom with a deep, formal bow for the honorable dignitaries I was greeting the first time.

Mr. Hideo Ishizaki, wearing a genuine Japanese straw hat for the perfect California summer season was, unmistakably, the president of the company. The three gentlemen accompanying him stood at least a half step behind, a sure sign of who was in charge!

"Sir, we've waited for you and are delighted and honored that you are allowing us to show you around California," I began. "We have already made pleasurable itineraries for you."

Strikingly dignified, Mr. Ishizaki bowed in response. I then greeted Mr. Yamashita-san, Bucho, the Director of the Export Department Division, and "company men" Mr. Yatabe-san and Mr. Kurokawa-san, returning them respectful bows. They were to be equally as honored as Mr. Ishizaki, whose familiar name was Shacho.

"Sah, ikimasho ..."

I led them to a fancy rental car parked curbside and opened the front passenger-side door for Shacho. Then I opened the back door for Bucho, smiling as I watched Yatabe-san and Kurokawa-san apologetically excuse themselves, and sit in the back seat. (In Japan, VIPs always ride in the back seat.) "Say, how do you like riding in the back seat like Big Shots?" I asked Yatabe-san and Kurokawa-san. They gave me embarrassed smiles, while Shacho seemed to take my joke in stride. Their laughter was definitely a release of tension.

I suggested they relax and even rest their eyes for the thirty minute drive to the hotel, since I would be driving on the "wrong" side of the road, to them.

At this time my encroaching blindness due to retinitis pigmentosa still left me a "tunnel" of clear vision which allowed me to drive, albeit very slowly and carefully. My loss of vision was gradual—as if a dog's tail was being snipped off very slowly, an inch at a time. By this time I could only see cars directly in front of me, not cars to either side. Soon I would have to give up driving altogether.

Checking them into the hotel, I explained that I would be picking them up at six o'clock for dinner, giving them nearly three hours to clean up and take care of personal matters.

I returned to my office, where Sam started shouting at me. "What in the world! Where are those "JAPanese? I want them here right now. You better not waste my time!"

"Sam," I started, amazed at his irritation over my having dropped our guests off at the hotel before the evening meeting.

"Don't Sam me!" he barked, glancing at his watch. "We still have a good two hours to talk business before we spend money on them tonight at that Japanese restaurant."

"By the way, I just want to remind you," I said, half reassuringly, half perturbed, "please, don't put the cart before the horse. As we agreed, whatever you do or say, don't blow it. Let me do my thing."

Isn't it said in America that the first impression is the most important impression? And that there is no second chance to make a first impression?

I was keenly aware that this first meeting would either begin a new relationship, or there would be no business. A meeting of two "strangers" would set the stage, establishing the "essence" of Eureka Northwest Lumber Company the Japanese were seeking to convey.

Normally, Japanese business deals require several meetings, with few, if any, business matters discussed in the early sessions, which are reserved for alluding to the "heart" and establishing the business relationship.

This is where Sam Goldstein should put his business on the line: carefully, humbly and sincerely. He needed to make this evening an enchanted one, as well as meaningful and productive, in order to establish his long-range goal of making money.

I had told Sam not to make chauvinistic claims of superior American culture and business practices, even if he thought his claims were true! All activities should revolve around the guests' interests, not around Sam's.

The hostess greeted our guests with a warm smile and led us to a private room where a lavish table was waiting for us to enjoy the unfolding of the evening.

"No!" I shouted in silence, momentarily halting. "Where in the world are Sam and Jeff? Didn't I make clear they were to be here, awaiting the arrival of our guests?"

We had blundered on the very first step of our "first date." I waited indignantly for Sam and Jeff to arrive, twelve minutes late and empty-handed. Sam had not brought a token gift for our guests, as I had requested.

The second cardinal "sin" had been committed. And yet the moment had arrived for the curtain to be drawn, revealing the stage, the backdrop, the characters, the props.

I made a slight bow to Mr. Ishizaki.

"Shacho," I began, with my utmost *keigo*, honorific form of language. Showing my highest respect, I introduced our guests of honor to Sam and Jeff. An air of arrogance filled the room, as Sam conceitedly extended his welcome to Mr. Ishizaki.

"How do you do. Are you folks ready to do business with us? Ha, ha, ha!"

I interpreted Sam's laughter to be "pretend" embarrassment. I then seated each guest according to the traditional Japanese hierarchical system. Whether or not Sam or Jeff understood what I was doing didn't matter at this point, but I wished they'd learn to be more humble.

We began the ceremonial exchange of *meishi*, business cards printed with names, titles, and company in Japanese on one side and in English on the other. This ceremony of welcoming our guests was a demonstration of our ultimate desire to share our "heart" throughout the evening. In Japan we say, "Let me touch your heart!"

Unfortunately, Sam had failed to bring any cards, creating a third breach of business protocol. Our guests presented their cards with humility of spirit and attitude.

"Yah, Tanemori-san, I accept your apology for your boss's blunder," said Shacho, in Japanese.

"Thomas, what about the flowers, fruit basket, cheese and bottle of wine?" Sam asked. He dropped his voice and whispered in my ear, "Why did you do it before we even talked about business?"

"Sam, that's enough!" I whispered back. "The subject is closed! Zip your mouth! All right?"

But Sam insisted, making a spectacle of his need to know why I'd bought the gifts and how much I'd spent.

"*Jah, Hajime masho!*" I insisted that the welcoming party should begin, and called for *Kanpai*, a toast of the hour. I poured ice-cold beer for Shacho, expressing my gratitude for his coming. I did likewise for Sam and Bucho, then Jeff, Yatabe-san and Kurokawa-san, in that order. I set the mood for *Kanpai*, and in return, Bucho led the next *Kanpai*. In unison, we toasted the joyous occasion, our well-being, and our wishes for an honorable venture together.

Then Shacho insisted I should be honored by accepting his empty glass. He poured cold beer for me to drink, and as I finished it, with a sense of esteem, I offered him my glass. Would he accept it without hesitation? This was a critical point!

Shacho accepted it graciously and enthusiastically, reflecting honor back to me and my employer! Our welcoming party was approved and appreciated. The *Kanpai* then continued for several minutes.

I realized, the way circumstances were unfolding, that we would soon be discussing the reason our honorable guests had come. We ravaged arrays of Japanese food, meticulously prepared and served. A mood of liveliness prevailed, excepting Sam and Jeff, who seemed to have lost the art of entertaining, or perhaps, of how to enjoy life.

Watching the proceedings, I noticed Bucho getting a signal from his boss. Bucho raised his glass and addressed me saying "*Ja, kono ippai de yarimasho kane.* Let's have one last *Kanpai,* just you and me."

This was the signal I had been waiting for. The process of business would now undoubtedly be less complicated, since we would speak the same language with a shared understanding of cultural values.

"Thomas, get going! I think we've spent enough time drinking and eating, and what's all the vowing between you and you-know-who?" Jeff whispered. "We need to see what kind of money these Japanese are talking about!"

Bucho presented a meticulously planned five-year proposal, a plan I considered bold, given that he hadn't heard of our capabilities, and that meeting the goals he set would require dedication and astute management. From his proposal, I assessed Japan's most needed products that we might provide, based on the abundance of forests and lumber products on the West coast and in Canada.

Even as green as I was to the lumber business, I could almost guarantee a way to fill each demand. I could see a successful business relationship blossoming from this first meeting of Ishizaki Seizai Lumber and Eureka Lumber. It would only require the patience and understanding of nurturing a *bonsai* tree.

Stressing over and over that the proposal from Bucho was *not* a contract, I briefly explained to Sam and Jeff where the offer was taking us.

"Thomas, show us what you can do," said Sam. "Whatever it takes, even making some concessions or compromising terms ... just get a signature on the dotted line from the Japanese. We're not spending hours for nothing! Do you get it?"

"Mr. Ishizaki," Sam suddenly said to Shacho, in a voice our guest undoubtedly felt was intimidating. The Japanese held their breath while Sam and Jeff huffed and puffed, and the mood turned from lively to ... dead still. Shacho sat in enigmatic silence.

Bucho, speaking for Shacho, reacted as if stunned. "Tanemori-san, *kore wa doyu koto nandesu ka*?" He sought an explanation for Sam's outburst. It pained me to see our guests exposed to stereotypical American business dealings.

Our guests began talking among themselves as Bucho again asked me what Sam had demanded. I heard our guest's comments, including their assessments of me. While I waited to return to negotiating, my stomach churned.

"Why?" Sam asked incredulously, when I told him the decision our guests had made. "Are you telling me that these blankety-blank Japanese are not going to commit to their proposals? It's just what I've been saying!"

He banged the table. "Thomas, you tell these 'slant eyes' they're not leaving here tonight without making some kind of deal worth all the hours and money spent on them."

"Sam, you don't mean what you're saying," I said, trying to remind him of the process we needed to follow.

"If they walk out tonight without buying anything … Thomas, you tell me who's going to pay for the food, drinks, and the gifts you've already bought?"

Our guests wanted to know what all the fuss was about. I was too ashamed to tell Bucho what was in Sam's heart, or of his demands.

I quickly turned to Jeff, warning, "You'd better stay out of this."

Then I looked squarely into Sam's eyes and said, "I'll pay for all this!" Then came another dead silence.

"Tanemori-ku …"

I could hardly believe it was Shacho, who winked at Bucho, then spoke to me as if he was a king extending his scepter to a subordinate seeking mercy.

"There is no need for you to be modest," Shacho said, "I already had a hunch about his demands. I will not burden you, Mr. Tanemori. Please let us hear exactly what he has in mind, right, Bucho?" He also addressed Yatabe-san and Kurokawa-san, who nodded in agreement.

I conveyed to Bucho what Sam had demanded from Shacho, then waited in shame for the answer, not raising my head even an inch!

Shacho returned to enigmatic silence! The Japanese discussion moments before had produced a consensus to comply with Sam's demand in order to *kao o tateru*—save my face. Ishizaki Seizai Lumber offered to buy one container of merchandise for about $35,000.

When I came to the office early the next morning to pick up the purchase orders, Sam was pacing the floor. Still fuming with anger and frustration, he insisted that I talk to the Japanese again to see if their five-year proposals could be resubmitted for consideration. I just looked at him.

"I should have followed my gut feeling not to hire you in the first place." Sam began ranting. "I just knew you damned Japs always stick together. You simply don't understand the real world—fighting for survival. It's no wonder the Japs lost the war!"

His remark reminded me of a Greek proverb: "When the fox cannot reach the grapes he says to himself, they are not ripe!" Or, as we say, "sour grapes!" I pitied Sam for thinking wealth could be purchased at the expense of others. Evidently he had never heard the Russian proverb, "The riches in the heart cannot be stolen."

"Sam, all I can say is you got what you asked for. You remind me of the giant who killed the goose that laid a golden egg every day. This goose hadn't grown up to lay an egg. But you were so greedy, you killed it for an appetizer." Our entire episode could be summarized by a Japanese proverb: "A man's teeth often bite his own tongue!"

I painfully acknowledged that by not reaching his heart I had failed Sam, and for that I was truly sorry. Looking at him with my heart, a teaching of Buddha came back to me: "There is no fire like passion, no shark like hatred, no snare like folly, no torrent like greed."

In the midst of this stormy night, I heard my Father's voice, "Takashi, remember who you are and follow your own heart, no matter what ... Be true to yourself no matter what others might think of you ..."

That compelled my heart-decision, and I had no regrets making it. With the blessing and approval of my Father, I walked into Sam's office with my my letter of resignation.

I sent a copy to Shacho, Mr. Ishizaki, on behalf of all the Japanese companies I had been privileged to work with. In short, it read:

September 24, 1990

Dear Shacho:

I deeply regret what transpired during our meeting. As I am seeking your indulgence and forgiveness, I trust this brief, candid letter will serve to explain why I left Eureka Northwest Lumber Company abruptly. I resigned my services as Cultural Consultant, Director of Exporting Division, and am no longer associated with the firm, as of 4:00 p.m. on Monday, September 24, 1990.

If I were to remain with this firm, it would be very difficult for me, as well as a disservice to the company, but more importantly, it would be a dishonor to you, Ishizaki

Seizai Lumber Company, and many other Japanese clients for whom I have great regards and respect.

Although the owner offered me great financial benefits and the promise of a great future position in the firm (he enticed me to stay with a quiet attractive offer), I decided to value my personal worth and integrity, and to honor you and Japanese companies.

Again thank you for the privilege of having served you. My sincere prayer for your success and healthy life, I am

Sincerely,
Takashi "Thomas" Tanemori

Reflecting on my experience with Eureka Northwest Lumber Company, I took a long, hard look at the truth represented by *Ikebana* and *Bonsai*. Japanese manners of business are ever so vital, not only in terms of corporate relationships, but as the core of human relationships.

I left the office with all the necessary papers to bring this nightmare event to closure. We scrapped all itineraries made for our guests' pleasure trip and our accompanying them. With thousands of my apologies accepted and documents signed, my final farewell to Mr. Ishizaki was short and sweet, but very personal.

"Mr. Tanemori," he responded, "You are welcome to visit us when you come to Japan!"

Shacho gave me his Japanese genuine straw hat as a token of his heart before leaving for Reno. I was awed to have witnessed his self-portrait so masterfully fulfilled. Nothing more was needed to describe the "essence" and capacity of his heart. The hat still hangs in my office, a token of my fond memories and as a reminder of the principles of *Ikebana* and *Bonsai*, principles to live by!

As I looked in the mirror, the words of Ronald Laing came to mind, echoing my thoughts and feelings: "Every human being, whether child or adult, seems to require significance, that is, a place in another person's world!"

Chapter Fourteen: The Epic Return to Hiroshima

August 6, 1945 to August 6, 2005

Returning to its birthplace,
the salmon is battered and bloodied
by the merciless rocks.
Only its heart is not bloodied.
It cradles the spirit of new life ...
the hope of a new generation.

LOOKING back, the last 60 years of my life have been like an embroidery—many different lengths of thread crisscrossing in many colors, adding to an iridescent tapestry of human dignity. What have I done for which my life can be measured and remembered—will a bust of bronze be erected in its honour in the heart of downtown? What epithet will be on my grave marker?

For me, in this journey of the heart, success is measured not by what we achieve, but by *who we become* as we cross many "bridges" along the way.

Success, in the journey of the heart, resides in discovering the depth of our capacity to love and the tenderness of friendships. And I can say, as I have made my epic return to Hiroshima, that I have discovered my life-journey has not been what many might have expected. Nor have I found the destination exactly as I had charted it. I should not be dismayed, nor disappointed, for "who I have become" is the true worth of my travels.

On a beautiful sunny day in September 1999, I found myself once again on the Geibi-Sen Line, riding the Black Engine. It was the same train that, 54 years before, had carried my shattered family to the dubious sanctuary of Kotachi Village.

Memories flooded back of bodies stacked like twigs along the railroad tracks, of the stench of charred and rotting human flesh, and of the gagging, sweet-sour smoke of the cremation fires. The moans of the injured and the wailing of hysterical children still reverberated in my ears.

Involuntarily, I shook from the memories, my body twisted in grief, and sobs convulsed me.

I was on a world tour with a group of artists and peace workers. Called the "First Light Journey for a Nuclear Free Planet," its director, Jim Berenholtz, had called to invite me to participate in the early spring of 1999, asking me to share my journey "from revenge to forgiveness." Jim and two fellow artists, Robert Kikuchi-Yngojo and Nancy Wang, were preparing a performance piece around my life story, called "Takashi's Dream."

Our journey for "First Light" began with a commemorative ceremony at the Trinity Test Site at White Sands, New Mexico, on July 16th, 1999. Here, 54 years earlier in the remote and forbidding desert the natives call *Jornade del Muerte*, Journey of Death, a small grapefruit-sized ball of plutonium had exploded with a ferocity unparalleled in human history, unveiling the power of a new bomb that would devastate two cities in Japan, indelibly marking the end of World War II, while thrusting mankind into a new era of nuclear arms proliferation and Cold War.

Now, more than five decades after that first atomic test, Japanese, American and Native American peace-workers linked arms to bless the earth and pray for mankind.

"First Light" continued its trek from the Trinity Site to Los Alamos, Santa Fe, and Albuquerque, and at each place I told my life story and took part in a ceremony of peace. In Santa Fe, I was stunned when the audience rose to a standing ovation after I shared my heart. This was the first time that an entire audience stood to applaud me, and my heart almost jumped out of my body at the surprising, unfathomed response.

Our journey continued to Three Mile Island in Pennsylvania, the site of a 1979 nuclear power plant malfunction that nearly led to a meltdown, causing radioactive material to be released into the atmosphere. I was saddened to hear of people who had suffered, not as a result of war, but from the peaceful use of nuclear energy.

Next, we met with legislators at the Pennsylvania state capitol of Harrisburg. I was astonished and touched to see, painted on the tile floor of the rotunda, my old friends, the crane and the butterfly.

The final stop of our U.S. tour was in New York City, performing at the KAMPO Cultural Center on Bond Street. As I ended sharing my life story there, a middle-aged woman named Valentina came up and handed me a bouquet of flowers, the first time I had received such a gift. Knowing I had touched her heart was revitalizing.

When Jim Berenholtz and his group of artists went to Europe, I waited to join them again in Japan to complete the "circle" of our journey. During my preparation to meet the group in Hiroshima, my heart was experiencing incomprehensible perplexity, as I prepared to speak to a group of people in Japanese for the first time in decades!

The day came when we all gathered at the Hiroshima Peace Museum, with great anticipation of a miracle. I had no idea what to expect, sharing my story in my native tongue with my countrymen.

There was still such bitterness and resentment in Japan. I was astonished when a tiny elderly woman came up to me, bowing deeply, after I had spoken. She was frail and stooped over and had to crook her neck to look up at me. But her eyes were clear and direct. In a surprisingly strong voice she informed me that, at the age of 91, she too, was a survivor of the bombing.

"Tanemori-san," she said in her lilting Hiroshima accent, "I have heard many, many survivors tell their stories and speak of their suffering and anguish. Unfortunately, many are still burdened with rage and pain. But when I heard you tonight, I felt that you are as liberated as a butterfly, soaring in the blue sky. Your spirit is free!"

Suddenly, the pain of separation from my fellow Japanese was lifted.

No! I had finally come home!

Our tour ended with a pilgrimage to Japan's most sacred peak, Mt. Fuji. Shortly after sunrise on August 22, 1999, the "First Light" group, accompanied by its Japanese counterparts, started the long walk to the top of Mt. Fuji. The night before, all 60 of us had been ferried by bus to

Station Five on the mountain's flank. From there, in single file, we hiked the narrow, winding trail to the summit.

In spite of my physical condition (I had undergone three major cancer surgeries, including a total gastrectomy) and the altitude (Mt. Fuji is 11,000 feet), I sprinted ahead of the others, driven by an inexhaustible energy that lasted the whole seven hour hike.

Reaching the top, we saw the skies become dark and angry. Almost as angry was the innkeeper at the summit who was not pleased to have 60 people all at once ascend to his establishment. We crowded into the shelter that night, eating cold *miso* soup (the innkeeper refused to reheat it) and sleeping on cold, smelly, pancake-thin futons, without clean sheets. During the night, I asked the innkeeper for a flashlight to guide me through the darkness to the bathroom, which caused him to explode.

"*Dame!*" he shouted, "nothing doing!"

Luckily, my friends were able to guide me, on hands and knees, around our sleeping companions and to the outhouse. All night long, the wind bellowed and howled like an angry giant, shaking and rattling the shelter walls so strongly that I feared they would be blown away.

The next morning, when the wind had died down, Jim Berenhotz led a peace ceremony, encouraging us to shed past resentments as the snake sheds its skin, and asking us to open our hearts to peace, forgiveness and love.

Later, every step we took back down the mountain was a step away from hatred and despair and towards love and hope. The final cleansing was a visit to the hot springs at the foot of the mountain. Luxuriating in the hot, spicy waters, I meditated on how the volcano's fiery power had been transformed to comfort and heal us.

The official part of the "First Light" Journey over, we said goodbye to our friends. I started my journey back to Hiroshima where, at long last, I was going to face my old nemesis, Satsuko, in Kotachi Village. Having not spoken with her since the fall of 1982, I called from Hiroshima to see if she would accept my visit.

At first Satsuko was angry and suspicious that I hadn't given her sufficient time to contemplate a visit. She flatly refused my request. But as I talked with her, her fears eased. Sensing my sincerity, she eventually relented.

With some trepidation, I stepped off the train in Kotachi, met my sister just outside the station, and before I could even say hello ...

"Takashi, Kottchine hayaku kinasai."

Satsuko yanked my arm and thrust me into a waiting car. Yuriko, her married daughter, was behind the wheel.

Satsuko, barking that she wanted me off the street before the villagers spotted me, slammed the door. The tires squealed, and we were off! Neither Satsuko nor Yuriko said a word as we drove down country roads to Yuriko's house.

"Hayaku hairi nasai?"

Satsuko practically dragged me by my arm, at lightning speed, into the house. "You may talk to me later," she practically growled, the way she had ordered me around ever since our Father died.

Her voice, heavy with turmoil, showed her deep disapproval of my coming. As the door closed, she turned to me. "Why in the world did you show up now, after years of not communicating?" she grilled me, demanding to know my motive for seeing her.

"Give me a second or two to catch my breath!" I shouted, internally. Rather than answer verbally, I bowed so low I felt as if my backbone was cracking. This was my apology for such long neglect.

"Takashi, sore wa dodemo yoi."

Satsuko turned to me squarely, took a deep breath, and let me have it. "Why have you come home on such short notice? Don't you understand that I am now living with my daughter and her family? I have a *giri,* obligatory responsibility, to protect them from intrusion. Especially since you have been silent for so long, you are like a stray bullet that, without warning, has just exploded in our lives!"

She paused, then launched again. "Has all the Tanemori blood been drained from your body? Has it been replaced by something else—American or Chinese blood? What were you thinking?"

"Haji o shirinasai? Don't you have any shame? Answer me," she demanded. She then told me how much

shame and humiliation she had endured because of me, long after I had left the village.

"Suman, Ne-chan," I said. "I am sorry, my sister." I bowed my head with contrition. Satsuko's tirade about my lifetime of inappropriate behavior continued while she served me fresh green tea and delicate Japanese pastries.

My body began shaking involuntarily as I bowed lowly. "My dear sister, I came here to beg your forgiveness and seek our reconciliation. I know I am not worthy of your kindness, or of being received into your home. Please forgive me ..."

Afraid to look up, lest her fury burn into my soul, I was convulsed by sobs. No matter what had happened between us, I could no longer stand the pain of being separated from her. I was begging her from the bottom of my heart.

Momentarily, time seemed to stop!

The tea was left untouched. Yuriko disappeared.

Then, her voice trembling, Satsuko opened her soul, "Takashi, you have no idea of the hell I endured to keep the Tanemori name in honor. I have spent every ounce of my blood to keep our name from being trampled in the dirt. I promised our Father before his death that I would live to see the day our Tanemori family tree would re-emerge with vitality. I could not allow it to die. I gambled my soul to preserve our honor."

She, too, broke down.

"I held my tongue from lashing out against all those *sen-gans.* I've played the role of the three monkeys—*mi-zaru, kika-zaru and iwa-zaru*—even against my soul, so that we might have a chance to survive the fiery darts of villagers who wished evil would befall the family. How they wanted to see the 'seed' of Tanemori die forever!"

From the day our Father died, Satsuko and I had been at odds with each other. The oldest of the Tanemori orphans, Satsuko had shouldered an enormous burden to keep our little family alive and together. Knowing the unfavorable position of orphans in Japan, she had done all she could to ensure that her siblings were obedient and traditional in their behavior.

Facing the harsh reality of our life, she had sternly monitored our every move. This led to ever-increasing conflicts with me. Angry, wounded and openly rebellious, I questioned everything, especially a traditional Japanese culture that valued unbroken filial bonds so greatly while icily ignoring innocent orphans. Even at age eight, being the first-born son of a *Samurai* had given me an indelible sense of self-worth. I had been outraged by our treatment.

"Takashi," she said, "I knew in my heart you and I walked different paths, but mine was the only way I saw the Tanemoris surviving, just keeping our heads above angry waters."

Looking back, I now realize that because Satsuko was a girl, and considered of lesser value, she had been forced to subjugate herself from the day she was born. Compromise was the only way she knew how to help us. As we both struggled to survive, our conflicts were inevitable and the chasm between us had grown greater and greater.

Her voice mingled with tears. "You are *hikkyo-mono*, a traitor," she shouted. "You left me behind as you committed the unpardonable sin of immigrating to America, land of our enemy. How could you, Takashi?" she pleaded.

By my conversion to Christianity, my marriage to a Chinese American, my becoming a Gospel minister, and my abandoning Japanese citizenship in favor of American citizenship—I had only added to her hostility towards me.

And my going blind was totally unacceptable! In Japan, disabilities were viewed as judgment or punishment for past wickedness. Therefore, my blindness revealed my personal and social sins and was a shame to be borne by the whole family. Again, Satsuko had to take the brunt of it.

She put her hands up in front of her, as if to stop me from speaking, and said, "You of all people, Takashi. You have received all due honor and the birthright of the Number One Son, and yet you have stood against me in every way. Why did you do it?"

I knew I had to give her time … to let her soul cry out. She wiped her tears, blew her nose, and went on.

"Takashi, don't you ever say or even think for a moment that the American Government helped us crawl out of the atomic ashes. Don't you have pride in your veins? We Tanemoris are neither beggars nor spineless jellyfish. We never waddled in the mud like swine. These hands dug trenches, these hands crawled up walls, and these are the hands that brought us Tanemoris to where we are today. We are Tanemoris! As the family crest says, we are the seed that by its own life and volition will grow into a prosperous forest in due season. You haven't forgotten, have you?"

Then, very somberly, but with her old warmth, she sat squarely before me and took my hands. "Takashi, you must listen." She paused, overwhelmed by her own tsunami of emotion. "We Tanemoris always share with others whatever we have in abundance. We also share whatever we have from nothing. Most of all, we Tanemoris always share from our hearts! And Tanemoris give 'heart.'"

Then she broke down in tears.

My heart was crushed by the heavy burden she had carried all these years, but I rejoiced in the truth of her spirit. How refreshing it was, like spring rain on a parched desert. I was so proud to know that we, although separated by a span of more than four decades and five thousand miles, had both been true to the teachings of our Father.

Unfortunately, she was unwilling to allow me to share my side of the story. Neither was she willing to feel my heartbeat, for she still questioned my motives for visiting her. She made me leave the Village under the cover of darkness, before the rooster had awakened. I was crushed. The gulf between us seemed immeasurable!

"Clickety-clock, clickety-clock," the engine of the train sounded like a Buddhist monk's mantra. Its sound was painful, and penetrated deep into my soul, until it finally faded into the distance.

By insisting that my sister offered me no chance to tell my story, I was, perhaps, not quite ready to listen to what she had to say. I would have heard my sister's heartbeat, had I listened truthfully, without pretence or any preconceived notion that I had the "answer." Oh, if I only had the heart to hear the depth of her soul's cry, it would have made such a difference!

Neither of us was willing to listen to the other's heartbeat during this outpouring of souls. We had yet to arrive at the point of "redemption," the rock of Niagara Falls where two rivers merge.

The train chugged and rumbled through another dark tunnel, churning up reminiscences of the past, stirring unfathomed feelings of loss. As the train's chugging muffled, I was returning to Hiroshima. Soon I would be back in America.

After returning to the States, confused and uncertain as to what I should do with an ogre sister who seemed so heartless, I fumed and stewed over my own pettiness. Fortunately, time was my friend, my companion, my healer!

At least time allowed me to return to my senses, accepting the fact that my sister should have her own life—whether or not I agreed with her or condoned her actions, and even if I rejected her folly of subjecting herself to the demands and pressures of Japanese tradition.

I pondered the paths we had taken during our years of postwar survival. We had not had the luxury to complain, nor to harbor self-pity, nor to contrast our lot with that of others in the community whom we thought lived better lifes. Yet there were obvious differences in our approaches to life in Kotachi village.

Satsuko's mechanism of survival had been subservience at any cost—as a slave or maid to the village leaders. Her actions appeared to me like those of a toy bird, bowing and bowing to drink water, and continuing to bow long after the village leaders had left!

By contrast, I had conducted myself with self-dignity, bowing to no one, nor allowing anyone to trample me without defending my noble manner, thereby upholding my self-respect! I had lived up to my reputation as a hooligan, quite contrary to the norms of social behavior. For failing to subject myself to village standards, I had paid the penalty of the harshest code of *mura-hachibu,* social ostracism.

I was not long back at my home in America, before I began to feel emotions building for the 60th anniversary of Hiroshima's bombing.

Those who survived the atom bomb and those born after the war have heard arguments on both sides justifying or condemning the use of nuclear weapons. A key question haunts us after 60 years of anniversaries—are these arguments still really necessary? What have we gained from all these arguments? What ground have they given us, allowing the world's citizens to move closer to harmony?

During the 1991 Gulf War, I had been invited to a San Francisco television station to be a panelist in a discussion about the conflict. From what I sensed, the majority of the audience was "anti-war."

Among the panelists was U.S. Senator Barbara Boxer, (D) California. With her sincere, emotional tone, she appealed to the audience to support a position against then-President George Herbert Bush for declaring war. She cited the devastation and suffering of the Hiroshima bombing to support her political viewpoint and personal agenda.

But I knew she wasn't in Hiroshima on that fatal morning. Nor at the time of our confrontation about war's impact on civilians had she ever been to Hiroshima. Her premise was but theory, and didn't "hold water" for me.

One fundamental flaw in her appeal was her lack of experience or understanding of the pain and suffering of survivors. She further attempted to disqualify my point of view—or heartbeat—that the atomic bombing, and indeed the origin of war itself, came from an internal darkness, the divisiveness and distrust of the human heart.

Her emotional appeal was high; the camera zoomed in! Many in the audience embraced her and her political viewpoint. I was, perhaps, the only one who stood up to her.

Nearly a decade and a half later, masses of well-wishing peace-lovers come to Hiroshima, as if the city belongs to them. Joining the majority of citizens living in Hiroshima are tens of thousands from abroad who converge there, with agendas of telling Hiroshima's survivors how they should deal with their suffering and wounds, and how to create peace.

I have great difficulty identifying with and embracing these "anti-war" citizens of the world. I venture to say that most of them have never known pain and suffering such as my family and I endured. Most likely, the majority of these people don't have the foggiest idea of the horrors of Hiroshima and Nagasaki.

Do they really believe they can bring "peace" to the world? Even if they have some empathetic understanding of the copious bloodletting of war, their participation is "anti," against something, but not "for" something! The question is: how can they bring peace out of the "war" going on in their hearts and souls? As a survivor of Hiroshima, who has since become a man of peace, I have empathy.

Perhaps I may be arrogant, but I wonder whether the majority of these hearts have ever experienced an inner-peace transformation (turning from revenge to forgiveness, as in my case).

You may ask why I refuse to take part in an event that many people are willing to go to great lengths to join.

I went to the 50th Anniversary of Hiroshima with Michi, my first guide dog, and I was stunned! I never expected such a gathering of countless faces, from whose mouths laughter and cackling came forth, instead of sighs.

And while there were many who genuinely consoled their own hearts and souls on behalf of the dead—the Japanese say *Ireisai,* moan for the dead—there were no supportive prayers for survivors of the bombing.

My heart was untouched by any of the speakers at this anniversary event. Without exception, for every person at the podium—whether giving an eloquent speech or saying a prayer—the rustling of the printed page from which they read betrayed their messages as coming from other than their hearts, their inner-souls. I came home to the States with Michi with a broken heart, vowing to avoid ever being a part of this mockery! I decided to never again take part in a "mob-gathering" for global peace.

Since the 50th Anniversary of Hiroshima, I have made several journeys back to Japan, alone, to my home city, hoping someone would hear my message.

That message is simple—global "peace" is not achievable by massive anti-war movements, nor through massed annual gatherings of *Ireisai*.

For all these decades, such misplaced efforts have, in their folly, equated the stopping of war, or the absence of war, with peace. Meanwhile, in many corners of the world, small wars rage and the precedents of war smolder, waiting for a gust of wind to fan them into destruction and death!

Contrary to the intentions of anti-war movements, we experience how easy it is to automatically take up weapons to settle our conflicts. Many of the wounds left by these conflicts never heal because of the failure of all parties to fully appreciate the roots of the conflict and, from them, to devise a solution.

Painfully, I have heard perennial pleadings from Hiroshima's citizens—pleadings borne of resentment, anger and bitterness—to the mass crowds that descend on the city every August 6th, to please stop coming.

And sadly, after each anniversary, the flock of thousands leave Hiroshima until the next year, echoing a cry of "no more Hiroshima," while wars continue.

I identify with so many survivors of Hiroshima and Nagasaki and their family members, who are searching desperately for *kokoro no yasuragi,* peace, or *yutori,* serenity. However painful it is, that they must reconcile with their individual pasts. As long as they live in "victim mode," they will regrettably be unable to live a "victorious life" and appreciate the tenacity of the human spirit.

Although it took four decades of my own struggle, I have become *kaiko*, emerged as a beautiful butterfly soaring freely, grateful for the life I am living.

> *"Cho-o-cho ...cho-o-cho, nanohani tomare ...*
> *Nanohani aitra, sakura ni tomare ...*
> *Hana kara hanae, asobe yo tomare;*
> *asobe yo tomare ... asobe yo tomare ..."*

[Butterflies, heavenly creatures, land on any flower you wish! Enjoy! And, when you are tired, rest for a while on the beautiful Cherry Blossom. When ready, fly again! Fly from flower to flower until you find the one that offers total joy—a resting place!]

At last, in discovering myself through my returned dream, my bitterness and longing for revenge was removed. I saw, unmistakably and irrevocably, that my enemies were not Americans, nor were they Japanese society.

The enemy was none other than myself—the darkness of my own heart!

My desire to avenge my Father's death vanished. I surrendered to my spirit, as the White Butterfly tipped the scales to the side of forgiveness. I experienced forgiveness, and the peace that flowed with it touched the deepest part of my soul!

For the first time, my life and my place in the world made sense to me. Such a realization required my inner transformation—all the resentment, anger, bitterness and consuming desire for vengeance paled against the overwhelming love I felt, as the White Butterfly touched my heart with its "magical" power. The clay that had blinded my eyes for forty years was broken and removed.

The Butterfly's message was clear and simple. At last, I fulfilled my promise to my Father, coming home to a place called "peace through forgiveness"—by letting go of my painful past.

I came through a raging storm to reach the calm "eye of the storm," where I have become able to see what is going on around me from a different perspective. I can now see myself as a true man of peace, who has come through storms much as bamboo weathers gales!

From my perspective, the peace for which the world longs is only achieved by individuals who similarly come through raging tempests to enter the "eye of the storm."

Hiroshimas continue to loom like dark shadows in our hearts, staring at us from our collective experience. Regrettably, this is the drama of our human family. Must we not consider what it would take to "shift" the world from our current warpath toward creating a safer, more peaceful place where six billion people of different nationalities can live side-by-side?

I have come to believe this is the time to learn from the *past* and act in the *present* with a heart of vision for the *future*. Here is the way this belief system has worked, on a smaller scale, in my life.

While considering the perplexing conditions of the world, I had an overwhelming desire to make things "right" with my sister and to reckon with my own past. I had survived the life of an *oyanashigo,* a street urchin—condemned as unworthy by Japanese society—only to commit a "crime" against my sister by constantly opposing her in order to survive in postwar Japan.

Alhough my reckoning with the past and my reconciliation with Satsuko were long overdue, I wondered how I could reach her, to let her know my heart yearned for reconciliation. I begged the *ishi no Ojizo-san,* a stone-Buddha standing at a turnpike in Japan, to show me the way. I knew I must find a way to Kotachi village, where my sister still lived, like a bird in a cage, submitting herself to the demands of Japanese tradition.

Then the tragic events of 9/11 struck. In the terrorist acts of this infamous day, Americans died, suffered pain and vulnerability in their homeland, the likes of which they had never before experienced.

Against this unfortunate backdrop, a handsome young man named Perry Thomas Hallinan appeared at the doorstep of my humble castle in Lafayette, California, where I now live with my second guide dog, Yuki.

Was I shocked? Yes, as he was a total stranger! However, I always welcome "strangers" to my place, opening my home and my heart. In doing so, the last four years have been the time of my life.

Perry spoke to me about his life-mission of producing video documentaries.

What first surprised me about Perry was his willingness to see events of the past from a personal perspective. Furthermore, I was impressed with the value he placed on combining our experiences and knowledge of history to give us a clearer understanding of who we have been, who we are now, and who we can become.

As we talked, we began to develop a relationship based on similar ideas and interests, and Perry began unfolding his ideas for a documentary entitled "Heart of Vision," to be a one-hour portrait of my journey and life's process of healing physical, emotional and spiritual wounds.

Perry began describing the video's key themes of transformation from revenge to forgiveness, cultural identity, and aging. He said my story was meant to bring a living perspective to our understanding of the human spirit when challenged by war and cultural divisions.

Before documenting my life-journey, Perry produced a short video about my physical and spiritual relationship with my guide dog Yuki. This not only covered some of my life and its lessons about the human experience, but also helped forge my relationship with Perry.

I must admit there was a time when I was very skeptical as to whether Perry and his production team could overcome their American perceptions and have a clear understanding of Japanese culture. Given the events of World War II, some Americans still hold stereotypes of Japanese as having slanted eyes, and on whose narrow noses, goofy-goggle glasses rest.

The enigma of Japanese culture in this new millennium is that deep traditions still lie beneath whatever modern, western trappings non-Japanese observers may perceive. Some westerners, seeing a young Japanese woman wearing "blue jeans and lace" instead of a *kimono*, might assume her values are modern and western. But to think such attire reflects the attitude of a westernized nation would likely be incorrect, as her undergarments probably reflect centuries-old tradition.

Conversely, the Japanese need to look at Americans the same way they see themselves, trying to understand the unique characteristics of another nation, while examining the values, goals, and standards by which they judge themselves. They must further consider to what degree they are willing to submit themselves to the process of global interdependence.

It is my firm belief that the progress of a nation can be retarded, forced to a standstill, or even retrogress, not due to inadequate knowledge or technologies, but due to a disconnected understanding of the nation's history, and of lessons which should be collectively learned by its citizens.

I have come to believe that the effects of past actions, persisting into the present, will directly influence the future of any nation, and that its progress depends on the will of its people to understand where it has been and to act in a manner which is of benefit to it and to other nations.

Humankind's track record of conflict and war reflects a well-worn path of behavior, a cycle that philosopher George Santayana noted a century ago, in an oft-used quotation: *Those who cannot learn from history are doomed to repeat it.*

I believe the root cause of human conflict is the inability of people to act beyond their own perceived self-interest. To act in such a selfish manner denies experiencing the sacred humanity of others, preventing the understanding required to meet mutual human needs and create peaceful co-existence.

The depth of this understanding necessarily depends on an understanding of history. The past must become valid and meaningful as we interpret the cause and effect of events, and apply these lessons as guides to handle present challenges. To this end, it is conceivable that we all must become historians to interpret events with honesty and truth.

It soon became obvious that Perry's documentary would transcend his original intentions. His working title of "Heart of Vision: I Lived Before You" would be about a spiritual journey each individual must embark upon, as well as the relationships that define that journey—between fathers and sons, mothers and daughters, from generation to generation—all told with the seasoning elements of human drama and romance.

In late April, 2005 I shared with Perry that the utmost desire of my heart and spirit in my life-journey was to make a final homage to Hiroshima. When I told him I wanted to return to the most sacred Tanemori shrine, the tomb where my Father is honored, he was delighted. The second reason for a pilgrimage to Japan was another attempt at reconciling with Satsuko.

Our Hiroshima plans put us on a hurried preparation schedule. In the second week of May, the Japanese Production Team of the HeartAttack Film Production Company began taping interviews of me in my humble home. Reflective silk flags were set up in my garden, giving it the look of a ship, especially because the flags were continually adjusted like a ship's sails to follow the sun while Perry rolled videotape. Out of ten hours of video shot, Perry edited a fifteen minute presentation to show at a project benefit in San Francisco in June, 2005.

Success regarding the second reason for the trip came to pivot on Perry's addition of Yukiko Judy Matsumura to our team. She would become the "bridge" for a meeting with Satsuko to try to span a chasm sustained for six decades.

Since 1999, I had thought it impossible for that abyss to be spanned.

I was confident in Yukiko. As my "twin soul mate," she was like the engineer of a bullet train with both hands on the throttle—her unceasing control would guide us through the complexities of this upcoming journey.

Mounds of last minute details took several days, and were totally exhausting! But even with all these preparations, one thing remained to be done.

I had to let Satsuko know we were coming. I knew she had been guarding her "sanctuary" from my intrusion with her very soul. But it struck me that she would see the inclusion of a third party as less of a threat to her.

Consulting with Yukiko, I agreed with her advice that Perry, a young American for whom my sister had no preconceptions, could make a preliminary approach by letter, charming Satsuko with his genuine heart. If Satsuko was honest with herself, she would receive such a letter as a message conveying Perry's heart, and nothing else.

There was a potential risk to this approach that could touch off the kind of explosion which had occurred when my sister heard of my plans to emigrate to America.

Satsuko's words from that day still rang in my ears: "America. Takashi, what in the world have you turned into, a madman? How could you sell your soul? Takashi, you are *Hikyo-mono*, a traitor!"

Knowing my sister as I thought I did, I guided Perry to write the letter in English and have two of his friends translate it into Japanese. This was a chance that had to be taken. Perhaps, at the moment she opened the letter, a gentle breeze from God or the merciful smiling of Buddha would whisper into her soul.

The letter from Perry reached her via Airmail Special Delivery. It proved to be a "miracle" of penmanship, with Perry's two friends capturing in Japanese the intended essence and spirit of the letter—that the American, wishing to share his heartbeat and spirit, implored her to open the door for her brother, Takashi, to make his way to Kotachi, to be received by her open heart.

My sister later told me she read the letter with great trepidation … not once, but three times. She confided to us that she had prayed to Buddha for understanding. If there was a quirk of chance for the Tanemori siblings to be reconciled, Satsuko had said Takashi would be the last one with which she would wish a reconnection.

We later learned my sister had great struggles opposing our visit when she discovered Perry and Jeremy were personally funding their own way to Japan. Whatever she did, however, cracked open a window to her soul, as a ray of light swung her way. And with that, the potential surfaced to crush her wish that I would be the last person to reconcile with her. Oh, the irony of human life!

Perry's Japan Production Team was comprised of three generations: I was the senior member; producer/video-photographer Perry, sound man Jeremy Biddle, and Yuki, my blonde guide dog, all came from America. Yukiko Judy Matsumura, my "twin soul mate," was the fifth member and her seven-year old daughter Kimina-chan, was our essential sixth member.

Chapter Fifteen: Crossing the Last Bridge

EARLY one morning in Tokyo, my eyes still not ready for the sun's brilliant rays, I meandered through the main lobby of Harumi International Hotel. Looking up, I saw Yukiko, her cell-phone to her ear, revealing a terribly serious countenance. She was on the phone with Satsuko. I could almost feel her waves of emotion and hear the sound of her heartbeat … the sound again of bass *Taiko* drums.

It was Tuesday, July 26th, 2005. We were embarking from Shinkansen, Nozomi, which means "Hope," on the best bullet train in Japan. We had left Tokyo before my emotional typhoon hit.

As the train approached Hiroshima, I was suddenly overwhelmed by a flood of memories of that fatal morning. The memory of a "sweet and sour" stench of burning human flesh returned to me in the train car, turning my stomach!

As the train pulled into Hiroshima station, emotions welled up from the depth of my soul. The 14 platforms were handling a flood of travelers. I noticed a number of foreigners, their presence signaling the gathering for the 60th Anniversary of the Hiroshima bombing.

Mr. Iori-san personally escorted us to the fourth floor, where his hotel's special Japanese guests stayed, to a most traditional, luxurious room—the very same room I had occupied the last time I was there, in 1999.

In our eyes, Iori-san was a magician. While preparing for our trip, Yukiko had exhausted herself, contacting every *Ryokan*, hotel, in the city, without success. Out of desperation, I gave her the name of Iori-san, whom I had known since 1984 when I was promoting California goodwill and agricultural products to the Far East. Not only did Iori-san find us glorious accommodations, but he also performed other "miracles." One occurred after Satsuko called Yukiko the night before we left Tokyo for Hiroshima. My sister told Yukiko she was planning to come to Hiroshima to meet with me and unload her feelings. The question was: where would we meet?

Yukiko was once again at her best! She immediately made the most of a serendipitous event when a strong knock was heard on the door, and with a smile but unaware of our dire predicament, Iori-san walked in.

"Iori-san," Yukiko's voice reverberated with urgency, "how good to see you! I was about to call you out of despair. Takashi's sister is coming, and we haven't been able to find an appropriate room to welcome her."

"Ah, sodesu ka?" he replied, as if Yukiko should have known the sun rises in the east and sets in the west.

He told her that of all the activities and events at Hiroshima Kokusai Hotel, nothing would happen without passing "before the eyes of Iori-san." He said to wait 10 to 15 minutes, as my sister had already left the Hiroshima train station and was on her way to the hotel. He extended his hospitality, which could be described as "second to none."

Yukiko waited for Satsuko in the main lobby. By the time she escorted my sister upstairs, a special 12th floor conference room had been prepared with cold drinks to cool her tongue, and a cold *oshibori,* a towel, to wipe her face.

Yukiko and Satsuko exchanged formal greetings, as this was their first face-to-face meeting. Oh, how I wished a camera had captured their facial expressions—the doubts, worries, reservations, uncertainties, suspicions and fears that must have filled the room.

As I waited to be invited into the room, I felt apprehension. Perry-san and Jeremy-san were quickly seated next to my sister. Then I was led into the room by the assuring hand of Yukiko, like a sheep being led to the slaughterhouse. I couldn't even raise my head, lest my gaze meet Satsuko's, and her fiery eyes sear my soul.

"One-e-chan, ohisashiburi desu ne. Okawari arimasen ka ...?"

Before I had a chance to complete my thoughts, Satsuko exploded like a volcano from the earth's core, rumbling through the depths of the Pacific Ocean.

"Don't you ever call me or even consider me your sister, for you are not my brother!" She stared at a blank wall uttering profanity! I dared not gaze at her blazing eyes!

As if shielding me with her own body, Yukiko frantically tried to stop the rain of arrows directed at me. She empathized with my sister, using the Japanese language of poetry and prose.

To settle her heart's conflict with me, my sister had no choice but to confront her emotions at their source. Her chest cavity shuddered violently, as if birds were flying from a cage. Clearly, the threat of Satsuko detonating again was still very much alive.

Our fate rested in Yukiko's hand, on her magical touch! The silence in the room grew deafening, as no one dared breathe!

What was taking place at this moment had to be the work of the Creator's handiwork—a great Weaver working on extraordinarily intricate embroidery.

Everyone has their responsibilities and their own pace of working. With enough time to plan, the creativity flows and pieces fit. This was the Divine guidance I had been praying for, that Yukiko's soul would stir and respond to the moment. I was unsure how all the elements would flow, connect and support one another.

My sister sat across the table from Yukiko, looking squarely into her eyes, probing deep into her soul. I sensed the energy in the room immediately shift. I had never heard the sounds that then came from my sister's lips, as if from the deepest chamber of her soul. where they had been sealed for the last 60 years.

Satsuko's voice crackled, much like the recording of August 15, 1945, when Emperor Hirohito verbalized his acceptance of defeat and surrender!

Satsuko poured out her soul to Yukiko-san. She spoke with disbelief about her life in Kotachi Village, and having to confront the "powers that be" to defend the Tanemori name when her brother immigrated to America. Her words, her emotions—some of which I was hearing for the first time—poured forth, uninterrupted, for what seemed to be hours. When she finished, we were exhausted, but without resolution.

Having emptied her emotional vessel without any resolution, my sister suddenly excused herself. She said she had lied to her daughter about coming to Hiroshima, and must be home before her daughter returned from work. We were stunned. Whatever had compelled her to face her thug brother had been a most excruciating and momentous decision toward finding her own inner peace, as she had vowed to our Father. We had all promised, in different ways, to honor his teaching and his spirit. We are the TANEMORIS!

"So long, my sister," I said as she left, wondering if she heard me. With my fading vision, I watched her depart. Her shoulders drooped with the burdens she had carried for 60 years. Could I blame her for what appeared to be posturing, for leaving us in Hiroshima without reaching resolution?

I suggested that Perry and Jeremy accompany Satsuko out to the lobby. Perry looked to Yukiko for assurance and she nodded for him to go.

The next day was overwhelming, unbearable. None of us spoke to one another, as the weight of her burden lay heavy on Yukiko, who felt she had failed us. Iori-san, very sympathetic to her, offered any assistance he might give.

We continued with our plans, going to the Shinto shrine three blocks from my childhood home. Remarkably, some of the stone walls, the gate, and the gate guardians remained from before the bombing. The rest of the temple has been rebuilt, and appears much as it did in 1945.

While we were conversing with the Head Master and his Number One Son—also a Shinto priest, whose main concern is to live up to his father's example by continuing to help people in need—Perry and Jeremy were granted permission to film whatever happened in the courtyard.

From nowhere, a drunken man stumbled into the courtyard and began playing with Yuki. He then stumbled over to Kimina, giving our youngest traveler a piece of candy. When we exchanged greetings, he asked if we were a TV news team. He then stumbled up to the Shinto Priest and spoke for a while. Through the camera lens, Perry captured the priest's warm smile and kindness toward the man. The drunken man then said goodbye to everyone and stumbled out of the courtyard.

Many people come in and out of our lives. Every one of them has something important to teach us. The lessons are learned if we listen truthfully to our thoughts and hearts during these interactions. No one has the full capacity to understand all the intricate moves that make for a life of wonder.

We said goodbye to the Shinto Priests and continued on to the Tenma River. Nearby had been the school where I had stood counting in the game of hide-and-seek with my friends on that fateful morning. This was the river I was taken to by the soldier who dug me from the burning debris. This was where I was reunited with my Father.

After lunch, our "spiritual" energy still at low ebb, we went to locate the area near the river where my school once stood. We found a wide open lot, the space where the school had been. This we discovered from a map recreated by a longtime resident of the neighborhood. I had known his family when I was a child.

In this open lot children were now playing a form of volleyball, but more like hitting a ball as hard as possible, trying to keep it in the air.

The play attracted Yukiko, a volleyball player in college. She became like a little ten-year-old girl as she played with the kids. Yuki got excited and joined in as well. She was a bolt of lightning, chasing the ball when it went astray. The children shrieked and scattered from Yuki's path. One of the young boys saw a challenge and played soccer with Yuki. An epic game ensued.

That evening, as we reflected on the day's events, our energy was renewed.

"Moshi, moshi."
Suddenly, the familiar greeting of a phone conversation snared our attention, and sent sparks flying around the hotel room. Yukiko was on the phone with Satsuko. I could hear my sister's voice on the other end of the line ...

We were dumbfounded to hear that Satsuko had invited us to Kotachi Village. She also welcomed us to pay homage at our family grave marker, my sacred temple where I used to meet my Father, and sustain my soul.

"Perry and Jeremy-san tachini kamera (video-camera) *o motte kitemo ii desu, to."*

She gave them permission to videotape whatever they wished for the documentary.

Mr. Iori-san, who had taken a half-day off from his busy schedule, arrived in the Kokusai Hotel's main lobby. He was ready to drive us the 63 miles of winding, narrow roads from Hiroshima to the Village of Kotachi.

Anticipating what might happen when we again met Satsuko, I felt great apprehension and dread. I could still see my sister's face when she had left the hotel two days before! Iori-san cast a smile at me, reassuring me that everything would happen as it should.

The heat that day in Kotachi Village was like none we had ever experienced. When Iori-san dropped us off, we thanked him for his generous help, said goodbye, and then I moved to my hallowed duty of bathing in my Father's spirit.

Satsuko hired two taxis to take us up to the hill where my Father, siblings and grandparents are buried. She gave us ice-cold hand towels to cool our faces, and a jug of water to pour over the marble grave marker for her family's and ancestor's spirits. Yuki found shade under a sakura tree.

Our stay was brief, as our group was acclimatizing to one another and the surroundings. For the first time, Perry and Jeremy, Yukiko and Kimina were seeing the village where my sister and I were orphaned after the war, where we had struggled to remain a family unit and survive.

We had received little help from society, and no government hand-outs! Neither did we have the luxury of waiting for the government, as can be the case in America, to assist us with the problems of survival. Instead, each one of us was responsible for merely existing!

Leaving the grave site, we headed to the home of Satsuko's daughter, Yuriko. Satsuko had moved there after selling her house and land to a commercial developer.

Although my sister was much more kindhearted, I could still feel an undercurrent of her energy toward me. After we took the cab back to her daughter's home, Satsuko grabbed my arm, with her old "Takashi, get in quickly before any neighbors ..." This time, she didn't finish.

I felt my fate was in the hands of these two young Americans, as Satsuko called them, and was especially influenced by Yukiko and her daughter. I think Kimina's innocent face softened my sister's demolishing tongue.

We weren't sure what to do with ourselves, standing in the hallway and dining room, and it was 10 to 15 minutes before all the "dust settled."

My sister, having overcome the painful moment, invited us to sit around the dining table. She also settled down, after freshly brewing green tea and serving Japanese goodies that struck my fancy.

I had no real grasp that the moment had arrived for Satsuko's last chance of reconciliation with her oldest brother. I was terrified, for fear of being considered ill-mannered, to even reach for the tea cup. Nor did I reach out to take any goodies, although I did smack my lips.

Satsuko then began to speak, directing her comments not to Perry, Jeremy, or to me, but to Yukiko-san, feeling that she had Yukiko's sympathetic ear. The long-sought moment had come for my sister to discuss face-to-face where and how we had erred in the past, and where we might meet on common ground.

Yuriko conspicuously left the room for her mother and me to talk without constraints.

Satsuko then zeroed in, pouring out her soul through Yukiko, whom she knew was there for her.

I knew I needed to focus on listening to Satsuko with my heart. Perry and Jeremy were silent, but gave total attention to what my sister was saying, though it was "totally Greek" to them. They were focused through the viewfinders of digital video and still cameras, capturing as best as possible Satsuko's great pain and anguish.

What kept my attention was my sister's very presence. I was sitting directly across from her, lowering my gaze from her piercing eyes, as her battered soul spoke to my heart.

For the next two-and-a-half hours Satsuko spoke, uninterrupted except for occasional nods or faint verbal responses from Yukiko, her affirmations that my sister's story was being received. Suddenly, I felt as if the Empire State Building's foundation had given in, and the whole skyscraper was crumbling from its weight.

"Takashi!" Satsuko shouted with a thundering voice as she leaned toward me over the dining table like a ferocious dog about to pounce on cornered prey! "Why did you do that to me ...? Once you left my sight, I was extremely grateful that you, of all people, finally got out from before my face. I would not see you ever again ... unless perhaps by some quirk I'd see your carcass in the parched desert, which would be no concern of mine."

She continued to vent. "Whatever your reasons, you returned to Japan, to Kotachi, without warning, and then went back to America, thinking you'd left no trace for me to find out. I didn't see you, but some villagers informed me of your activities, reminding me of your sinful, hooligan life of the past."

Her body was shaking reflexively, to the point of convulsion. "Each time you came and went, I had to face the leaders and villagers, prostrating myself before them and begging their sympathy on behalf of our Father's spirit for my thug brother."

Of course, I had no problem identifying and relating to all of her accusations. I knew that I had been rebellious, ungracious and contrary to the villagers' expectation. I also knew, deep inside, that my actions had kept me alive. They had been my path to survival.

Suddenly, from Satsuko's lips came the most excruciatingly painful sound I had ever heard. "Taka-chan," she said, controlling her emotions at the point of breaking, "I know what you have done is inexcusable, unjustifiable and unforgivable, but I understand that that was the only way you knew in order to survive alone. But, there was ..."

Unexpectedly, she halted and composed herself.

I looked toward her with trepidation and then searched Yukiko's luminous eyes for "rescue" from the fire of my sister's glare.

Satsuko's emotion shifted from hurling scorching accusations at me. "This is not anything between you and me. This is about what the villagers did to the Tanemoris," she said, then hesitated.

"It's a good thing you did not know all that happened. I have shielded some things in one compartment of my soul, never to be revealed to you, for I knew what you would do to the villagers if you learned of them. A chain of events might have led the Tanemoris into judgment like that of the 'Scarlet Letter,' subjecting us to *mura-hachibu,* banishment from the community!"

I focused my attention, trying to listen with my heart. But from her words I couldn't begin to spell out the difficulties she must have had with me on account of the villagers, nor how she had subjugated herself to their will, all to keep the honorable Tanemori family name unsoiled.

"Takashi," she asked, tears welling in her eyes. These tears were different than those shed from anger toward me. "Do you remember how little time the village leaders gave us to cremate our Father?"

I nodded my head, vaguely recalling the morning of September 4, 1945.

She composed herself, asking me to listen carefully, for she would not have the energy to repeat or explain her feelings about what she was going to divulge.

"Do you remember the incident surrounding our sister Masuyo's cremation?"

"What do you mean about Masuyo's cremation …?" I inquired, breaking my silence in angry indignation.

Satsuko was about to reveal what had been locked in her soul for sixty years.

"I was willing to wade in against the Village leaders," she said. "I would have no problem at all if their souls burned in hell … forever!"

I never expected what came next from her lips, a secret that had lain concealed and incarcerated for a lifetime in the pit of her soul.

"Satsuko Ne-e-san," Yukiko pleaded, casting her tender eyes toward Satsuko, searching for understanding. I looked to Yukiko for consolation while my sister continued, uninterrupted.

"I was on watch for Masuyo's cremation," began my sister. "The fire was crackling and embers flew against the dark canvas, as white smoke ascended to drift into the village. From the pile of wood, I determined the cremation would take another half-night."

Satsuko choked on her emotions as the words poured out. "I heard a number of villagers, with several leaders, coming to the cremation site with *oke*, tubs, full of water. They started dowsing the fire without asking or explaining to me what they were doing."

"Please explain to me, what in the world are you doing! It is my sister's cremation. Tell me …" She had clutched the leader, begging for understanding.

Satsuko covered her face and continued. "I hysterically stood between the fire at my back and their madness. I begged and begged for them to stop putting out the fire and let the cremation finish."

Her voice quivered, "Several more villagers came, all carrying tubs of water, adding further injury to my already wounded soul. I screamed, "Why?"

One of the elders responded, "One of the important village leader's loved ones passed away and has to be cremated as soon as possible. Your #%$@&* sister is preventing us from doing so."

"No! I will not accept that as lawful conduct. Whether or not this is a village leader, you are not above the law, nor should your family have any exclusive privilege over other villagers. Let my sister Masuyo take her final journey without interruption by your madness!"

Satsuko could not allow the leaders' imposition. She clung like a *suppon,* a snapping-turtle, to her post by the fire. But being a 14-year-old girl, she was unable to prevent the dowsing, and Masuyo's cremation was suspended.

My sister told me that she, too, had promised our Father to *kake,* gamble her own soul, to withstand any efforts to destroy the Tanemori name.

She emptied her soul upon us, expecting we would listen with our hearts! As I did, an uncontrollable energy surged deep within! As my sister had said, it was a good thing I was unaware of the disrespect that had disturbed Masuyo's final journey.

As my fury rose, I thought, "Oh, let the gate of hell open widely to swallow those who have done this to Masuyo, Satsuko, and the Tanemoris!"

Yukiko, Perry, Jeremy and I heard Satsuko say many things, stunned by her choice of words. Unable to fully grasp the depth and breadth of her emotion, my sister's presence still sunk deep into our hearts as her body shook violently, her energy escaping, releasing extraordinary pressure that had been locked inside for so long.

Satsuko was freed from her burden, and as she turned to Yukiko, her soul aroused a melody I had never heard from my sister until that moment.

"Yukiko-san, *arigato*. For it was because of you that I was able to open the gate to my soul. For all these years, no one knew that I had chained this secret in my innermost soul, that not even my children should know."

Then there was a great hesitation. She looked into the distance, as if seeking a place of refuge. I sat directly across from her, yet unable to reach her, even to touch her hands. I was stunned to hear her confess her soul, stunned to hear the reality of a journey she had chosen to endure alone.

"Even if I had created a moment to pour out my soul to my children, they could not have truly understood. They would only have heard my shrieking and the sundering of my soul. I could not allow my children to suffer, for this suffering was to be solely mine."

"Now that I have released my soul, I am ready to hear the beckoning of my Father, if he should call me home."

"I felt I could trust my soul to your hands, Yukiko-san. I knew in my heart you were able to give understanding ears to listen to my heartbeat. Without such trust I would still be in my own captivity, never to find inner-peace."

How painful it had been for Satsuko to accept "fate," struggling under Japan's social structure with its stranglehold on those who resisted the "powers that be"!

I had neither words nor fortitude to empathize with her soul! I kept my distance while Yukiko and Satsuko did most of the talking. As I pondered the revelations of the moment, it struck me how similar Satsuko's approach to life had been to mine. Due to the teachings of our parents, we had both survived our hardships.

At this point Satsuko's miniature dog startled Kimina. The little girl screamed and slid across the floor to her mother. Yukiko, with Kimina in her arms, excused herself from the room, while Satsuko scolded the dog. The dog licked its lips.

After returning and apologizing for her daughter, Yukiko said something I could never have anticipated. "I am so glad that I am Japanese, a Japanese woman, nurtured and maintained as I am by Japanese culture, without any outside influence."

I think she meant she had not come to live in America to become tainted by its culture, as I had. At least, that's what my sister thinks about my "disconnected" lifestyle. My behavior over the years has not been acceptable to her, nor to Japanese tradition.

"My dear sister," I said, carefully looking into her eyes "why have you kept this secret about our sister buried in your soul? You are *hikyo-mono*. You have contravened the teachings of our Father, thinking as the oldest you must take the role of 'father' and 'mother,' that you alone must carry the weight and responsibility to face the villagers and their leaders. Tanemoris are to share their heart, no matter what. Remember Father's teaching? 'When you share your joy with others, it will multiply, and when you share the burden, it will reduce by half.'"

My sister looked at me tenderly, and said, "My dear brother, it was meant to be, as I am your older sister and had made a promise to our Father to guard the Tanemori name. It was my journey and mine alone."

She had accepted the facts of the fate that befell her. She went on to say that if it weren't for the death of our

Father, her life would have been different, easy and comfortable, the life every child hopes for, with expectations of growing up to contribute to society.

"I can truly say now, it was I who was left behind, and not Masuyo *Ne-e-chan*," Satsuko declared. "Masuyo wouldn't have survived the raging storms in Kotachi village—the "devilish" villagers and leaders—for she was much more tenderhearted, and would have succumbed to their pressures."

How true it was that Satsuko possessed the spirit of a wild tigress to protect her cubs, the enduring energy of a dragon, and the strength of a bamboo grove, to let the world's storms rage by so many times and still return upright in the sun!

Satsuko continued her survival saga.

In fulfillment of her promise to our Father, no matter what happened, she had been like a lion, an angry ox, a dragon, and even, as I had accused her, the "water-drinking-bird," bowing to the powers-that-be.

Having heard the bawl of her soul, I had never felt such a need to quickly to find a hole to crawl in and hide. I was so ashamed for my conduct, and having caused my sister to endure so much adversity and suffering for these many years. I wondered if she had questioned whether daylight would ever break through the dark clouds ...

Oh, the strength of my sister, Satsuko!

She had kept this "truth," causing her to be ever-vigilant of the honor of the Tanemori name. It was as if she was the Japanese Black Pine that I loved so much, its tap-root burrowing into the heart of the earth while its top branches reached heaven above, braving the four seasons!

How in the world had I allowed the expanse of the Pacific Ocean and decades of separation to make me "deaf, dumb and mute" to my sister? I had "masked" myself from her as she had "masked" herself from me, so that we never really saw each other. It was like Noh's dance: we had acted according to the mask each of us wore—keeping our real selves from each other.

Satsuko was the matriarch of the Tanemoris—no one dared challenge or be seen as contemptuous of her, as I was known to have been. According to Japanese tradition, no one could make a decision, without Satsuko's knowledge, that would impact any member of the family. Perhaps Satsuko was being kind by having Sachiko sit beside me, to provide comfort and support.

The teachings of our Father, which I call the *Codes of the Samurai*, Satsuko, even to this day, refused to accept, saying, "Takashi, how could you understand what he taught us, especially when you were so much younger than I? By his nurturing, I learned how to survive. I learned by him and from his life. He lived before us, before his children."

That is the promise my Father made me vow to uphold the night before he passed away. Bear in mind that I was only eight years old. Yet with my understanding today, I know how important it was for Father to make sure that he had correctly passed on his *Codes of the Samurai*.

Since bidding farewell to my Father on September 3, 1945, I had carried one physical icon of his legacy—the photo of him in his *kimono* emblazoned with the family crest, *Maruni Tachi Aoi*. I had also carried inside me his gift of the *Codes*, which sustained me in my darkest times. They were what kept my heart intact and helped preserved the essence of who I am.

My Father's teachings also had served to guide me to pass on to my children that which I received from him—"Live by duty, responsibility, and accountability, bonded by honor, love and principles."

While my journey from Revenge to Forgiveness had been difficult, my epiphany, reliving my dream before the bombing in Hiroshima, became the tap-root of my desire to reconcile with my sister.

And now, here I was, reconciled with Satsuko, cognizant that she had undergone her own transformation and reconciliation, bringing harmony the Tanemori family had not known for three generations. Despite the differences between us, differences that almost destroyed us, we are undeniably united by our spiritual journeys of the heart.

Now I understood more deeply what Yukiko-san had said about being glad she had always remained a Japanese woman in heart and spirit.

I also have overwhelming joy and gratitude for the members of the Japan Production Team who were instrumental in my journey, serving as bridges between people—between generations, between men and women, sisters and brothers, animals and humans, between the spirit and material worlds.

For me now, the message of life is clear and simple. We can settle human conflicts and differences, national enmity, ethnic hatred, and cultural divisiveness, without resorting to violence or war. Choosing a path of revenge, with its endless cycle, spirals only into death.

I have come home to the real promise I made to my Father: a place called "Peace, through Forgiveness," by letting go of my painful past.

I believe a journey to peace must begin in each individual heart. Only when we bring light into the darkness of our own hearts can we truly heal. Only when we ourselves find inner peace can we become a force for peace in the world.

In the words of my Father, "Takashi, learn to live for the benefit of others, then we will all benefit; this is the key to living peacefully with each other."

It begins with one person … like a tiny pebble dropped in the lake, creating countless rings toward the shore, rings uniting to the strength of a *tsunami*!

My sister's last words to me reminded me of the process a Japanese sword undergoes in the hands of the blacksmith. Fiery trials temper its blade until the moment when the "spirit" of Amaterasu, the sun-goddess, enters the steel. Only then does the steel take on its true intended character.

Satsuko had said to my heart, "Taka-chan, I am able to say from the bottom of my heart how deep the 'valley of death' appeared during our life in Kotachi village. I burrowed through the mountain with these hands and was finally able to provide for, protect and guide the Tanemoris through perilous times, when society wished me dead."

"*Demo ne, Taka-chan,*" she continued.

I sensed in her voice a cry of victory, of gratitude and fortitude.

"Whatever I had done," Satsuko said, her eyes welling with tears, "since we said 'so long' to our Father, I have had nothing to regret! I have done my best, that which was demanded of me by the promise I made to our Father. I have kept his spirit in my own life-journey, for I have always known who I am and followed the light of my heart with all due responsibility and accountability for the consequences of my actions and deeds. If, for any reason, I should be called home, called to our Father, I am ready to tell him I am coming. I am not ashamed of how I lived, for I have lived my life as I was entrusted it."

My proof of reconciliation came with Satsuko's "Taka-chan," her tender voice reassuring me of our reconnection, knowing clearly that we are Tanemoris!

It was then, for the first time ever, I asked Satsuko, *"One-e-chan,* may I?"

I was somewhat embarrassed as I offered my sister a shoulder massage. But my offering was such a reward! I had never seen Satsuko display such a beautiful smile! Her reaction was my greatest discovery of hidden treasure!

My sister's shoulders, drooped with burdens she had carried alone for so many years, were hard like lead. It seemed to take forever to soften them.

In doing so, what energy surged into my hands and heart! We had both longed for this moment of *kokoro no Kaihou,* reconciling of estranged souls. It was as if two mighty currents of water had been running separate parallel courses, each obscured from the other by emotional and cultural barriers, until this day.

Satsuko excused herself and hurried upstairs.

Waiting for her return took an eternity. The freshly brewed green tea she had poured was still waiting for me, untouched. We all looked toward each other with trepidation. Then we were caught in an array of surprises, as my sister made her grand entry back to the dining room.

She was dressed in a traditional *kimono,* carrying props. She needed to dance a traditional Japanese dance.

As the music flowed, I was astounded. I had never heard music propel me in such a way through time and space. I was carried back to the past, as Satsuko danced flawlessly. She danced as an *Otoko-buyo*, a male dancer. Every move, every facial expression was perfectly succinct with each mood of the melody. I was spellbound, lost in an enchanted world I had never known existed.

I had been so separated from my sister that I was unaware she had trained and performed as a *Shisho*, a master of traditional dance, for more than 30 years. Only now had Satsuko modestly revealed to us that she was a revered master of dance in the region where she lives.

When she completed the dance, Satsuko hurried back upstairs and returned with several family photo albums she guarded like Fort Knox. In these albums was another treasure—many pictures of myself as a young boy, of my brothers and sisters, grandparents and cousins—most of whom I was seeing for the first time! My guess is that Satsuko and Chisako carried the albums out of Hiroshima when they evacuated in the weeks before August 6th, 1945.

My sister and I looked over the photo albums alone, without speaking, for perhaps as long as 45 minutes.

Perry then asked me to be his translator, explaining what Satsuko had communicated from her heart. What he heard shook him, Jeremy, Yukiko, and, most of all, me.

We were all gathered around my sister, poring over the family photos, hearing her stories, bathing in her spirit. We all saw and sensed the split of the single river, Satsuko and me, into two bodies of water, and all the disharmony spread over the many years since.

Satsuko's sharing was the utmost demonstration of her gratitude to Perry, Jeremy and Yukiko, as she honored them with the gift of her soul.

We celebrated with *sake*, and enjoyed the Japanese goodies she offered. Little Kimina, although she had limited understanding of what had transpired before her eyes, certainly knew she was a part of our team. She said she was the team's fifth member, as Yuki was to take up the "tail," as number six. Kimina had every right to be proud, and we were glad she was part of our journey.

As further evidence that Satsuko and I had reconciled, she invited us all to stay with her. Yukiko and Kimina were to sleep upstairs, while the men were to bunch up in the *tatami*-room, where we had viewed the photos of my parents and my sister Masuyo.

I could almost see that after meeting my sister, and experiencing what she had become during the postwar years in Kotachi Village, and hearing her proudly exclaim "WE ARE TANEMORIS," Perry would need a few more days to reflect upon his direction in making the documentary.

Satsuko had freely shared much of her personal history, and we had heard her individual experiences, interpreted and applied through the eyes of our own life stories. I saw with great understanding how her experiences had profoundly altered her values, direction and lifestyle.

We can truly say now *Tadaima*, live for the moment, to each other, to the Tanemoris.

Tadaima.

The "seed" of the Tanemoris is like that of the Japanese Black Pine Tree. The pine's tap-root reaches the heart of the earth and its branches reach toward heaven, as the name we proudly bear.

The Tanemori seed has its own power and volition and in due season it shall prosper into a forest. My sister allowed no villagers or village leaders to soil our family name, keeping it with honor and dignity.

For me, for the Tanemoris here in America, the seed has been planted in Mother Earth, has set its tap-root in foreign soil, and is ever-growing, giving shade to weary travelers during the heat of day and shelter for birds to perch and rest their wings on at night, a parallel to the Mother Land of Japan.

A metaphor comes to mind of the relationship Satsuko and I now share. Our relationship has been that of an extraordinary river, the Enoki, flowing through the valley cradling Kotachi Village.

The river splits at one point, the divided waters running parallel courses around obstacles of geology. Figuratively, the parallel streams of Satsuko and Takashi have run around the obstacles of Japanese society. Over time, these obstacles have been cleared or worn down, allowing the parallel streams to merge back into a single flow, continuing a course into the Bay of Hiroshima, the "home" from which the water once came!

And so shall be the family crest: *Maruni Tachi Aoi!*

"Be in peace, my Beloved Father!"

Now, understanding the events that shaped and directed my personal life, I realize more than ever the importance of humanity as a whole taking a similar path. As I look at the relationships between Japan, the land of my birth, and America, my adopted home, it behooves us all to squarely regard our history and honestly, truthfully act upon our understanding of it.

If there is any hope for harmony and unity, for members of the world's nations to coexist side-by-side, they must see others as they see themselves, and be willing to understand seemingly enigmatic differences in values, goals, and moral principles.

Many open wounds do not heal because of the failure of all parties to fully understand and appreciate the history that defines the roots of conflict and leads toward solution. And it has become obvious that the ROOT cause of human conflict is the inability of people to move beyond their own perceived self-interests and truly experience the sacred humanity of "others."

Perry, Jeremy and Yukiko have seen the Tanemoris transcend estrangement through reconciliation. There have been rich experiences in the lives of these two siblings—drama and romance, heartache, tears, sacrifice and hysterical laughter. However, the main story is one of a spiritual journey each individual must embark upon, and of relationships between fathers and sons, mothers and daughters, and between generations.

That story, that journey, manifested itself due to Satsuko's immense will, spirit and strong heart. Oh, the strength of my sister, Satsuko! She has kept this "truth" that caused her to be ever-vigilant, guarding the honor and dignity of the Tanemoris!

To transcend our conflicts, Satsuko and I had to embrace our history and offer forgiveness, while being true to ourselves and living our lives for the benefit of others. Along the way we not only redeemed our lives, but we found reconciliation for the two countries that both wounded and nurtured me. In the process, we have benefited from becoming the persons we now are, willing to share our souls through our heartbeat.

I finally understand that, even though I am now almost completely blind, due to the late embers of the naked sky of Hiroshima so long ago, it was when I first saw with the "vision of the heart," that I was truly able to "see."

Your time spent as I shared my journey is the most precious "gift" you can give me.

Personal Journey

*At first, I had no knowledge, purpose or destiny
as I entered into this world.
Safely cradled in the arms of my Mother,
did I wonder. "Who am I or Why?"*

*I have walked crooked roads and valleys,
climbed steep hills, and dived into deep waters.
My soul has been tempered by life's fiery trials
and by wonder of nature beyond measure.*

*Rains fall on both the good and the wicked;
I am like a trembling sparrow
in the hands of the Master ...
My heart fills with innumerable blessings.*

*A trembling migrant bird,
watched over by the Creator,
my heart fills with countless blessings for
food, shelter, clothing and friends who touched my
                                        life.*

*Battered by the raging storm,
I've learned to enter into the center (the "EYE" of
                                    the storm),
the quiet place from which I was able to see
the world in a different perspective,
like a baby cradled in the arms of its mother.*

Like the fixed point of a compass guiding a ship,
I held the vision of a distant harbor safely in my
                                              heart.
My Father's spirit, guiding me home through
                                              troubled Seas.
Knowing such things are riches for the soul.

Finding "Truth" in my pilgrimage
from "cradle to grave," the span of life,
lies not in which path I wandered.
I have never been alone.

Discovering my life-journey
in many stumbling steps,
"who I become" along the way.
is the greatest treasure!
or
is the true worth of all my travels.

I finally see my home in the distance.
Looking to the above with gratitude ...
There is my Father in the doorway-safe harbor;
He bends closer and whispers, "You are my heart."

Thank you for listening to my heart,
Takashi "Thomas" Tanemori

AFTERWORD

THE PAGES of history bear witness that the decision made by Harry S. Truman, former President of the USA, on July 25, 1945, at the Potsdam Conference, to use the atomic bomb on Hiroshima, did not only cause the demise of my home, my city and my family, but radically changed the course of humanity and ultimately ushered in the Nuclear Age.

Instead of experiencing the permanent global peace which was intended, we have, for the last 60 years, painfully endured many raging wars, in every imaginable form: cultural, religious, economic, political and personal. We have been continually raiding, burning and bombing in the name of some public or private agenda, creating tragedies in which innocents are routinely and randomly maimed, killed, or enslaved.

As a survivor of Hiroshima, I find it deeply disturbing that we so easily take up weapons—something which is accepted as the norm—and go to war so quickly to settle our differences. The rhetorical questions one must ask are:

What is the ultimate outcome of war ... any war?

How can we expect to create or promote global peace when we ourselves are at "war" within our own hearts?

What, then, must we do to "shift" the world from our current path of self-destruction, toward creating a safer and more peaceful world for our children, and for all the children of the world, so that six billion people of different nationalities can live side-by-side in *Heiwa*, peace, in harmony and equality?

My vision consists of finding ways to understand the root cause of human conflict, to honor both the past and the present, and to express my love for the two countries that both wounded and nurtured me. It is a vision which seeks for a solution to human conflict, through a rite of passage marked by the discovery of love, forgiveness and the healing of the human heart.

The message is clear and simple. We can settle conflicts and differences, national enmity, ethnic hatred, and cultural divisiveness, without resorting to violence or war in the grip of an endless cycle of revenge. May we share with the rest of humanity how to find the way to hope and peace!

I can boldly say that my journey reaffirms that even tragedy can lead to peace, love and forgiveness, giving hope and light, and experiencing how precious it is to dedicate one's life to the healing of human hearts and souls.

> *At the dawn of the 21st century,*
> *we honor this passage through darkness.*
> *We must have the courage to enter*
> *the void again ... and again,*
> *emerging with the gift of new life.*
> *Healing only comes through learning to forgive*
> *and by making peace with our past.*
> *Only then, will the wind whisper:*
> *"Hibakusha, you have not lived in vain!"*

I was only 48 years old when, suddenly, I had to confront for the first time how close I had come to death. As I looked at the faces of my three children, tender young shoots regarding me in the intensive care unit, watching over me vigilantly, a glass window separated our two worlds. Their eyes seemed filled with jewels, as they silently communicated their love, their hope and their fear.

I was swiftly taken back to September 3, 1945, the night before my Father was taken. I remembered how important it had been for him to make sure that he passed on the *Seven Codes of the Samurai* correctly, which in turn helped me to survive decades of darkness, which in turn kept my heart and soul intact. That night he also reminded me that we must repay our debts to our ancestors by passing what we have received on to our children: to live by duty—responsibility and accountability—bonded by honor, love and principles. Now, the questions are: What have I passed on to my children? What do they know about who I am—as their father? Do they really know who I am? What legacy am I leaving to them, if there is any?

It was then that I resolved to leave my *testament,* my personal journey in this book. This book is the result of a promise that I made to myself, and to my Father on his deathbed, on September 3, 1945.

This book is my life journey from the past to the present, woven with the intricate fabric of my life, combining the traditional Japanese cultural "homogeneity" with the contemporary, pragmatic diversity of Western-American cultural "heterogeneity."

My life has been described with cultural sensitivity blended with both personal and historical events brought about by the atomic bomb—by which I was thrust into the rubble of postwar Japan. I reveal how the war affected me in the struggle for survival against the merciless discrimination of my fellow Japanese after the war, and in my eventual immigration into the United States to seek revenge. I also expose the blatant racial, ethnic, social and cultural prejudice of my adopted homeland, America, the land of my enemy.

It is a demonstration of how a heart twisted by hatred and the lust for revenge can be transformed by forgiveness, and can attain peaceful wisdom in order to practice the important work of healing human hearts.

The radiant strength and dignity of the Crane and the beauty and elegance of the Butterfly are the central mysteries which give this story universal meaning and convey a message of forgiveness and hope for peace that is sorely needed at this time.

Also important is the significant contribution this story can make by increasing cultural understanding and mutual respect between Japanese and American citizens.

For American readers, the book provides valuable insights into the Eastern culture and history that have shaped the personality of the Japanese people.

Japanese audiences will be fascinated by the presentation of a Japanese teenager (and adult) learning to adapt to the awkward heterogeneous culture of the US in the years 1956 to 2005.

My story also bridges enigmatic cultural dichotomies between Japanese and American citizens, helping both parties to see their cultural differences.

Ultimately, therefore, this book, however emblematically it may be written, is written as a testament as important as my life: "Preventing another World War II is an important legacy that mankind asks of us, and Peace is the only real gift that we can give them!" This is my *task*; this is my *prayer*; and this has become the *touchstone of my life*.

The human soul is stronger than any nuclear bomb!!! The dramatic and emotionally charged nature of the story is inspirational testimony—finding *KOKORO NO YASURAGI*. It foreshadows the final victory of the tenacious human spirit and life—the symbolic fulfillment of *"No More Hiroshimas."*

Therefore …

It is my hope that this historical presentation may bring urgently required understanding that may lead us, as citizens of the world, to become more honest with ourselves and with our own history.

This would help us to be more straightforward, truthful and honest in our dealings with other nations in the future.

Most importantly, it is my heartfelt wish for all of us to resolve this historical conflict, preparing ourselves for the final "war." This war, the most difficult one of all, we have yet to fight. In this war we must bring ourselves to recognize that the time of recrimination is long over and that reconciliation must take place if there is any hope for the future, for the survival of the human race.

It is time for us to make peace by learning to forgive. It is for the sake of our children, and of the world, that we ought to learn from the silkworm to sacrifice our life for the strand of silk-threads: the threads of many colors, adding unto each other to benefit humanity with an iridescent tapestry of human dignity.

I am Takashi "Thomas" Tanemori, a "Noble Man," the name my Father gave me, and I am a survivor of Hiroshima. After immigrating into America, from postwar

Japan, to find a new life and purpose, I have since become a naturalized citizen.

My life is the result of the two different cultures of Japan and America. I have been brought up by these two cultures which have dramatically influenced and shaped me. On one hand the teaching of the *Seven Codes of the Samurai* taught to me by my Father kept my heart and soul intact, and his teaching has also helped me to see the complex world we live in from a different perspective.

Paradoxically, for me, the "path" of Hiroshima has taught me this most important lesson: those of us who have lost the most in war are also the ones who have the most to gain by putting aside our feelings of revenge, by going beyond our own cocoon, by learning to forgive, and by making peace with our own painful past.

As a result of my blindness, caused by the long-term consequences of the radiation from the explosion so long ago in Hiroshima, I currently live with my Guide dog, Yuki, in Lafayette, Berkeley, California. I am the founder of the Silkworm Peace Institute, a non-profit organization that promotes peace through forgiveness, art exhibitions, and public speaking.

I hope to make the world a safer and more peaceful for our children, and for all the world's children. On that last fleeting moment, on September 3, 1945, my Father asked me to live my life as he lived his own for his children, "Takashi, learn to live for the benefit of others. This is the simplest way to have peace in the world." I finally understand how going beyond my personal suffering and helping others leads to healing.

© 2008 Takashi Tanemori with John Crump